Conflict, Crime, and the State in Postcommunist Eurasia

CONFLICT, CRIME, AND THE STATE IN POSTCOMMUNIST EURASIA

Edited by

Svante Cornell and Michael Jonsson

PENN

UNIVERSITY OF PENNSYLVANIA PRESS

PHILADELPHIA

Published by
University of Pennsylvania Press
Philadelphia, Pennsylvania 19104-4112
www.upenn.edu/pennpress

Printed in the United States of America
on acid-free paper
10 9 8 7 6 5 4 3 2 1

Library of Congress Cataloging-in-Publication Data
Conflict, crime, and the state in postcommunist Eurasia / edited by Svante
E. Cornell and Michael Jonsson. — 1st ed.
    p.   cm.
    Includes bibliographical references and index.
    ISBN 978-0-8122-4565-3 (hardcover : alk. paper)
    1. Political violence—Economic aspects—Eurasia—Case studies.
2. Organized crime—Political aspects—Eurasia—Case studies.
3. Insurgency—Economic aspects—Eurasia—Case studies. 4. Civil war—
Economic aspects—Eurasia—Case studies. I. Cornell, Svante E. II. Jonsson,
Michael.
JC328.6.P6   2014
364.106095—dc23   2013022395

Contents

Chapter 1

The Nexus of Crime and Conflict

Svante Cornell and Michael Jonsson

Over the past decade, the political economy of armed conflict and terrorism has been accorded increasing attention by both academic and policy circles. Indeed, following the end of the bipolar world order, a symbiosis has appeared to develop between organized crime, on the one hand, and nonstate violent actors, on the other. Conflict diamonds in Africa, narco-guerrillas in Colombia, and narco-terrorists in Afghanistan have all entered the vocabulary of the international media.

Indeed, the end of the Cold War led to a dramatic decrease in state support for insurgency and terrorism. The "East" lost its financial ability to support insurgent groups abroad; the "West" lost its interest in doing so.[1] Insurgent groups have therefore to a larger degree been on their own, forced to fend for themselves and raise the money for their insurgencies from other sources than foreign funding. Many have done so through donations from diaspora groups; others have turned to self-financing, looting natural resources or engaging in illicit forms of commerce.[2]

In a globalized world where organized crime can move across national boundaries with increasing ease, the weakness of law enforcement in conflict zones provides suitable conditions for such crime. But crime and conflict do not only coexist in a geographic space. Indeed, there is a mounting body of evidence suggesting the systematic involvement of conflicting parties in organized criminal activity. Examples of the involvement of terrorist groups and belligerent parties in civil wars, especially in the developing world, in organized criminal activity have mounted over the past decade.

While this issue has attracted substantial levels of media attention, the scholarly community in the social sciences did not accord it much attention until a decade after the end of the Cold War. Indeed, scholars have for a variety of reasons found it conceptually difficult to grapple with the political economy of armed conflict. For example, the theoretical and methodological traditions in the social sciences find themselves ill suited to deal with murky, secretive milieus such as those involving both organized crime and armed conflict. The discipline of peace and conflict studies is relatively new, while organized crime is traditionally studied not by political scientists but by criminologists, trained in a combination of sociological and psychological methods. As a result, the structure of the academic community was ill prepared for identifying and studying the problems occurring in the interface of armed conflict and the illicit economy. These problems have been compounded by the lack of reliable systematic data on countries in civil war in general, and organized crime in countries with weak or corrupt law enforcement agencies in particular. An enduring challenge is how to estimate the size of organized crime in the absence of convictions because such patterns are equally consistent with low levels of organized crime, very weak law enforcement, or corrupt judicial systems.

By the end of the 1990s, the World Bank had put together a group of scholars to study the political economy of armed conflict; in the first decade of the twenty-first century, the academic literature has only gradually begun to direct attention seriously on this issue. As it did so, the discourse initially centered on the role of natural resources in the onset and duration of conflict, with African "conflict diamonds" perhaps the most widely publicized example.[3] Much of the research undertaken has tended to focus on the narcotics trade. This is natural for several reasons. First, the interaction between protracted civil war and the cultivation and trafficking of narcotics is increasingly observable around the world. This is particularly the case regarding coca and opium, the crops from which the most potent and profit-bringing psychotropic substances, cocaine and heroin, are produced. Today, the bulk of the global cultivation of opium and coca is taking place in conflict zones, while the trafficking of their derivatives has come to heavily involve insurgent and terrorist groups operating between the source and destination areas of illicit drugs. This was not always the case: in the 1960s, countries such as

Turkey, Iran, and Bolivia produced much of the world's opium and coca without experiencing armed conflict. But presently the production of these drugs is concentrated in Afghanistan, Burma, Colombia, and Peru—four countries that have been ravaged by some of the world's longest-lasting civil wars.[4] This trend raises important questions as to the reasons behind this phenomenon and its implications.

Second, while the cultivation of drugs is particularly well suited to the conditions of armed conflict, the drug trade stands out by the extremely high profits to be made, and the boost in military capacity a party to a conflict stands to benefit from being involved in the drug trade. Hence, the drug trade—rivaled only by the looting of gems and other valuable natural resources—often forms a kind of "plow" whose value spurs various groups to open up trafficking routes, which can later be used for smuggling many other commodities and persons.[5]

In the instances where the academic debate has touched on this issue, drugs have been accorded interest as a limited part of a broader discussion on the economic explanations of civil wars and the relationship between natural resources and armed conflict. In particular, drugs have been included in subcategories such as "lootable resources" together with, for example, diamonds. The results of such research have tended to show that lootable resources, including drugs, have no link to conflict initiation, but that they are positively correlated with conflict duration.[6] The number of countries involved in large-scale production of opium and coca is nevertheless low, and obtaining reliable data on drug cultivation and production across time and space presents considerable difficulty. Consequently, these results remain tentative.[7] But the suggested link raises a number of important questions regarding the dynamics whereby narcotics and conflict interact, which are presently not well understood—and thereby also on the dynamics of the broader interaction of armed conflict and organized crime. Research has contributed significantly to our understanding by showing that lootable resources such as narcotics do not cause but do lengthen conflict, but the specific mechanisms whereby this takes place remain to be explained; equally important, the implications of this linkage for conflict resolution and postconflict stabilization remains to be studied.

The assumption in the literature is that lootable natural resources extend conflict by strengthening the weaker party, normally the insurgent force, enabling it to escape defeat.[8] But does the interaction between organized crime and conflict alter the capabilities, cohesion, and motivations of the parties to a conflict?[9] And what happens during the postconflict period in cases where insurgent groups funded by organized crime transform into powerful political parties? Recent research has suggested that insurgent groups that offer economic incentives to recruits attract opportunistic joiners and thereby over time lose control over its cadres. But these findings are tentative and the argument remains controversial.[10] A better understanding of the specific mechanisms of interaction between the drug industry and armed conflict would provide important implications for the prospects of conflict management and resolution. Therefore, this volume applies the political economy literature to the conflicts in postcommunist Eurasia. In contrast to previous research, the case studies focus not solely on the armed conflict, but extend the analysis to cover the postconflict period, tracking how organized crime evolved, particularly in cases where former insurgents transformed into political actors.

Natural Resources, Civil War, and the Crime-Conflict Nexus

Traditional conflict theory has tended to focus on a "grievance" approach, seeing intrastate conflict as emanating from movements seeking the redress of injustice, or from collective fear.[11] Indeed, war has tended to be portrayed as a result of "information failure": the underlying assumption being that war benefits no one, it must therefore be an outcome that actors seek to avoid, hence an irrational decision. By contrast, a number of emerging studies have focused on economic incentives as the driving force in intrastate conflict.[12]

From Greed or Grievance to the "Feasibility of Conflict"?

Paul Collier and his colleagues argued that civil wars are caused by economic rather than sociopolitical factors, and by loot-seeking rather than by justice-seeking.[13] As Collier and Hoeffler note, this economic approach to understanding civil war differs from political science approaches by focusing on a different motivation for violence—greed, not grievance—and a different explanation for the outbreak of war, atypical opportunities and not atypical grievances.[14] The economic approach focuses on the opportunities that arise to belligerents, especially insurgents, during times of civil war. While war leads to great material losses on a societal basis, this does not mean that "war is a disaster for almost everyone concerned." As David Keen argues, war is not simply the breakdown of order, economy, and social organization, but "the emergence of an alternative system of profit, power, and even protection."[15]

To put it simply, war has functions for some actors. The insecurity and unpredictability of war, coupled with the breakdown or weakening of law and order, implies a turn to a more opportunistic society; an increase in criminality; the disruption of markets; and opportunities for what Collier calls "rent-seeking predation."[16] These consequences are immensely detrimental for society at large, but provide specific opportunities for armed groups to reap significant economic benefits: some people manage to do well out of war.[17]

This so-called "greed theory" of civil conflict has nevertheless been criticized as simplistic and not holding up to closer scrutiny, especially as regards the onset of conflict.[18] Empirical research has argued that few if any conflicts have been initiated only or mainly as a result of economic incentives. An influential study argued that "combatants' incentives for self-enrichment and/or opportunities for insurgent mobilization created by access to natural and financial resources were neither the primary nor the sole cause of the separatist and non-separatist conflicts analyzed."[19] Likewise, in a summary of the findings of fourteen cross-national econometric studies of resources and conflict, Michael Ross concludes that "there appears to be little agreement on the validity of the resources-civil war correlation."[20] Indeed, there is strong disagreement on whether natural resources at all increase the risk of war. As Ross argues, these inconclusive results are likely the result of differing methodologies and differing data.[21] Critics have also argued that "greed" theory is too reductionist to be applied to a complex phenomena as civil war, and particularly the motive of insurgents, since it is based on the idea of Homo Economicus, representing an abstraction of merely one dimension of human behavior.[22] Methodologically, these quantitative studies only identify under what economic circumstances conflict onset occurs, or what economic indicators are correlated with longer-duration conflicts. To move from such correlations to causation and discussing motives, one needs additional data, most suitably collected through case studies. For these reasons, Collier et al. have also shifted attention, moving from a discussion on motives (greed or grievance) to feasibility, that is, under what economic conditions civil wars can viably be financed.[23]

Differentiating Resources

Lumping together all kinds of natural resources does not appear to be meaningful. Moreover, the focus on natural resources also omits the possibility that actors in armed conflicts reap benefits from unrelated economic activity, such as smuggling goods and human beings. There are also types of funding sources for insurgent groups that are not necessarily demand-driven or market-based. These include diaspora funding (which often entails some level of force or extortion), extortion or taxation of local businesses, robberies and kidnappings, diversion or taxation of development aid, and sometimes low-level forgeries or white-collar crimes.[24]

As far as natural resources are concerned, the division of resources into smaller categories, especially between lootable and nonlootable resources, generates more interesting results.[25] Ross concludes from a study of fifteen cases that alluvial diamonds and drugs are the resources most strongly associated with civil wars occurring between 1990 and 2000.[26] He argues that the level to which a commodity is linked to conflict depends on its lootability, obstructability, and legality. Drugs, like alluvial diamonds, are easy to appropriate by a limited number of individuals, as compared to oil, gas, timber, or minerals, and are hence lootable. Given their high value to size ratio, they are not easily obstructable—unlike oil, minerals, and timber, which require much more time and complicated enterprises to be looted. The illegality of drugs also makes them benefit insurgents disproportionately, since they are less susceptible to influence by international prohibition regimes, unless governments (such as the Taliban in Afghanistan during 1996–2000) are willing to endure international sanctions and isolation. Moreover, this argument extends to nonnatural economic resources as well, notably the smuggling of goods and people that involve an element of illegality. Indeed, the more illegal an economic activity is, the more suitable it becomes for nonstate violent actors, which do not operate under international law. Human trafficking is a case in point, as is the smuggling of controlled commodities such as cigarettes.[27]

The research record so far only indicates a link between lootable resources and the duration of conflict, not the onset of conflict. Humphreys, for example, found no statistical link between diamonds and the initiation of war.[28] Noting a link between "valuable contraband" and conflict duration, Fearon found that rebels relied extensively on contraband financing in 17 of 128 cases of conflict. These cases had median and mean conflict durations of 28.1 and 48.2 years, respectively, while the remaining 111 conflicts had 6.0 and 8.8.[29] Indeed, as Ross sums up the field, most evidence suggests that gemstones and narcotics are linked to the duration of conflict, but not to the initiation of conflict.[30] Previous research by Svante Cornell of nine narcotics-producing states, of which seven experienced armed conflict, has indicated that the same holds true for the production of narcotics. Rather than generating or being generated by drug cultivation, the study found that armed conflict qualitatively and quantitatively transforms existing drug cultivation. Importantly, the study found that armed conflict is itself deeply affected by the narcotics industry, which tends to strengthen the capacity of insurgent movements while weakening that of the state.[31]

The Crime-Conflict Nexus

These studies suggest a causal link between narcotics, a form of organized crime, and enduring conflict. They do not, however, explain convincingly why this should be the case. The basic inference is that the presence of narcotics increases the capabilities of insurgents. But is this the entire story? Increased capabilities could be conceived to imply a greater possibility for a negotiated solution in protracted conflict, once both parties realize that there is little possibility of victory—William Zartman's "hurting stalemate."[32] Why, then, should conflicts involving narcotics be so intractable? Recently emerging theory from the field of organized crime is helpful in suggesting an answer to this missing dimension.

Studies in the late 1990s observed a globally increasing linkage between organized crime and violent nonstate actors, in particular terrorist groups.[33] This relationship, termed the crime-terror nexus, was initially coined by Tamara Makarenko for the study of terrorist organizations, but is equally applicable to regular insurgencies.[34] For the purposes of this study, the term "crime-conflict nexus" is therefore more appropriate. The crime-conflict nexus refers to an increasing confluence of groups originally espousing either political or criminal motivations. Ideologically and criminally motivated groups have traditionally been seen as forming opposing ideal types of armed groupings.[35] The ideal type of groups that challenge state authority with violent means in the pursuit of a political goal is one of striving for a self-defined higher cause. Such groups are therefore traditionally understood as being disinterested in—or even principally opposed to—the pursuit of profit through organized crime, including drug trafficking.[36] Transnational criminal networks, on the other hand, are motivated simply by pursuit of monetary profit and status. Clearly, their interests may be more than simple economics, since money is not necessarily an end in itself but a means to achieve status, influence, security, and even territorial control. Earlier research by Phil Williams has argued that they are "economic rather than political organizations, [and therefore] do not pose the same kind of overt or obvious challenge to states that terrorist groups do."[37] Their primary aim, unlike terrorist or insurgent movements, is not to directly challenge the state. Bruce Hoffman eloquently notes the dividing line between these two opposing ideal types: "the terrorist is fundamentally an altruist: he believes he is serving a 'good' cause designed to achieve a greater good for a wider constituency [whereas] the criminal serves no cause at all, just his own personal aggrandizement and material satiation."[38]

This traditional division into mutually exclusive ideological and criminal ideal types lies at the basis of the academic division between political science and criminology, as well as bureaucratic divisions between law enforcement and national security. As Williams notes, the perception is that "crime is a domestic problem; and law enforcement and national security are based on very different philosophies, organizational structures and legal frameworks."[39] As a result, transnational organized crime has not been viewed as a national, let alone international, security issue. This view has nevertheless become increasingly misleading, as the observable situation has changed. For example, Williams's argument would not be able to explain the challenge that essentially economically motivated criminal entities have posed to the Mexican state. More recently, Williams has also partly changed his view, agreeing that there are "hybrid forms of organizations," pointing to the Revolutionary Armed Forces of Colombia (FARC) in Colombia and D-Company in India as an insurgency and an organized crime entity, respectively, that exhibit mixed motives.[40] As Thachuk observes, organized crime groups traditionally "rarely co-operated with terrorist groups, or engaged in their activities, as their goals were most often at odds . . . many of today's terrorist groups have not only lost some of their more comprehensible ideals, but are increasingly turning to smuggling and other criminal activities to fund their operations."[41] Likewise, organizations such as the World Bank have begun highlighting how organized crime and other nonpolitical armed actors have expanded in the vacuum left by weak or failing postconflict states to a level where they now pose a serious threat to human security and state stability in many postconflict societies.[42]

Two separate phenomena have contributed to this: the decline in state funding for insurgency and the global expansion of transnational organized crime. The end of the Cold War drastically reduced the availability of state financing for terrorist and insurgent movements.[43] Without the bipolar confrontation, simply being in opposition to a communist or noncommunist regime no longer translated into financial support from a superpower or its proxies.[44] Insurgent groups hence needed to find other sources of funding to survive. Organized crime appeared an attractive and lucrative way of obtaining necessary funds. International efforts to root out terrorism financing after September 11, 2001, caused a further decline of state financing, pushing nonstate violent actors further toward organized criminal financing.[45] Meanwhile, the rapidly developing processes of globalization, which have made transportation and communications easier, have enabled the gradual expansion of transnational organized crime globally.[46] From having been more geographically circumscribed and specialized, transnational criminal networks now operate across continents, in alliances with similar groups elsewhere, and engage in any form of criminal activity that combines high profit and acceptable risk.[47] The criminal opportunities arising to insurgent groupings therefore increased over the 1990s, and globalization opened markets to crime in the most distant conflict zones. Specifically, globalization has facilitated the expansion of organized crime through several different mechanisms. The increased levels of global trade allow organized crime groups to hide their merchandise in licit shipments; improved communication technologies make it easier to coordinate not only licit but also illicit trade across great distances; increases in financial flows make it harder to spot money laundering operations; and decreased border controls and cheaper transportations of goods and persons further facilitate transnational organized crime. Whereas there are multiple initiatives to improve international policing, political issues, and the inherent challenges of intelligence sharing and acting on Interpol Red Notices all contribute to a situation where organized crime groups are gradually becoming transnational while law enforcement agencies continue to be overwhelmingly based on nation-states and limited to their jurisdictions. Furthermore, as Naím points out, demand-driven organized crime pits international networks against national bureaucracies.[48]

The interaction between criminal and political groups is therefore presently best conceptualized as a continuum rather than separate phenomena. In this respect, Makarenko's analytical construct of a security continuum that places pure organized crime at one end of the spectrum and pure ideological groups at the other is helpful.[49] It shows the wide variety of possible interactions between criminal and political groups. Between the two ideal types, the continuum allows for a "gray area" where different variations and combinations of the two exist. Interactions between organized crime and ideological struggle can take place either through cooperation between criminal and ideological groups; or through the involvement of an ideological group in

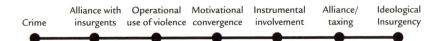

Figure 1. The crime-conflict continuum.

crime or vice versa, as suggested in the crime-conflict continuum depicted in Figure 1.[50]

Research has suggested that the practice of cooperation between groups at opposing ends of the spectrum tends to give way to self-involvement—mainly due to the lack of trust between groups and the greater profitability of self-involvement.[51] It should be noted, however, that the continuum mainly describes observed behavior rather than motivation, which is notoriously difficult to pin down. In essence, the continuum assumes that growing involvement in organized crime on the part of an ideologically motivated organization leads to modifications of the organization's motivations.

Thus, the logic of the continuum is that the need for sources of finance forms the first impetus for the involvement of politically motivated groups with organized crime; and that such involvement also tends to affect the groups' motivational structures. Once involved in crime, groups may continue to further their original interests—but crime can also become an end in itself, rather than just a method of financing.[52] Particularly in protracted conflicts, the continuum expects entire groups or parts of groups to shift their focus increasingly toward the objective of profit. That is, the organization or movement either gradually shifts its nature to a predominantly criminal one, or acquires a criminal nature at the side of its ideological nature. Thus, some groups are found in a situation where "organized crime and terrorism are indistinguishable from one another."[53] Profit through crime, often specifically the drug trade, becomes a motivation in its own right for the existence and cohesion of the movement.[54]

An added value of the continuum model is that it allows for the movement of groups across this continuum over time, enabling the tracking of the evolution of a group's involvement in crime as well as of its motivational structures. Clearly, this issue is relevant not only for drug production or transit states but for insurgent/terrorist groups in the developed world as well—the Ulster Defense Association and Ulster Volunteer Force being only two examples of movements that continued their involvement in organized crime long after a formal peace agreement had been signed.[55] However, the continuum is incapable of explaining why some groups appear to rapidly witness a change in motivational structures, while others appear to sustain long-term involvement in organized crime without an observable impact to the organization's primary motives. In other words, the question why some insurgent groups are "corrupted" by money while others are not remains unanswered.

Indeed, not all armed groups are equally "criminalized" by their involvement in organized crime. For example, armed groups such as the Kurdistan Workers' Party (PKK) in Turkey and FARC in Colombia have been heavily involved in heroin and cocaine trafficking, respectively. In spite of this, neither group has shown significant shifts in their basic motivations—neither pays wages to combatants, their leaders typically live under modest circumstances (with the exception of PKK leader Abdullah Öcalan during his exile in Syria in the 1990s) and both groups continue to pursue their original political aspirations in a way that is inconsistent with any wholesale "criminalization" of their leadership.[56] This relative discipline is largely explained by the nature of these organizations. Both are left-wing insurgencies that have put a strong emphasis on personal sacrifice by their combatants, and both are largely hierarchical organizations that closely monitor both their members and the income generated by drug trafficking, routinely pursuing and executing individuals suspected of stealing from the organization. By contrast, the paramilitary umbrella organization United Self-Defense Forces of Colombia (Autodefensas Unidas de Colombia; AUC) in Colombia was always loosely organized, motivated more by its involvement in drug trafficking than its nominal counterinsurgency mission, paying wages to members and seeing extensive intra-organizational strife and murders as midlevel commanders sought to expand their turf and maximize their incomes.[57] Furthermore, the criminalization of armed groups is not a one-way street—for example, the Provisional IRA even withdrew from drug trafficking to Northern Ireland after this trade made it profoundly unpopular with its core constituency.[58] By contrast, certain units inside armed groups may be specifically vulnerable to motivational changes. Individuals working with financing inside armed groups tend to be better educated, exposed to less risk of combat, and given more opportunities to engage in graft inside the armed group as they manage large sums of money under circumstances where it is very difficult for the senior leadership to monitor their actions. Hence, finance officers in armed groups are exposed to significant principal-agent problems.[59] This aspect can also impact entire units inside armed groups that work specifically with financing through organized crime, such as Sendero Luminoso's local committee in the Upper Huallaga Valley.[60] Last, whereas much research has focused on drug cultivation and other lootable commodities, as Picarelli and Shelley point out, there is a wide array of types of organized crime that nonstate violent actors can engage in to obtain funding. These range from market-based crimes (trafficking in narcotics, valuable commodities, goods, and humans), to violent crimes (extortion, kidnapping, robberies) and simpler forms of white-collar crime (fraud, intellectual property theft, aid diversion, and counterfeiting). Each of these types of crimes has advantages and drawbacks from the point of view of the organization, including technical expertise required, risk of detection, availability, competition, and potential pay-off.[61] Surveying the financing methods of a wide array of terrorist groups, Picarelli and Shelley also argue that "while still important, narcotics can no longer be seen as the predominant source of funding terrorism."[62]

Implications

Involvement in crime can be seen as fundamentally changing the equation of an armed group's relationship to state and society. Whether or not its motivations are affected, crime enriches the group and its leaders, enabling the acquisition of more sophisticated weapons, the employment of more fighters, the corruption of state officials, and the better propagation of group ideology to the population. Hence crime and its proceeds makes the group a more dangerous adversary to the government, and often results in a further weakening of the state—particularly if it enables insurgents to assert territorial control over parts of the state's territory that is usable for criminal activities. In this sense, crime and drugs are instrumental in enabling a group to threaten the security of the state at its very foundation—the monopoly of the use of force and control over territory.[63] As laid out in this chapter, insurgency financing through organized crime can also impact the internal dynamics of insurgencies, potentially affecting discipline in relation to civilians, creating principal-agent problems with specialized financing units, changes in tactics, target selection, or modus operandi or even wholesale motivational change inside the group.

The existing debate on natural resources and armed conflict does not significantly address the possibility of motivational change in insurgent groups. In fact, much of the literature generally takes a "snapshot" of a group, considering it at best either motivated by greed or by grievance, but does not consider the possibility of motivations changing over time. Indeed, the crime-conflict nexus offers the possibility that insurgents may initially be motivated by grievance, but that the opportunity of economic profit in the course of conflict can change both the group's financial condition as well as its motivational structure. This in turn affects the evolution of the conflict, the development of the group itself, and the prospects of various measures of conflict resolution. Indeed, asserting whether an insurgent group has gone through significant changes in motivation will have important implications for ways to handle the group. Simply put, offering redress to the stated grievances of an insurgent group will do little to end the conflict in case the group has changed its primary motivation to the criminal. Indeed, in such cases, the very proposition of political compromises, including offers of power-sharing or regional autonomy, could be misplaced as the insurgent groups have developed an interest in the continuation of conflict. A traditional, grievance-based understanding of the conflict would hence be likely to lead negotiators in the wrong direction. Likewise, much of the existing literature focuses on the onset and duration of the conflict, and relatively little on the postconflict period. Thus, with the exception of Colombia and Afghanistan, little attention has been allotted to what becomes of the leadership and combatants of crime-funded insurgencies in the aftermath of armed conflict. If the argument that motives change due to involvement in organized crime is taken at face value, this would suggest potentially serious consequences, particularly in countries where former insurgents become the new political leaders—as happened in many of the conflicts covered in this book

Conditions for the Crime-Conflict Nexus

The crime-conflict nexus can and does operate with any form of organized crime, but the specific case of the cultivation of illicit drugs stands out for a number of reasons: they are immensely profitable, especially in processed form; they are renewable as they can be continuously cultivated year after year; and they are by nature illegal, given the existence of a strong international legal regime that outlaws the large-scale cultivation of drugs with very specific and controlled exceptions. Thus, the drug industry requires territories outside state control for cultivation, a fact that is true also for the looting of natural resources such as timber or gemstones. However, the trafficking of drugs, gemstones, or humans, and most other forms of crime, do not similarly require control over territory.

Thus, the different manifestations of the crime-conflict nexus are likely to occur only under certain conditions. Armed conflict and its consequences, such as the collapse of law enforcement and the loss of state control over territory, create an impetus for the rise of all forms of organized crime. But the option of drug cultivation or the looting of natural resources may not be present in all conflict areas. All are dependent on the availability of the resources in question; if there are no lootable resources, insurgents will not be able to exploit them. Similarly, drug cultivation is a relatively complicated process. While not technologically advanced, it does require certain skills. Opium cultivation, for example, is a complex, labor-intensive occupation, with many natural hazards.[64] This makes it likely to take place only where a previous tradition of cultivation of narcotic plants exists. In the absence of cultivation tradition, suitable climatic conditions, and market outlets, armed conflict is likely to make other forms of organized crime more attractive.

Insurgent groups seeking sources of finances are likely to turn to organized crime only if that option is preferable to alternative modes of financing, which could include external support from states or diasporas, the extortion of civilians, or the abuse of development assistance.[65] Thus, it is opportunity that makes insurgent groups turn to organized crime. That being said, insurgent groups seldom if ever rely on a single revenue stream. In fact, most armed groups that engage in drug trafficking typically have other sources of funding. The PKK engages in heroin trafficking, but also receives extensive funding from the Kurdish diaspora in Europe; FARC is involved in cocaine trafficking, but also used to receive substantial income from kidnappings and extortion, and possibly financing from Venezuela; and various groups in Afghanistan and Pakistan receive training and financing from the Pakistani Inter-Services Intelligence (ISI) and Iran, as well as robberies, extortion, and other types of organized crime.[66]

The link between organized crime and conflict is plausible in both conflicts over territory and conflicts over government, but is likely to have different dynamics. In separatist wars, insurgents are tied to a specific territory, and hence have little choice of terrain or theater of operations. They can protect local drug production to bolster legitimacy; and in a protracted conflict with control over territory, encourage drug production. If their territory is located at a crucial crossroads of trade, they may attract trafficking flows across territory under their control. In a conflict over government, however, insurgents have a greater potential to choose their theater of operations across the country, and a choice whether to press for territorial control over specific areas. This provides greater flexibility in selecting areas of operation. As far as drug trafficking is concerned, protecting drug cultivation could in these situations play a bigger role for building popular legitimacy, as rebels may have less inherent popular support than insurgents struggling for ethnic rights.[67] Conflicts over government, where insurgents may not have a secure home territory, could also be more likely to generate a focus on acquiring income through trafficking of a variety of commodities. Hence if an insurgent movement does not have stable control over a fixed territory, it would be more likely to seek to involve in a form of organized crime that itself is flexible and requires the right networks and connections, but is not linked to a specific territory.

Combining the findings of research on the natural resources and armed conflict, and the crime-conflict nexus, a number of propositions for the relationship between organized crime and conflict can be inferred.

- The origins of conflict are based on grievance and not greed. Even large-scale organized crime, whether drug production or various forms of smuggling, is unlikely to cause a conflict.
- The conditions of armed conflict provide an impetus for organized criminal activity. Where a tradition of drug cultivation exists, conflict will tend to generate an increase in the production of drugs; where no such tradition exists, the growth of smuggling operations of various forms should be expected, especially if a conflict zone is located between the origin and destination areas of major smuggling flows of drugs, human beings, or various commodities including weapons.
- The growth of organized criminal activity, at first a spillover effect of conflict given the decrease of state control, forms a strong incentive for insurgent groups to involve in organized crime to reap profits. This involvement tends to go from alliance with or taxing of organized criminal activity to direct involvement.
- Once involved in the drug trade, insurgent groups are likely to see their motivational structures affected to some extent , with elements of the group acquiring an economic motivation that compounds or supplants the ideological one.
- In postconflict situations where the armed group has been involved in organized crime, there is a much higher risk of transitions from political to criminal violence and the emergence of weak or failing states. If the armed group emerges victorious from the conflict, there is an even higher risk of the state itself becoming criminalized and consequently of subsequent state failure.

Postcommunist Eurasia

The linkage between organized crime and conflict is a global phenomenon with a series of focal areas around the world. The northern cone of Latin America is perhaps the best-researched area, where the interaction between narcotics and conflict in Colombia and Peru has long been known. Western and Central Africa is another area strongly affected, where looting of diamonds, timber, and other natural resources in conflict zones has been widely observed. A third area is the "golden crescent" of Southeast Asia, with the Burma-Laos-Thailand border area until recently exhibiting strong elements of both organized crime and armed conflict, something that has nevertheless normalized to some degree.

Postcommunist Eurasia is the newest, geographically largest, and most strategically located area of overlap between organized crime and armed conflict. Indeed, the specific circumstances of the breakup of the communist bloc in Eurasia contributed to the emergence of a series of protracted armed conflicts; to the rapid growth of transnational organized crime across the width of the postcommunist area; and inevitably to the interaction of armed conflict and organized crime in these conflict zones, with important implications for the processes of conflict resolution as well as political and economic development in Eurasia as a whole.

The conflict zones of Eurasia are located along some of the most important smuggling routes of the present day. Indeed, they link the areas of origin and destination of a number of smuggling operations. The postcommunist area links the world's largest source of opiates, Afghanistan, with its main destination market Europe, with Russia in particular developing into a destination. It links the source areas for human smuggling from Asia and the Middle East to Europe, while increasingly becoming a source area for human trafficking. Meanwhile, it also links the most significant source area of WMD trafficking, Russia, to its major destination, the Middle East. Finally, it links the source of much of the world weaponry—Europe and the northern postcommunist states—with destination markets farther south.

The Collapse of Communism, the Building of Statehood, and Organized Crime

As the Italian experience until the 1990s has shown, organized crime can pose a substantial threat even to industrialized, developed states. In this context, it should come as no surprise that organized criminal networks are able to pose a much more significant threat to weak and developing states. While this is the case, the states of postcommunist Eurasia have a common experience of the political and economic transitions from communist rule, as well as the processes of state formation that resulted from the disintegration of the communist federations that the Soviet Union and Yugoslavia constituted. This transition, involving the collapse of existing state institutions and the requirement of building entirely new ones, was an auspicious moment for organized criminal networks, whose roots in the Soviet period enabled them to strongly benefit from the instability of the transition period.

Indeed, organized crime and corruption were constant features of the Soviet Union.[68] A criminal elite had formed in the Soviet labor camps already in the 1920s and 1930s, something that was boosted by the 1921 penal code, which identified political opponents and not regular criminals as the main threat to the state.[69] This raised the position of criminal groups in society. Informal criminal groupings known as thieves in law, *vory v zakone*, were formed. The origin of these groups in the labor camps is also a reason for the very violence-prone nature of post-Soviet organized crime. The background in this most brutal part of the Soviet system made the subculture around the criminal groups hardened and resilient to a level not experienced in the Western context.

Criminal elites, moreover, developed a symbiotic relationship to parts of the communist elite. The latter had power, but the policies of communism limited the opportunities for politicians to personal enrichment. The criminal forces therefore shared their wealth with political figures in exchange for political protection. The political elite needed the criminal groups, and vice versa.[70]

When the Soviet system collapsed in 1991, the competition over control of resources that developed lacked a clear definition of legality and illegality. Indeed, during the Soviet period, capitalism per se was illegal. With the collapse of the discredited ideology of Communism, capitalism not only was legalized but turned into the societal norm. Hence, most business activity that had been classified as illegal, as "speculation," during the Soviet period was legalized overnight; yet some forms of business activity remained illegal. The borderline between legality and illegality was moved, but societal understanding, as well as respect, for this border was largely absent. As a U.S. Justice Department report observes:

> Organized crime in the Soviet era consisted of illegal enterprises with both legal and black-market connections that were based on the

misuse of state property and funds. It is most important to recognize that the blurring of the distinction between the licit and the illicit is also a trademark of post-Soviet organized crime that shows its ancestry with the old Soviet state and its command-economy system. This, in turn, has direct political implications. The historical symbiosis with the state makes Russian organized crime virtually an inalienable part of the state. As this has continued into the present, some would say it has become an engine of the state that works at all levels of the Russian government.[71]

The collapse of communism allowed the entrepreneurs from the shadows to emerge into the limelight. It should be noted that the shadow economy had some prestige in the communist period, particularly in ethnic minority areas, because it openly ignored political repression and challenged the political regime by its very existence. The criminal world was associated with wealth, as well as resilience in the face of repression and Russian rule.

Moreover, when Soviet president Mikhail Gorbachev's reforms in the late 1980s allowed for some elements of private enterprise, the criminal groups were the main elements in Soviet society that had a thorough understanding of the thinking underpinning a market economy. This, and their readiness to resort to force, put them in a favorable position to benefit from privatization processes. Meanwhile, the decline of security services across the former communist space led to the firing of tens of thousands of former security officers, whose expertise and networks were strongly in demand among criminal circles. Hence the salience of organized criminal figures in the economy and politics of postcommunist states in the 1990s, a process affecting most if not all postcommunist states, which was nevertheless gradually overcome in the more developed countries to the west, which also enjoyed substantial support from European institutions, including the prospect of integration into the EU and NATO. But in the states of the former Yugoslavia and Soviet Union, the problem instead became entrenched. Crime came to permeate society and politics. When Otari Kvantrishvili, a former wrestler and one of the largest figures of Russian organized crime in the early 1990s, was murdered in 1994, his funeral was broadcast on live television. To music from the *Godfather* movie, high political figures marched silently in the funeral procession, illustrating the acceptance and glorification of organized crime in society. Russian president Boris Yeltsin stopped at offering written condolences.[72] Of course, crime has since then grown more discreet and less overt, but by no means less dangerous to the political system.

If Afghanistan, by the time of the collapse of the USSR, was already in the process of full state collapse, the southern republics of the Soviet Union and Yugoslavia were also in a particularly vulnerable position. To begin with, they were economically weak, with much of their budgets having been subsidized by the richer republics of the respective federation. They were also located on the outskirts of the federations, whereas their economies were disconnected from their neighboring, noncommunist states. Finally, they lacked most institutions normally associated with statehood, having to build key institutions such as tax codes, border guards, and police authorities themselves or inheriting nonfunctioning institutions from the communist period. This exacerbated the collapse of their economies, and accentuated their vulnerability to organized crime. To further complicate the process, the ethnic and regional tensions that emerged and led to the wars across the regions completed the picture. In this situation, in the former republics of the Soviet Union and Yugoslavia where conflict erupted, there was often an acute lack of, or weakness in, local institutions with the resources to organize large-scale collective violence. Hence, organized criminal networks, with their access to weapons, links of violent members, and preexisting organizational structures, were often relied on to defend their ethnic brethren while benefiting financially from the resulting power vacuum.

The Conflict Zones of Eurasia

The conflict zones of Eurasia have both similarities and differences. Most have an origin in the late Soviet period, but break down in terms of the point of contention of the conflict, some being over territory, others over government, and the identity being politicized, ethnicity and religion. They break into two clusters. The eastern cluster of conflicts is motivated mainly by the politicization of religion, involving the civil wars in Afghanistan and Tajikistan, joined by the insurgency of the Islamic Movement of Uzbekistan (IMU). The western cluster involves ethnopolitical wars in the South Caucasus, Moldova, and former Yugoslavia.

- Afghanistan is included in this study because its conflict was a direct result of the communist government and Soviet occupation, but also because of the crucial role its opiate industry plays in Eurasian

organized crime. In Afghanistan, a complex civil war over government
dates back to the withdrawal of Soviet troops in 1989, politicized
mainly around religious identity, but with a substantial ethnic aspect.
This conflict has gone through numerous phases, involving substantial
Western involvement since 2001, but is mainly characterized by
the collapse of central governmental authority that is yet to be
meaningfully rebuilt.

- Tajikistan, to Afghanistan's north, experienced a state collapse not
  unlike that of Afghanistan, with a civil war over government waged
  between 1992 and 1997. This conflict, fought mainly along regional
  and ideological lines, ended with a power-sharing agreement that saw
  the temporary integration of the opposition into governing structures,
  but also their subsequent marginalization.
- The insurgency of the IMU on the territories of Kyrgyzstan and
  Uzbekistan has been closely linked with both the Afghan and Tajik
  conflicts. Nevertheless, in spite of close linkages, the insurgency is
  clearly dissociated from those two conflicts given the specific goals of
  the movement. While a much less serious conflict in terms of intensity
  and duration, the IMU is included in this study mainly on account of
  the significant depth of its linkages to organized crime. The IMU was
  decimated by Operation Enduring Freedom in Afghanistan in 2001,
  after which its remnants moved to northwestern Pakistan's tribal areas;
  it has transformed into a purely terrorist movement with little capacity
  to conduct ground operations in Central Asia.
- The Chechen wars were initiated as a dispute over territory, but
  motives and identities transformed during the conflict. After the
  Chechen side won the initial conflict (1994–1996), during the Second
  Chechen War and its aftermath religion has become increasingly
  central to the conflict. Even though high-intensity fighting has ended,
  there is still a simmering low-intensity insurgency based largely
  around an Islamist agenda that has spread to neighboring regions,
  particularly Dagestan.
- The war in Bosnia-Herzegovina occupies a middle ground between
  these two clusters, a tripartite conflict over territory where religion
  was also strongly politicized. This was particularly true for the
  Bosniak side, which received a significant influx of Islamist fighters
  and funding from Islamic charities. With an estimated 250,000
  casualties, this was together with the war in Afghanistan and

Chechnya the most high-intensity and atrocious of the wars analyzed in this book. Like Kosovo, the conflict ended following a decisive Western military intervention and the region has since hosted a substantial international peacekeeping force and received a steady flow of development assistance.

- In Georgia, two conflicts over territory, between the Georgian government and the autonomous areas of Abkhazia and South Ossetia, erupted during the collapse of the Soviet Union. These conflicts have remained unresolved along cease-fire lines since that time, and further exacerbated by Russia's invasion of Georgia in 2008, after which Russia recognized the independence of the two territories and for all practical purposes occupied them.
- Moldova has been affected by a conflict very similar to those in Georgia, with the eastern region of Transnistria seeking to secede from Moldova. As in Georgia, the conflict remains unresolved. While Western powers have sought to move toward a resolution, Russia's close links to Transnistria have effectively precluded an agreement.
- Kosovo has some similarities with the conflicts in Moldova and Georgia, being a conflict over territory involving the quest for separate statehood on the part of a formerly autonomous minority population. The main difference, however, is the international involvement in Kosovo and the support for conditional independence that it has gained from the international community.

Methodology and Case-Study Design

The main aim of this book is to study the crime-insurgency nexus in the Eurasian civil wars, analyzing both how this connection affected the insurgent groups and the conflict dynamic, and also what legacies it has had during the postconflict period. Each case study will do so by briefly providing a background to the individual conflict itself, as well as to the particular forms of organized crime involved. Moving from there, the case studies will seek to investigate the form of interaction between parties to conflicts and organized crime, seeking to gain a better understanding of the effects this interaction has had on the conflicts, and its implications for the conflict zones and countries during the postconflict period. Hence, the book is organized as a structured comparative case study, facilitating comparisons across the region while presenting detailed analysis of events on the ground, drawing on primary sources from all the conflicted-affected regions.

This approach has both clear advantages and certain limitations. Drawing on in-depth regional expertise, the book offers a wealth of empirical data and insight difficult to acquire for any single researcher, or using purely quantitative indicators. As such, it can unearth similarities in causal patterns and mechanisms across countries that would be very difficult to identify using single-case studies or purely quantitative methods. The downside is that many established analytical approaches become inapplicable and findings may be diverse and difficult to present parsimoniously. However, limiting the study to the Eurasian region with its collective experience of communism and focusing on the immediate aftermath of the break-up of the Soviet Union and Yugoslavia yields a sample of cases to which this method can be usefully applied. The book concludes with a chapter analyzing the implications of these cases both for the crime-insurgency literature and for policy, especially the planning of future peacekeeping and postconflict reconstruction missions.

Chapter 2

Afghanistan's Endless Conflict and
the Development of the Opium Industry

Svante Cornell

When the Soviet Union ended its occupation of Afghanistan in February 1989, peace did not follow. Instead, Afghanistan faced further destruction and turmoil as a civil war erupted in the aftermath of the Soviet withdrawal. It was not until 1996, when the Taliban movement gained control over a larger part of Afghanistan, that some stability was brought to the country. The exception was the northern region, where fighting between the Taliban and the Northern Alliance still carried on. In 2001, a new phase of the Afghan conflict was initiated when the U.S.-led Operation Enduring Freedom-Afghanistan was initiated, and rapidly led to the fall of the Taliban regime. Throughout the period of Taliban rule, Afghanistan had become a safe haven for Islamist militants of different nationalities. Groups like Al Qaeda and the IMU participated on the Taliban side in the Afghan conflict, and used the country as a base for activities abroad. A decade later, the country remains marred by conflict, with added uncertainty as NATO has committed to a withdrawal of combat troops by 2014.

During the thirty-year period in which Afghanistan has experienced armed conflict more or less incessantly, the country was transformed into the world's largest producer of opiates. UN statistics show that opium production in Afghanistan took off in the mid-1980s; during the civil war and Taliban rule, opium production rose from 1,570 metric tons in 1990 to 4,565 metric tons in 1999.[1] In the post-Taliban era, the international presence in Afghanistan has failed to make a dent in the spectacular growth of opium production and heroin refining in the country.[2] From 2007 to 2009, opium production ranged from 6,900 to 8,200 metric tons; crop disease led the number to fall drastically in 2010 to 3,600 tons, a figure that would nevertheless still have been considered a bumper crop in the 1990s. Indeed, climate and crop disease have appeared to contribute much more significantly than interdiction to the fluctuation of opium production in the country.

Afghanistan stands out among the cases discussed in this volume, as it is the source of the most valuable illicit commodity driving the interaction of conflict and organized crime across Eurasia. Given the dilapidation of Afghanistan's licit economy, the opium industry also has an inordinately large role in the country's overall economy. As such, the opium economy has so penetrated the fabric of Afghanistan's economy and politics that most armed as well as political groupings have some form of involvement with it. This is valid both for insurgent groups fighting the state and for those forces that are allied with or constitute the country's state institutions. Naturally, drug production and trafficking are not the only forms of organized crime associated with Afghanistan's conflict: the smuggling of gemstones and timber, among others, have mushroomed during three decades of war, and have been sources of financing for various armed groups. Nevertheless, the opiate industry has had the gravest effect on the country by far, and will be the focus of this chapter.

Soviet Occupation and Civil War

The war in Afghanistan derived from the communist coup d'état in 1978 and the ensuing revolt against the new political regime. The rebellion, starting in the countryside, continued to grow and soon spread to the cities. During 1979, the uprising developed into a serious threat to the young pro-Soviet regime in Kabul. The Afghan army was on the brink of a breakdown, unable to suppress the insurgency and regain control over the country. At that point, the Soviet leaders took the decision to upgrade the Soviet presence from military assistance to a full-scale invasion.

During the first years of the invasion, Soviet forces successfully took control over major cities and main roads. To put further pressure on the rebels, the military launched offensives into areas with mujahideen activity. The counterinsurgency operations forced the Mujahideen to seek refuge in inaccessible mountain areas. When the military withdrew from the areas, the Mujahideen would return in the classic fashion of guerrilla warfare. In a similar manner, the military controlled the country in daytime while the rebels held sway during the night. In this period, there were no large-scale battles as the insurgent groups were vastly out-muscled by the Soviet forces: such confrontations would have been devastating and pointless for the rebels. Instead, the Mujahideen fighters relied on tactics based on ambushes and small-scale operations against the overwhelming enemy.[3]

The insurgency contained a variety of religious and political groups. The most important insurgency group was the Hezb-i Islami (Gulbuddin; HIG) under Gulbuddin Hekmatyar, which owed much of its capabilities to being favored by the Pakistani military and intelligence services.[4] At the early stage of the conflict, the insurgent groups, with camps and bases in the border areas near and inside Pakistan, began to receive arms and funding from different contributors to fight the Soviet Union and the regime in Kabul.[5] In the beginning, few expected the ill-trained and badly equipped Mujahideen fighters to be able to inflict any serious damage to the Red Army, much less to defeat it. This would later change as more and more sophisticated weapons and military equipment poured into Afghanistan.

By 1983, the Soviet forces had managed to take over the country but were not in total control of the territory. They had consolidated their presence in Afghanistan by controlling the major cities and main roads and entrenching themselves in bases around the country. Still unable to repel the insurgency by hunting down the rebels, the military initiated the next phase of the war by implementing a new strategy, emphasizing Soviet air superiority and targeting the support structures of the insurgency. The Soviet counterinsurgency strategy of the mid-1980s mimicked the warfare of the mujahideen through disrupting supply lines and punishing local support for the rebellion. This kind of warfare laid waste to the Afghan countryside. Besides destroying the rural economy and infrastructure, it forced millions of refugees to flee to the neighboring countries.[6] It was among the Afghan refugee youth in *madrassas* in Pakistan that the Taliban movement was later born.

The Soviet occupation left Afghanistan devastated and planted many of the problems that still plague the country. The human devastation has already been noted; suffice it to observe that over two million Afghans were killed in the war, close to 10 percent of the population; 40 percent were turned into refugees; and between five and seven million landmines were scattered across the country. Politically, the occupation left a large vacuum: the central authorities lost their already precarious relationship to the countryside, but more important, the demographic implications of the war fundamentally altered structures of authority in Afghan society. Traditional sources of authority such as elders lost their leading role as communities were depopulated, while power shifted to the younger mujahideen, who in turn increasingly came under the sway of radical ideologies that even further undermined the traditional authority structures. This helps explain the near-hegemony radical Islam has commanded in Afghan society from the 1990s on. The radical forces were the ones to fight the Soviet occupation; moreover, the most radical among them, such as HIG, received the bulk of foreign funding and were therefore disproportionally strengthened by the war.

Yet another effect of the occupation was to worsen ethnic relations among Afghanistan's heterogeneous communities. As in the USSR, Soviet authorities promoted the role of ethnicity in society and politics, and Afghans found that ethnicity became an increasingly important factor in daily affairs. Other foreign actors contributed to this phenomenon as well: Pakistan mainly supported Pashtun fighters, the West poured money to ethnic Tajik warlord Ahmad Shah Masoud, while Iran alone supported the Shi'a rebels in the Hazarajat.

Thus, the Soviet withdrawal led to a protracted civil war. Given the differences between rival mujahideen groups, the pro-Soviet regime managed to survive for three years, during which time the Afghan state practically disintegrated. This is important because the collapse of the Afghan state implied that from 1992 to 1996 it was meaningless to speak of an Afghan state being criminalized: the state in reality consisted of specific and shifting alliances of warlords that happened to control the capital. Indeed, the bewildering nature of the conflict is illustrated by the fact that the major forces involved in the civil war had all at some time been both allied with and fighting against all other factions.

Even with the emergence of the Taliban movement and its success in achieving control over most of the country's territory, as well as in the post-Taliban era, it is only meaningful in a limited sense to talk about an Afghan state, especially in the outlying regions. Power has locally been exercised as much or more on the basis of informal power holders—warlords, tribal leaders, and so on—who have often been co-opted by the state, which lacked a better option to secure nominal control over the territory. This, then, is the context of the role of the heroin industry in the successive conflicts in Afghanistan.

Main Actors in Afghanistan's Conflict

Just listing the wide array of organizations and movements that have been parties to the Afghan conflict since 1979 would be the subject of a study in its own right. This chapter will very briefly describe the main forces in the different periods of conflict: the Soviet occupation, the civil war, and the post-2001 phase. Their roles are all the more bewildering since these forces have at various times been in and out of government—a term that, as noted, is problematic since the Afghan state essentially collapsed following 1989.

The Soviet Occupation and the Civil War, 1979–2001

Throughout the 1980s and 1990s, the groups involved in the resistance against Soviet occupation broke down into radical versus moderate, and along ethnic and sectarian lines. These became the major belligerents in the civil war that followed—supplemented in 1994 by a major new force, the Taliban movement, and its foreign allies, most notably Al Qaeda.

The groups that gained the greatest prominence and staying power belonged to radical Islamic currents. These were chiefly the Hezb-i Islami and the Jamiat-i Islami. The Jamiat-i-Islami borrowed its name, and much of its inspiration, from the Pakistani group with the same name. The Afghan grouping, emerging in 1972, was led by Professor Burhanuddin Rabbani; two key figures that formed its core were Gulbuddin Hekmatyar, a Pashtun from the northern city of Kunduz, and Ahmad Shah Masoud, a Tajik from the Panjsher valley, who would emerge to be key players in the resistance as well as in the civil war, when their vicious rivalry led to the destruction of Kabul. Hekmatyar remains a significant force today. However, Rabbani's thinking did not initially embrace violence and militancy; as a result, following the exile of the Islamists from Afghanistan in 1973, Hekmatyar broke off to form the Hezb-i Islami, advocating a much more militant approach to the secular Afghan authorities.[7] Hekmatyar was also more radical than Rabbani both in his authoritarian personality and in his ideology, which was much more hostile to Afghan traditions he deemed to be non-Islamic. Ethnic divisions also played a role. Jamiat came to be closely identified with the Tajiks of Afghanistan's northeast, particularly under the military leadership of Ahmed Shah

Masoud, and their remnants form a key faction of the post-2001 government led by Hamid Karzai. By contrast, Hezb-i Islami came to be mainly composed of Pashtuns of the south, as well as from Kunduz, Hekmatyar's birthplace and a Pashtun enclave in the north. Hezb-i Islami itself broke into two factions, as Mohammad Yunus Khalis broke off from the main group following the Soviet invasion, and became known as Hezb-e-Islami Khalis (HIK) as opposed to Hekmatyar's HIG. Khalis's group was focused on the southeastern areas around Nangarhar; it was nevertheless much smaller than Hekmatyar's, and was absorbed into the Taliban in the mid-1990s. While Khalis died in 2006, HIK remains significant as his former deputy, Jalaluddin Haqqani, is very much a force in the insurgency presently, leading the eponymous Haqqani network.

The HIG was the perhaps strongest and best-organized force in the mujahideen resistance to the Soviet Union, largely because of Hekmatyar's managerial skills and the fact that it benefited from the lion's share of foreign funds for the resistance.[8] Pakistan's leadership under General Zia Ul-Haq favored HIG over the moderate groupings, whose tendency toward Pashtun nationalism was worrisome to Pakistan.[9]

These were the three main groups, but not the only ones. Others included Abdul Rasoul Sayyaf's Wahhabi-leaning Islamic Union, as well as traditional and moderate Sunni groups that sought not an Islamic republic but the restoration of the monarchy. These, which included Syed Ahmad Gailani's Mahaz-i Melli, Sibghatullah Mojaddedi's National Liberation Front, and Mohammed Nabi Mohammadi's Harakat-i Inqelab, were increasingly marginalized throughout the conflict and did not survive the 1990s. Their leaders command generally greater respect among the Afghan population than the radicals, and their leaders, such as Mojaddedi, have been appointed to high ceremonial positions in the post-Taliban era; yet their effect on the conflict was less marked and they will not be discussed in greater detail here. This is also the case for the Shi'a groupings in the central Hazarajat, which fought the Soviets separately with Iranian support and who were constantly marginalized and excluded by the Sunni groupings. A grouping that does remain relevant today is the mainly Uzbek forces of Junbish-i Milli, led by Abdul Rashid Dostum, a supporter of the communist regime who defected in 1992, allying on and off with Masoud's forces. Dostum has been known as one of the leaders most prone to shift allegiance for short-term gain. Nominally chief of staff to the Afghan army's commander-in-chief, he continues to dominate his core areas around Mazar-i-Sharif and Sheberghan as of this writing.[10]

By comparison, the Taliban movement emerged much later, in 1994. By this time, total anarchy reigned in southwestern Afghanistan as local sub-commanders fought for influence, control, and territory. The movement consisted of young Afghan students from the Pakistani madrassas. Their stated goal was to liberate Afghanistan from bandits who controlled the roads and harassed the population. The movement drew rapid support from powerful economic interests in the transport and smuggling business, as well as from Pakistan, which was actively looking for a new force to support given Hekmatyar's unreliable nature.[11] Moreover, the Taliban came from a different religious tradition from the other factions: they were a product of the religious schools of the Jamiat-e Ulema-e Islam, a strict Orthodox movement belonging to the Deobandi tradition, a South Asian Islamic current strongly influenced by Wahhabi ideas—a fact explaining the lavish Saudi funding for the schools.

The collapse of the Afghan state that resulted from the infighting among various factions in the Afghan civil war—chiefly between Jamiat and HIG—provided the conditions for the emergence of the Taliban. By 1996, when Pakistan had dropped its support for Hekmatyar and fully endorsed the Taliban, the movement gained control of Kabul as well as most of northern Afghanistan. Only at this point would it be meaningful to speak of an Afghan state again, since the Taliban movement focused strongly, and with some success, on restoring central authority in its own hands during its brief tenure in power. That said, the Taliban takeover also opened the door for the return to Afghanistan of Al Qaeda and Osama Bin Laden. Forging a deep alliance with the Taliban, Al Qaeda became an additional factor in the Afghan conflict, exerting a substantial influence on the Taliban.

The Post-2001 Conflict

Following the American-led invasion in late 2001, the Taliban movement collapsed. It reemerged in a more decentralized shape in 2003, following America's invasion of Iraq, alongside HIG and the Haqqani network, and took up a leading role in fighting the U.S. and the Afghan government. Since 2002, therefore, the conflict in Afghanistan has morphed into one where, once again, former foes are united. On the one hand, HIG, the Haqqani network, the Taliban, and Al Qaeda have aligned, joined by their regional allies such as the Pakistani Taliban, and the Islamic Movement of Uzbekistan (discussed in this author's chapter on the IMU in this volume). This alliance is porous, and the Taliban itself is considerably less centralized as a movement than it was in 1994–2001; while its central leadership largely resides in Pakistan—to that split into the separate Quetta and Peshawar *shuras*—commanders in Afghanistan itself are acting with relative autonomy. That said, in spite of this fluidity, the movement appears to have retained a functioning chain of command. However, opinions have diverged on whether to seek a negotiated solution with the Afghan government, for example.[12]

On the other is the Afghan government, led by Hamid Karzai. That government, in turn, is far from a homogeneous entity. Quite contrary, while Karzai is a Pashtun, the erstwhile Northern Alliance of Jamiat and Junbish forces (especially the former) have exerted a disproportional influence, benefiting from their role in the overthrow of the Taliban. Aligned with them are a wide array of local warlords, mainly Pashtuns across the south, whose prominence dates to the pre-Taliban years, and who have formed an uneasy relationship with the central government and the U.S.-led coalition.

To this should be added external forces. This mainly refers to the U.S.-led international coalition, which has propped up the Afghan government and which could scarcely have survived without it. But it also includes Pakistan, whose role in the conflict is paramount but defies easy definition. While Pakistan has cooperated with the United States and the Afghan government, there is overwhelming evidence that institutions of the Pakistani state have hedged their bets by supporting elements of the insurgency, not least the Haqqani network. Similarly, the Afghan government accused Pakistan of being connected to the assassination of former Afghan president Burhanuddin Rabbani in September 2011, when he played a leading role in seeking peace between the Afghan government and the Taliban.[13]

The Emergence and Evolution of Afghanistan's Drug Industry

The role of the Afghan drug industry as a driving force in the crime-rebellion nexus in the entire region spanned by this book is such that it deserves a somewhat more detailed background. Opium was according to myth brought to Afghanistan by Alexander the Great over two millennia ago,[14] yet it was only in the 1980s that opium production in Afghanistan began to acquire the character of an export industry. This in turn was the result of several distinct developments that converged on the country: a drought in the Golden Triangle in 1978, which led to an increase in production in Southwest Asia; the gradual decrease of opium cultivation in Southwest Asia as a whole in the 1950s to 1970s, most dramatically with draconian laws implemented in Iran and Pakistan in 1979–1980; and the Soviet invasion of Afghanistan, occurring at roughly the same time, and the instability and war economy that followed.

Afghanistan had seen only a measured growth in opium production. By the early 1970s, Afghanistan harvested an amount of opium roughly equal to Pakistan, and exceeded its neighbor's production only in 1979. Yet rapid changes in attitude to opium developed in Pakistan and Iran, and that occurred simultaneously with the Soviet invasion of Afghanistan and the 1978 drought in the countries of the Golden Triangle. All these trends combined to shift production into Afghanistan. While Iran, Pakistan, and Turkey imposed severe drug control laws, the government of Afghanistan headed by the People's Democratic Party of Afghanistan (PDPA) lost control over the opium producing areas in the countryside.[15]

The Soviet Invasion and the Drug Trade

This did not mean an end to drug problems in Afghanistan's neighbors; far from it. Iran and Pakistan instead became the main transit routes for increased opium production in Afghanistan and Pakistan,[16] as well as a major focal point for the refining of opium into morphine and heroin. Cultivation hence left Pakistan but developed across the border in Afghanistan, while laboratories refining the opium sprung up in the Federally Administered Tribal Areas of Pakistan's Northwest Frontier Province, which operate under a special autonomous status leaving them outside the jurisdiction of Pakistani law. Hence Iran and Pakistan turned into refining and trafficking countries for opium that was increasingly grown in Afghanistan.

The collapse of the traditional economy that occurred with the Soviet occupation forced farmers into opium cultivation for their survival, while the general economic collapse removed any opportunities to receive credits. Opium gradually became the only crop for which farmers could receive credits to help survive winter, given the role of the opium traders and the cash they possessed. Meanwhile, mujahideen commanders adopted the practice of forcing farmers to grow poppies early on. Especially those groups that were not favorites of the Pakistani Inter-Services Intelligence (ISI), which channeled practically all the funding to the resistance, came to be deeply involved in the opium trade—such as Helmand warlord Nasim Akhundzada.[17] As seen below, however, so did the forces that received lavish ISI funding to secure financial independence.

Opium proved a sustainable commodity with a higher price and guarantee for credit and investment in times of war. Even despite the destruction of most of the transport infrastructure in the war, armed groups had a direct interest in maintaining the transport systems necessary for the opium trade.[18] Various mujahideen groups who fought the Soviet invaders used opium as a leading source of money to buy weapons, equipment, and ammunition. As the war became protracted and the rural subsistence economy was destroyed, the drug-based economy became even more pronounced, the growing urban populations became increasingly dependent on government assistance, and opium gradually became the most reliable income for the warlords. The practice of warlords pressuring farmers into growing a cash crop that could be taxed emerged.

By the late 1980s, there were no social and legal constraints left for many peasants and landless laborers, who for a decade had been increasingly involved in opium cultivation. These groups were developing expertise, markets, and infrastructure for the opium trading system.

The pro-Soviet governments of Afghanistan under Mohammad Daud, Nur Muhammad Taraki, Babrak Karmal, and Najibullah in the 1970s and 1980s took superficial measures to reduce the land under opium cultivation. Najibullah's government, the last pro-Soviet administration of Afghanistan, set up a high commission that devised an economic policy allocating subsidies for wheat and seeds and providing technical assistance to farmers. This policy resulted in checking to a very limited extent the expansion of Afghanistan's drug production.[19] In 1991, the UN opened a mission in Kabul, and U.S. State Department representatives reportedly sought to negotiate with the Mujahideen commanders in Pakistan to reduce the cultivation of opium. However, in the light of the ongoing war and the frequent changes in government, these measures were doomed to failure.[20]

Civil War and the Explosion of the Drug Trade

Once foreign support for the jihad died out as the Soviet Union retreated, so did the external money supply to the Mujahideen. These groups then started to use rural areas of Afghanistan for drug production, areas where the lingering Soviet-backed Afghan government had virtually no control, let alone support.[21] Increasing sales of opium and a "drugs for arms" trade gradually turned into a formalized and structured economic system in the areas that slipped out of government control.

Following the Soviet collapse, the war changed its character, as the factions now vied for power rather than simply using guerrilla tactics against Soviet forces. The factions hence sought to improve their arsenal, turning into an escalating arms race that nurtured the growing war economy. The existence of large quantities of weapons had the effect of leading the factions to seek to top each other with heavier and more sophisticated ones. This generated an arms race that introduced heavy artillery, rockets, and anti-aircraft weapons into the conflict. If in the early 1980s, the tribesmen were armed with First World War-style Lee Enfield rifles, a decade later Hekmatyar had the capability to devastate Kabul with artillery and Katyusha rockets. This escalated financial needs and contributed to the factions turning to the drug trade.[22]

Diminishing support from outside contributors escalated the growth of the narco-economy when groups involved in the civil war had to find alternative forms of financing. This led to a growth of areas used for poppy cultivation as the actors involved in the Afghan conflict made opium a cornerstone in the war economy. Often, battles between warlords seem to have been caused in part by struggles over the control of opium production. The objective for campaigns in areas of opium cultivation was in many cases to control production for financial reasons.[23]

Whereas the war in the 1980s had the primary objective of defeating the regime in Kabul and the Soviet forces, the civil war of the 1990s was a struggle for power among warlords, and no single faction was strong enough to dominate the country. This undermined state power, allowing warlords and regional leaders to use the cultivation of and trade in drugs to increase their influence and control. The economic power that derived from the opium trade was in some aspects a different approach for the insurgent groups to take part in the business of narcotics. Instead of being one of the sources of income to finance the armed struggle, opium cultivation and trade developed into a central part of the conflict and the war economy.[24] At this time, the drug trade grew to meet the demands of the changed conditions of the conflict, placing the economic structures of the drug trade at the heart of the war economy. The trafficking of narcotics thus filled the gap created by declining external financing. In the same process, the economic base for the conflict became gradually more located to Afghanistan itself, where it created its own beneficiaries in terms of traders, drug barons, and warlords. The combination of the close relationship between local elites, mafia, and warlords and the destruction of other sources of income transformed the trade of illicit drugs into a tool for maintaining influence and to create a powerbase.[25] This was fueled by the ongoing arms race between the factions of the war that were in a constant need to strengthen their military capacity.

By the early 1990s, opium producers and traders had therefore entrenched their positions in Afghanistan's domestic economy as the annual growth rate in opium production accelerated from about 14 percent in the 1980s to over 19 percent in the first half of the 1990s. In 1991, thanks to Afghanistan's opium production, the Golden Crescent (including also Pakistan and Iran) surpassed the producers of opium from the Golden Triangle (Myanmar, Laos, and Thailand) and rose to the top of the world's opium producers.[26] The year 1994 in particular was a peak year, with 3,500 tons of opium produced on 70,000 acres, a figure not reached again until 1999. Continued conflict between the mujahideen groups, and the collapse of the state, made opium an ever more viable method of generating income, and increasingly replaced the decrepit Afghan currency for savings and exchange.

Developments on Afghanistan's northern borders added a new dimension to the drug situation. The collapse of the Soviet Union led to the emergence of new, weak states in Central Asia, three of which bordered Afghanistan. Having to build state institutions from scratch, plagued by economic dislocation and widespread corruption, the Central Asian states were an appealing new smuggling route just as the Iranian government began to invest serious resources into monitoring its border with Afghanistan to fight drug trafficking. Prior to 1991, Afghan opium had flowed through Pakistan and Iran to international markets, as the closed Soviet border made smuggling unattractive.[27] But the collapse of the Soviet Union provided an opportunity for Afghan opiates to find their way to new markets in Russia and Europe.

Especially important in this regard was the civil war in Tajikistan, discussed in greater detail in Johan Engvall's contribution to this volume. Tajikistan began to experience, in microcosm, similar patterns of warfare, state collapse, and drug-fueled insurgency as in Afghanistan itself. Tajik military commanders on both sides in the civil war hence became increasingly involved in the trafficking of Afghan opiates; and the close linguistic and increasingly political connections between Afghan and Tajik actors facilitated the development of this new smuggling route.[28] By the mid-1990s, the first seizures of opiates began to be observed in Central Asian republics. Yet the smuggling routes inevitably took several years to develop, something that was to happen following the Taliban takeover of power in Afghanistan.

Production Trends, 1995–2011

The Taliban takeover did not initially affect opium cultivation greatly. From 1994 to 1995, the area under cultivation actually decreased from 71,000 to

54,000 ha, a level roughly maintained through 1998 with minor variations. In 1999, by contrast, the area under cultivation skyrocketed to 91,000 ha, an all-time high at the time, followed by another bumper crop of 82,000 ha in 2000. Already at this time, enduring trends could be seen: opium cultivation was concentrated in several provinces in the country—chiefly Helmand, which already produced roughly half of Afghanistan's opium, and Nangarhar, which produced a quarter.

In 2001, by contrast, the Taliban ban on opium cultivation led to a dramatic 97 percent reduction in the cultivated area. While the ban did not survive the toppling of the Taliban regime, it did lead to a brief diffusion of opium cultivation across the country—driven mainly by the rapid growth of cultivation in Badakhshan province in the north following the Taliban ban. In 2002, production was already back to 2000 levels, and from 2004 onward, cultivation began to grow considerably again. Thus, 131,000 ha of opium were cultivated in 2004, reaching 193,000 ha in 2007—a record that still stands, figures having fallen to the 120,000–130,000 range since then, historically still extremely high figures. As far as regional distribution is concerned, northwest Afghanistan briefly became a significant growing region in 2004–2006, but subsequently production once again concentrated largely to the southwestern provinces of the country, as production steadily declined both in Badakhshan and the northwest. At first, the pattern looked very similar to the late 1990s, with Helmand once again taking from half to two thirds of the cultivated area. The main difference, however, lay in the decline of Nangarhar as a major poppy producing area. The province was even declared poppy free in 2008, although opium once again appeared in 2010–2011. Instead, opium production spread to the provinces surrounding Helmand, especially Kandahar, Farah, and Oruzgan. By 2012, then, Afghanistan's southwest area had consolidated its position as the undisputed opium capital of the world.

Militant Groups, the State, and the Drug Trade

The attitudes of the parties to the conflict in Afghanistan toward the drug trade have ranged from ambivalent to enthusiastic, and have changed over time among and between groups. The location, cross-border linkages, and organizational skill of the various groups have also played a major role in providing an opportunity for involvement in this key industry of the country. The most complex picture is that of the Taliban attitude to opiates, which ranged from initial ambivalence over a short period of total prohibition while in government, to endorsing the industry once again following Operation Enduring Freedom,.

The Mujahideen Groups

Even before the withdrawal of Soviet troops, warlords began fighting not only the Soviets but also each other for the control of the opium trade. The most prominent example is the perhaps most notorious Afghan warlord, Gulbuddin Hekmatyar. Hekmatyar's Hezb-i Islami gradually became deeply involved in opium production as well as heroin processing, and even fought other groups, such as Helmand warlord Akhundzada.[29] HIG's involvement in the heroin industry was initially denied by U.S. authorities, who were focused exclusively on the goal of combating the Soviet presence in the country, but later gradually acknowledged.[30] The American disengagement from Afghanistan led to an abrupt cut in funding for the Mujahideen factions, pushing Hekmatyar and others to rely ever more on the drug trade for financing their struggle for power.[31] Indeed, even before the Soviet pullout, Hekmatyar was fighting other Mujahideen factions over lucrative arms and opium trade routes. His group controlled a substantial number of the laboratories producing heroin that were scattered along the borderline between Afghanistan and Pakistan. The raw opium for these laboratories was sourced from opium fields primarily in Nangarhar, Kandahar, Zabul, and Paktiya provinces, regions under the control of the forces loyal to HIG. Of course, Hekmatyar typically opposed any government in Afghanistan—including the Soviet-backed government, the Mujahideen government headed by Rabbani, and the Taliban Emirate. As of this writing, Hekmatyar continues to fight the U.S.-supported government of Afghanistan and the presence of foreign troops, and to remain involved in the drug trade—although he has also indicated his willingness to participate in peace talks.

Many other warlords and political leaders were directly engaged in drug production and trafficking during the civil war. In the northeast of Afghanistan, seven large zones of opium production were under the control of field commanders loyal to Rabbani and Masoud. In this part of the country and especially in the Northern Alliance stronghold of Badakhshan, huge fields of opium and hemp were flourishing.[32] The Islamic government of Afghanistan headed by Rabbani officially appealed for the destruction of poppy plantations, yet this never led to any concrete policies as field commanders and high-ranking officials remained deeply involved in the drug trade.[33] As will be seen below, their involvement in the drug trade did not abate when they entered the Afghan government from 2002 on.

The Taliban in the 1990s

As noted above, the Taliban's attitude to opium has been highly ambivalent. Before taking control of Kabul in 1996, the Taliban stated their ideological opposition to the consumption of opium and the manufacturing of heroin, but not to the production and trading in opium.[34] While in control of government, the Taliban developed an increasingly negative attitude to opium: they were exposed to heavy international pressure to curtail opium production, as well as the lure of international recognition if they did. This culminated in near-total eradication of opium in 2001.

The very origins of the Taliban speak of this ambivalence: one the one hand, the movement sought the moral high ground and thus expressed its opposition to opium. On the other, it has been shown that forces with a stake in the opium industry contributed to financing the Taliban's takeover of power. Gretchen Peters details how the U.S. Embassy in Islamabad was informed in February 1995 that Haji Bashar Noorzai, a member of a known drug trafficking family who subsequently ended up serving a life sentence in the United States, was an early financial backer of the movement.[35]

And while the Taliban displayed an ambivalent attitude to the drug trade, its leaders nevertheless realized the economic importance of the opium economy to Afghanistan—both in terms of the taxes they could levy on the trade, and the lack of alternative livelihoods for the hundreds of thousands of people living off the opium economy. As a result, the Taliban government taxed the growth and sale of opium like any other agricultural produce, and is estimated to have made between $10 million and $50 million annually on the opium trade through levying taxes, and possibly more through individual commanders' involvement, though that may not have translated into the movement as such receiving the funds.[36] In the absence of a functioning economy, the opium trade was by far the biggest economic activity in Afghanistan and the largest income source of the Taliban government, along with the tax on the transit trade.

While in power, the Taliban until 2001 continued to allow the powerful warlords to continue their business. The opium industry's incomes were all the more important given the few other comparable sources of revenue, particularly as the Taliban fought a prolonged war in the north. A larger ban on the lucrative production and trade with opiates had the potential to turn powerful segments of the population, as well as its backers, against the

Taliban regime.[37] The economic realities of Afghanistan hence appear to have made the Taliban tolerate the trade and production of opium.[38] Still, this resulted in some religious and moral difficulties for the Taliban, and in order to justify the lack of action against the increasing narcotics industry, the Taliban banned drugs that were produced for the domestic market, such as hashish. Opiates, which were produced primarily for foreign markets, would still be allowed since they were not, according to the Taliban's convoluted reasoning, used by Muslims or Afghans—an erroneous conclusion at that, given Afghanistan's growing addiction problem.[39]

Upon coming to power, the Taliban government was able to stabilize the territories that it controlled through brutal suppression of dissent and any challenge to its authority. That stabilization resulted in a short-term trade boom, including both licit and illicit trade, and an increase in agricultural production. For example, wheat production by 1998 had risen to a level close to that existing prior to the outbreak of war in 1979–1980. The Taliban did establish the governing authority of a single government over most of Afghanistan's territory, facilitating long-distance trade and the exploitation of natural resources such as granite, timber, and marble—but the opium industry benefited equally from this stability.

However, since coming to power in 1996, the Taliban had gradually been building their effort to counteract the cultivation of opium. Taliban leader Mullah Muhammad Omar had in fact never had a particularly lenient attitude to opiates. When the Taliban came to power in 1996, the area under opium cultivation in Afghanistan, which at that time primarily corresponded to the southern, Pashtun areas dominated by the Taliban, decreased from about 70,000 ha to 54,000 ha.[40] In November 1996, shortly after taking over Kabul, Taliban foreign minister Mullah Muhammad Ghaus sent a letter to the UN International Drug Control Programme (UNDCP) asking for international help for the struggle against drugs, which he termed necessary for this task. The Taliban also publicly declared their opposition to the production, processing, trafficking, and abuse of opiates.[41] By September 1997, the Taliban issued a declaration banning the production and trade in opium. In October, the UNDCP formalized a written agreement with the Taliban in the matter, while it drew up a crop substitution plan for Afghan farmers.[42] Only a month later, UNDCP executive director Pino Arlacchi offered the Taliban $250 million in aid over ten years if they successfully eradicated opium production.[43] In May 1998, an American Drug Enforcement Agency (DEA) official visited Kabul and discussed cooperation to combat drugs.[44] Showing the political nature of the issue, Mullah Omar in 1998 offered the eradication of opium against international recognition, but was not taken seriously.[45] In spite of this impasse, Taliban authorities in February 1999 issued a ban on heroin production and destroyed 34 laboratories in Nangarhar province.[46] In September, they asked all farmers to cut production by one third, as a step toward eradication.[47] Then, in early 2000, the Taliban moved ahead with wholesale eradication of opium.

This eradication has widely been considered a ploy to raise prices; however, while such considerations may have played a role, it is clear that the Taliban from 1996 onward followed a relatively consistent line: offering to cooperate on opium, and taking gradual steps toward beginning eradication, in the hope of gaining international recognition and assistance.

It is useful to compare the involvement of the Taliban with that of the Northern Alliance, where opium cultivation grew by 158 percent at the time of the Taliban ban. The major difference was one of degree: Northern Alliance troops were directly involved in the production of opiates, whereas the Taliban primarily benefited by collecting taxes from farmers and traders on their profits. Evidently confronted by the power of domestic drug mafias, the Taliban appear before 2001 to have entered into tacit agreements with drug traders. Agreeing to pay a 10–20 percent tax on their profits, drug mafias secured their impunity. The Northern Alliance, by contrast, established heroin production laboratories in Kunduz, and successfully took advantage of the 2001 opium ban enforced by the Taliban. Limited only by market demands, the power of drug mafias, and the amount of opium that could realistically be cultivated in areas under their control, the Northern Alliance was free to raise the area under opium cultivation in Badakhshan province from 2,458 ha in 2000 to 6,342 ha in 2001. Northern Alliance involvement in the drug trade would have serious consequences for the return of opium production to Afghanistan following Operation Enduring Freedom, in which it took a central position.

Thus, the Taliban did have more ambiguous plans than most of the participants in the civil war on the opium issue. But they were far from able to put an end the lucrative drug trade. Like other actors, they ended up taking advantage of the germinating narco-industry even though they remained ideologically opposed to it.[48]

The Neo-Taliban

The reconstituted and more decentralized Taliban movement, reemerging in 2003, abandoned its prohibition of opium, instead embracing the opium economy. As will be seen, the leading question today is whether the move-ment's motivational factors have been affected by its deepening involvement in the opium economy.

The production of opium and narcotics has deliberately been used by the neo-Taliban insurgency in order to raise funds for the struggle, but also to destabilize the southern parts of Afghanistan. A decade after the U.S. inter-vention, large sections of the country are once again controlled or influenced by the Taliban. And in the past several years, as described above, opium cul-tivation patterns have come to follow Taliban-controlled areas closely. After having spread across the country in the first years following Operation En-during Freedom, opium production has gradually once again concentrated in the Taliban heartland.

Poppy cultivation has the effect of decreasing the Afghan government's control over Afghanistan, not only by strengthening rebels but also as a direct tool of denying the government access to parts of the country. By encourag-ing local leaders, warlords, and farmers to continue poppy cultivation, the insurgent groups support the interests that seek to prevent eradication. The absence of substitutes to the lost revenues from opium cultivation following eradication has made farmers even more dependent on poppy cultivation for their survival.[49] Indeed, eradication policies force farmers to either give up their livelihood or to fight against eradication, which automatically puts them into the category of insurgents.[50] In effect, Taliban commanders have been known to coerce farmers into planting poppies. Thus, coalition officials have increasingly come to see the organic relationship between the neo-Taliban and the drug trade in the south of the country feeding each other and com-bining to undermine central government influence.[51] In the light of such a strategy, the narcotics industry once again transforms from simply being a source of income to being a weapon or a tool of the insurgency.[52]

The ways the neo-Taliban are involved in the opium industry have changed little. Gretchen Peters's survey-based research in southern Afghani-stan indicates that the main forms of involvement continue to be the taxation of opium cultivation and trade, as well as providing "protection" to the culti-vation and transport of opium.[53] The case of Haji Bashir Noorzai, one of the original funders and close advisors to Mullah Omar, exemplifies the impor-tant role organized crime continues to play in the Afghan conflict. Noorzai was briefly detained by U.S. authorities in 2001, then released, but arrested in 2009. The U.S. indictment alleges that in the early 2000s, Noorzai led a heroin-trafficking organization that had close connections with the Taliban and provided them with military material and manpower in return for protecting his operation.[54]

Furthermore, there is evidence of the Taliban insurgents actually running heroin laboratories themselves, rather than simply taxing the organized criminal groups that engage in the production of heroin. Thus, on several occasions, coalition forces have stumbled on enormous drug caches following battles that forced insurgents to flee a locale.[55] Conversely, when dedicated counternarcotics units raided heroin labs in southern Afghanistan from 2004 onward, in the words of a commander of the British-led Force 333, they were "guaranteed to be attacked," as the drug traffickers called in support from the local Taliban subcommander to come to their rescue.[56] DEA agents have also successfully arrested and prosecuted several Taliban members involved in the heroin trade.[57] Furthermore, leaked documents have revealed that the UN Office on Drugs and Crime (UNODC) believes the Taliban keep large stockpiles of opiates as a form of savings for a rainy day.[58]

The linkage is borne out by comparative research studying the incidence of terrorist attacks across Afghanistan's provinces. James Piazza found a statistically significant correlation between the level of opium poppy cultivation and the likelihood of terrorist attacks in a given province; moreover, he found that the causal link is unquestionably that opium cultivation makes terrorist attacks more likely, and not the other way around.[59]

It is clear that this increasingly symbiotic relationship between the Taliban and the drug industry has raised the insurgency's capacity significantly. Estimates of the Taliban's yearly profit from the drug trade range from $120 million to $300 million. While this is generally accepted, the real question is whether the Taliban's motivations have changed as a result.

Researchers have tended to be skeptical of this possibility. Antonio Giustozzi, for example, acknowledges that the Taliban cooperated with both growers and traffickers, and that they have been observed to protect drug shipments. He nevertheless argues that the drug trade remains secondary as a source of funding, supporting this assertion with three arguments: first, traffickers would be unwilling to allow the Taliban to take on a more direct role in the drug trade; second, the Taliban hierarchy would not have been able to withstand a large-scale inflow of drug money to midlevel commanders; and third, the Taliban do not control the border with Pakistan and Iran, key to smuggling and thus profits.[60] By contrast, however, Peters makes a strong case that the Taliban are not only increasingly dependent on the drug trade, but that they "were no longer fighting for Allah, but for the almighty dollar."[61] Peters supports her argument with numerous interviews with Afghans involved in the drug industry as well as coalition officials. In her survey of Afghans involved in the drug industry at various levels, 80 percent of respondents agreed that Taliban fighters are mainly interested in financial gain, not fighting for ideological reasons. Indeed, in a country where few employment opportunities are available, the Taliban are known to pay their fighters wages beginning at about $100 per month, considerable sums in Afghanistan. Moreover, Peters's research includes examples of Taliban subcommanders skirmishing with one another over the right to tax opium production in specific locales. She also cites coalition officials whose intelligence indicates that a small and shrinking proportion of Taliban commanders are ideologically motivated.[62]

Peters makes a credible analogy between the evolution of the Taliban and that of the FARC in Colombia:

> The Taliban and the Revolutionary Armed Forces of Colombia . . . both got their start like modern Robin Hoods, protecting rural peasants from the excesses of a corrupt government. Strapped for cash and needing the support of local farmers, both groups began levying a tax on drug crops. Over time in Colombia, the FARC was slowly sucked into the coca trade. . . . As one senior U.S. official who moved from Colombia to South Asia put it, "it's like watching a bad movie all over again."[63]

While analysts appear to disagree on the full impact of the Taliban movement's embrace of the drug trade, it is plausible that this deepening involvement is having a substantial effect on the movement itself, its motivations, and goals. While this does not mean that the Taliban will revert from its aim of evicting Western forces or imposing its form of Shari'a on Afghanistan, it does mean that the organization itself has morphed from a purely ideological one—if it ever was—to one with more complex motivations, in which maintaining the opium industry is likely to rank high among its priorities.

The Afghan Government

All studies of the actors in the Afghan drug trade agree that whatever the involvement of the Taliban in the opium industry, it is dwarfed by the involvement of government officials at all levels. Studies have shown that Afghan police and military units systematically tax the opium trade much the same way as the Taliban do.[64] More troubling, perhaps, is the U.S.-sponsored Afghan air force's alleged direct involvement in transporting drugs across the country.[65]

The involvement of high officials has systematically compromised efforts at counternarcotics. Numerous reports detail how captured drug traffickers, including those tied to the Taliban, have often been released upon placing a call to high officials, or been found innocent by courts. Indeed, those convicted of drug-related crimes in Afghanistan appear to invariably have been small traders that had no connections or resources to ensure their release. By contrast, conviction of large-scale traffickers is practically unheard of—and when it occurs, arrangements appear to be rapidly made for their "escape."[66] In a pattern similar to many other drug-affected countries—Mexico comes to mind—the counternarcotics authorities themselves appear to have become deeply involved. An investigative report by the Toronto *Globe & Mail*, for example, detailed allegations of collusion by Afghanistan counternarcotics czars with the drug trade.[67]

Serious allegations have been directed at many senior figures, involving a number of provincial governors and central government officials. Perhaps most famously, detailed reporting emerged in 2008 suggesting that President Hamid Karzai's brother, Ahmed Wali Karzay, had become one of the country's largest drug traffickers, alongside his duties as head of the Kandahar provincial council.[68] Similar accusations have been directed at leading Afghan officials like Muhammad Qasim Fahim, vice-president and leader of the Northern Alliance;[69] Ismail Khan, Gul Agha Sherzai, Sher Muhammad Akhundzada, and Rashid Dostum, the onetime strongmen of Herat, Kandahar, Helmand, and Mazar-i-Sharif respectively.[70] Akhundzada was removed from office in 2005 at Britain's behest after drug enforcement officials found tons of drugs in his compound. Akhundzada was nevertheless given a senate seat by President Karzai, and his brother appointed deputy governor following his ouster.[71]

These examples suggest the characterization of Afghanistan as a "narco-state," which U.S. Secretary of State Hillary Clinton employed when testifying to Congress upon her nomination in January 2009.[72] In a scathing 2008 article in the *New York Times Magazine*, former U.S. counternarcotics official Thomas Schweich wrote that "Karzai was playing us like a fiddle: the U.S. would spend billions of dollars on infrastructure improvement; the U.S. and its allies would fight the Taliban; Karzai's friends could get rich off the drug trade."[73]

Schweich's conclusions are incontrovertible. However, there is an important subtext to the reality, which Schweich also makes painfully clear: the problem of the Afghan government's involvement in the drug industry cannot be understood in isolation from the international community's conscious decision to desist from making counternarcotics a priority. Indeed, countless counternarcotics officials and analysts detail how all efforts to have the coalition in Afghanistan focus on counternarcotics—or even to appreciate the linkage between the insurgency and the drug industry—have been systematically undermined by U.S. and British military officials that continuously insisted on prioritizing the fight against Al Qaeda and the Taliban at the cost of counternarcotics. These military officers were in turn supported by various NATO members who feared the security of their troops should they engage in counternarcotics. Thus, Pentagon officials insisted on "sequencing": defeating the Taliban and Al Qaeda militarily as a first step, after which other entities would move in and handle the drug problem, which they did not consider the business of the military.

Given the resources available to the coalition forces, this approach is understandable: the United States diverted most of its military attention to Iraq until 2008, ensuring that the military lacked the resources that would be required for a combined effort to target both the insurgency and the drug industry. With such scarce resources, they needed to prioritize, and therefore focused on the main mission, defeating the Taliban.

This strategy may have been understandable in 2001 as it was based on the assumption that directly attacking the drug trade would increase the size of the insurgency. In particular, key local Afghan paramilitary factions crucial to the prosecution of the war were themselves involved in the drug trade; moreover, the drug trade did and does provide a source of income that the international community was not in a position—financially or logistically—to displace. That said, this strategic decision failed to appreciate the dangers that the drug industry posed both to Afghanistan's short-term stability and long-term development; and indeed, the extent to which the drug industry would ensure the revival of the Taliban insurgency.

While there have been various plans for counternarcotics in Afghanistan, as former Afghan interior minister Ali Jalali has noted, there is no agreement among donors on the priorities among these.[74] Western forces initially supported the least promising avenue for counternarcotics, namely eradication.[75] This was bound to fail, as the drug industry is demand-driven. It is the consumption of drugs in Western economies that is the primary driver of the industry, generating the huge profits that middlemen and traffickers make, which in turn generates supply. This makes eradication inherently problematic, as a disruption in supply is likely only to have short-term effects, pushing production into other countries or regions that would in turn be destabilized. Afghanistan itself was victim to such a displacement in the late 1970s; and within Afghanistan, this dynamic can be seen in the strong shifts in production across provinces over time. Moreover, eradication targets the farmers, who are utterly replaceable from the perspective of opium traders; in fact, it punishes and marginalizes the most socially vulnerable element in the opium industry. By 2010, the coalition forces had moved away from eradication and began focusing on interdiction and the destruction of laboratories, a much more promising avenue. Moreover, as the arrest of Noorzai and growing counternarcotics operations in provinces such as Helmand suggest, coalition forces by 2009–2010 appeared to take the role of the opium industry more seriously. Of course, by then, it was too late. The drug industry had been joined at the hip with both the insurgency and the Afghan government.

Western policies for most of the period since 2001 thus reflected not only a reluctance to tackle the drug problem, but a conscious strategy to avoid making counternarcotics a priority. In fact, coalition officials often consciously enlisted the help of known warlords and drug traffickers—from Haji Juma Khan to Bashir Noorzai to Ahmed Wali Karzai—as informants and allies in the struggle against the Taliban.[76] In this environment, it would be unreasonable to expect the Afghan government to be able to accord priority to counternarcotics. Quite to the contrary, Karzai was left in a position where he had no choice but to dovetail with the U.S. strategy and cut deals with warlords and drug traffickers that held sway in the country's various provinces— having them under some form of control within the government's structures, rather than as free agents operating against the government. Inevitably, however, this strategy led the Afghan state to rot from within.

Implications for Afghanistan's Future

While this chapter has shown the intricate connection between the Afghan conflict and the country's drug industry, it should be noted that the roots of the conflict had next to nothing to do with narcotics, or any form of organized crime. Indeed, it was the war that brought large-scale production and trafficking of narcotics to Afghanistan. This corroborates the proposition outlined in the introduction that conflicts tend to emerge as a result of grievances rather than greed. Thus, Afghanistan is a textbook case for the second proposition, that armed conflict provides important impetus for the growth of crime. Indeed, the cultivation of opium was embedded in Afghanistan's neighborhoods, especially Pakistan and Iran; stronger antinarcotics regimes in these countries combined with the armed conflict in Afghanistan to shift production into that country.

The case of Afghanistan also aligns well with the notion that once substantial organized crime has established itself in a conflict zone, insurgents are almost by necessity drawn to it. Afghanistan may be an extreme case of this phenomenon, given that the decades of war gradually eliminated many sources of livelihood, not only making Afghanistan one of the poorest countries in the world, but also boosting the narcotics industry to an economic role hitherto unseen in any other country. Effectively, once the value of the opiate industry surpassed that of all other areas of economic activity, armed groups could scarcely afford eschewing participation for fear of being marginalized. However, the evidence suggests that far from all factions engaged in the trade themselves; self-involvement and taxation of drug cultivation and trafficking have both continued to persist alongside one another as means of benefiting from the drug trade.

The most difficult question to pin down is to what extent involvement in organized crime has affected the motivations of insurgent groups. Here, the evidence is mixed. While there appears to be much to suggest that the motivations of the Taliban movement have moved away from ideology and toward the goal of economic profit, it does not appear that the movement as a whole has lost its ideological motivations. Instead, it appears that the goal of economic profit has established itself alongside with, rather than in the place of, ideology as a driving force behind the insurgency.

Finally, Afghanistan also illustrates with all clarity the peril of an insurgent group deeply involved in the drug trade transitioning to a position in government. When the Northern Alliance benefited from the U.S. invasion of Afghanistan to establish itself as the core force behind the post-Taliban government, it effectively brought with it the practice of deep involvement in the drug trade into Afghanistan's government institutions. To put it simply, these institutions never recovered from that initial burden, severely delaying and undermining the process of state-building in Afghanistan.

This chapter has shown how all major political forces in Afghanistan are deeply involved in the opium industry. The Taliban derive a dominating share of their income from opiates; while the regional warlords as well as central authorities that compose the Afghan government play an even greater role in the industry. This, in turn, hampers the legitimacy of the Afghan government and the prospects for its consolidation and development, which in the final analysis further contributes to instability and conflict. The conflict in Afghanistan cannot be understood without due attention to the opium industry: the two are intimately intertwined.

This state of affairs has serious implications for the future of Afghanistan. Indeed, Afghanistan epitomizes the strong and growing global trend toward the concentration of drug cultivation and production in unstable states and conflict zones. Once introduced in a conflict zone, as occurred in Afghanistan in the 1980s, the drug industry entrenches itself and forms a formidable impediment to peace, long-term development, and meaningful reform. The drug industry further generates strong vested interests seeking to prevent the full integration of the country into the global economy and that are in fact dependent on a certain degree of unrest, a weak central government, and lax border control for its operations. In this context, it is simply impossible for Afghanistan to develop into a functioning and stable state integrated into the global economic and political system as long as the drug trade persists in the proportions it presently carries.

As for the prospects of the development of Afghanistan's drug industry, the hopes of the international community after the fall of the Taliban that opium production could gradually be dismantled in a matter of several years have been proven a fallacy. Such assumptions grossly underestimated the degree to which the opium industry had become engrained in the fabric of Afghanistan's economy; the level to which armed factions and warlords in Afghanistan were dependent on the drug trade; the corruptive effect it had on the development of the Afghan state; and the complicated processes by which counternarcotics can succeed.

The elephant in the room, undoubtedly, is the singular negligence with which Western powers approached the opium industry as they effectively took control of the country in 2001. In fact, it is no exaggeration to assert that the Western powers directly contributed to the resurgence of the opium industry, by explicitly centering on counterterrorism and making counternarcotics a secondary priority contingent on not disturbing the war aims of fighting the Taliban and Al Qaeda.

Sadly, there are "no quick fixes" to Afghanistan's opium industry.[77] It is likely to remain an important factor and to that increasingly entrenched in the political structures of Afghanistan, impeding the development of Afghanistan into a functioning state on the road to economic development, and sustaining its armed conflict into the foreseeable future. For the international community, this means that Afghanistan will be the world's major source of opium for the foreseeable future.

Chapter 3

Tajikistan: From Drug-Insurgency to Drug-State Nexus

Johan Engvall

Tajikistan has been the post-Soviet state perhaps most affected by organized crime and its impact on the country's security. This is due primarily to three interrelated factors: the extreme weakness of its state institutions; its proximity to Afghanistan, whose opium production skyrocketed as Tajikistan gained independence; and its protracted civil war in 1992–1997. The main cleavage of the civil war was between the unreformed communist government and a loose alliance of opposition groups, including Islamists, nationalists, and those claiming to be democrats. Both sides were coalitions of militias formed primarily along regional lines. After the end of the civil war, the political economy of the heroin trade had transformed from a means of financing armed groups in conflict to an entrenched component of postconflict state-building and a crucial source of power and wealth. This trade has become far more organized and large-scale under a settled political order compared to the violent order of the 1990s. Indeed, it has become one of the most important factors shaping whether relative stability or violent confrontation is the order of the day.

The Civil War, 1992–1997

About the time the Soviet system collapsed, Tajikistan was probably the worst prepared republic for running its own affairs as an independent state. During Soviet times, it was one of the poorest republics, with an economy heavily subsidized by Moscow. The Soviet legacy of central planning meant that the economy was the polity, and political power equaled control over economic opportunities. By the time of independence, a struggle for control over the state and its resources emerged in most post-Soviet states.[1] Contrary to what happened in Central Asia's other post-Soviet states, Tajikistan's political elite failed to achieve a stabilizing agreement between the rival interests in society, which led to a civil war that lasted for five years, from 1992 to 1997.[2]

The conflict involved the country's neocommunist government and an opposition composed of Islamists, democrats, and nationalists, which indicates that the opposition did not come together based on any ideological commonalities. The common ground, and for that matter the differences, had their origin in the country's subethnic divisions and local loyalties reinforced during seventy years of Soviet rule and the uneven access the Soviet authorities granted to different regionally based interests. Tajikistan was created somewhat artificially in the early Soviet period: the unnatural construction left large Tajik-populated areas in southern Uzbekistan but incorporated mainly Uzbek-populated areas of the Fergana valley. Four administrative regional entities were created: Leninabad, later renamed Soghd, in the north; the region under the jurisdiction of the capital Dushanbe, now known as the region of Republican Subordination; Khatlon in the south; and the autonomous region of Gorno-Badakshan in the east. These administrative provinces were not monolithic either in ethnic terms or with regard to traditional clan identities. Indeed, during the civil war, warring parties often represented solidarity groups located in valleys in the same province, something that increased the intensity of the conflict. A clear example is the case of the Hissar and Gharm valleys, both in the region of Republican Subordination. The conflict in these areas proved among the bloodiest in the five-year long conflict. The two major parties were the local political elite from Kulyab, in the south, and its counterpart in Gharm, located in the central province.

The Kulyabi grouping was the main force within the neocommunist government, known as the Popular Front of Tajikistan (PFT), mainly assisted by the Hissar grouping from the west. The Gharm faction constituted the backbone of the Islamist forces, supported by the Pamir group from

Gorno-Badakhshan and collectively termed the United Tajik Opposition (UTO). Yet, under both the PFT and UTO umbrellas there were rival interests among myriad relatively small armed bands. The Soviet-time privileged Khujand elite from the Soghd region in the north of the country, which since the 1930s had dominated the republic's political power structures, took a more neutral stance in the conflict,[3] even though it can be concluded that they had their loyalties with the PFT. The civil war never reached the northern part of the country, which was shielded by the high mountain ranges stretching across the central parts. Furthermore, it should be noted that as the conflict evolved, a cacophony of armed groups emerged, some of them based on patronage networks, others based on parts of the dissolved former Soviet police and security structures, and yet others pure criminal gangs with a history of illicit activities since the late days of the Soviet Union.[4] In short, rather than being ethnic or ideological in nature, the conflict was in essence a local turf war over which elite would control power and resources in the post-Soviet system.[5]

In comparison to other conflicts during the same period, such as in the Balkans or the Caucasus, the civil war in Tajikistan only marginally attracted the international community's attention. This is one of the main reasons for the comparative lack of detailed information and research regarding the civil war itself. Rough estimates indicate that at least 50,000 people died as a direct consequence of the war, while some estimates show figures closer to 100,000. Irrespective of which figure is correct, the Tajik civil war remains, on a par with Chechnya, the bloodiest of all post-Soviet wars. In addition, far more people lost their homes and other property. The war's most intensive and brutal phase was during its first years, chiefly 1992 and 1993. The decisive victory was already won after a few months of extreme brutality, when the government forces won a decisive military victory and forced the opposition to retreat from the capital Dushanbe to the mountains.[6] Thereafter, years of low-intensity warfare took over.

During the war, central state power in Dushanbe collapsed, and the state lost its relevance to the life of its citizens, particularly in economic terms. The economic system saw unprecedented deterioration as the Soviet command economy also collapsed, opening the way for new forms of informal and illicit economic relations to develop.[7]

A peace settlement between the warring parties was negotiated with the help of the international community in June 1997. The settlement seemed very brittle at first; nevertheless, overall peace and order prevailed. The treaty, a power-sharing agreement in essence, established that the government would be composed of a coalition of political parties and that the political opposition would have 30 percent of the government seats. In reality, this quota was never met, and that opposition was gradually marginalized. The government came under the domination of a mainly Kulyabi elite, led by President Emomali Rakmonov, something that has caused resentment among the political opposition as well as the once dominant Soghd region in the north, with a substantial ethnic Uzbek minority, which is now largely excluded from access to the central power apparatus.

Actors

During the past decade research on the connection between the struggle for economic resources (legal and illegal) and armed conflicts has emerged. The findings in a case study of Tajikistan support this research. A deeper look at the conflict dynamics indicates more complex patterns of conflict relationships, where political goals were occasionally a rhetorical cover for what appear to be other private and criminal motivations.[8] It should be noted that the conflict did not emerge out of causes linked to organized crime, but as a result of a power struggle between the different territorially based factions. It is nevertheless equally clear that more or less all the warring parties were involved in the narcotics trade from Afghanistan. During the civil war the narcotics industry was free from any control, and both warring sides recruited criminals for the purpose of enhancing their own interests. According to the U.S. Department of State 2001 *International Narcotics Control Strategy Report*, "The disruption of normal economic activity during the 1992–1997 civil war gave rise to a warlord class whose leaders jostle for control of the lucrative narcotics trade. . . . Influential figures from both sides of Tajikistan's civil war, many of whom now hold government positions, are widely believed to have a hand in the drug trade."[9]

The Popular Front of Tajikistan (PFT)

According to Kirill Nourzhanov, the leadership of the PFT can be divided into three groups.[10] One was the paramilitary leaders of the Kulyab region, closely tied to organized crime chief Sangak Safarov. During the Soviet period, Safarov spent twenty-three years in prison for a variety of criminal offenses. Despite his lack of political or military leadership experience, he nevertheless managed to control a paramilitary force composed of Kulyabis. He later had a violent scuffle with his once close ally and crime boss Faizali Saidov, which left both commanders dead.[11] After Safarov's death, several career criminals took over control of his forces. Prominent figures were Yakub Salimov, Ghaffor Mirzoyev, and the Cholov brothers.[12] Salimov, who became Tajik minister of interior in 1992, has been referred to as the founder of the first large-scale Tajik drug trafficking group. He reportedly used his control of the police force to organize opiate smuggling from Afghanistan through Gorno-Badakshan and on to Dushanbe and even into Russia.[13]

The second group consisted of allies of the Kulyab clan, led by ethnic Uzbeks Mahmud Khudoberdiyev and Ibodullo Boimatov, both of whom fought the opposition forces and did not participate in the peace negotiations. They even staged several attacks against government forces after the signing of the peace treaty, demonstrating that there were forces among the government allies who were opposed to a political settlement of the conflict. The Khudoberdiyev and Boimatov attacks on the government could also be described as related to unwillingness to give up the profits generated by the war operations. It has been reported that in 1998 Khudoberdiyev even attempted to take full control over the Khujand province to maintain the narcotics monopoly established during the war.[14] Boimatov, on the other hand, took over the politically and economically important state aluminum factory in the city of Turajonzada.[15] The two maintained political and economic control over the province's vital functions, which briefly gave them prominent societal positions following the civil war.[16]

The third group contained small-time criminal leaders whose primary activity was to plunder, kidnap, and extort local businesses.[17] These groups were typical examples of roving bandits roaming the lands during a period of anarchy. When the situation in Tajikistan stabilized in the mid-1990s, such groups disintegrated rapidly as they were outcompeted by large-scale warlords with a comparative advantage in violence and financial strength.[18]

The United Tajik Opposition (UTO)

While Russia and Uzbekistan supported the PFT government in Tajikistan, the UTO developed close relationships with actors in neighboring Afghanistan. A considerable number of the UTO military operations were initiated from Afghan territory, which showed its close ties to Afghanistan's Northern Alliance, then in charge of the areas bordering Tajikistan. The IMU was one of the groups that supported the UTO both morally and militarily. The "coordinator" between the UTO and Afghan factions, as well as a UTO field commander in his own right, was Mirzo Ziyoev. He was well known for his leadership skills and close relationship with both Northern Alliance leader Ahmed Shah Masoud and the leaders of the IMU, Juma Namangani and Tohir Yuldashev.[19] After the 1997 peace treaty, Ziyoev was instrumental in the establishment of IMU bases in central Tajikistan, areas under his control.[20] The IMU was thereafter able to launch multiple attacks against government forces in both southern Kyrgyzstan and Uzbekistan in the summers of 1999 and 2000. Ziyoev's support for the IMU operations is considered key to their relative success.[21]

Ziyoev's close connections to the Northern Alliance and the IMU during the 1990s resulted in wide-range speculations of his involvement in large-scale drug smuggling through Tajikistan. His connections with the IMU have fueled such allegations, given the fact that the IMU, as discussed in Svante Cornell's chapter on the IMU in this volume, functioned partly as a criminal organization, showing operational patterns associated with those of organized crime groups.[22] The UTO's connection with the IMU and other paramilitary groups (e.g., the Northern Alliance) resulted in important economic benefits for the opposition, mainly through "taxation" of smuggled goods.[23]

After the civil war, Ziyoev was given the helm of the specially created Ministry for Emergency Situations. His paramilitary forces were submerged into government forces under the direct control of his ministry. Until the ministry was disbanded in late 2006, Ziyoev stood out as by far the most powerful representative of the revolutionary UTO phalanx in the government. Among Ziyoev's close allies were the brothers Makhmadruzi and Muhammadshokh (better known as Shokh) Iskandarov, who originated from Tojikobod and represented the Karategin clan from the Rasht district in the eastern part of the central province. Makhmadruzi was the political leader of the democratic opposition party, which joined the coalition government after the civil war. Most notably, he was director of the state monopoly TajikGaz until 2003. He was arrested in Moscow in 2005 and later extradited to Tajikistan, accused of illegal possession of arms and embezzlement of US$40 million during his time as director of TajikGaz.[24] Makhmadruzi's brother Shokh was long suspected of being in control of a major part of the narcotics trade in the Karategin valley, where he held the position chief of border police on the Kyrgyzstan border. He occupied this post during the IMU operations in southern Kyrgyzstan in 1999 and 2000, which further strengthens the evidence of continued close ties between the UTO and the IMU even after the peace treaty.[25]

Shokh also developed close ties with Kyrgyz Member of Parliament Bayaman Erkinbayev, who has been credibly shown to have been a major drug lord in southern Kyrgyzstan until his death shortly after the 2005 Kyrgyz revolution. According to the Kyrgyz police, his death was a direct consequence of the fusion of his political and criminal interests.[26] In 2007, Shokh was reportedly released from his position in the border guard, and retreated to his native home in the Rasht district.

Other UTO warlords believed to have a heavy hand in the drug trade, not least after the peace treaty, are former military commanders based in Gorno-Badakshan. In Soviet times, this was an autonomous region with an economy directly subsidized by Moscow largely without the intermediary of Dushanbe. Since independence, the province, inhabited by Pamiris, who speak a language distinct from Tajik and adhere to the specific Ismaili branch of Islam, has remained largely outside the central government's writ. Reports have identified four warlords—Tolib Ayombekov, Imomnazar Imomnazarov, Mamadbokir Mamadbokirov, and Yodgor Mamadaslamov—as the real authority wielders in the province. In summer 2012, a violent armed confrontation took place when government troops were sent to Gorno-Badakshan in an attempt to curb the powers of these warlords,[27] an episode that will be further discussed later on.

To summarize, warlords representing the PFT as well as the UTO were involved in the heroin trade during the civil war. Still, it is probably true that the importance of the heroin trade was comparatively greater for the opposition forces than for the government-aligned militias that benefited from the external backing of both Russia and Uzbekistan. Both these external players more than anything else feared that radical Islamists would take power in Tajikistan. Among UTO warlords, financing from the Afghan heroin trade and shelter in their bases in the mountains strengthened their ability to continue low-intensity warfare, and reduced their incentives to negotiate a settlement of the conflict.[28]

Types of Organized Crime

The primary type of organized crime in Tajikistan is without doubt the heroin trade. Even so, in Central Asia in general and Tajikistan in particular, drug smuggling is a relatively new phenomenon. During Soviet rule, the external borders were secured against any type of systematic intrusion. After 1991, the

smuggling of goods has steadily been on the increase, and since the beginning of the 2000s the region has become a major center of drug smuggling,
primarily heroin produced in Afghanistan. The UN Office on Drugs and
Crime (UNODC) *World Drug Report* estimates that in 2009, 365 metric tons
of heroin produced in Afghanistan were trafficked to the international market. Of this total, 160 metric tons were trafficked to Pakistan, 115 to Iran, and
90 to the Central Asian countries.[29] Thus, according to UNODC, one-fourth
of Afghanistan's heroin is trafficked through Central Asia, of which Tajikistan
is widely recognized as the main entry point.[30] Once heroin enters Tajikistan
via the porous border with Afghanistan, it moves through Kyrgyzstan and,
to a lesser extent, Uzbekistan before transiting Kazakhstan into Russia. The
bulk of the drugs trafficked through this northern route is destined to supply
heroin consumers in the former Soviet countries, primarily Russia, although
some also reaches Europe. However, for European consumer markets, the so-
called Balkan route from Afghanistan through Iran, Turkey, and the Balkan
states to the EU remains the leading smuggling corridor.[31]

Nowhere in the former Soviet region have the conditions for criminal
activity been as propitious as in Tajikistan. The collapse of the old political
order, in combination with the inability to set up new institutions, the civil
war, and an unprecedented economic recession, created favorable conditions
for organized crime. The state's ability to collect taxes was practically nonexistent, which in turn resulted in inability to build up costly institutions such
as the army, police, and border controls.[32]

According to Paoli et al., the types of drug traffickers in Tajikistan have
shifted with the rise of the illicit drug business as the country's most profitable
economic activity. During the initial phase in the early and mid-1990s, drug
trafficking was rather unorganized, often consisting of individuals or small
groups of people, and represented a means of survival.[33] As drug smuggling
expanded, small- and medium-sized drug trafficking groups were better able
to cope than individual traffickers. Until today, many such groups, generally
consisting of ten to fifteen people, operate along the Afghan-Tajik border.
However, these groups are small fish compared to the large-scale organized
crime groups that have come to dominate the drug trade in Tajikistan. The
emergence of large groups has been facilitated by a more ordered political
system. They are fully in tune with law enforcement agencies, and the financial exchange between organized crime groups and state agencies is standard-
ized; this cooperation is essential for their ability to deal with what has been
estimated at more than a ton of heroin a month.[34] The fact that no major drug

cartel has been brought to trial, while only small-scale dealers are arrested, provides an indication of the impunity of drug barons due to their direct or indirect political clout.[35]

Aside from the drug trade, weapons smuggling and human trafficking have become lucrative illegal activities, increasing drug lords' incentives to diversify their illicit activities. Weapons smuggling, for example, was a direct consequence of the war and the state's inability to control the distribution of weapons. The trafficking of women is another large problem for Tajikistan. The International Organization for Migration (IOM) estimates that thousands of women from Central Asian republics are smuggled yearly for the purpose of the sex trade. In the year 2000 alone, around 1,000 Tajik women were thought to have been smuggled, primarily to the Middle East and Russia.[36]

From Crime-Insurgency to Crime-State Nexus

Tajikistan's current political system remains heavily formed by the civil war settlement. In fact, it is not possible to understand the presence of criminal elements in state structures without taking the civil war and peace agreement into consideration. Undoubtedly, the peace treaty of 1997 resulted in the preservation of the Tajik state, which was on the brink of destruction as a unified state. The negotiation process involved high-ranking warlords on both sides of the table, who brought with them a variety of criminal agendas. In other words, the leaders of the warring factions became legitimate political leaders overnight. Different state institutions practically became private property as the spoils were divided, and the leaders and former warlords became semi-independent sovereigns, often with specific control over parts of the country's territory. In this way, organized crime did not need to fight its way into the state structures, it simply became part of them through the peace negotiations. The treaty thus transformed the role of organized crime from a part of the anarchic war-time condition to a legitimate, although unofficial, part of the political system in Tajikistan.[37]

The years immediately following the peace agreement can be described as stability on a sword's edge; it involved a horizontal power struggle between ministries and government institutions, now led by rival former warlords. This situation stood in contrast to the broader political development in the region, where state power revolved around a single authoritarian ruler. The fragile stability that characterized this period stemmed from the brittle power balance among elites.[38] Indeed, for years after his election President Rakhmon was referred to as "President of Rudaki Avenue" since his administration was largely incapable of enforcing its decisions a mile from the presidential palace.[39] Due to the fragile peace agreement, Rakhmon's power base was not initially consolidated enough to break the institutionalization pattern marked by decentralized privatization and criminalization of state institutions. After the peace treaty, several field commanders from the government and opposition side alike continued to control territories in which neither the central government nor international observers could enter without permission of these warlords.[40] Yet, during the postconflict period, President Rakhmon pursued a subtle political campaign wherein he gradually eliminated his political rivals and succeeded in establishing himself as the country's uncontested leader.

Rakhmon's Consolidation of Power

The relatively unknown and politically inexperienced Emomali Rakhmonov, who later de-sovietized his name to Rakhmon, came to power in 1993, the year he was elected president for a five-year period. From the outset, he was dependent largely on support from the remnants of the Russian army and the local warlords and crime authorities of the Kulyab region (which captured the state apparatus during the civil war and have remained in charge ever since), such as Sangak Safarov, the most powerful military leader, and Safarali Kenzhaev, a PFT founder.[41] In 1999, Rakhmon was reelected by 94 percent of the vote for another seven years in a deeply flawed election process. Furthermore, in June 2003, he reassured his power position through a referendum by opening the possibility of being reelected for another two seven-year terms as president (which would enable him to stay in office until 2020). In November 2006, he succeeded in assuring the first additional term, expiring in 2013, in an election without much competition. Given all the complexities and difficulties Rakhmon faced during and after the war, the fact that he maintained his power position is remarkable, as is the way he transformed himself from a little-known political puppet into an authoritarian leader.[42]

There is no evidence or credible allegation of Rakhmon's direct involvement in the drug trade. The economic base for his power seems to be connected mainly to control over profitable legal industries, such as aluminum production, or legal economic flows, such as foreign aid. He controls the key ministries and sectors of the country through an extensive network of family members and clients closely linked to his family and his native town.[43] Rakhmon cunningly removed his political opponents through a series of political and legal tricks. Former minister of interior Salimov was sentenced to fifteen years in prison for drug trafficking.[44] Another high-profile case involves the notorious warlord turned head of the Presidential Guard Ghaffor Mirzoyev.[45] Mirzoyev was accused of a string of crimes, but although these accusations may well have been true in the first place, the power struggle seems to have been the primary reason for his removal from Tajikistan's political scene and lifetime imprisonment. A plausible version describes this case as linked to one of Mirzoyev's close associates, long time Dushanbe mayor and speaker of parliament Makhmadsaid Ubaidulloyev. Mirzoyev is part of the Kulyab clan's "Parkhar" grouping, led by Ubaidulloyev.

Mirzoyev served as head of the Presidential Guards until his dismissal in January 2004. This move sought to distance Mirzoyev from the 3,000 troops that had been under his command and whose loyalty President Rakhmon obviously doubted. Mirzoyev initially barricaded himself in the palace with his forces, but eventually accepted the post of director of the Tajik Drug Control Agency (DCA), the smallest of the government bodies that provided control over armed forces, a criterion Mirzoyev demanded in order to accept his dismissal. Mirzoyev was nevertheless arrested already in August 2004 on charges of murder, illegal business activities, and possession of a large amount of weapons, as well as attempting to overthrow the regime.[46] Indeed, the move to the DCA seems to have been only a tactical move to eventually remove Mirzoyev completely from the political scene. The clear aim of this strategy was to eliminate the potential danger posed by the 3,000 well-armed presidential guards, who were loyal to Mirzoyev. Mirzoyev's loyalty to Rakhmon seems to have been trusted only until the rivalry between Rakhmon and Ubaidulloyev grew stronger. The connection of this entire episode to state infiltration is the credible allegations that Mirzoyev was implicated in drug trafficking during the civil war, even allegedly being able to build up his fortune and construct restaurants and casinos with drug money.

Dushanbe mayor Ubaidulloyev on his part was always considered part of the highest echelons of Tajikistan's political elite, and a real challenger to Rakhmon. Some experts even claim his power consolidation efforts at the turn of the millennium surpassed Rakhmon's.[47] However, in both Western and domestic media, Ubaidulloyev was accused of having close ties to the drug trade in the region,[48] which would have given him substantial economic support. Previously, he had major interests in the country's most profitable resources—the Turjonzada aluminum factory and the cotton industry. In the early 2000s, numerous rumors pointed to a power struggle between

Ubaidulloyev and Rakhmon, both natives of the Kulyab region but representing two rival factions. Rakhmon has headed the Danghar faction, while Ubaidulloyev led the Panghar group, to which Mirzoyev belongs. According to reliable reports, Mirzoyev and Ubaidulloyev attempted to orchestrate a coup d'état against the president, which was thwarted by Mirzoyev's arrest.[49]

Rakhmon's systematic purging of the political opposition on the basis of their involvement in the drug trade or other illicit activities seems to indicate a clear-minded strategy. According to Erica Marat, it is possible that Rakhmon intentionally surrounded himself with individuals involved in criminal activity in order to use this information in case of insubordination.[50] While this may be true regarding his present ruling tactics, it does not account for his initial years in power when his destiny was largely in the hands of those warlords that had put him in power with the purpose of having a non-warlord representing Tajikistan in the international arena and attracting external economic and political support, while the warlords from the Kulyabi region themselves were the real authority wielders on the domestic arena.[51]

Following General Suhrob Qosimov's resignation after fifteen years as head of Tajikistan's Special Force Brigade in February 2007, there are no more political and military heavyweights from the PFT in leading government positions.[52] In principle, Rakhmon's position in power has increasingly come to resemble the position of the presidents of neighboring Central Asian countries, with a single patron-client pyramid of power centered around the president at the expense of competing pyramids.[53] How, then, did the president manage to defeat these formidable violent entrepreneurs and establish himself as uncontested number one in the hierarchy of the Tajik power system, and what, if any, role did the heroin trade play in this process? In a pioneering analysis of how Rakhmon elevated his status from a puppet in the hands of warlords to master of the country and the total elimination of the old guard of war commanders from the PFT coalition, Jesse Driscoll stresses three factors. First, Rakhmon maximized his leverage over the warlords from his ability to divide their interests against one another. In particular, he realigned domestic institutions and economic policy to inhibit cooperation among warlords from different territories. Second, he took advantage of Russian economic and military support in the 1990s to marginalize unwanted groups. Finally, the PFT warlords' positions were weakened by Rakhmon's ability to co-opt rebel factions in his patronage system; in exchange for loyalty, they were allowed shares in the lucrative heroin trade.[54] Thus, in Tajikistan, economic flows from the heroin trade function as a strategic rent to be distributed among influential elites similar to other external flows like foreign aid or oil.

This does not mean a peaceful order, however. The risk of violence is constantly there, in particular when access to lucrative shares is redistributed, something that appears to have increased in recent years. Take for example former minister of emergency situations Ziyoev. After leaving the government, Ziyoev returned to his native Tavildara valley in the Rasht district, where he continued to be an influential unofficial leader. In summer 2009, he was killed in a special government operation disarming an illegal armed group suspected of terrorism and drug trafficking in Tavildara, with which Ziyoev was associated[55] The name of another UTO warlord—Shokh—would resurface in 2008 in connection with another influential player: Mirzokhuja Akhmadov, a former junior UTO commander who was appointed head of the local department of the anti-organized crime unit in the Rasht district. In this position, he reportedly kept the central government's authority at bay.[56] In 2008, the central authorities sent a column of paramilitary police to deal with Akhmadov. Upon its arrival in Gharm, Rasht's main settlement, a firefight erupted between central government forces and Akhmadov's bodyguards. The commander of the central government troops, Colonel Oleg Zakharchenko, was killed and the government had to retreat. In May the following year, former UTO commander Mullo Abdullo, who had rejected the 1997 peace treaty and been in exile in Afghanistan, returned to Tajikistan with an Afghan-based guerrilla group. The government launched military operations in the Rasht district to sweep out the insurgents. Clashes erupted in July, which claimed the life of Ziyoev. The government declared victory in August, and it was reported that 11 guerrilla fighters had been killed and 49 captured. Mullo Abdullo, however, survived for another year until he was killed in a government crackdown following a jailbreak conducted by many of the rebels captured and convicted the previous year.[57]

An even more recent episode of violence occurred in another stronghold for former UTO warlords—the Gorno-Badakshan Autonomous Province— in late July 2012. The military operation began after the government accused the UTO warlord Tolib Ayombekov, at the time chief of a major border post near Gorno-Badakshan's capital Khorog, of arranging the murder of General Abdullo Nazarov, head of the provincial national security service. A battle between government troops sent in from Dushanbe and local armed groups left about 50 combatants dead. Various experts and observers interpret the violence as having both a political component (to establish central government control over Gorno-Badakshan and eliminate the local strongmen who have continued to be the real power wielders in the province some fifteen years after the peace treaty) and a criminal component (senior government officials desiring to consolidate control over the drug trade in this major hub for heroin smuggling at the expense of the warlords).[58] In Tajikistan, these two factors are mutually reinforcing as the boundaries between the state and the private and between the formal and informal are elusive. A citizen's perception communicated to the news agency Eurasianet brings the point to the fore: "It is simple: one gang of drug traffickers is fighting with another gang of drug traffickers over their turf. Both wear official Tajik uniforms."[59]

A Narco-State?

Since organized crime operates in the shadows, it is hard to assess the extent of its influence on the country's political system. Accusations of involvement in organized criminal activity are often tossed around during internal political confrontations between different factions and high-level officials. Tajikistan is a prime example of this type of system, in which virtually no one is innocent and criminal charges can be brought against anyone believed to be disloyal. At the same time, as long as influential actors do not go into opposition or defect from the informal rules of the game, their illegal activities are generally accepted.[60] In short, this is both a mechanism for keeping order and for manipulating political competition. Nonetheless, there is highly relevant information that is passed around, containing anecdotal evidence of the direct involvement of officials in organized crime. Regarding drug smuggling, there are several specific cases that illustrate how different state representatives, particularly in the security forces, use their official positions to enrich themselves, thus undermining the functioning of state structures. Some of the cases revealed are described here; however, it must be mentioned that these cases represent just the tip of an iceberg, since officials can use their elevated positions to cover up their involvement in organized crime.[61]

A case that received international attention in 2000 involved Tajikistan's ambassador to Kazakhstan. The envoy was caught twice trying to smuggle heroin through Kazakhstan. During his second and last arrest, Kazakh police found 62 kg of heroin and US$1,000,000 in cash in the ambassador's car. Shortly after the incident, the police also arrested the ambassador's associate, the trade representative at the Tajik embassy in Astana, who was caught with

24 kg of heroin. The International Crisis Group (ICG) commented on the incident by concluding that the amount of seized heroin indicates the approval of smuggling by officials from the law enforcement authorities.[62] In August 2002, another case was documented when a former deputy defense minister was convicted of smuggling heroin in a military helicopter.[63]

The role of the Russian military also merits discussion. After the collapse of the Soviet Union, the Russian military remained stationed in Tajikistan. In May 1993, Presidents Boris Yeltsin and Rakhmon signed a bilateral agreement stipulating the Russian military's task to guard the Tajik-Afghan border.[64]

Soon enough, the Russian border troops' most important task became to fight the inflow of opiates from Afghanistan. However, at the beginning of 2000, rumors began to spread that the role of the Russian military was not entirely benign. Even though its presence in the region contained parts of the drug trade, it seemed that parts of the Russian army were involved in the trade they were supposed to fight. The primary goal of Russian smugglers was to supply the domestic Russian market with high-grade heroin from Afghanistan.

Some experts are convinced that segments of the Russian military have been a destabilizing factor in Central Asian political and security development since the beginning of the 1990s.[65] A former military intelligence officer stated that a significant amount of Afghan drugs were smuggled by the Russian military using heavy military helicopters. Supervision of these flights was limited, and secret agreements were allegedly made with customs officers, making inspection of goods transported from Tajikistan to military bases in Russia only a formal procedure.[66]

Only in 2004 were these suspicions widely substantiated. News agencies reported that a twenty-five-year-old Russian military officer from the border guards was arrested in the vicinity of Dushanbe with 8 kg of heroin. Shortly after this incident, information leaked that the Tajik Ministry of Interior's Special Forces for counternarcotics arrested several officers in the Russian military with substantial amounts of drugs on them. During a special operation, a high-ranking Russian military officer was arrested with 12 kg of heroin.[67] Moreover, Western intelligence sources have noted that appointments to serve in Tajikistan were very attractive to Russian officers, who were ready to pay significant sums of money informally to be posted there. Presumably, the reason was the opportunity to make a fortune during deployment there.[68] The mandate for the Russian border guards in Tajikistan ended in the summer 2005, and the responsibility was taken over by Tajik troops.

It would be unjust not to mention the Tajik state's efforts to fight the drug trade. It is clearly visible from the official statistics that Tajikistan is the Central Asian state with the highest drug seizure rates.[69] The United States and the UNODC finance the DCA, which has been widely lauded as a comparatively corruption-free institution. Nevertheless, this institution has not been free from flaws. In 2004, a high-ranking military officer working in the DCA in Zarafshan valley was arrested with 30 kg of heroin. After this incident, the police found 6 kg of unrefined opium in the officer's home. According to sources in Dushanbe, the arrest was a direct result of an ongoing conflict between state institutions over the control of the drug trade in the country.[70] Further evidence that the agency is vulnerable to power struggles was the brief tenure of former warlord Mirzoyev as head of the agency, as discussed above. Mirzoyev's appointment led to a collapse of morale in the organization and dwindling seizures. His dismissal and arrest in August 2004 alleviated the problem, but the episode raised concerns over the Tajik leadership's commitment to drug control. Since then, the leadership of the DCA was returned to the respected general Rustam Nazarov, and it is widely regarded as the best functioning law enforcement agency in the country, although concerns exist regarding its long-term viability, given that it is entirely foreign sponsored. Furthermore, it has been pointed out that it is largely functioning on its own with little institutional cooperation with other Tajik law enforcement agencies.[71]

The fact that drug-related corruption in the country affects state functioning is well known. According to official sources, between 2000 and 2005, 800 civil servants were arrested on charges of drug trafficking.[72] Some reports have even shown that enclosed networks operating within law enforcement agencies are themselves involved in the drug trade, usually using the confiscated drugs and selling them along to the highest bidder.[73] In their careful discussion of the topic, Paoli et al. notes the hierarchical structure of drug corruption in Tajikistan:

The bribe taker, who has often bought his own post, is required to pass a share of his earning to the boss who helped him. In such a system there is little stigma to a functionary taking a bribe, it is improper only when he takes more than he is supposed to. According to the DCA, for example, as of 2000, the position of head of the Interior Ministry Department in one of the districts bordering Afghanistan cost about $50,000. With the bribes extorted from drug traffickers, however, the position holder can quickly earn the money paid in advance and give a share of his revenues to his supervisors as well.[74]

The existence of illegal networks within law enforcement agencies such as police, customs, security agencies, and military has had devastating effects on their functioning. Drug corruption inhibits the operational ability of government institutions; the state's ability to fight organized crime and the drug trade are neutralized. On the other hand, it is obvious that drug trafficking and corruption mirror the widespread poverty in the country. The average monthly wage for a police officer in Tajikistan is estimated at about $50, which provides incentives to accept a bribe for turning a blind eye to drug shipments.[75] Moreover, in a system in which crime and politics are intrinsically linked, the actual seizures and arrests made must be treated with caution: these are not necessarily reflective of the actual corruption problems, as they may well be the result of political or criminal rivalries in government institutions rather than anything else.

The drug trade also has vast economic consequences for Tajikistan. The World Bank estimated at the beginning of the twenty-first century that over 30 percent of Tajikistan's economic activity was connected to the drug trade.[76] Another study, conducted by the UN Development Programme (UNDP), estimates that yearly income from drug trafficking in the country accounts for between US$500 million and 1 billion, compared to a GDP of US$ 2.1 billion.[77] The drug trade's effect on the Tajik economy is exceptional among countries not producing narcotics themselves. Indeed, the share of drugs in the Tajik economy far exceeds that in Colombia, where the cocaine industry never accounted for more than 5 percent of the GDP. Indeed, only Afghanistan at its peak in 2006, when drug trade according to UNODC estimates was equivalent to 60 percent of the total economy,[78] probably had a higher share of the economy related to drugs. To this should be added, in Tajikistan's case, the fact that drug/warlords immediately following the peace agreement transformed their illegal assets into the legal economy.[79]

The influence of organized crime on politics and economy has, according to several Central Asian experts, developed into a sophisticated organizational system that penetrates state structures across the region. In this context, resources are diverted from the public good to private interests. The implication is a weakness in fulfilling even the most basic commitments of a state toward its citizens. At the same time, this leaves a vacuum that enables criminal organizations to become an alternative provider of social services to the population, a direct rival to state authority. These informal providers of social services are seen not as criminals but as figures comparable to Robin Hood.[80]

Conclusions and Theoretical Implications

There is widespread consensus that criminal interest played next to no role in the initiation of the civil war, which had its origins in real power struggles between local elites in Tajik society. Over time, however, as the conflict erupted just as Afghanistan overtook Myanmar as the world's leading producer of illicit opiates, taxation of the lucrative trade or direct organization of smuggling activities became a major source of financing for war operations. Moreover, in a country where political power and economic strength are indistinguishable, it became crucial for building up political power and establishing positions as leading power brokers.[81] In a country lacking substantial profitable licit economic sectors and with a weak natural resource endowment, smuggling simply stands out as a major source of economic strength. As such, there is a strong impetus for aspiring political leaders to take part in illicit activities, since refraining from doing so would severely weaken their position vis-à-vis actors that do not refrain from participating in organized crime. As long as Afghan opiates continue to cross Tajikistan's borders in large amounts, there is no reason to expect organized crime to decline, either in society or within state structures. In a country as poor as Tajikistan, it simply constitutes such a lucrative source of income compared to regular economic activity that there will always be actors willing to take part in it.

To understand the political dimension of the drug trade in Tajikistan, a focus solely on the links between organized crime and insurgency is clearly insufficient. What stands out since the end of the civil war is not the link between conflict and drug trafficking, although violent episodes and insurgencies since 2008 suggests that the potential for instability continues to exist and that President Rakhmon's degree of control and authority outside Dushanbe remains low. Instead, the more pronounced feature in the case of Tajikistan is the increasingly institutionalized symbiosis between organized crime and the state, leading some scholars to warn of the emergence of a narco-state. While the drugs-state nexus obviously has a multitude of negative consequences for how the state behaves and performs, it may be worth pondering whether state-crime relations in some ways actually have promoted stability and alleviated the risk of violence. In other words, drug trafficking, even when it takes gigantic proportions as it has in Tajikistan, is not a threat to the security and stability of a country per se. From the perspective of the political system, shares in the lucrative trade work as a stabilizing mechanism, a way of keeping order. The risk of confrontations or violence in this system is closely linked to redistributions of illegal economic resources. The violence in Gorno-Badakshan in July 2012 demonstrates this point, clearly indicating the inherent dangers if the leadership does not want to share the profits any longer. In short, it bears noting that in the political economy of contemporary Tajikistan the ideal-typical distinction between political and criminal violence is very difficult to maintain when applied to the real situation on the ground. From the perspective of the illicit drug trade, it has expanded under a settled political order; it has become more rationalized, organized, and profitable under the protection of officials at the highest echelons of state power. Seen in this light, we should not expect this state-crime merger to be a temporary phenomenon; it may very well be so entrenched in the political system that it may persist for a very long period of time.

Chapter 4

The Islamic Movement of Uzbekistan

Svante Cornell

The Islamic Movement of Uzbekistan stands out among the objects of this study, as it is not so much a study of an actual conflict as of a transnational movement. While the IMU never succeeded in engaging the government of Uzbekistan in a protracted conflict, it has, over the years, been active in conflicts involving four countries: its native Uzbekistan, Tajikistan, Afghanistan, and Pakistan. The IMU played a supporting role in two conflicts studied elsewhere in this volume, in Afghanistan and Tajikistan; nevertheless, in spite of alliances with the UTO and subsequently Al Qaeda and the Taliban, the IMU has remained a distinct organization and the leading radical Islamist group in post-Soviet Central Asia. The group first drew attention with a series of daring raids on Kyrgyz and Uzbek territory in 1999–2000, and was then engulfed in the war in Afghanistan in late 2001, from where it was forced to move across the border into Pakistan's Tribal Areas. What makes the group of particular interest for this study are the consistent allegations of its systematic involvement in organized crime since the late 1990s.

Roots of the IMU

The roots of the IMU date back to 1990, in the city of Namangan in Uzbekistan's Fergana valley. A group of men in their early twenties representing the Islamic

Renaissance Party (IRP), led by Islamic scholar Tohir Yoldash and former Soviet paratrooper Juma Namangani, built a new mosque in the city and tried to enforce Islamic dress code and behavior. They increasingly fervently demanded the declaration of Uzbekistan as an Islamic state—a demand rejected by the government of Islam Karimov. The group split off the IRP and formed the Adolat (Justice) Party, which managed to gain prominence in the Fergana valley during 1991, by channeling the political mobilization of the population toward political Islam, restoring order through street militias, and in fact attempting, sometimes successfully, to challenge local government and law enforcement bodies and take over their roles.[1] Adolat also received emissaries from Saudi Arabian religious charities.[2]

The government, apparently unable to judge the strength of the Islamic feelings in Fergana or devise a strategy to deal with the mounting challenge, remained passive for several months. Only in March 1992 was Adolat outlawed and a crackdown ensued, forcing its leaders into exile in Tajikistan—where Yoldash and Namangani aligned themselves with radical forces in the Tajik opposition and participated on their side in the civil war. Namangani's military prowess—he had been a Soviet paratrooper fighting in Afghanistan—made him useful there, and he took the Tavildara valley in northeastern Tajikistan as his base. Meanwhile, Yoldash toured the Islamic world, including Chechnya, Turkey, and Pakistan, playing an entirely different role than Namangani: Yoldash was the IMU ideologue, where Namangani was its guerrilla leader. The IMU opposed the 1997 peace accords that ended the Tajik civil war, and both Yoldash and Namangani decided to break with their former Tajik allies. A serious crackdown on Islamic movements in the Fergana valley was in full strength at this moment, prompting an exodus of potential recruits that ended up with Namangani in Tajikistan.[3]

With this new strength, Namangani moved to Afghanistan, where the Taliban were now extending their power, and formally founded the IMU in Kabul in 1998. In early 1999, a series of bomb explosions rocked the Uzbek capital of Tashkent and almost killed President Karimov. The IMU was blamed for these terrorist attacks, though its culpability has yet to be convincingly determined. At this point, a part of the IMU under Namangani moved back into Tajikistan, asserting its position in the Tavildara valley bordering Kyrgyzstan's section of the Fergana valley.

The IMU Military Operations

The IMU military operations of 1999–2000 are key to understanding the organization's nature, as questions have been raised regarding the purpose of these raids. As such, they deserve closer scrutiny. In August 1999, the IMU conducted its first military incursion into the Batken region of Kyrgyzstan, catching the Kyrgyz military by complete surprise and prompting a mobilization of the Uzbek army. Namangani, who organized the incursion, managed to secure an informal permission to transit the Tajikistan-Kyrgyzstan border. The time was chosen during delicate negotiations between the Tajik opposition and the government on the implementation of the 1997 peace accord; Tajik authorities, under these conditions, were unwilling to confront Namangani, particularly as the IMU had close ties with the former opposition fighters that the authorities were negotiating with.[4]

The IMU contingents launched an attack that focused on the Batken region of Kyrgyzstan, as well as on the Vorukh and Sokh enclaves in the southern area. These are small islands of territory belonging to Uzbekistan and Tajikistan respectively, but entirely surrounded by mountainous territory belonging to Kyrgyzstan and with little or no road communication to their respective homelands. These enclaves have been the subject of much discord between the three states, posing difficult questions of transportation, road links to the mainland, administration, and so on. These enclaves are also known for their strong Islamic sentiment. Of the enclaves, Sokh is the largest, comparable to the Gaza strip in size (125 mi^2/325 km^2) and with a population of 43,000, whereas Vorukh has a population of 25,000.[5]

An IMU detachment estimated at fifty members occupied a mountain village in the Batken region in early August 1999. A first IMU action conducted by twenty-one militants then took a mayor and three government employees hostage on August 9 in a village in the Osh district, also in southwestern Kyrgyzstan. They initially demanded the release of political prisoners in Uzbekistan. However, the Kyrgyz government secured the release of the hostages on August 13 for a $50,000 ransom and a helicopter to fly them to Afghanistan.[6] A larger group of fighters then moved in on the Batken region, capturing a meteorological station and the commander of the Kyrgyz Interior Ministry Forces.[7] On August 23, the IMU seized further hostages, including four Japanese geologists. On October 25, the hostages were released, the IMU reportedly managing to extract a sum of $2–5 million from Japan in exchange.[8] After receiving the ransom, and as increasing snowfall was threatening to close the mountain passes, the IMU detachments retreated to Tavildara, aided by the mediating intervention of the IMU's old ally from the civil war in Tajikistan, now Tajik minister of emergencies, Mirzo Ziyoev. Uzbek pressure had now built up on Tajikistan so much that the authorities spent significant efforts to convince Namangani to leave the valley for Afghanistan. Hence several Russian army helicopters air-lifted the main IMU contingents, including militants' families, from two camps in Hoit and Sangvor into Afghanistan, where Namangani and his men spent winter in camps in Kunduz and Mazar-i-Sharif.[9]

A year later, the IMU struck again. In August 2000, Namangani arrived back in Tavildara with several hundred men. He launched a series of significantly more sophisticated attacks, mainly into Kyrgyzstan, but the scale and geographical spread of the incursions was much larger than the previous year. The southern Surkhandarya district of Uzbekistan was targeted, as were the mountains just north of Tashkent. However, the main thrust was in a simultaneous launching of several coordinated diversionary offensives of units of 50–100 men each, across the mountains separating Tajikistan and Kyrgyzstan, toward Batken and the Sokh and Vorukh enclaves. Several foreign mountain climbers, including four Americans, were taken hostage, but all were able to escape their captors.[10] As operations ended, Namangani was again flown to Afghanistan by helicopters belonging probably to the Tajik Ministry of emergencies.[11]

Making Sense of the Incursions

These two episodes raise numerous questions regarding IMU intentions in staging them. Whereas in 1999, the IMU took the Central Asian militaries by surprise, already in 2000 both the Uzbek and Kyrgyz armies were considerably more prepared. Kyrgyzstan had in fact consistently ignored military reform in the 1990s, but after the Batken incursion of 1999 it was forced to invest large resources, including significant amounts of foreign aid, in order to improve its border guards capacity and special operations forces. But as much as they startled the Central Asian region and led to efforts by regional governments to shore up their defense structures, the IMU incursions were in both cases too small to pose a serious long-term threat to the governments or territories of Central Asian states—shedding doubts on their real motivation, among others, since the incursions only woke up the Central Asian militaries and exposed their weaknesses.

One explanation that has been advanced is that the IMU sought to replicate the "Tajik model"—to force the Uzbek government to negotiate and share power.[12] Yet the IMU detachments apparently did not seek to enter the Uzbek section of the Fergana valley. They could easily have moved into Uzbekistan in 1999, but chose not to, in spite of that being their main officially stated aim. Kyrgyz National Security Minister Misir Ashirkulov has conceded that "the Uzbek militants could have easily penetrated into Uzbekistan using mountain tracks."[13] The self-avowed state of the Kyrgyz army in 1999 was such that it could in no way have stopped the well-armed militants should they have chosen to continue into Uzbekistan instead of occupying Kyrgyz mountain villages for weeks.[14]

Since the militants neither expected to nor tried to take control of the Fergana valley with their numerical strength, the argument that the IMU sought to force the Uzbek government into negotiations is implausible. While the militants did not move into Uzbekistan in 1999, they did conduct high-profile but minor skirmishes on Uzbek territory in 2000. These seemed to have been more of a public relations purpose, to embarrass the Karimov government by showing the IMU ability to surface close to Tashkent. Moreover, had the IMU had serious political intentions, it would likely have kept the hostages instead of quickly surrendering them for ransom. It has been advanced that the hostages produced a rift within the IMU, with the more religious parts led by Yoldashev wishing to hold onto them, and Namangani interested only or mainly in the ransom.[15]

Another explanation is that the IMU moves were dictated elsewhere—by the Taliban high command or by Osama Bin Laden. This explanation bears some logic; this was the time when the Taliban were aggressively trying to wipe out the Northern Alliance in Afghanistan, which was squeezed back into a small territory near the Tajikistan border. As the Northern Alliance received most of its assistance through Central Asia and specifically Tajikistan, the IMU operations could conceivably have been designed to sow unrest there in order for the Taliban and Al Qaeda to finally eliminate the remaining threat to their power over Afghanistan. Yet another possibility is that the IMU had identified the mountainous and impoverished southwestern Kyrgyzstan, around the Batken region in particular, as a most fertile ground to begin their building of an Islamic state in Central Asia. The area has ethnic enclaves as mentioned above, which had been positively disposed to Islamic movements earlier; the IMU may have sought to cut off the area from Kyrgyzstan to create a self-proclaimed Islamic state there, from which they would spread into the Uzbek parts of the Fergana valley.[16]

These reasons are plausible as a part of the puzzle explaining the timing and nature of the IMU actions. Still, an IMU desire either to destabilize Central Asia or to establish itself in southwestern Kyrgyzstan does not account for the militants' decision to rapidly agree to accept a ransom for the hostages, and be airlifted back to Afghanistan to bide their time to come back to the area once again, with a much higher alert and readiness by local military forces. These questions suggest that there is a missing link in the analysis.

The IMU and the Drug Trade

Several aspects of the modalities of the IMU incursions suggest that they were in fact conditioned to a great extent by the narcotics trade from Afghanistan. These include both the geographical areas targeted, the timing of the attacks, and the tactics used. The transit of Afghan opiates became an increasing problem in the region in the mid-1990s, as traffickers increasingly faced efforts by the Iranian government to curtail trafficking through Iran, the erstwhile chief smuggling route, making that route dangerous and therefore expensive. Central Asian states, with their porous borders, newly established state authorities, and corrupt climate, became a major new trafficking route.[17] The first seizures of heroin and opium occurred in 1995–1996, and quickly grew in size; in 2002, the five Central Asian states seized 5,5 tons of heroin, mainly in Tajikistan.[18]

The highway between Khorog on the Tajik-Afghan border and Osh, the largest city in the south of Kyrgyzstan, became known as the major transit route for drugs into Central Asia in the late 1990s, very much because it was the only major highway linking the Afghan border to the population centers of the region. The Khorog-Osh highway by the late 1990s came under increasing scrutiny by the Kyrgyz government, aided by the UN Drug Control Programme, which identified Osh as a major drug transshipment point and sought to limit the smuggling through the highway in a joint project among regional states called the "Osh knot," beginning in 1997.[19]

Meanwhile, as production of opium in Afghanistan skyrocketed while Turkey, Iran, and Pakistan cracked down on drug trafficking, increasing quantities of opiates were being smuggled into Central Asia. The Taliban's coming to power in 1996 initially led to a minor decrease in opium production, but from 1996, as discussed in this author's chapter on Afghanistan in this volume, opium production steadily grew to about 2,700 metric tons in 1997 and 1998 until it reached a record 4,600 tons in 1999, roughly double Europe's estimated yearly consumption of opiates. Afghanistan at this point accounted for 79 percent of global opium production.[20]

Concomitantly, traffickers now sought new routes into Central Asia in addition to the Khorog-Osh route. A new important route became the Batken route, by which drugs crossed the Tajik-Kyrgyz border from Jirgatal and Gharm in Tajikistan.[21] Importantly, Jirgatal and Tavildara, the strongholds of the IMU during the civil war in Tajikistan and from where it launched its two armed incursions, lie along this route. This region was of particular interest to traffickers due to the mountainous character and remoteness of the region, the weakness of Kyrgyz law enforcement there, and, most important, the existence of the Vorukh and Sokh enclaves as well as additional, smaller enclaves such as the Qalacha and Khalmion areas in Kyrgyzstan administered by Uzbekistan, and Chorku administered by Tajikistan. The enclaves suffered from a power vacuum, as neither the state they are geographically located in nor the state legally administering them was able to exert strong government authority there.[22] As a result, the enclaves became major hubs of the drug trade, as well as a storage point for heroin.

But the enclaves were also serving as forward bases for IMU militants. Already in 1997, militants were freely crossing from Tajikistan across the Korgon gorge, spreading their message and recruiting locals across the Batken region but especially in the territorial enclaves.[23] The militants apparently established routes for crossing the border with the help of the major so-called "drug barons" of the Osh region.[24] Indeed, the major destination for drugs in Kyrgyzstan was the city of Osh, where organized crime networks with well-established international contacts re-exported the merchandise toward Russia and Europe.[25]

The geographic juxtaposition of the IMU camps and activities in the late 1990s with the main areas of drug trafficking into Kyrgyzstan point at the very least to a symbiosis between the group and drug trafficking networks. The 1999 events suggest that the IMU has also in all likelihood been a leading actor in its own right in the drug trade.

The timing of the August 1999 events is indicative, as it occurred during the very narrow timeframe between the harvesting of a record batch of opium in Afghanistan in June, and the closure of the mountain passes due to snow from late September onward. In fact, in the complex political climate of Afghanistan and Central Asia at the time, the IMU was in a singularly well-placed position to control the drug trade from Afghanistan to Central Asia. The IMU had well-established links with the Taliban government and Al Qaeda, as Bin Laden even allegedly provided the IMU with funding in the order of several million dollars.[26] The group had obtained bases in

Mazar-i-Sharif and Kunduz in northern Afghanistan, as well as offices in the diplomatic sector of Kabul and in Kandahar, the Taliban spiritual capital. In addition, the IMU had close contacts with its old comrades-in-arms in the former Tajikistan opposition, now formally in government. The Tajik government, as discussed in Johan Engvall's contribution to this volume, in turn had close links with the ethnic Tajik-led Northern Alliance under Ahmad Shah Masoud. In a situation where opposing political forces were controlling the main producing areas of drugs and the transit countries in Central Asia, the network of contacts built up by the IMU enabled it to freely move across Afghanistan and Tajikistan unlike any other known organization.

The 2000 attacks further illustrated this fact: they again occurred roughly a month after the last opium harvest in Afghanistan. This allowed time for the processing of opium into heroin, which had increasingly come to be carried out in northern Afghanistan, before smuggling it out of the country. Moreover, the launching of simultaneous but small-scale incursions by comparatively small groups of fighters into Kyrgyzstan, but also Uzbekistan, makes the most sense if seen as a diversionary measure intended to create instability and confuse law enforcement and military forces, thereby allowing for the use for trafficking of several mountain passes originally used by Tajik refugees fleeing the civil war to Kyrgyzstan in the mid-1990s. These passes had since been taken up by traffickers of drugs, arms, and humans.[27] The IMU had made a practice of staging August incursions, but this did not take place in 2001. While other factors may have been at work, it is an interesting coincidence that 2001 was the year the Taliban ban on opium had gone into effect: there was no harvest in Taliban-held Afghanistan the IMU could smuggle out to Central Asia. There are nevertheless numerous reports that large stockpiles of opiates remained in the country following the large harvests in 1999 and 2000, and arguments that the Taliban eradication was only carried out to reverse the fall of opium prices.[28] As discussed in the chapter on Afghanistan in this volume, this analysis is doubtful. Yet even if there were stockpiles, this nevertheless does not necessarily mean that the IMU was in control of them. As such, the lack of an insurgency in 2001, the year of opium eradication, strengthens the case of a criminal connection to the previous incursions.

An increasing consensus has developed that the IMU was strongly involved in the drug trafficking from Afghanistan toward Osh in Kyrgyzstan, where the opiates were likely handed to trafficking networks that could ship them farther north and west. Bolot Januzakov, at the time head of Kyrgyzstan's National Security Council, asserted in 2000 that the IMU controlled the majority, perhaps up to 70 percent, of the heroin entering Kyrgyzstan.[29] Drug control experts concurred with this figure.[30] Ralf Mutschke of the Criminal Intelligence Directorate of Interpol labeled the IMU "a hybrid organization in which criminal interests often take priority over 'political' goals," adding that "IMU leaders have a vested interest in ongoing unrest and instability in their area in order to secure the routes they use for the transportation of drugs."[31] During and after the 1999 incursion, law enforcement officials noted a three-fold increase in trafficking attempts. Januzakov in late 2001 noted that the volume of drugs trafficked into Kyrgyzstan increased significantly after the 1999 incursion.[32] Organized crime and terrorism expert Tamara Makarenko has noted that

> All the events perpetrated by the IMU prior to September 11 indicate that the primary motivation of the IMU, under the leadership of military commander Juma Namanganiy, were criminal. Since 1999 the IMU was predominantly under the control of Namanganiy. Although he has been described as a "born again" Muslim, there are no indications that he was a strict Muslim with any associated allegiances. On the contrary, prior to dedicating his life to the IMU it is believed that Namanganiy was involved in the drugs trade. As such, under his leadership, it is not surprising that the IMU was focused on securing its role as a leading trafficker of opiates into Central Asia.[33]

It should be noted that the IMU never lived up to the reputation of a monolithic, hierarchically structured organization. Most studies of the movement seem to indicate at least two focal points coexisting, not without friction, within the IMU: the more guerrilla-oriented and criminal part of the organization led by Namangani and the more religious part controlled by Yoldash.[34] As such, a set of different motivations likely were behind the IMU's actions. As Frederick Starr has termed it, the IMU is best understood as an "amalgam of personal vendetta, Islamism, drugs, geopolitics, and terrorism."[35]

The IMU After September 11

The IMU was heavily cut down to size at the battle for Kunduz in November 2001, as its fighters defended the last Taliban stronghold in the north of the country. Its military leader, Juma Namangani, was killed by U.S. forces in the battle for Kunduz, while a great part of its fighting force was eliminated. The remnants of the IMU then splintered into three groups, according to interviews with former members.[36] Of these, one scattered across South Asia and another back to Central Asia, while a core group led by Yoldash sought refuge in the Tribal Areas of Pakistan, particularly in South Waziristan, where they stayed until 2007 under the protection of Waziri Taliban leader Maulvi Nazir. During the period, the Uzbeks and other Central Asians that composed the IMU became entrenched in South Waziristan, where many are known to have married local women, acquired property, and engaged in economic activity from agriculture to trade and smuggling.[37] Furthermore, Yoldash by this point dropped the focus on Uzbekistan and Central Asia as the organization's first priority, aligning instead with Al Qaeda's global jihad. This led to a further split, with some former IMU fighters under the leadership of Najmiddin Jalolov and Suhayl Baranov to found the Islamic Jihad Union (IJU), which subsequently orchestrated a series of suicide bombings in Uzbekistan in 2004.

Importantly, it appears that Yoldash's rump IMU—its numbers are variously estimated at three to five thousand members—had become dependent on funding from Al Qaeda and the Taliban. In other words, together with its military defeat in northern Afghanistan, it had also lost its control over the conduits of opium into Central Asia.[38] Thus, it is possible that Namangani rather than the more theological Yoldash controlled the IMU's involvement in the drug trade; but in any case, Yoldash's loss of independent funding—together with the substantial physical distance from Uzbekistan—may have played a large role in his decision to alter the fundamental objectives of the organization.

However, while respected for their toughness, the Uzbeks began to make enemies locally, as locals complained of their increasingly dominant attitude, attempts to force locals to behave according to their understanding of Islamic law, which did not square with Pashtun customs, and physical abuse, including assassinations, of locals.[39] Furthermore, the Pakistani Taliban leaders apparently became irritated by the refusal of the Uzbeks to join the fight against the NATO forces in Afghanistan, which was Nazir's priority.[40] The Pakistani government, at the time seeking to drive a wedge between local Taliban factions and foreign fighters, succeeded in the urge to have Maulvi Nazir oust the Uzbeks.[41] Yet they did not go far: benefiting from the long-standing tribal rivalries in Waziristan between the Mehsud and Wazir tribes, Yoldash managed instead to gain the protection of Pakistani Taliban leader

Baitullah Mehsud, who had fought with the Uzbeks in Afghanistan and who one source argues "lived with the Uzbek, who became his biggest ideological inspiration."[42] Thus, the IMU benefited from Mehsud's closer ideological affinity to the internationalized Salafi Islam espoused by the IMU, which contrasted with the more local Deobandi practices of Nazir.[43] Nevertheless, large numbers of IMU members are believed at this point to have left Pakistan and blended into Taliban units in southwestern Afghanistan.[44]

The bliss did not last long, however. Shortly after the conflict, Mehsud was named the primary suspect in the assassination of Benazir Bhutto in December 2007, leading the group to come into the crosshairs of the Pakistani state. Indeed, IMU members appear to have been frequently deployed by Mehsud against targets in Pakistan. Thus, the IMU was identified as being behind the assassination attempt against Afrasiab Khattak, leader of the Pashtun nationalist (and secular) Awami National Party in 2008.[45] By 2009, the prominence of Uzbeks and other Central Asians in the operations of the Pakistani Taliban was again noted in the Pakistani operation to remove the Taliban from the Swat valley. By summer 2009, Yoldash's rump IMU had become a key focus of the United States as well. In August, both Meshud and Yoldash were killed by predator drone attacks, effectively decapitating the IMU. The next month, IJU leader Jalolov was also killed by a drone attack.

Yoldash's death meant that the IMU now had neither of its founding leaders alive, and this appeared to lead to further fragmentation of the movement. On the one hand, research has shown a further internationalization of the IMU. As Jacob Zenn has noted, only four of the 87 IMU members that the organization claim were "martyred" during 2011 were from Uzbekistan.[46] Thus, the trend of melting away of the IMU into the region-wide jihad appears to continue.

On the other hand, the setbacks the IMU suffered in 2007–2009 appear to have led some members to seek a return to Uzbek-populated territories, where they would not be as vulnerable and exposed as they turned out to be in Pakistan. In 2009, shortly following the exodus of Uzbeks from Waziristan, International Assistance Force and Afghan forces were forced to seek to halt the IMU from establishing itself in Kunduz province in northern Afghanistan.[47] From that point on, a greater level of IMU activity became noticeable in northern Afghanistan, as well as in areas of Tajikistan, including those with a considerable Uzbek population.[48] By late 2011 and early 2012, ISAF forces in Afghanistan again reported considerable increases in encounters with the IMU—at least 37 operations targeting the group in 2012 alone.[49] It is no coincidence that most reports of IMU activity were centered in the provinces vacated by the United States and Germany in that period—Badakhshan, Balkh, and Panjshir.[50] It is also notable that allegations of involvement in the drug trade have increased following Yoldash's death. This should come as no surprise: Yoldash was in many ways the link between the IMU and the financiers of the global jihadi movement, enabling the group to receive funding from what the U.S. Treasury Department termed "Gulf-based donors."[51] That said, the IMU was also implicated in several daring attacks on Pakistani military installations through late 2012, suggesting that the organization has far from severed its ties with, and important role for, the Pakistani Taliban movement.[52]

The post-9/11 period shows a considerable change in the IMU's nature: one that suggests a return to a more ideological orientation and away from the group's criminal focus of the late 1990s. This is not to say that the IMU's involvement in drug trafficking has ceased. Pakistani authorities have stated their belief that the organization relies on drug trafficking for its funding; similarly, in 2011 Tajik DCA officials stated that "we would often detain Tajik nationals for smuggling drugs, and then it would turn out that they are the ones wanted by our security service as IMU militants."[53] The difference is that the IMU no longer appears to wield any significant control over major drug flows. A Center for Strategic and International Studies study concluded:

> Extensive interviews in the region suggest that the IMU currently exerts far less, if any, control on the Central Asian narcotics trade today. Instead, the trafficking is led by a mixture of corrupt government officials, former Tajik field commanders, and entrepreneurs coming together in what one senior official characterized as "increasingly well-coordinated, organized groups."[54]

Thus, from 2002 on, there appears to have been a parallel decrease in IMU involvement in the drug trade and an increase in its ideological profile. The question, of course, lies in the causal direction between these phenomena. Was the IMU's increasing ideological profile conditioned by its loss of control over trafficking corridors and its ensuing dependence on funding from ideologically motivated sources? Or was it, at least partly, driven by the death of Namangani and the hegemony of the more ideological Yoldash over the organization? While important, there is no conclusive answer to these questions. A combination of the two is likely the answer, but it is difficult not to conclude that IMU's evolution over time has to a large degree been opportunistic—it has followed the money, so to speak.

Conclusions

Though having suffered the death of its erstwhile leaders and seen multiple splits and splinters, the IMU continues to be a force to be reckoned with across Central and Southwest Asia. Indeed, the IMU remains unique in its geographic reach, operating on a large territory that includes several opium-producing areas of Afghanistan as well as the southern Central Asian republics and the Federally Administered Tribal Areas of Pakistan. This has provided the IMU with opportunities and networks to remain an important force both in the ongoing Jihadi movement and in drug trafficking in the region. Aside from its opportunities to do so, the IMU has—particularly following Yoldash's death—few options but to engage in the drug trade, as it has likely seen a decrease in its alternative sources of funding. Al Qaeda hardly possesses the means to keep subsidizing its Central Asian subsidiary, and international efforts to stop terrorist financing are likely to have made it harder for ethnic Uzbeks in Saudi Arabia to support the organization, as they did earlier. Drug trafficking is therefore likely to remain the major source of funding for the IMU, even if a return to a stronger ideological motivation appears to have occurred.

The risk is therefore apparent that the drug trade will allow the IMU—or a successor organization—to acquire the financial wherewithal to survive and even possibly regain strength should unrest grow in Central Asia in coming years. Indeed, from 2009 onward, there are indications that this has begun to occur. The key question, of course, is how the IMU will be impacted by the impending U.S. withdrawal from Afghanistan. Will it move back to Afghanistan's north and into Central Asia, or continue to maintain its commitment to the Pakistani Taliban cause? The answer will in no small part be related to whether ideological or criminal motives will prevail among the organization's leaders.

The IMU stands out among organizations covered in this book due to the flexibility of the organization's profile. It has moved not only from an ideologically motivated group in the direction of a criminal motivation, but has also moved back along the same continuum. As such, this opportunism stands in contrast to the resilience and hierarchical nature that the organization has proven over the past two decades.

While officially claiming to seek the reestablishment of a political order that existed 1,400 years ago, the IMU is, as one of the most prominent examples of the integration of transnational organized crime and violent anti-state movements, a decidedly postmodern phenomenon. Prior to September 11, 2001, the IMU was showing clear symptoms of an organization whose motivational structures were gradually changing from the ideological to the criminal. With the death of the leader that was most involved in the drug trade, the group moved back in an ideological direction. With the death of its most ideological leader, the IMU now may be moving back in a more criminal direction. Clearly, elements of both could survive in symbiosis in the organization, as they seemed to do in the period before September 11.

The IMU's development illustrates the dangers of ignoring the security ramifications of the international production and trafficking in narcotics. Treating the drug trade as a domestic law enforcement issue and thereby rejecting its implications for national, regional, and international security has only allowed the situation in Central Asia, just as in the Andean region or in Southeast Asia, to deteriorate. Transnational organized crime has in the past decade become far more sophisticated and multifaceted than it once was. It is a rising threat especially to the security of weak states; yet the financial power it possesses and its links to human trafficking and terrorism clearly make it an issue that deserves attention in the security debate also of industrialized countries.

Chapter 5

From Chechen Mafia to the Islamic Emirate of the Caucasus: The Changing Faces of the Insurgency-Organized Crime Nexus

Murad Batal al-Shishani

Given the complex circumstances of a war-torn and non-self-governing region such as the North Caucasus, developing an accurate understanding of the challenge posed by organized crime can be daunting. Assessing the overlap between organized crime and insurgency in the region requires observing three determining factors in this relationship: the structural problem in the region, the reflection of events in Moscow that impact the political dynamics in the region, and the stereotyping of North Caucasians, and in particular Chechens, by Russia within the long history of enmity between the two parties.

After two wars that lasted a decade in Chechnya, the structural problems of the North Caucasus and the potential ethnic or territorial conflicts—which could yet flame up at any time—make the region an ideal area for the growth of organized crime. Furthermore, violent incidents occur on a daily basis—not only in Chechnya, but across the entire region.

Following the collapse of the Soviet Union, the absence of the effective governing authorities made Russia, as a whole, a fertile ground for criminal activities. The number of identified criminal groups increased remarkably in the mid-1990s, after which the increase slowed down. Along with other political dynamics, an increase in organized crime groups affected the situation in the North Caucasus, and these groups came to play a significant role in the region by using it as a hub to facilitate their activities.

Generally, the phenomenon of "organized crime" in Russia started with the collapse of the Soviet Union in the early 1990s. It had been associated in part with various ethnicities. The "Chechen mafia" emerged as the largest of these groups and as a representative of the link to the North Caucasus.

The Chechen mafia went in two directions; the first linked to the various Russian security services, and the second defected to join the independence movement emerging in Chechnya at the time. Both groups played a key role in determining the shape of the nexus between organized crime and insurgency in the North Caucasus.

Also worth noting is that the nature of insurgency had changed by the beginning of the Second Chechen War in 1999, and after 2005 it has moved to neighboring republics with the Islamic banner and expanded into Dagestan, Ingushetia, and Kabardino-Balkaria. This included a new source of funding for Islamist insurgency that affected the nexus between organized crime and insurgency in the North Caucasus.

In that context, this chapter discusses the organized crime and insurgency nexus in the North Caucasus, arguing that it was not clearly linked, as the so called "Chechen mafia" represented a unique form of organized crime in Russia whose social structure was similar to the structure of insurgents in Chechnya, but whose origins and motivations were different. This phenomenon also reflected a stereotyping of Chechens that was systematically carried on state-controlled Russian media outlets.

Background

The North Caucasus, with a population of roughly six million, is the southernmost region of the Russian Federation, bordering Georgia and Azerbaijan. The region consists of a number of nominally autonomous republics with an area of 72,000 km²,[1] dominated by several distinct ethnic groups. In the west, the Turkich Balkar and Karachai share, with the Circassian peoples (Kabardin, Adygey and Cherkess) the republics of Karachai-Cherkessia and Kabardino-Balkaria; the Ossetians in North Ossetia; the Vainakh peoples (Chechens and Ingush), who form the overwhelming majority of the republics of Chechnya and Ingushetia. Dagestan, the largest republic on the

Caspian coast, itself has several dozen distinct nationalities, of which eight are nominally titular, sharing power in the government institutions of the republic. All these republics are subject to the Russian federal government, although they have movements that are seeking independence.

Although the entire region is affected by violence, the rate of attacks is higher in republics with larger grievances that formalized in armed movements such as in Ingushetia, Dagestan, and Kabardino-Balkaria. These armed groups, following the Second Chechen War, subjugated themselves to the Islamic Emirate of Caucasus (IEC), an entity formed in 2007, which helped them enhance their funding, capabilities, and geographical expansion.

There are common elements among the peoples of the North Caucasus, such as history, religion, customs and traditions, and culture (music, singing, dancing), that stimulate the idea of unity between them.[2] Historically, a number of movements among North Caucasians have sought to unite their region, and they had a long history of joint resistance against the Russian advance in their territories.[3] However, this changed under the Soviet rule that dominated the region after 1917.

Since Sheikh Mansour declared a "holy war" against Russia in 1785, the history of the region witnessed various attempts to unit its peoples: Imam Shamil and his State of the Imamate 1829–1851; the 1877 revolution of Chechnya; the Emirate of Caucasus Mountains; and the Caucasian "Mountain" Republic in 1917. This history was cited repeatedly by forces calling for the unification of the region. Similarly, Islam is considered to be a unifying factor among North Caucasians; apart from Christian Ossetians, they are all Sunni Muslims, and Islam was an important factor that shaped their resistance movements against the Russian advance.[4]

However, Sovietization policies largely dismantled the idea of a united Caucasus. The Soviet nationalities policy, especially during the Stalinist era, dismantled the region into several distinct autonomous republics and regions, which merged, seemingly randomly, the peoples of the region. This later resulted in a number of border disputes in the years before and after the Soviet collapse.[5] When Mikhail Gorbachev introduced "Perestroika" and "Glasnost" policies, individuals sought to restore their properties and nations began to seek the reunification of their territories.[6]

This resulted in several border disputes in the region, such as between Dagestani Laks and Chechens in the areas of Khasavyurt and Nolak, which are predominantly Chechen and were merged with the territories of Dagestan during the Stalinist era. There were disputes between the Karachay and

Cherkess, and the Balkar and Kabardins, as they had been merged into one republic despite being ethnically different. There was also a much bloodier dispute between the Ingush and Ossetians over the Prigorodny area, which degenerated into armed conflict in 1992.[7] These border disputes were largely ethnic in nature, illustrating how following the collapse of the Soviet Union, ethnic feelings emerged more strongly than religious feelings in the region.[8]

On September 6, 1991, Chechnya declared its independence. All Soviet institutions were dismantled, and the National Conference of Chechen People elected a Soviet general in his late forties as a leader of the Congress. General Jokhar Dudayev was the first Chechen-origin general in the Soviet army, a remarkable achievement given the discrimination against non-Slavs in the military, especially the deported peoples such as the Chechens. Dudayev was married to a Russian woman, a fact that made him trusted by Soviet authorities, and he was gradually promoted until heading a Soviet Strategic Missile Unit based in Estonia, where his embrace of the Estonian popular movement raised his profile among nations in the Soviet Union.

The charismatic Dudayev was elected president in October 1991, and in return Moscow enacted emergency rule in Chechnya and sent special forces to impose it. Dudayev was able to stave off that attempt to remove him from power, and effectively presided over a de facto independent state until the outbreak of war in November 1994, when Russian forces invaded Chechnya.

Although Dudayev did not create alliances with organized crime groups, his policies paved the way for the activities of these groups. Dudayev believed that independence was linked automatically with prosperity, and assumed that the independence of Chechnya would create a strong economy.[9] Hence, Dudayev kept talking about a "second Kuwait," in reference to Chechnya's oil wealth, and set up an economic program that was based on breaking the state monopoly on production, especially in the oil sector, and opened the door to foreign investment, aiming to attract investors from abroad.[10]

By making economic freedom synonymous with political freedom, Chechnya—newly transforming from the Soviet planned economy—became an open market for various Western and Asian goods, as well as for illegal economic activities and suspicious transactions, often based out of Moscow.[11] Chechnya also became an attractive hub for organized crime groups and their supporters in Moscow.

As one author observed the situation, "the undefined status of Chechnya's territory in 1991–1994, before the Russian invasion, made the region a free-trade zone for all type of contraband including drugs and weapons. This signified the inability or unwillingness of General Jokhar Dudayev's government to provide order in Chechnya; but it was also an illustration of the use that Russian elites had for an ungoverned territory through which they could conduct illicit activities."[12]

On December 11, 1994, Russian troops invaded Chechnya. In the following months, most of Chechnya's territories were destroyed and occupied. Thousands were killed and fled the country. The Chechen popular resistance movement formed, and resorted to urban and guerrilla warfare. In practice, Chechen resistance was divided between the formal small army units that had been formed by Dudayev, and the popular groups that emerged after the Russian invasion. Both groups were based on *taip* (Chechen clans), traditional Sufi orders or *Wird*, and geographical area. Arab fighters also joined the Chechen insurgency, but their presence at that time was limited.

Despite the fact that Arab fighters played a role in the first war and participated in liberating Grozny, which earned them respect from the Chechens,[13] the first war from 1994 to 1996 was primarily a nationalist uprising, with Islam merely playing a subsidiary mobilizing role.[14] Indeed, Arab fighters had a marginal role in the outcome of this war. It was only in the aftermath of the victory and by securing de facto independence that the notion of an Islamic state started to gain traction as a plausible outcome of the war.[15] This is when Arab fighters started playing a major role in Chechnya.

The war with Russia destroyed everyday institutions in all of Chechnya and ruined 80 percent of the Chechen economy, which resulted in high rates of unemployment and an economic depression. This consequently paved the way for external influences in Chechen politics, and gave rise to the Arab fighters' Salafi-Jihadi ideology, which attracted frustrated young men, whose only prospects following the brutal war with Russia seemed to be unemployment and economic deprivation.

In the first war, Dudayev distributed funds to field commanders to secure his control and command. However, with his death by a Russian guided missile in 1996, Zelimkhan Yandarbiyev assumed the presidency and announced that Chechnya would be an Islamic state with Shari'a courts, causing charity organizations and individuals from the Middle East, particularly from the Gulf States, who favored Salafi-Jihadis, to become active in Chechnya. Nevertheless, in elections in early 1997, Yandarbiyev lost to the secular nationalist Aslan Maskhadov, who had been Dudayev's chief of staff.

These organizations and the Arab fighters that streamed into Chechnya at this time played a significant role in Chechnya in the face of Russia's reneging of its promises and agreements. This was particularly the case with Russia's promises to help rebuild Chechnya in the Khasavyurt Agreement of 1996, which former Russian president Boris Yeltsin declared had put an end to an ongoing 400-year-old conflict.[16] These infringements were perceived as Russian tactics that sought to undermine Maskhadov, Chechnya's first democratically elected president, who was opposed to the radical Islamists, as well as to the criminal activities that had begun to increase in Chechnya by then.[17]

From 1997 on, the Arab fighters established an alliance with Chechen field commander Shamil Basayev, who had also sought the presidency but lost. This alliance was supported financially by the Saudi-born fighter Amir Khattab,[18] and was protected by Basayev. However, the alliance was provisional since both parties had different ideas concerning the ultimate unification of the North Caucasus. It was the formation of this alliance that encouraged the Salafi-Jihadi forces in Chechnya to invade neighboring Dagestan in September 1999 to support a few small Dagestani villages that had declared Shari'a law and isolated themselves from the rest of the republic. That invasion gave Russia the pretext it needed to start what it called a war on terrorism, which was characterized as a religious war, as opposed to the first war, which had been framed in a nationalist context.

The presence of jihadists in Chechnya also inflamed the opposition between traditional Sufis and Salafi-Jihadists, and the situation came to a head in 1998, when shots were fired between them. For the first time in decades the Sufis, especially followers of the Qadiri order, began to lend support to Russia, in view of the perceived Salafi-Jihadi threat. The most significant shift came when Chechnya's former mufti, Ahmad Kadyrov, switched to the Russian side, and headed the pro-Russian government that Moscow installed in Grozny after the beginning of the second war, starting in 1999.

While the first war was considered to be a nationalist struggle, the second war was characterized and exploited as a religious war by Russian propaganda. The role of Arab fighters, along with their alliance with Basayev, was manifested particularly in female suicide operations. Chechen females, covered in black dresses and thus earning the nickname "black widows," participated in hostage crises at the Dubrovka Theater in Moscow in 2002, and in the Beslan School carnage in September 2004.

The Russian military's brutal response, the division in Chechen society, and the labeling of the Chechen resistance as terrorism especially in the post-9/11 environment, all contributed to weakening the Chechen insurgency, and empowered the pro-Russian Chechen government of Kadyrov in its attempts to enforce the slogan of a "normalizing" Chechnya—as it endorsed a new constitution for the republic, and in spite of the numerous reports of widespread human rights violations coming out of the republic. When Kadyrov was assassinated in 2004, his son Ramzan became the actual strongman of the republic, a position he has consolidated fully at the time of this writing.

As Kadyrov's forces were able to assert control over Chechnya and marginalize the insurgency, the latter countered by spilling over into neighboring republics and by, in effect, implementing Basayev's idea of the unification of North Caucasus in creating alliances with emerging local groups in the other republics. As a logical consequence, the IEC was established in 2007 as an umbrella for the North Caucasian armed groups. The Caucasus Emirate's leader, Dokka Umarov, is among the few leaders of the Chechen independence movement who remain alive.

High rates of poverty and unemployment, widespread corruption, incessant power struggles, and Moscow's failure to present a nation-state project that attracted and integrated the different nationalities of the North Caucasus, have all played a major role in boosting a form of regional integration that increased the role of Islam as a factor of unification within the armed groups in the region, culminating in the formation of the Caucasus Emirate.[19] By contrast, the erstwhile secular nationalist Chechen leadership has transformed into an exile phenomenon.

The Main Actors

The current actors in the North Caucasus region emerged after the collapse of the Soviet Union. The Chechen wars played a major role in this emergence. While Russia, the local governments, and the North Caucasian insurgent groups are the main actors in the region, organized crime developed simultaneously and overlapped with the other actors.

Russia and the Local Governments

Despite structural problems and the failure of integration, partly caused by Russia's own policies, Moscow considers the North Caucasus region strategically important, given its proximity to the South Caucasus and the Islamic world, and its crucial location at Russia's only warm water ports.

The importance of the region for Russia became obvious after the declaration of Chechen independence when it launched two wars against Chechnya in one decade. Russia feared that an independent Chechnya not only would lead to Russia's loss of the entire North Caucasus—the so-called "domino effect"—but also put in jeopardy other non-Russian territories, including Muslim-majority Tatarstan, where separatist sentiments were strong. The Chechens would either succeed in gaining independence, with widespread repercussions, or fail and be integrated with Russia.[20]

After suffering a resounding defeat in the First Chechen War, the Russian authorities seized the opportunity for revenge. The Second Chechen War was provoked, in part, by the burgeoning alliance between Arab fighters and radical Chechens. This was exploited by the Russian government, which used it to justify a savage war in Chechnya by calling it a war on terrorism. Ironically, Russian policies contributed to isolating and exiling the legitimate and moderate Chechen nationalist movement. With the Second Chechen War, in which former intelligence officer Vladimir Putin came to power promising to restore Russia's superpower status and to fight Islamic fundamentalism in Russia, the Chechen independence movement became synonymous with international terrorism, particularly after September 11.

Since coming to power, Putin implemented a new strategy in the North Caucasus in the form of two policies: one increased the role of the Russian security services in the region, while the other returned the region to central government by abolishing elections for the heads of the various republics. Instead, these were now appointed by the Kremlin. Putin officially portrayed this as a necessary response to the deadly seizure of a school in Beslan by North Caucasian militants in September 2004.[21] Since then, the Kremlin has fully controlled the regional governments in the North Caucasus.

However, this control has been questionable, particularly in Chechnya. Its strongman, Ramzan Kadyrov, has walked a fine line between personal loyalty and subservience to Putin, on the one hand, and institutional distancing from Russia, on the other. Indeed, while repeatedly stating his absolute loyalty to Putin and delivering embarrassingly high numbers of votes for the ruling party at all elections, Kadyrov has also begun to appeal to Chechen nationalism and sought to Islamize Chechnya. This has included seeking the prosecution of Russian officers responsible for civilian deaths in Chechnya;[22] to have the Russian military expelled from the republic;[23] and to assert Chechnya's economic and political autonomy including the creation of a Chechen oil company that would deny Moscow the revenues of Chechnya's oil industry. Kadyrov has urged women to comply with Islamic dress codes, spoken favorably of Shari'a, and referred to women as men's property—all in violation of Russian law.[24]

In addition, Kadyrov has diverted large funds from the Russian federal government, whose auditors have called attention to the disappearance of millions of dollars in state subsidies to Chechnya. Thus, while Kadyrov has stabilized Chechnya on the surface, its stability rests on the personal relationship between Kadyrov and Putin, and it is an open question whether the stability of the republic would outlive the departure from power of either man.[25]

Elsewhere in the North Caucasus, Moscow has sought to achieve a "vertical of power" and assert control over the region. The main feature of the new ruling elites is loyalty to Moscow rather than, as had been the case, roots in the local politics of the region. This has generated additional friction between Moscow and the inhabitants of the North Caucasus. Their leaders are now responsive mainly to Moscow's demands rather than to their own needs. In Ingushetia, the independent-minded leader Ruslan Aushev was replaced in 2002 by an Ingush Federal Security Service (FSB) officer with little connection to the region, Murad Zyazikov, whose mismanagement and repression alienated considerable parts of the population and brought many young Ingush into the arms of the insurgency. In Kabardino-Balkaria, Putin similarly appointed a Moscow-based businessman with roots in the republic, Arsen Kanokov, to the presidency in 2005, with the explicit purpose of appointing a person without links to the "clan politics" of the republic. However, Kanokov's lack of a popular base in the republic led the situation to deteriorate further.[26]

As the *Economist* noted, the socioeconomic situation in the region, which fuels the insurgency and provides the insurgents with new recruits to the Caucasus Emirate, is related "to the Kremlin's policies in the mainly Muslim north Caucasus. While Chechnya has been brutally pacified, the region is in a simmering civil war. Republics such as Dagestan and Ingushetia are formally part of the Russian federation, but have long ceased to be treated as such either by Moscow or by their own inhabitants. Corruption and the failure of everyday politics have made governance in the north Caucasus completely ineffective."[27] For instance, more than 300 attacks were recorded in Dagestan and Ingushetia alone in 2010. As of November 2012, 574 violent deaths have been reported in the North Caucasus; also, recent reports indicated that security services in the region are involved in kidnapping civilians.[28] Needless to say, the government institutions of the North Caucasus are rife with corruption, and open to the infiltration of organized crime.

Insurgency

The insurgency in the region started in Chechnya after the first war in the mid-1990s. It consists of two parties: nationalists and jihadists.

The nationalists have been divided into two factions: the soft-liners and the hard-liners. The former were represented by Chechen presidents Dudayev and Maskhadov. Currently, they are represented by Ahmed Zakayev, living in exile in London. This faction believes in a secular nationalist regime in Chechnya. While the soft-line nationalists led the fight against Russia in 1994–1996 and in 1999, they believe that negotiating with Russia is the best way to resolve the conflict. Maskhadov indeed sought a balanced relationship with Russia and opposed calls for a pan-Caucasian state.[29] After the first war ended and he was elected president, he denounced attacking the Russian forces under the pretext of "Jihad."[30] This faction adopted a Westernized policy, but relented due to the growing strength of Islamist and nationalist hard-liners, although national elements are still present in the Caucasus Emirate insurgency.

The hard-line nationalists are represented by the followers of Chechen warlord Shamil Basayev, who was killed in 2006. He allied the jihadists and Arab fighters in 1998 and placed great importance on the unification of the North Caucasus, which partly explains his subsequent alliance with the Islamists.[31]

Islamism in Chechnya was represented by a group of Chechen elites whose political attitudes led them to look to the Middle East, and to adopt the concept of political Islam. One of the most well-known members of this faction was Zelimkhan Yandarbiyev, Dudayev's vice president, who became interim president in 1996–1997 following Dudayev's assassination. Yandarbiyev was assassinated in Qatar in 2004. This Islamist faction was then assimilated by the Arab fighters or Salafi-Jihadists, but their influence reappeared in the Caucasus Emirate. Following the first war, in 1997–1999, the jihadists opened training camps and Islamic schools, and implemented Shari'a courts. Their influence was rejected by Chechens, and their presence there has been decreasing since 2003.[32] Beginning in 2007, when Umarov announced the formation of the Caucasus Emirate, it has served as an umbrella to all insurgency groups in the North Caucasus including various factions of the Chechen insurgency. Yet in practice, it is questionable to what extent the

Caucasus Emirate is a hierarchically organized entity. Indeed, it relies heavily on autonomous resistance cells across the region that arise spontaneously, and is in this sense more of a loose network than an institutionalized entity.

Rise of Organized Crime in the Region

The situation in the North Caucasus region shows various factors that feed organized criminal activity. In a report written for the Canadian Criminal Intelligence Service, Julia Novitskaia and Stewart Prest listed several factors that feed organized crime, including conflict, governance, economics, and demographic shifts. These factors create a vacuum of power that make a state "vulnerable to influence [and] encourage the growth of corruption and criminality."[33] For instance, 80 percent of the North Caucasus population is estimated to live below the national poverty line,[34] and the region is experiencing high rates of corruption.

In 2010, a criminal case became public in Chechnya involving "the embezzlement of 3.5 million rubles (more than $115,000) in budgetary funds allocated for the construction of a school-hostel for deaf and hearing-impaired children in Grozny."[35] Yet few instances of corruption are publicized in the region, given the widespread use of repressive measures by government officials. Yet it is widely known that the Kadyrov government itself siphons off large amounts of money from federal subsidies, which in Chechnya as in its neighboring republics constitute over three-quarters of the republican budget. Thus, the reconstruction work that has taken place in Chechnya is done in Kadyrov's own name rather than attributed to the federal government; and Kadyrov himself proclaims to be unaware of the source of financing for the cultural and sports events with foreign stars that regularly take place in Grozny.

As a result, the level of subsidies to the North Caucasus has generated a growing popular movement in Russia wanting to stop the government from "feeding the Caucasus."[36] A leaked Russian government report in 2006 cited that the shadow economy constituted an estimated 44 percent of Dagestan's economy, as opposed to 17 percent in Russia as a whole; 50 to 70 percent of Dagestanis with some form of employment were thought to work in the shadow economy.[37]

The activities of organized groups in the North Caucasus reflected the developments in Moscow. In the mid-1990s, 40–50 percent of Russia's economy was estimated to be controlled by organized crime,[38] and Russian government sources themselves estimated that "the mafia controls 40 percent of private business and 60 percent of state-owned companies."[39] For example, Chechen rebels benefited from the corruption in the Russian army establishment. They were buying their arms from individual soldiers as well as from military armories and Russian manufacturing plants.

While these figures show the influence of organized crime in post-Soviet Russia, the North Caucasus was also witnessing the creation of the self-proclaimed independent Republic of Chechnya, and links were created between ethnic Chechens involved in organized crime in Moscow and the new Chechnya. However, it was not a clear, simple relationship as Russian authorities described it—they called it simply, the "Chechen mafia."[40]

Indeed, the conflict in the region developed in isolation from the widespread organized crime. While groups from both the North and South Caucasus were heavily represented in the organized criminal structures of the late Soviet period, the origin of the conflicts in the region is based squarely on grievances. The Chechen (and later North Caucasian) insurgency was motivated by political and to some extent economic grievances, unlike organized crime groups that are motivated by economic interests or greed. Thus, when the insurgency sought to seize weapons depots or acquired weapons from corrupt Russian troops, their purpose was to carry out their armed struggle rather than to sell these weapons. It is worth mentioning that Soviet economic policies toward the peripheries, including the North Caucasus republics, caused a job-seeking migration among North Caucasians to the cities and industries of Russia proper, where the organized crime groups later known as the Chechen mafia, were established. This indicates the distinction between insurgency and organized crime groups in terms of origins as well as in terms of motivation.

The Chechen "Mafia"

Organized crime groups in Russia can be divided into three major categories: "classic," whose structure is similar to traditional organized crime groups around the world; "governmental," which consist of elements within the security services, particularly cadres of the Ministry of Interior (MVD) and Federal Security Service (FSB), and private security agencies that run substantial criminal activities; and "national," which represent ethnically based, not least Chechen, groups that "initially set up explicitly to protect Chechen business interests but then diversified their activities and membership."[41] The Chechen mafia got its start with the refusal by Chechen businesses in Russia (that were involved in finance, banking, oil, metallurgy, and bulk sales) to pay for protection, which is known in Russian slang as *krysha* (literally roof). Initially, this was to remain independent "for the sake of honor," even when this meant open confrontation with organized crime groups. Chechen businesses instead developed their own networks that later "became virtually the only category of business that could resist *krysha* (though some Chechens did affiliate themselves with governmental syndicates)."[42]

The reputation of the Chechen network, in the words of one analyst, "spread among foreign executives, who began to include Chechens in investment projects—Chechens with experience in protection became the preferred source of it over time, and Chechen groups formed initially to protect Chechen business became Mafia groupings."[43] Chechen organized crime started in Moscow in the late 1980s and was a reflection of the changes in the Soviet empire. While nativization was on the rise in the USSR, ethnic-based crime groups formed in that era, with Azerbaijani, Armenian, Georgian, and Dagestani ones being prominent among them. The main Chechen group was the Lozanskaya group (named after a Moscow restaurant that the group used as its headquarters). The bands mainly controlled car-dealing and hotels. The group became influential, and its growth did not go unnoticed by the KGB. It was infiltrated then. Before the First Chechen War, all leaders of the Lozanskaya group maintained close ties both with the separatists' leaders and Russian security agencies at the end of 1994.[44] However, the Lozanskaya group was divided sharply by the war in their homeland; several of its leaders, including Lecha Islamov, Balaudi Tekilov, and not least Khozh-Akhmed Nukhayev, supported the separatists, while Ruslan Atlangeriyev and Mustafa Shidaev supported the FSK (federal counter-intelligence service).[45]

According to organized crime specialist Mark Galeotti, "Moscow was worried that Chechen gangs elsewhere in the country would become a dangerous fifth column. After all, for a while under the infamous "Khoza" (whose real name was Nikolai Suleymanov), the Chechens had been the most active and possibly even most powerful gang alliance in Moscow following a turf war in 1988–89."[46]

Khoza (which means "sparrow" in the Chechen language) played a major role in mobilizing and supporting opposition to Dudayev, and until his death in 1994 he led efforts to fight against the independence movement. This wing of the Chechen mafia was used by Russian secret services against the Chechen separatist movement; thus, as Galeotti argues, Chechen organized crime was "strikingly unaffected by the two Chechen wars."[47]

The role of organized crime persisted after Dudayev's presidency. Maskhadov, once elected, tried to distance himself from former members of crime groups, unlike Dudayev, who tried unsuccessfully to carry them to support his new state.[48] Also, the former members of the Lozanskaya group who had supported the Chechen state and refused to collaborate with Russian secret agencies were killed in suspicious circumstances.[49] The situation was such that "many Chechens returned to fight for their homeland or supplied money or weapons, but the actual criminal organizations did not."[50]

However, criminal activities increased noticeably between 1997 and 1999, the interwar years in Chechnya. Some insurgents, particularly those linked to warlord Arbi Barayev, got involved in the kidnapping "business." It should be noted that Barayev was one of the key forces that sought to undermine Maskhadov, and even engaged Maskhadov's troops in firefights in 1998. During the second war, Barayev lived freely in a town under Russian control until his death in 2001—although he was responsible for the killings of captive Russian soldiers. Barayev lived only a few miles from a Russian checkpoint, and his car is reported to have had had an FSB ID allowing him safe passage.[51]

Maskhadov sought to prevent any linkage of organized crime groups to the de facto independent Chechnya, but he was simultaneously under pressure from the Islamist-nationalist alliance's demands to establish an Islamic state. Thus, Maskhadov was unable to counteract the growing instances of kidnappings, while Moscow, in turn, was encouraging such criminal activities, among others, by paying ransoms to undermine Maskhadov's authorities. The kidnappings were a reflection of the state's weakness as well as an activity that suggests a change in the motivational structure of some insurgent groups. That said, it is clear that the mainstream of the resistance remained focused on confronting the Russian advance and building an independent state.

Social Structure and Stereotyping

The social structures that laid the foundations for the insurgency and for the organized crime groups in the North Caucasus, and particularly in Chechnya, are similar. The Chechen organized crime syndicates tend to call themselves a *bratva* (brotherhood), rather than a mafia.[52] This is due to its social structure based on the *taip* (clan), the primary social unit in Chechen society; while it was weakened as the chief organizing principle of Chechen society by the deportations, it not only defines personal identity but also provides a practical alternative to the state in a range of ways, from protection to economic opportunity.[53]

This was also the case for the insurgency groups in Chechnya, which all were based on taip networks. Furthermore, the immigration movement to Europe from Chechnya was facilitated by taip-based networks.[54] The fact that both Chechen guerrilla fighters and organized crime are based on kinship creates an overlapping confusion, and this encouraged stereotyping in Moscow.

Russian authorities and state-owned media outlets in Moscow used the term "Chechen Mafiya" to criminalize Chechens' political and economical activities. "Even in regions where there are very few Chechens, police reports talk of dominant Chechen gangs. To some extent this could be written off as propaganda, as Moscow demonizes the Chechens, or simple racism that lumps all North Caucasian peoples as 'Chechen.' "[55]

Stereotyping of Chechens in Russia has a historical context that reflects the protracted conflict between both parties; in each historical stage of this conflict, Chechens were labeled by a different name in order to demonize them, such as: "barbarians" (in the Tsarist era), "enemy of people," "bourgeoisie," and Wahhabis. In the early 1990s, Chechens commonly were linked to the "Mafiya." As John Russell has concluded,

> the Russians were liberal in their use of the epithets "criminal" and "crazy" and their synonyms in describing their Chechen opponents, laying special emphasis on Mafia connections and drawing attention to a fanaticism bordering on madness. The "criminal" label was pinned on the Chechens, first and foremost, owing to the identification of their taip (clan) system with that of the Mafia.[56]

Chechen Mafia or Bratva?

By the mid-1990s, according to mostly Russian reports, the Chechen mafia started to "play a prominent role in narcotics trafficking, car thefts, black marketeering, oil and gas diversions and other crimes," and more significantly, "in the arms trafficking associated with the Caucasus and other areas."[57] Furthermore, when the Russian army launched a military campaign against de facto independent Chechnya in 1994, it was described as an operation against "gangsters" and to "restore order" in the republic.

In fact, the statement was a mix of Russian propaganda and the reality on the ground. Andrew Meier, who considered the Chechen mafia the real reason for invading Chechnya, stated that "by 1994 Chechen criminal organizations had built up the most lucrative and far-reaching network of contraband goods in the former Soviet Union. Their smugglers' manifest now runs from weapons to cars to counterfeit money to prostitutes. Narcotics—opium and hashish from neighboring Central Asia—rank at the top."[58]

Reports assumed that there was a "strategic linkage" between the Chechen mafia in Moscow and the Chechen guerrillas in Grozny, stating that "the Chechen Mafia has reportedly supported Chechen terrorists by financing groups within the separatist region. In return, Chechen rebels have supposedly organized and implemented bombings within Moscow."[59] Also, others suggested that the "criminalization of the Chechen resistance occurred in part as a result of the difficulties the rebels have had to seek funding for their struggle. Indeed, in the mid-1990s, a large portion of the Chechen resistance's funding came from semi-legal or illegal Chechen business in Russia, including the notorious Chechen organized crime groups."[60]

Also, by then some of the Chechen organized crime members had joined the Chechen government, and others had also returned to Chechnya to join the resistance movement to fight against the Russian advance in Chechnya. That was another indicator of the overlapping between organized crime and the insurgency in the North Caucasus. However, organized crime and the Chechen insurgency were separate phenomena.[61] Indeed, neither of the writers mentioned in the foregoing paragraphs showed evidence either of a criminalization of the resistance, or of organized crime being the main reason—rather than simple propaganda—for Russia's decision to launch the 1994 intervention.

Post-9/11 Developments

From the early 2000s, Russia succeeded in installing a pro-Moscow regime in Chechnya led by former Chechen Mufti Ahmed Hadji Kadyrov and, following his assassination, his son Ramzan. Kadyrov, like many Chechens, opposed the increasing influence of Islamists inside Chechnya. Benefiting from the 9/11 attacks by Al Qaeda in New York and Washington, Moscow cracked down on the separatist movement in Chechnya; leaders were assassinated, and the Russian army fully occupied Chechnya in the name of the "war on terror." After Putin came into power, the power of the security services continuously increased, a development directly connected to their role in the war in Chechnya. This resulted in an increase of the strength of "governmental" mafia in Russia.[62] Therefore, the Chechen mafia members who supported the national movement were weakened, whereas the MVD and FSB cadres involved with organized crime groups rose in prominence.

While the situation inside Chechnya normalized, in relative terms, as mentioned above Chechen guerrilla fighters spilled over to the neighboring republics. With the establishment of the Caucasus Emirate as an umbrella for North Caucasian armed groups, a new generation of North Caucasian insurgents emerged, whose identities were initially little known to the Russian security services. With nearly 300 attacks or instances of insurgency-related violence tied to the Caucasus Emirate in 2010 alone, it is apparent that the Chechen-inspired jihad is spreading through the North Caucasus even as it recedes within Chechnya itself. In descending order, the main sites of such violence in 2010–2011 were Dagestan, Ingushetia, Kabardino-Balkaria, Chechnya, and Karachai-Cherkessia.

These developments occurred in a context in which international Salafi-jihadists considered the North Caucasus region an important strategic priority. Starting in late 2007, they showed a renewed interest in the region after their earlier role in the area (represented by Arab fighters in Chechnya) had diminished around 2003, when the U.S. invasion of Iraq drew most of their attention. This interest takes various forms, most notably with remarkable new activity in cyberspace after a lengthy period without postings on jihadist websites. Since early 2008, jihadist web forums began to circulate numerous items on Chechnya and the North Caucasus. An integral part of this Internet campaign has been an emphasis on translating jihadist materials into Russian—a crucial element, since many local North Caucasian jihadists cannot read Arabic.[63]

Another indication of the aims to link the Caucasian armed groups to the global jihadi movement was seen in an exchange of letters between Abu Muhammad al-Maqdisi and Anzor Astemirov (aka Amir Sayfullah), leader of Yarmuk Jama'at in Kabardino-Balkaria and an ideologue of the Caucasus Emirate, who was killed by security forces in March 2010. The letters concerned Astemirov's translation of al-Maqdisi's books into Russian. Astemirov also sent al-Maqdisi the Caucasus Emirate's ruling against the London-based prime minister of the nationalist Chechen Republic of Ichkeria (ChRI), Ahmed Zakayev, declaring him an apostate. The ruling was approved by al-Maqdisi. Astemirov also asked al-Maqdisi about a Shari'a ruling on participating in the Olympics. The 2014 Winter Olympics are scheduled to be held in Sochi, a city in present-day Krasnodar Krai, previously home to Muslim Circassians who were driven out from the region with enormous casualties inflicted by Russian imperial troops in the nineteenth century. Al-Maqdisi ruled that participation was prohibited. Astemirov's request for direct advice from jihadist ideologues such as al-Maqdisi demonstrates increasing attempts to tie the Caucasian armed groups, which are still driven by local grievances, to the global jihad.[64]

The Failed Nexus

As mentioned earlier, the relationship between insurgency and organized crime groups was never clear. The Chechen insurgency did benefit from former members of the Chechen mafia, but in that case, the insurgents had already left the crime groups. Also, this was a situation in which Chechen guerrilla fighters were seeking funding. However, speculations were raised whether the North Caucasus insurgency would turn into a "black hole" or be "Afghanized" in terms of the crime-insurgency nexus. Due to several factors that clarify the relationship between insurgency and organized crime, however, such a nexus did not materialize.

Russia's New Regional Policy in the North Caucasus

While North Caucasian organized crime was infiltrated and exploited by the Russian secret agencies to demonize the separatist movements in the region (Chechnya in particular), the post-9/11 regional policy of Putin produced a new alternative to control the region.

Putin moved to effectively abolish federalism in Russia, as local governors, including the presidents of autonomous republics such as those in the North Caucasus, became appointed figures instead of elected. What followed from this was the removal of local leaders with local backing in the republics of the North Caucasus, and the appointment in their place of nominally native officials with a history in the Federal Security Services."[65]

As discussed above, this development took place in all the republics of the North Caucasus. While augmenting Moscow's control over these republics, it also inflamed frustration among locals, increasing the popularity of the Islamist insurgency.[66] About 1,800 individuals were killed in the years 2010 and 2011 as a result of the violence in the region, and more than one thousand were injured during same period.[67]

With this policy, the growing power of the security structures rendered the functionality of the relationship with organized crime groups useless. For instance, the last of the Lozanskaya group's founders, Atlangeriyev (a personal friend of Ahmad Kadyrov's), was allegedly killed by Ramzan Kadyrov because he refused to pledge allegiance to him.[68] Moreover, reports suggest that a crime group in Chechnya had helped in killing famous Chechen warlord Basayev, which indicates the divergence between insurgency and organized crime groups.[69]

Self-Criminalization

The resistance in Chechnya—and now in the North Caucasus as a whole—has shown an inclination toward so-called self-criminalization, especially from the beginning of the millennium,[70] thus some reports suggest that arms seizures were more common than drug trafficking. This can be explained by the need for weapons. Self-criminalization implies that rather than allying with crime groups, insurgent and terrorist groups get involved in activities similar to those of organized criminal groups. In July 2004, for example, Basayev seized a weapons depot in Ingushetia, distributing the weapons to Chechen insurgents. Furthermore, Caucasus Emirate attacks gradually came to target law enforcement officials in the various republics of the region, including those tasked with countering organized crime. However, it should be noted that such bodies in the North Caucasus are intelligence entities that are designated to fight against the insurgency as well. To some extent, such naming reflects the Russian government's attempts to conflate insurgency and organized crime, and thus the stereotyping of Chechens in general.

Importantly, the insurgency benefited from the corruption of the Russian forces, and did not need the meddling of organized crime groups. This shows the reflection of corruption in the Russian army and how it fed the wars in Chechnya:

> In many ways, the war has degenerated into a large criminal operation with numerous players with varying interests; paradoxically, the cooperation between nominal enemies in this conflict has become a *sine qua non* for the continuation of conflict, since it is primarily from the Russian forces that Chechen insurgents acquire their weapons, food, and other commodities. By 1997, twenty Russian generals had been arrested on various corruption charges, while impunity remained widespread.[71]

For instance, Russian authorities recently implemented new thinking to fight against insurgency apart from the military solution that has been used in the last decade in the region. A project aims to attract $22 billion from investors for building ski slopes and sandy beaches in Dagestan and Kabardino-Balkaria. The authorities believe that project could secure 300,000 jobs for locals; however, some observers believe that corruption could affect the project as "corruption comes from Moscow, and there is certain mutual understanding between corrupt officials in Moscow and their brothers in the Caucasus."[72]

A New Form of Insurgency

While the taip was a basic social unit that formed the armed groups and organized crime groups in the North Caucasus, there was a high potential for overlap between both groups' members. But since the establishment of the Caucasus Emirate, a new network has been produced that fits more of a pan-Caucasian format. All groups under the umbrella of the Caucasus Emirate are ethnic-based with an Islamic banner, but this banner is unifying them in a way that distributes the pressure and security campaigns against them.

Moreover, these groups are showing an inclination toward jihadist ideology, and in return, jihadists around the globe have shown an interest in the region and in creating an alliance with the Caucasus Emirate. At the same time, the policies imposed by the international community to cut the funding of jihadist groups led the insurgency groups to seek funds locally. Whether they resort to seeking assistance from organized crime groups in the North Caucasus is a matter of how strong the crime groups are. Hence it is expected that the Caucasus Emirate will keep relying on local sources (including the corruption of Russian authorities and self-criminalization).

Conclusion

The topic of organized crime in the North Caucasus is complicated by the long history of conflict in the region, which involves stereotyping, propaganda, and manipulation from the parties in the conflict. The presence of the Chechen mafia as an influential force and the fact that some of its members are involved in the Chechen separatist movement enhances the assumption of a crime-led insurgency in Chechnya—but the dynamics of organized crime in the region suggest that its linkage with security services is stronger than its links to the insurgency.

While both crime groups and the insurgency reflect the social structure in Chechnya, the state of crisis in Moscow also has been feeding their influence. For instance, the corruption in the Russian army forces fed the conflict in Chechnya. However, the new Russian regional policy in the North Caucasus—accompanied by the creation of a transregional insurgent movement with ideological ties to Salafi-jihadists around the globe—suggests that overlapping between the insurgency and organized crime groups is unlikely.

However, with the insurgency expanding geographically in the North Caucasus, it is expected that "self-criminalization" attacks (seizing weapons, kidnaping officials, etc.) will continue. This also means a larger geographical space for insurgency in the future.

As long as grievances among North Caucasian residents persist, the insurgent movement will continue to grow in the region. This was seen in the expansion of insurgency in Chechnya to the neighboring republics of the North Caucasus in the form of the Caucasus Emirate, which has proven able to develop different ways to secure resources that provide continuity to their struggle. On the other hand, North Caucasian organized crime groups have been more associated with developments in Moscow, which explains the decline of its affiliation with the insurgency. The policies of Moscow and the local governments in the North Caucasus, however, are feeding the insurgency, which indicates the likelihood of continued violence in the region.

Chapter 6

Georgia's Conflicts: Abkhazia and South Ossetia

Niklas Nilsson

During the years following independence from the USSR in 1991, Georgia developed into a weak state, which saw a high degree of collusion between organized crime and state institutions. Considerable networks were established, consisting of criminal groups and paramilitaries in Georgia and the secessionist regions, with external links to actors in the North and South Caucasus. State actors such as police and customs authorities were to a large extent involved in smuggling and other illegal activities. These networks were protected by high officials in the Georgian government and the de facto authorities of the secessionist regions. Hence, a situation evolved where criminal elements were to a large extent integrated with the Georgian political system and where criminal activities brought significant revenues for political actors on the Georgian side, while they were a vital part of the economies of the secessionist regions.

Organized crime thereby contributed to creating economic incentives against negotiated solutions to the conflicts and cemented the positions of the conflicting sides. As Charles King has argued, the economic benefits of maintaining the conflicts ensured that throughout the 1990s, neither side had any strong incentive for reaching or implementing peace agreements.

After what came to be known as the Rose Revolution in 2003, the Georgian government has employed a wide range of measures to rebuild the Georgian state and integrate with the Western security community, which have included reforms to legalize the economy and come to terms with the influence of organized crime, both on the unresolved conflicts and on the Georgian state. These efforts have contributed to significantly reducing the involvement in organized crime on the part of actors in the Georgian state, and thus weakened a vital link in the criminal networks. While the reforms reduced the incentives on the Georgian side to retain the status quo in the conflicts, they also provided Georgia with the economic and political means to actively seek a change in realities on the ground and reintegrate the two regions into the Georgian state. In combination with increasing Russian support for the two regions, in large part a reaction to Georgia's decidedly pro-Western foreign policy orientation, Georgia's conflicts with the two secessionist regions from 2004 increasingly developed into a bilateral confrontation between Georgia and Russia, eventually culminating in the war of August 2008.

The analysis of the impact of organized crime on Georgia's conflicts in this chapter focuses on developments in the 1990s and early 2000s. It is during this period that the state penetration of organized crime in the Georgian case was at its highest, and had a distinguishable effect on the conflict dynamics around Abkhazia and South Ossetia. Developments after 2004 replaced the incentives on the Georgian side to retain the "frozen" character of the conflicts for the personal gain of key political actors, with a new logic aimed at tilting the balance as far as possible in favor of a solution within the Georgian state.

Independence and Conflict

On October 28, 1990, Soviet-era dissident Zviad Gamsakhurdia's party—the Round Table for National Liberation—won the parliamentary elections and Gamsakhurdia became speaker of parliament. The new government adopted several nationalizing policies, among those language laws intended to make Georgian the only state language, and minorities were frequently referred to as "guests" on Georgian territory. These policies caused protests among most minority groups, and were met with counterreactions, especially among Ossetians in the South Ossetian Autonomous Oblast and Abkhazians in the Abkhaz ASSR.

In March 1991, a referendum was held throughout the USSR on the preservation of the Union. Georgia prohibited its population from taking part in
the referendum, which was nevertheless held in Abkhazia and South Ossetia,
resulting in a vast majority voting in favor of remaining within the USSR.
Georgia instead declared independence in April 1991 and had previous to
this declared itself "a unitary state with no internal boundaries," in effect abolishing the three autonomies of Abkhazia, South Ossetia, and Ajara.[1] Gamsakhurdia was elected president shortly thereafter. Tensions in South Ossetia
escalated and violent confrontation on a large scale erupted during 1991, to
the point that the regional capital, Tskhinvali, was regularly shelled and surrounded by Georgian paramilitary troops. However, development into full-
scale war was interrupted by the outbreak of a brief civil war in Tbilisi in
December.

On January 6, 1992, Gamsakhurdia was ousted by paramilitary forces that
had grown influential during his tenure, and fled Georgia. Eduard Shevardnadze, former foreign minister of the USSR,[2] was invited by the paramilitary forces that had ousted Gamsakhurdia to assume leadership. However,
Shevardnadze failed to immediately take control of the paramilitary forces
and hostilities in South Ossetia resumed, with overt Russian support for the
South Ossetian side. Shevardnadze and Russian president Boris Yeltsin then
signed a cease-fire agreement on South Ossetia, which came into effect in
June 1992. Mounting tension since 1989, meanwhile, caused the situation in
Abkhazia to escalate into full-scale war during the summer of 1992, after the
Abkhaz leadership declared Abkhazia independent. Georgian paramilitaries entered Abkhazia and occupied its capital, Sukhumi, forcing the Abkhaz
leadership to retreat. However, they soon conducted a counter-offensive,
heavily armed with Russian military equipment and reinforced by volunteers
from the North Caucasus. Russian involvement in the conflict on the Abkhaz
side increased throughout the war, and when a cease-fire came into effect in
October 1993, the Abkhaz leadership was in control over almost the entire
territory of the former Abkhaz ASSR.

Conflict and Organized Crime in Georgia

During the political chaos following Georgia's independence from the USSR,
the civil war in Tbilisi in 1991, and the civil wars in Abkhazia and South Ossetia, the Georgian economy deteriorated rapidly, according to World Bank

estimates, with an average GDP decline in 1990–1995 of 29.6 percent per year.[3] A war economy developed, where state actors became intertwined with warlords and organized criminal groups, creating a situation where the state in practice stood powerless to actors gaining considerable revenue from a lawless climate and protracted conflict.[4] Endemic corruption and political instability, combined with a lack of government control over the state's territory, brought a high degree of collusion between organized crime and state institutions, in turn limiting both the state's ability and its interest in effectively combating smuggling, drug trade, and other organized crime.[5] This was a forthcoming phenomenon during Shevardnadze's presidential period, from 1992 to 2003.[6]

In an overview of organized criminal activity in Georgia in the 1990s, Glonti distinguishes between Political Crime Societies, largely organized as political interest groups aiming to control economically lucrative aspects of the state, and Ethnic Crime Societies, aiming to assert control over a certain territory.[7] Georgia had, during Soviet times, established a comparatively high representation in the *vory-v-zakone* (thieves in law, *kanonieri kurdebi* in Georgian) community in the USSR, which is often stated to have had a special institutionalized position in Georgian society, as compared to other former USSR republics.[8] In 1990, a third of the thieves in law operating in the USSR were of Georgian ethnicity, however, most resided outside Georgia.[9] One of Georgia's most notorious thieves, Jaba Ioseliani, had in 1982 been a key proponent of a change of strategy for the Georgian thieves to decisively infiltrate politics and business. The thieves thrived during the emergence of private businesses under Perestroika, as they successfully infiltrated and exercised control over most aspects of political and social life in the late 1980s and early 1990s, and essentially replaced many functions of the state in the early 1990s.[10] Thus, the process of organized crime infiltration into the state had begun long before Georgia's independence from the USSR. The strategy of criminal groups to establish connections to politics and business placed them in a favorable position to practically "capture" the state during its collapse in the early 1990s.

The brief civil war in Tbilisi, December 1991–January 1992, instilled a climate of complete lawlessness in the Georgian capital. The dissemination of small arms during the conflict and the complete absence of any meaningful law enforcement due to the collapse of the state made Tbilisi a haven for criminal activity, where robberies, kidnappings, and looting for a period became features of everyday life. This climate initially caused an out-migration of the resident thieves to Russia and Europe, while they maintained their contacts with emerging criminal groups in Georgia. New criminal groupings were formed and expanded, practically forming armed militias.[11] In parallel, paramilitary groupings, corresponding to Glonti's political crime societies, had prior to Gamsakhurdia's ousting been formed to safeguard the interests of various elite groupings. As usually the case among "private armies" formed during the breakup of the USSR, the absence of a functioning state provided for such paramilitary groupings forming around narrow political or economic interests, attracting members from the criminal world, and relying on their own capabilities to exploit the shadow economy. They thus largely supported themselves through various forms of criminal activities, including looting and extortion from locals during the conflicts.[12]

Primary among these were the National Guard, headed by Tengiz Kitovani and formed by armed volunteers, and the Mkhedrioni, led by the aforementioned Jaba Ioseliani, which consisted of various criminal groupings. The paramilitary and semicriminal nature of these organizations, along with the lack of government capability to build and finance proper military forces, had an impact on the course of war in both Abkhazia and South Ossetia. Baev makes the case that both wars were to a significant extent caused by "the struggle between competing elite groupings for control over lucrative and profitable resources," that the destruction of these resources during the course of war was instrumental in bringing an end to the conflicts, and that the protracted status quo can be attributed to an "inability of the central authorities in building up the necessary military organization."[13] Points of escalation in the South Ossetian war were largely linked to the power struggle in Tbilisi; however, the impoverished region did not provide a sufficient resource base to support the paramilitary forces, which were therefore not motivated to carry out the operations ordered by Gamsakhurdia.[14] This would suggest that the greed-driven aspects of the conflict played a part in ending immediate hostilities—key actors on the Georgian side simply lost interest in reasserting control over South Ossetia due to lack of lootable resources.

Gamsakhurdia quickly fell out with the paramilitary leaders. The Mkhedrioni were outlawed and Ioselinani imprisoned in February 1991. After Gamsakhurdia's compliance to integrate the National Guard with the Soviet Interior Ministry after the August coup in Moscow, Kitovani broke with Gamsakhurdia and withdrew his troops from Tbilisi. A jailbreak in December freed Ioseliani and many of the Mkhedrioni. Kitovani and Ioseliani, along with former prime minister Tengiz Sigua, whom Gamsakhurdia had fired in August 1991, then ousted Gamsakhurdia during a brief civil war in Tbilisi in the end of 1991, and formed a Military Council governing Georgia until Shevardnadze's arrival as president in 1992. They were then included in the State Council under Shevardnadze, who initially had to rely on the paramilitary forces as the state's sole source of military power. Kitovani was appointed minister of defense and Ioseliani's Mkhedrioni engaged in the brutal suppression in Western Georgia of Gamsakhurdia's supporters, the Zviadists, well into 1993 when the latter were effectively quelled with the help of a Russian intervention following Georgia's defeat in the war in Abkhazia.[15]

While it is unclear whether Shevardnadze ordered the National Guard's invasion of Abkhazia in July 1992, or whether Kitovani acted on his own initiative, Baev argues that the main driving factor behind it was the conflicting desires by the central authorities and local clans in power to gain control over Abkhazia's profitable agriculture and tourism businesses. However, these resources were largely destroyed during the course of war, thus weakening the Georgian paramilitaries while the Abkhaz side sustained victory through attracting external support from Russia.[16] Looting and robberies of the civilian Abkhaz, Armenian, and Georgian populations was a prominent feature of the warfare conducted by Georgian and Abkhaz militias.[17] While the paramilitary leaders had initially expected to control Shevardnadze, he was eventually able to consolidate his control over the state and its security and armed forces. The National Guard was integrated into the Georgian armed forces and Kitovani dismissed as minister of defense in 1993, while Ioseliani was imprisoned and the Mkhedrioni disbanded in 1995 after an attempt on Shevardnadze's life.[18] Many Mkhedrioni members later allegedly joined the Forest Brothers, a Georgian militia operating in Mingrelia and southern Abkhazia.[19]

Apart from the breakaway regions of Abkhazia and South Ossetia, the government exercised limited control over several additional parts of the country. Relying on his private militia, local strongman Aslan Abashidze had established de facto sovereignty over the southwestern region of Ajara, economically relying on smuggling and illegal trade. The Pankisi Gorge on Georgia's border with Chechnya had long been sheltering Chechen refugees, but it was during the period of 1999–2002 also a haven for Chechen rebels and transnational criminal networks.[20] The latter in practice reportedly "rented" the gorge through bribing high officials in the Georgian government and used it as a transit zone for the drug trade.[21] Moreover, the government lacked administrative control over several other regions, of which Svaneti in the Northwest and Javakheti in the Southwest of Georgia were the most obvious examples.[22]

Even though Georgia over time stabilized during Shevardnadze's presidency, the infiltration of organized crime into state structures became a lasting problem, reflected in extremely widespread corruption and the involvement in criminal activities among high officials, as well as among the military and police forces.[23] Much as in other former Soviet republics, privatization of public property through "voucherization" from 1995 onward provided opportunities for criminals to acquire state property at low prices.[24] To protect their business interests and participate in the law-making process, powerful criminals were able to enter parliament through financing electoral campaigns in exchange for inclusion in party lists.[25] The shadow economy was in 2003 estimated to comprise between 35 and 70 percent of Georgia's total economy.[26]

The perhaps most obvious example of the connections between organized crime and state institutions were the activities of the Ministry of Interior (MOI) during this period. Through a developed system of protection rackets and bribes, the MOI police controlled large parts of the trade in tobacco and gasoline and the retail trade, while the various law enforcement units were deeply intertwined with criminal groups.[27] Officials within the police also had connections to counterparts in the breakaway regions, benefiting from the control of theft and transport of cars from Tbilisi for sale in Abkhazia and South Ossetia, among other activities. A similar scheme was carried out in the Pankisi Gorge, where police officers would exchange stolen cars for narcotics, later to be sold in Tbilisi.[28] Tobacco and gasoline were among the most rewarding contraband products, and practically all imports of these products were under the MOI's control. High officials within the MOI were also evidently involved in the drug trade.[29] Corruption was highly organized, displaying a pyramid-like structure where individual police officers were obliged to pay a part of the collected bribes to their superiors, who then transferred money upward in the system, to the head of the unit, head of department, and finally officials in the MOI and the interior minister himself.[30]

During 2001, a series of events, including tension in the Pankisi Gorge, operations by Georgian and Chechen paramilitaries in the Kodori Gorge in Abkhazia, and the assassination of a popular journalist—all with suspected involvement of the MOI and the security services—and a raid by the security services against the Rustavi-2 private television channel, caused substantial public protests and demands for the resignation of the officials viewed as responsible. This in turn forced Shevardnadze to dissolve the government and appoint new ministers and officials on several posts, especially within the MOI.[31]

Transnational Trafficking in Drugs, Arms, and Radiological Materials

In the early 1990s, Georgia and other states in the Caucasus became seriously affected by transnational drug trafficking, since their limited territorial control and extremely weak state authorities made the region a profitable transit area for drugs bound for Europe. The Caucasus is located where two of the main smuggling routes for heroin from Afghanistan to Europe intersect, which has brought a sustained presence of transnational networks involved in narcotics trafficking in the region. Drugs enter Georgia through its southern borders with Turkey, Armenia, and Azerbaijan, which in the mid-2000s became more significant drug routes than the conflict zones.[32] Another important inroad for the heroin trafficked through Georgia is through Dagestan bordering Georgia in the north. The Chechnya-connected Pankisi Gorge also has long played a key role as an inroad for heroin. The Black Sea ports of Poti and Batumi in Georgia, or Sukhumi and Gudauta in Abkhazia, have served as transshipment points for drugs bound for Eastern Europe. Reforms of the Ministry of Interior and Security Services undertaken in 2001, reestablishment of control over Pankisi in 2002, and reforms undertaken after the Rose Revolution in 2003, have improved government capabilities to curb the drug trade, but the problem remains.

The smuggling and trade in small arms and heavy weaponry has been yet another feature of organized crime in Georgia. Arms have been transited to Europe and the Middle East through the Caucasus and smaller amounts of sophisticated weaponry have been smuggled through the South Caucasus to Chechnya.[33] Small arms are in great supply in the entire Caucasus, as an effect of the inflow of arms during the civil wars in the early 1990s, but chiefly due to the takeover of Soviet weaponry during the breakdown of the USSR.[34] The largest quantities of arms in transit in the South Caucasus in the mid-2000s originated from the Russian military bases in Georgia and Armenia, and were often obtained through purchase from the Russian military.[35]

Smuggling of radioactive materials originating in Russian nuclear facilities[36] has also taken place across Georgia's insecure borders. Thirteen criminal cases have been brought against smugglers of these materials in Georgia since 2002; however, such smuggling is normally perpetrated by loose networks and rarely displays involvement of established crime groups.[37]

Smuggling Networks

In the conflict economy developing in Georgia and the secessionist regions, the key source of income from smuggling and other illicit activities seems to have been control over the extensive smuggling networks that developed in the early 1990s, rather than any specific resource. While narcotics, weapons, and human beings have certainly been transited along these routes, trade in consumer goods such as petroleum, timber, wheat flour, cigarettes, and even hazelnuts have constituted the key sources of income for criminal networks in Georgia, Abkhazia, and South Ossetia, as well as regular inhabitants of these territories. It is also important to note that these networks started as wartime informal trade, which in the case of Abkhazia became illegalized under an economic blockade introduced by Georgia and Russia in 1994, and expanded to a full Commonwealth of Independent States (CIS) embargo in 1996—but which Russia gradually abandoned. In South Ossetia, lack of a clear demarcation line provided for an intensifying informal trade that was partly due to the extensive interests of Georgian state actors in maintaining it, unregulated until 2004.[38]

These networks were over time consolidated and came to involve locals, criminal groups, law enforcement bodies, and officials in both the Georgian government and de facto authorities of Abkhazia and South Ossetia. In Abkhazia, relatives of Abakhazian leader Vladislav Ardzinba were positioned to control all lucrative branches of the Abkhaz economy, including various forms of smuggling. Pasha Ardzinba was in control of timber export from Sukhumi's ports, while Zurab and Aka Ardzinba were engaged in petroleum smuggling, imported from Russia and transferred to Georgia. Levan Ardzinba controlled a cigarette factory and exports of cigarettes without excise marks to Georgia and Russia, and allegedly had extensive contacts with actors on the Georgian side, ranging from the Forest Brothers to businesspeople and government officials.[39] President Shevardnadze's nephew Nugzar Shevardnadze was a key interlocutor in petroleum smuggling from both Abkhazia and South Ossetia on the Georgian side, while officials in the Georgian Ministries of Interior and Transport, as well as the governor of Shida Kartli, were deeply involved in smuggling from South Ossetia.[40] Lokha Chibirov, son of former South Ossetian de facto president Lyudvig Chibirov, was in turn a key sponsor of smuggling on the South Ossetian side.[41] Thus, as the smuggling networks through Georgia's conflict regions consolidated, they came to provide a highly fertile ground for collusion and shared interests between criminal groups and representatives of the Georgian state, as well as the de facto authorities in Abkhazia and South Ossetia.

It should be noted that smuggling through the breakaway regions has frequently been politicized. The Georgian government, in its efforts to attract international participation in the resolution of these conflicts, is naturally interested in underlining the international security problems attached to two entities existing outside Georgian or international jurisdiction, and especially the possibility of such territories functioning as operational bases for organized crime and important transit points for trafficking in drugs, weapons, and nuclear materials. Since the presence and influence of organized crime in these regions poses important questions about the legitimacy of their respective leaderships and claims to independent statehood, the de facto governments of South Ossetia and Abkhazia have been as interested in downplaying their links to criminal activities as the Georgian leadership has been in publicizing them. However, the problem of smuggling in Georgia has by no means been confined to the two secessionist regions. For example, only 20 percent of the fuel traded illegally in Georgia before 2003 was estimated to have been transited through Abkhazia or South Ossetia, as even larger quantities entered Georgia through Azerbaijan or the Poti port. Also, the inflow of heroin from South Ossetia before 2004 comprised about half the quantities entering Georgia through Dagestan and Azerbaijan.[42]

Government and Politics in Abkhazia

After breaking away from Georgia, the Abkhazian leadership has officially underlined its ambition to become a recognized and independent state, while it has in practice remained highly dependent on Russian political and economic support. Vladislav Ardzinba was elected chairman of the Supreme Soviet of the Abkhaz ASSR in 1990 and was after the war elected Abkhazia's first president in 1994. Ardzinba staffed Abkhazian authorities with his own family members, allowing their access to and domination over the region's resources. His rule lasted until February 2005. After presidential elections in October 2004, a protracted power struggle took place between Raul Khajimba and Sergei Bagapsh, and the latter assumed the presidency in a power-sharing deal with his rival. Both Ardzinba and Moscow openly favored Khajimba, while Bagapsh enjoyed support from the two main opposition movements in Abkhazia (Amtsakhara and United Abkhazia) and from a large part of the ethnic Georgian population in the Gali district.[43] The obvious involvement of Moscow in the election process caused public resentment and provided Bagapsh with additional support. Yet Khajimba's position allowed him and his subordinates to maintain control over most of Abkhazia's security and defense bodies, ensuring that these remained under the control of actors loyal to Moscow. Bagapsh stated the ambition to maintain a close relationship with Russia, but also took a firmer stance on Abkhazian independence. Thus, while the change of president in practice meant little in terms of Abkhazia's foreign policy orientation, the events surrounding the elections nevertheless to some degree displayed a previously unanticipated capability of Abkhazia to oppose Russian involvement in its politics. Abkhazia has to a certain extent developed a participatory political system within the Abkhaz ethnic community, granting ethnic Abkhaz society influence over the political process. However, the system still largely excludes the ethnic Georgian population and to some extent the ethnic Armenian population. Bagapsh died in May 2011 and was succeeded by Alexander Ankvab, who won the presidential election in August 2011 against Moscow's preferred candidate Sergei Shamba—though Moscow's interference in the election was much less visible than in 2004.

Economy and Smuggling in Abkhazia

The Abkhazian economy is in large part based on agriculture, with a substantial cultivation of citrus, tomatoes, and hazelnuts. However, in recent years, the tourism industry has gained importance, as Abkhazia is increasingly attracting Russian investment and tourists.[44] Abkhazia's budget in 2010 reached US$128.5 million, of which Russian subsidies constituted 60 percent in 2009.[45] As an effect of trade restrictions introduced by the CIS in 1996, Abkhazia was long prevented from entertaining formal economic relations with the outside world. Abkhazia was not allowed to import or export commercial goods, and land, sea, and air communications were closed to Russia as well as Georgia. However, some trade with Turkey existed through the Sukhumi port. Russia started allowing for increased movement across its southern border in 2002, and in 2006 foreign citizens were allowed entrance to Abkhazia through Russia, while the Sukhumi port has gained importance for Abkahzia's maritime trade across the Black Sea.[46] Combined with the provision of Russian citizenship and pensions for a large part of Abkhazia's population, this was widely viewed in Georgia as steps toward Russian annexation of the region.

Abkhazia contains two particularly unstable areas. The first is the Kodori Gorge, controlled by a local warlord until summer 2006, when Georgian authorities established control over it, which they subsequently lost in the 2008 war. The second is the Gali region, which before the war was mainly populated by Georgian Mingrelians. A limited number of Mingrelians returned to their homes following the conflict. Gali is a tense and unsafe region, and a large part of the criminality and violence there is directly or indirectly linked to local organized crime.[47] After the end of the war in 1994, Georgian and Abkhaz criminal groups established a functioning cooperation and well-defined areas of interest, even though violent skirmishes have occurred.[48] Thus, similar to other areas plagued by nominally ethnic conflicts, such as the Balkans in general and Kosovo in particular, organized crime groups based around ethnic identities had no problem to cooperate with networks from ethnic groups they were nominally in conflict with.

In the Gali region, smuggling and other organized criminal activity has been controlled by Abkhaz groups with connections to Abkhaz authorities, Georgian criminals, and former members of Georgian paramilitaries previously supported by the Georgian government, that is, the White Legion and Forest Brothers. Especially for the Forest Brothers, headed by David Shengelia and whose activities were allegedly supported and protected by Tamaz Nadareishvili, former leader of the Abkhaz government in exile, smuggling across the cease-fire line with Georgia was long a means for financing guerrilla activities in Abkhazia and gradually turned into their primary occupation.[49] After the Rose Revolution, these groups lost their protectors in the Georgian central government and have since officially been disbanded. The reestablishment of control over Kodori during summer 2006 scattered the local paramilitary group Monadire (Hunter). These groups have thus formally ceased to exist, even though many of their members are likely to have persisted in their criminal activities.[50] The Georgian and Abkhaz groups active in Gali cooperated in illicit trafficking and regularly engaged in extortion and theft from the local population. Control over production of and cross-border trade in hazelnuts has been a lucrative source of income.[51]

Apart from Gali and the Kodori Gorge, in 2004 different Abkhaz criminal groups operated in clearly defined areas, dividing the region among four main groups; the Western Abkhazia group, the Gagra group, the Gudauta group, and the Chechen-Abkhazian group controlling Eastern Abkhazia. These controlled trade in oil, tobacco, and commercial goods, and were also involved in drug production and trade.[52] It was allegedly impossible to distinguish between Abkhazia's official police and security structures, criminals, and politically motivated groups, as they were all to a significant degree involved in, and benefited from, criminal activities.[53] Another important actor in illicit trade through Abkhazia were the Russian peacekeeping forces deployed through the CIS Peace Keeping Force (CISPKF). The CISPKF controlled all official bridges and were therefore in control of all heavy traffic across the borders, a fact frequently utilized for gaining revenue. Abkhaz and Georgian smugglers were accustomed to paying bribes at the Russian border controls, in practice making the CISPKF a broker between smuggling networks on the two sides, as well as an important component of these. Illegal goods have allegedly also been transported in Russian military vehicles and aircraft, which could not be searched by Georgian border guards.[54]

Before 2008, the main smuggling routes to and from Abkhazia ran across the Psou River to Russia, across the Inguri River to Georgia, and at sea through the ports in Sukhumi and Gudauta. During harvest season, thousands of Abkhaz travel across the Russian border to sell citrus and hazelnuts on Russian territory, trade in which constitutes their main source of income. Smuggling of weapons, cigarettes, gasoline, stolen cars, and narcotics has also taken place across this border, though it is difficult to estimate the volumes trafficked. A "waterproof" system existed for crossing the Psou River without passing Russian border controls.[55]

Smuggling also took place across Abkhazia's de facto border with Georgia, consisting of the cease-fire line in the war along the Inguri River. The main passage over the river was a bridge with Abkhaz, Russian, and Georgian border controls, which mainly allowed for petty smuggling, in the form of women living in the Gali district frequently crossing the cease-fire line to Georgia carrying bags of cigarettes.[56] Locals in the Gali district in large part made a living out of transporting hazelnuts across the border to sell them in markets on the Georgian side.

The river could nevertheless be crossed at numerous other locations. Large quantities of drugs, gasoline, and cigarettes were reportedly smuggled across the border, under the control of Georgian paramilitaries in Abkhazia, in cooperation with Georgian police and regional authorities on the Georgian side.[57] However, measures to reduce the Georgian side's involvement in smuggling has seemingly decreased this activity, making Abkhazian ports more likely as smuggling routes. While this may have had an effect on the livelihoods of petty smugglers, the effect on Abkhazia's economy is likely to be marginal, as especially Russian subsidies and tourism have emerged as key sources of income for Abkhazia.

Government and Politics in South Ossetia

If the Abkhaz government has pursued an agenda underlining the goal of Abkhazian independence from both Russia and Georgia, the same cannot be said for South Ossetia. The region is in practice completely dependent on Russian political, economical, and military support. Moscow has at all times been highly involved in South Ossetian politics, most blatantly through positioning Russian security services officers in the de facto government and security structures.

Lyudvig Chibirov was chairman of the South Ossetian Parliament from 1993 to 1996, and South Ossetia's first de facto president from 1996 to 2001. Chibirov's family and especially his son Alexei, deputy head of the republic's KGB, maintained a good position to exploit illegal trade and smuggling. Chibirov and his family in large part built its power on a tight relationship with the Tedeyev clan, one of South Ossetia's most powerful families. However, before the presidential elections in 2001, the most influential Tedeyevs turned to supporting and financing the campaign of businessman and former member of the Soviet national wrestling team Eduard Kokoity. After Kokoity's victory, key members of the Tedeyev clan occupied prominent positions, among others head of the Security Council, and took over control of South Ossetia's customs service and traffic along the Transcaucasian Highway to Russia.[58] However, in 2003 Kokoity acted to strengthen his control over the de facto republic and its security structures. He also turned against the Tedeyev clan, and several members of the family were removed from their positions.[59] Kokoity since then acted to further consolidate his powerbase in South Ossetia, with extensive Russian support.[60] His presidential term ended in 2011 and elections were held in November. Kokoity's planned successor and Moscow's preferred candidate Anatoly Bibilov failed to secure a victory against former education minister Alla Dzhioyeva. The results were annulled by South Ossetia's Supreme Court, sparking a series of street protests by Dzhioveva's supporters, and Dzhioyeva was later hospitalized after a police raid on her headquarters. Repeat elections were held in March and April 2012, resulting in the victory of former South Ossetian KGB chief Leonid Tibilov, who managed to position himself as an alternative to the circle around Kokoity.

Economy and Smuggling in South Ossetia

Much of South Ossetia's agriculture was destroyed during the conflict, and has to date not been reconstructed. The region enjoys fewer links to the outside world than Abkhazia, and its economy has to a large extent been dependent on trade in contraband, which also makes it more vulnerable to border controls. South Ossetia's GDP was in 2004 estimated at US$15 million, of which a large part, according to Ossetian officials, was collected through customs at the border with Russia.[61] However, Georgian sources state that only about 10 percent of the income collected from customs was estimated to reach the region's budget, while the rest was direct income for members of the South Ossetian government and administration.[62] In 2010, South Ossetia's budget was stated at US$140 million, however, consisting of 98.7 percent Russian aid.[63] Massive embezzlement of the Russian contributions for humanitarian aid and postconflict reconstruction has remained a problem Russia has unsuccessfully sought to curb through key political appointments.[64] Before 2004, some Georgian observers claim, as much as 70–80 percent of South Ossetia's fiscal income may have come from illegal trade.[65] South Ossetia had been one of the primary inroads for illicit goods to Georgia, where the Transcaucasian Highway was a main transportation route and income source for South Ossetian authorities, smuggling networks, and ordinary residents, of both Ossetian and Georgian ethnicity. The main passageway for goods into South Ossetia is through the Roki Tunnel on the Russian border, outside the control of Georgian authorities. The Georgian side before the 2008 war repeatedly accused Russia of using this tunnel to provide South Ossetia with weapons.[66]

Large portions of the contraband were, until 2004, sold at the Ergneti market outside Tskhinvali, which annually transited an estimated 450,000 tons of contraband worth about US$130 million.[67] This market formed the main economic link between South Ossetia and Georgia, displaying a broad range of goods for sale to Georgian individuals and businesses, for further transport and sale in Tbilisi and other parts of Georgia. The goods above all comprised provisions in the form of wheat and wheat flour, dairy products, gasoline, and cigarettes. However, drugs and weapons were among the merchandise sold at the market.[68]

The market was divided into a Georgian and an Ossetian part, where the former was reportedly controlled by three Georgian members of parliament and the governor of Shida Kartli,[69] while the son of former South Ossetian leader Chibirov played a key part on the South Ossetian side.[70] Organized criminal groups maintained a strong presence at and around the market.

Georgian and Ossetian criminal groups engaged in trade with Ergneti as their main meeting point and were in turn linked to Chechen networks, above all in the gasoline trade. Trade via Ergneti to Georgia was long controlled by a criminal group under a leader nicknamed Robota, offering protection for transport of smuggled goods through the company Express Services LTD. The group was under the protection of the former deputy head of police in Shida Kartli, and allegedly had additional protection in the State Chancellery, which intervened to prevent investigations against Robota's group.[71] The involvement of the Russian peacekeeping forces of the Joint Peacekeeping Force (JPKF) played a role in the networks,[72] however, a less important one than that in Abkhazia. This is above all due to the fact that the South Ossetian de facto border with Georgia was until 2008 less defined and hence did not allow for as strict controls, and JPKF checkpoints could more easily be avoided by smugglers.[73] Moreover, it seems that police and customs authorities on both sides were engaged in sophisticated cooperation with the criminal networks to extract revenue through bribes and escorts of smuggled goods,[74] and several of the criminal groups controlling trade through Ergneti were considered to have enjoyed protection from officials both in the Georgian president's administration and the Ministry of Interior until 2003.[75]

The Ergneti market was long a black hole in the Georgian economy, since smuggling caused enormous fiscal losses in customs and taxes. In December 2003, the Georgian government launched an extensive antismuggling operation aimed at establishing control over the inflow of illegal goods from South Ossetia and by extension undermining the South Ossetian leadership. The Ergneti market was closed down in May 2004, and the Ministry of Interior started setting up roadblocks and transporting troops to the region to confiscate illegal goods. Tbilisi motivated the operation by stating that economic interests and revenue from smuggling were the primary obstacles to conflict resolution. The assessment was that limiting smuggling would cause a breakdown of the South Ossetian economy and deplete the de facto government's public support base. However, aside from being the primary income source for the South Ossetian leadership, smuggling revenue was also of vital importance to ordinary citizens in Georgia and South Ossetia, while the trade provided an avenue for people-to-people interaction in the conflict zone.[76] In spite of Georgian pledges to compensate economically for the losses incurred by the operation, the South Ossetian leadership successfully mobilized the Ossetian population against the perceived Georgian aggression, dramatically strengthening Kokoity's popularity. During July, a series of skirmishes erupted between Georgian and South Ossetian troops, which lasted until August 19, when the Georgian side pulled back.[77] The Georgian government has maintained that an important reason for the outbreak of violence was pressure placed by the closure of Ergneti on South Ossetian authorities and smuggling networks.[78] However, increased financial support from the Russian state as well as Ossetian businessmen in Russia proved sufficient to prevent the region from economic collapse.[79]

War Economy and Persisting Status Quo

The conflict economies that developed in Georgia, as well as South Ossetia and Abkhazia in 1991–2003 likely contributed to maintaining the status quo in the conflicts. The extensive and profitable networks that developed between criminal groups, illicit traders, and state structures on the Georgian, Abkhazian, and South Ossetian sides created considerable interests in reproducing the existing situation on the ground. In Georgia, the conflict economy had a considerable impact on the state-building process, as the composition and staffing of political and security institutions were often based on the loyalty of employees to sustaining the existing system and delivering profits to their superiors.[80] Moreover, the conflict economy contributed to the weakness of the Georgian state through producing severe limitations to taxation, and the violence accompanying the smuggling networks contributed to a lawless climate in the conflict regions. In sum, the failure of the Georgian state to make any credible efforts at resolving the conflicts is linked to both the general criminalization, weakness, and lack of legitimacy of the state during this period, and the existence of lucrative opportunities for state actors to benefit from the unresolved nature of the conflicts.

Illicit trade has also constituted an important source of income for the Abkhazian and South Ossetian economies. As a conflict economy, South Ossetia provides an example, to a higher degree than the Abkhazian one, of how income from illicit trade has become a factor "freezing" the conflict, as a very large part of the region's economy has consisted in revenues from illicit trade in all sorts of contraband. South Ossetia's isolation from the outside world and its dependence on access to Russian and Georgian markets caused a situation where the dividing lines between South Ossetian authorities and smuggling networks were extremely vague. Criminal groups have had direct links to the South Ossetian leadership and have thus likely been capable of influencing the conflict resolution processes. South Ossetian reactions to the closure of the Ergneti market are an illuminating example in this regard. Both the Georgian and South Ossetian sides appear to have viewed trade in contraband as a crucial factor in maintaining the status quo. For the Georgian government, impeding this trade was a key factor in weakening the South Ossetian leadership and preparing the ground for the region's reintegration with Georgia. However, to the South Ossetian leadership, this was a direct attack on the region's independence. Both sides seemingly viewed income from smuggling as a decisive factor in the conflict and the attempt to block the main smuggling route to Georgia came very close to causing a relapse into war in the region. While actors within the Abkhaz leadership during the period are believed to have entertained strong connections with organized crime as well, the economy to a larger extent relies on domestic production and tourism, aside from Russian subsidies, and has proven capable of sustaining other income than from transit rents alone. Georgian capabilities for damaging the Abkhaz economy through combating smuggling have thus been far more limited than was the case in South Ossetia.

Revolution and Reform after 2003

After the Rose Revolution in 2003, the new Georgian government undertook a program of fundamental reform of key state institutions in an effort to rebuild the state. Important aims of these reforms were to legalize the economy, constrain corruption, and limit the collusion of Georgia's state institutions and criminal activities. The energetic anticorruption campaign commencing in 2004 included introduction of legislation based on U.S. and Italian anti-organized crime methods allowing for plea bargaining and property confiscation, and legislation introduced in 2005 that made membership in organized criminal groups (especially those of the thieves in law) illegal.[81] Arrests of high officials and powerful criminals on corruption charges ensued, forcing them to repay money earned through corruption to the state. While criticism has been raised against the aggressive and violent implementation of these methods, as well as the frequently nontransparent allocation of confiscated funds, they arguably served to drastically reduce both high-level corruption and the connections between organized crime and the state.[82] Indeed, Georgia by 2009 had advanced to a score of 4.1 on Transparency International's

Corruption Perceptions Index, from 2.3 in 2005 and 1.8 in 2003, and presently ranks higher than several EU members.[83]

Two specific components of these reforms were especially relevant in reducing the state's involvement in smuggling through the conflict regions. These include reforms in the security structures, especially the police; and reform of the customs authorities. Georgia's police reform was carried out with extensive international financial support. It provided for the discharge of corrupt high officials within central and regional police authorities, thus removing several sources of protection for established criminal networks. Funding was also allocated to police authorities for developing capacity and efficiency in combating organized crime.[84] The Ministry of State Security was disbanded and its remains were merged with a rebuilt Ministry of Interior. A general reorganization of the police departments was carried out and several thousand police staff made redundant. The flagship initiative of this reform was the abolishment of the Transport and Traffic Police, one of the country's most corrupt and distrusted authorities. Overnight, 16,000 traffic police officers were dismissed and replaced by a newly formed Patrol Police Department employing 2,400 mostly younger police officers not previously implicated in corruption, with considerably higher salaries than their predecessors.[85] The Patrol Police is today among the most publicly trusted state authorities in Georgia.[86]

The customs authorities were another notoriously corrupt government agency and provided a serious challenge in the anticorruption campaign. By replacing 80 percent of the customs officials, raising their salaries, and providing a greatly simplified law on customs tariffs, customs services have improved greatly, featuring an increase in customs revenue from US$202 to US$908 million between 2003 and 2010.[87] Yet, one of the major challenges to reforming border security in Georgia has been to find a suitable balance between these and other aspects of state building. The improvement of border protection has clearly been subordinated to the modernization and reform of the armed forces and police, while it is also weighed against other state building priorities such as facilitating trade and maintaining interethnic stability.[88] An example of the promotion of trade as a priority over border security is the approval of the Transports Internationaux Routiers (TIR) carnet system for sealed transit traffic through the country. Since the system allows for transit of goods without controls at border crossings and ports, it may also be used for illicit trafficking, provided smugglers gain access to transportation under

TIR vouchers.[89] Georgian efforts to secure its borders have also had an impact on the state's relations with its Armenian and Azerbaijani minorities. Government relations with these minorities are fragile, and policies perceived as affecting them negatively are frequently understood as discrimination on an ethnic basis. Since these minorities are accustomed to engaging in trade across the borders with Armenia and Azerbaijan, tightened border controls, confiscation of goods, and operations to crack down on smuggling caused frustration and led to several local clashes during 2004 and 2005. The desire to avoid further instability likely caused Georgian authorities to refrain from more decisive efforts combating smuggling across its borders with Armenia and Azerbaijan, such as closing down the Red Bridge market. This argument also has relevance to the unresolved conflicts, as stricter enforcement of control over the Abkhazian sea border would escalate tensions, while the attempt to crack down on smuggling from South Ossetia escalated into a brief relapse into warfare in 2004.[90]

Significant U.S. support under the Georgia Border Security and Law Enforcement Program (GBSLE) has provided the Georgian Border Police with training and equipment. Yet, the Border Police, contrary to the reformed Patrol Police, has maintained a reputation for engaging in corruption, and thus continually posed an impediment to border security in Georgia. In Georgia and most other post-Soviet states, border security is a lucrative line of work due exactly to the opportunities for extracting bribes at border crossings. In January 2009, Georgia's ministry of interior undertook a reorganization of the Border Police, transferring several of its duties to the Patrol Police. Yet, according to cables from the U.S. embassy in Tbilisi, the reorganization was undertaken in a haphazard manner including layoffs of trained staff, and may partly have been politically motivated since the Border Police had retained a higher degree of independence from the government than other police branches and several of its higher posts were occupied by members of the political opposition.[91] While measures to reduce corruption and increase transparency in Georgia's border management are certainly needed, there is a risk that a transfer of border management duties to a branch of the police not trained for this purpose will induce an unnecessary loss of competence and capacity.

The success of these reforms in Georgia is often attributed to the decisive and occasionally ruthless approach by the new Georgian government, along with an extensive public mandate to come to terms with the problem of corrupt state institutions. This was combined with significant international political and economic support for the reforms, and their significance in Georgia's foreign policy as an integral part of the Georgian modernization project, ultimately aimed at providing Georgia a place in the European security community. A recent study commissioned by the World Bank lists the Saakashvili government's strong exercise of political will; rapid and comprehensive implementation of reforms; "frontal assault" on corruption; replacement of corrupt staff; efforts to limit the state bureaucracy; openness to unconventional solutions; internal coordination; ability to adapt general solutions to a local context; ability to replace bureaucracy with technological solutions; and communication of the reforms to the public as key factors in the Georgian government's success.[92] Yet, it should be noted that while the success in decriminalizing especially the police and reducing corruption through rapid and unorthodox reforms is generally recognized, it has also frequently been related to a critique of the Georgian authorities of prioritizing measures to strengthen the state over strict observation of the rule of law and democratization.[93] Moreover, reform of the state structures has not been all-encompassing. Corruption has not been eradicated, and lack of independence and integrity of the judicial system is frequently quoted as a remaining problem. Nontransparent privatization processes provide fertile grounds for corrupt practices, and connections between organized crime and politics are still a feature of Georgian society, even though such connections are today reportedly more common in the parliament than within government bodies.[94] The new government appointed by Prime Minister Bidzina Ivanishvili after the October 2012 parliamentary elections has highlighted the establishment of an independent judiciary as one of its main priorities.

Yet, following the reforms, Georgian observers state that the corruption still existing within the police seems much less organized and opportunities for Georgian police and customs authorities to take active part in smuggling networks have been circumscribed, although such activities persisted several years after the Rose Revolution.[95] For example, in March 2005, one year after the closure of the Ergneti market, the chief of police in Shida Kartli, all his deputies, and all Shida Kartli district chiefs of police were dismissed for alleged involvement in smuggling through the region.[96] The chief of police was, however, appointed chief of the military police and later deputy minister of defense.[97] During 2005, Georgian police carried out raids against border checkpoints at Sarpi on the Georgian-Turkish border and the Red Bridge Crossing between Georgia and Azerbaijan, arresting several customs officials on corruption charges.[98] These and other cases imply that problems connected to the involvement of the police and customs in smuggling remained problematic well into the mid-2000s.[99] Also, the reforms unintentionally added to the recruitment base for organized criminal groups, since they caused the dismissal of about 16,000 police officers with significant experience in smuggling and established contacts with the criminal world.[100] Many had already been connected to organized crime while on the government payroll.

Even though it is difficult to estimate the extent to which smuggling has decreased, the efforts to decrease the involvement of Georgian state actors in the smuggling networks has seemingly been successful. An observed tendency of smuggling to assume less organized forms[101] can be taken to indicate changes in the role of Georgian state actors, since this involvement has long been a precondition for the functioning of the extensive smuggling networks. Yet, as long as involvement in smuggling activities is profitable to state actors, there will be incentives for taking part in it. Some observers claim that criminal groups are displaying tendencies of establishing new connections with parts of the police forces, as well as with protectors in the state apparatus.[102]

State Decriminalization and the August 2008 War

As stated above, the collusion between the Georgian state, organized crime, and the breakaway regions was a distinct feature of the political and economic system that developed in Georgia during Shevardnadze's administration. Indeed, this endemically corrupt system led many observers to term Georgia a "failed state." While the interconnections between the shadow economy, the conflicts, and the Georgian state likely provided incentives on all sides to retain the status quo, it is hardly the only reason for the relative lack of violent confrontation during this period. One related, and at least as important factor was the extremely low capacity of the Georgian state to affect the situation on the ground. Notable changes in this situation took place after the Rose Revolution in 2003. First, the far-reaching reforms conducted under Saakashvili's government did serve to significantly reduce the state's involvement in activities possibly sustaining the conflicts. Previously important opportunities to gain revenue through involvement in criminal activities were significantly reduced and individuals implicated in such activities, in the Ministry of Interior and elsewhere, were removed from office.

Second, the increased capacity of the Georgian state through the reorganization of power ministries—not least the army, which received significant funding and training from the United States ahead of its deployment to Iraq—provided altogether new possibilities for the Georgian government to affect the balance on the ground in the conflict regions. Combined with a zealous ambition on Saakashvili's part to reintegrate Abkhazia and South Ossetia with Georgia, the new situation allowed the government to employ a wide array of assertive and accommodating measures against the two regions. The former included the attempt to reassert influence over South Ossetia under the pretext of an antismuggling operation in 2004 and the capture of the Kodori Gorge in Abkhazia in 2006, and the latter comprehensive peace proposals to the Abkhazian and South Ossetian leaderships and restoration projects close to the cease-fire lines to demonstrate to the inhabitants of these regions the benefits of returning to Georgian jurisdiction.

Third, when following the Rose Revolution it was becoming clear that Georgia would direct its foreign policy exclusively in a Western direction, including ambitions to gain membership in NATO, the character of the conflicts gradually transformed. From constituting secessionist conflicts within Georgia, albeit with heavy Russian involvement, their significance was reduced to points of leverage in an emerging bilateral conflict between Georgia and Russia. The Georgian side's understanding was that Russia's support for the regions was detrimental in preventing a resolution to the conflicts and increasingly resembled a Russian annexation of Georgian territory. At the same time, the Russian side viewed its influence over the regions as important assets in preventing Georgia's integration with Western security structures, hence serving Russia's national interests.

The years 2003–2008 consequently saw a rapid deterioration in Russian-Georgian relations, where the conflicts were constantly at the center of attention but where their significance obtained a much larger geopolitical dimension. In spring 2008, three developments made the situation especially acute. First, Kosovo's declaration of independence in February implied a diplomatic defeat for Russia, but also provided a "precedent" for its policies toward Abkhazia and South Ossetia. Second, Russia's lifting of the sanctions previously imposed on Abkhazia in March was viewed in Tbilisi as the start of an official Russian policy to annex the two regions, triggering a military buildup and increased deployment of Georgian troops along the cease-fire line with Abkhazia, while Russia reinforced its military units in both territories with heavy equipment, railway troops, and paratroopers. Third, while the NATO Bucharest summit in April did not provide Georgia and Ukraine with the Membership Action Plans they had expected, the alliance stated that the two states would become members at some point in the future. This was taken by Russia as an acute threat that needed to be addressed.

This is not the place to elaborate at length on the immediate causes of the war starting on August 7.[103] However, the Georgian decision to respond to shelling of Georgian villages from the South Ossetian side through a military incursion into the region and the subsequent Russian invasion of both South Ossetia and Abkhazia had little to do with the microdynamics in the conflict zones themselves. Rather, it was the consequence of Georgian concerns about a permanent Russian annexation of its territory, and Russian desires to prevent a neighboring country from joining NATO—the latter fact admitted publicly by Russian president Dmitry Medvedev in 2011.[104]

The war also fundamentally altered realities on the ground in both conflict zones. Russia recognizes their status as independent states, as do Venezuela, Nicaragua, Nauru, Vanuatu, and Tuvalu, while the rest of the international community considers them Georgian territory. Russia has consolidated its military presence in the regions as well as its control over their de facto governments. The cease-fire remains unstable, with occasional incidents along the cease-fire lines. In the foreseeable future, it is difficult to envision any solution to these conflicts involving their reintegration with the Georgian state.

To conclude, while the current situation makes assessment of organized criminal activities in and around the regions themselves more difficult, it also underlines the decreasing importance of such activities for conflict dynamics. The impact of organized crime and state criminalization on the dynamics of Georgia's conflicts were forthcoming during Shevardnadze's time in power, but reduced considerably as the Georgian state was reformed and strengthened. The renewed capacity of the Georgian state, as well as the increasingly bilateral and geopolitical nature of the conflict, gave way to a new dynamic, eventually culminating in the 2008 war.

Still, for the de facto leaderships of Abkhazia and South Ossetia, involvement in and benefits from organized criminal activity remains a question of credibility. While affected by organized crime, Abkhazia is not dependent on income from these activities, as it can in large part rely on domestic agricultural production and tourism for its economical survival. Abkhazia has also to some extent shown an ability to resist Russian involvement in its politics, granting it a certain degree of credibility as an actor in its own right. In contrast, South Ossetia displays a higher degree of criminalization, its politics are practically dictated by Russia—or caught between divergent Russian interest groups—and its economy exclusively relies on a combination of incomes from smuggling and Russian subsidies.

Conclusions

The origins of Georgia's conflicts can largely be considered as grievance-driven. The resurgent Georgian nationalist project and demands for independence in Georgia during the breakup of the USSR clashed with countering nationalisms and independence claims within Georgia's autonomies. As Coppieters has argued, the weakening of the Soviet center allowed Georgia, peripheral in the USSR, to assert its independence from the center while the weakness of the independent Georgian state in turn allowed the peripheries of Abkhazia and South Ossetia within Georgia to assert their independence from the Georgian center.[105] These conflicting independence claims emboldened Georgia under Gamsakhurdia to roll back the autonomy of Abkhazia and in particular South Ossetia, which in turn proclaimed independence from Georgia.

The general collapse of the Georgian state, in which the conflicts in Abkhazia and South Ossetia were a considerable contributing factor, provided a fertile ground for the growth of criminal groups, and collusion between these groups and authorities on the Georgian, as well as the Abkhazian and South Ossetian sides. Control over smuggling networks through the conflict regions has been a key resource for all actors involved, and the vested interests in maintaining these networks likely created disincentives both to resolving the conflicts and returning to large-scale warfare. Yet, while trafficking in contraband such as drugs, weapons, and human beings has certainly been a feature of smuggling through Georgia and the conflict zones, the key goods transited have been "normal" consumer goods such as agricultural produce and petroleum.

The rapid growth of organized crime in Georgia, as well as the breakaway regions, emerged as an effect of the collapse of the USSR and the extreme weakness of the Georgian state during the process of gaining independence. However, it is difficult to discern the extent to which crime groups in Georgia appeared separately from, or in concordance with, the formation of politically motivated actors. While organized crime in the form of thieves in law had penetrated the Georgian state long before Georgia's independence, many of the new criminal groups in Georgia and the breakaway regions emerged around the interests of local economic "clans," on whose support political actors depended in realizing their goals. Likewise, several of the leaders and participants of the paramilitary forces who did most of the fighting during the wars had criminal backgrounds and many of these were later incorporated into the regular armed forces or political leaderships of Georgia and the breakaway regions. Jaba Ioseliani and the Mkhedrioni are a case in point, an organization in large part recruited from the criminal underworld, led by a person with genuine criminal credentials who took part in governing Georgia as part of the Military Council ahead of Shevardnadze's arrival. In sum, the formation of organized crime groups is not easily separable from political actors in the conflict.

Throughout Shevardnadze's administration, no decisive efforts were made by the Georgian state to regain control over the breakaway regions, nor by the breakaway regions to gain international recognition or formal independence, or merging with the Russian Federation. Hence, few steps were taken to realize the political goals (sovereignty/independence) driving the warfare in 1991–1994. While this can be interpreted in terms of a balance of power in which neither side had the means for reaching these objectives, profits from the war economies arguably also had a considerable effect on the motivational structures of all actors involved. The postconflict situation was such that neither side had a strong motivation for altering the existing situation on the ground.

The collusion between organized crime and political leadership established during the conflicts became a prevailing feature of the societies developing in both Georgia and the breakaway regions after the conflicts. A lawless climate, endemic corruption, high rates of crime-related violence and a virtually nonexistent Georgian state outside the capital led many observers to term Georgia a failed or failing state during the Shevardnadze era. Reforms made after the Rose Revolution in 2003 managed to turn many of these shortcomings around by severing the ties between the state and organized crime and significantly reducing corruption within state institutions. In Abkhazia and South Ossetia, the increased dependence on Russian aid following the 2008 war can paradoxically be said to have reduced the importance of criminal activities for the budgets of these regions, while simultaneously reducing the credibility of their claims to independence.

Chapter 7

Moldova: The Transnistrian Conflict

Alexandru Molcean and Natalie Verständig

The conflict between the self-proclaimed regime in the Transnistrian region of the Republic of Moldova and the Chisinau legal authorities in the early 1990s has until today remained unresolved. While violence receded after relatively short-lived fighting, the failure to reach a negotiated settlement has turned the Transnistrian conflict into one of the frozen disputes that emerged following the breakup of the Soviet Union. In the absence of a permanent settlement, illegal economic structures have been given the opportunity to flourish in the region, posing a threat to the country as well as the surrounding region. More specifically, the existence of an unrecognized breakaway region on the territory of the Republic of Moldova is a serious threat to the country's efforts to consolidate its statehood and develop a stable and prosperous economy. Its inability to control a large part of its external border or exercise effective power over the Transnistrian region, 12 percent of the territory, has problematic consequences for Moldovan sovereignty. Beyond the obvious negative consequences, such as the lack of stability and security in the country, as well as reduced economic development, the conflict generates additional immediate threats. The existence of two separate entities with different tax codes, customs, and legal systems creates an ideal environment for organized crime.

At the same time, it is important to note that organized crime within Moldova has not been static but has undergone a process of transformation since the breakup of the Soviet Union. Illegal crime networks operating in the territory have evolved from Soviet-era "thieves in law" structures in the 1990s, with a focus on violent crime, to more organized criminal activity, focused mainly on "white collar" crimes, controlled by political and economic elites in Tiraspol and Chisinau.

Regarding the types of organized crime in the region, smuggling is argued to be the main form and most pervasive type of illegal activity. Smuggling is intricately related to the border issue, where large quantities of goods are illegally transferred through the region. Other forms of organized crime include trafficking in drugs, human beings, and arms as well as trade in nuclear material and various economic frauds. Arms trafficking in particular has been a major source of income; both for the criminal networks themselves and for the de facto authorities in Tiraspol. All these types of organized crime can to a large extent be seen as negative spillover effects of the unresolved conflict, both in terms of poor border control and extensive corruption.

The establishment of the EU Border Administration Mission (EUBAM) has indeed addressed these issues by tracking trade and putting major trade routes under stricter control, and its existence continues to help to deal with the problems faced in the region. However, it must also be considered that its extension implies that smuggling and trafficking are still viewed as serious problems that require increased attention.

The Transnistrian conflict continues to represent a major destabilizing factor not only in Moldova's development, but within the entire region as well. Threats posed by the unsettled status of Transnistria reach far beyond the borders of the country, both when it comes to security and stability as well as when dealing with organized crime. There is a deep inter-linkage between various political and economic processes in the region and the settlement of the conflict, which in turn has a direct impact on the level of organized crime.

The Transnistrian Standoff

While there is disagreement as to the real causes of the conflict, which arose in the Moldavian SSR in the early 1990s, it can be argued that the nationalist sentiments spreading across the Soviet empire—as a result of Mikhail Gorbachev's reforms—were used as an efficient political instrument by different groups within the country. Nationalist movements representing the Moldovan-speaking community started demanding a closer relationship with Romania and on August 31, 1989, the local legislative body altered its policy on languages. For the first time in fifty years, the government officially recognized that Moldovan is the same language as Romanian and that Latin characters were to be used for Moldovan as well. Moldovan became the state language whereas Russian was given the status of "inter-ethnic communication language" and the language officially used between Soviet states.[1] On April 27, 1990, the Supreme Soviet of the Moldavian SSR adopted the traditional tricolor flag (blue, yellow, and red) with the Moldavian coat of arms and changed the national anthem to "Deșteaptă-te, române!"—the Romanian national anthem before 1946 and after 1989. Later that year, the name of the country was changed to "Republic of Moldova," removing the words "socialist" and "Soviet."

These changes were not accepted in all parts of the country, especially in the Eastern Transnistrian region located on the left bank of the Nistru River. During the Soviet period, military industries and units of the 14th Army were located in Transnistria that induced an influx of immigration from other parts of the USSR. As a result, the people on the left bank felt they were part of the majority in the Soviet Union and rejected the idea of being turned into a minority group within the Moldovan state.[2]

Russian-speaking industrial workers from the region formed a protest movement against the new language laws. Igor Smirnov, a native of the Far-Eastern Kamchatka peninsula who arrived in Tiraspol in 1987, eventually became leader of the worker protest.[3] The councils of the largest cities located on the left bank of the river Nistru also rejected the language laws and denied the legitimacy of the Chisinau authorities. On September 2, 1990, the so-called Second Congress of the Peoples' Representatives of Transnistria declared its independence and proclaimed the establishment of the Moldavian Transnistrian Republic.[4] While this was not accepted by Soviet leadership, the lack of reaction from the USSR and Moldova essentially allowed the new authorities in Tiraspol to take control over the region.[5]

Understanding that an effective consolidation of power would be significantly helped by a military presence, Transnistrian leaders started in the early 1990s to form paramilitary units—initially by strengthening the existing Soviet volunteer and workers' units in the region. By 1992 these units were converted into the National Guard, which was portrayed as an elite force. Additionally, local territorial units were reinforced by external paramilitaries that mainly included Cossacks from the south of Russia.[6] During the armed conflict, these volunteers as well as those coming from other regions were paid from the local budget, receiving 3,000 rubles per month.[7] However, the presence of the 14th Army in the territory proved to be essential for the Transnistrian side. While originally being subordinated to Moscow, the 14th Army declared loyalty to the secessionists in Tiraspol and provided crucial support to the local military and paramilitary units by arming and training them.[8] Many 14th Army officers formally resigned and joined Transnistrian militias, while the commander of the army, General Gennadii Yakovlev, even headed the Transnistrian military forces.[9]

The Russian support and transfer of arms to the Transnistrian side, along with the lack of military skill and experience on the Moldovan side, implied that unlike in most other civil conflicts, the secessionist side was in fact superior to the central authorities from which it was seeking autonomy. The decree on establishing the National Army of Moldova was signed by President Mircea Snegur only in September 1991 and while the intention was to set up a military force of around 15,000 professional soldiers,[10] it is unlikely that this was achieved by the time the conflict had escalated into an outright war.[11]

A short but intense war broke out on March 2, 1992, when Snegur launched military operations to ensure the Republic of Moldova's sovereignty over the uncontrolled territory. This decision was a direct result of the increasing number of violent incidents between Moldova's police and separatist forces. The launch of military operations was followed by several armed confrontations between the two sides, the most severely affected areas being Tighina (Bender), Cocieri, Coşniţa, and Dubasari. The fighting intensified in June 1992 when the parties fought for control over the city of Tighina. Eventually, under the command of General Alexander Lebed, the 14th Army (now operating under Russian president Yeltsin), attacked with artillery and defeated the Moldovan forces in Tighina, forcing a peace arrangement but also securing the de facto establishment of the Transnistrian regime.[12] On July 21, 1992, a cease-fire was signed between Moldova and Russia and a tripartite peacekeeping force composed of Russian, Moldovan, and Transnistrian troops was set up to oversee the security zone established between the two territories.[13]

The most common estimates cite the total casualties on both sides of the conflict at 1,132—barely passing the hurdle for being classified as a war.[14] This can be contrasted to the devastating 250,000 lives lost during the war in Bosnia-Herzegovina. Still, however, the Moldovan conflict had and continues to have significant implications on the political situation in the country.[15]

Since the cessation of violence, several attempts have been made by different parties to achieve a negotiated settlement without any considerable successes. Negotiations were initiated in 1993 under the auspices of the Organization for Security and Co-operation in Europe (OSCE) following a so-called five-sided format; in addition to the two conflict parties, Ukraine and Russia were to function as guarantors of an eventual settlement, with the OSCE equally associated in the negotiations.[16] Nevertheless, in 2012 Transnistria remains a de facto state claiming sovereignty over this small territory.[17]

Actors

The Moldovan Government

Although no tangible results were achieved following two decades of continuous negotiations, an important observation is that Transnistria has managed to survive as a de facto state. At the same time, the Republic of Moldova has failed to achieve political viability and economic prosperity.[18] This weakness has been exploited by other actors since the start of the conflict. At the end of the 1980s when tensions first started to arise, Moldova was still a formal member of the Soviet Union and its leaders lacked the strength and knowledge necessary to suppress and avoid escalation of the conflict. Moreover, following the breakup of the Soviet Union, the newly formed Moldovan government was preoccupied with issues related to its own independence and international recognition. By the time Chisinau gained the strength and understanding of the implications of the secessionist movement, the momentum was lost. Other actors involved in the conflict had reacted more promptly; Transnistrian leadership had secured its position by subordinating the military force in the region and Russia had seized the opportunity to maintain direct influence in the region.[19]

The approach adopted by the Chisinau authorities in regard to the Transnistrian conflict failed to reach its two main goals; settlement of the conflict and withdrawal of the Russian troops.[20] One view is that the government made a mistake by focusing primarily on the military (withdrawal of the Russian military) while neglecting the more practical issues such as the widening gap between the population on the two sides, anti-Moldovan propaganda of the Transnistrian leaders,[21] and the establishment of statelike structures in the separatist region. Only from 2005 to 2006 did Chisinau start to realize that lower-level confidence-building measures could contribute to an improved political climate, and as such bring the two parties closer to a settlement.[22] In the following years, the Moldovan authorities launched several civil society initiatives that arguably led to the promotion of mutual confidence and security between the two populations.[23]

The Transnistrian De Facto Government

Since a cease-fire was established over the Nistru River, the Tiraspol leadership has had one overriding priority: to have its de facto independence officially recognized by Moldova. This unwillingness to give up their hold on power through a negotiated agreement explains the persistence of tension and low-intensity conflict between Chisinau and Tiraspol.[24]

Until 2011, economic and political power in the breakaway region had over time been consolidated by Igor Smirnov. Smirnov came to power through elections in 1991. He had previously been in charge of one of the largest industrial plants in Tiraspol, "Eloktromas," while at the same time being the chief of the local city council. Smirnov was reelected as Transnistria's president in 1996, 2001, and 2006. While in power, particularly during the 1990s, Smirnov continued to consolidate control over a large part of political and economic life of the region by making extensive use of his prerogatives and status. Furthermore, a significant portion of power in Transnistria came under control of Smirnov and members of his family.[25] Smirnov's son Vladimir was appointed chief of the Transnistrian Customs Committee, a position he held for twenty years. During this time Igor Smirnov managed to exercise direct control over the legal and illegal inflow of goods to and from the region. Another of Smirnov's sons, Oleg, held a leading position in the largest Transnistrian bank, Gazprombank,[26] later involved in numerous money laundering scandals.[27] In 2011, Evghenii Sevciuc won the local presidential elections on a political platform largely based on anticorruption policies.[28] However, it remains to be seen how these policies will be put into effect, since some newly appointed heads of Transnistrian law enforcement bodies seem not to meet even basic professional integrity requirements.[29]

An important actor in Transnistria's economic and political arena is the Sheriff Corporation. Founded in 1993 by former Soviet Ministry of Interior officers in Tiraspol,[30] Sheriff has managed to secure a position of privilege in the region. In 1996 it signed an agreement on 'mutual cooperation' with the Transnistrian government, opening the door for the corporation to monopolize trade by establishing a network of supermarkets, gas stations, and Moldova's most successful football club—boasting a massive training complex and stadium outside Tiraspol. Sheriff also controls a large regional bank, owns the only telephone and Internet service provider in the region, and is involved in many other areas of production.[31] Since its foundation, the Sheriff Corporation has had a strong criminal profile and based many of its commercial activities—especially in the 1990s—on corruption, smuggling, money laundering, or counterfeiting scams.[32]

Russia

Russia is considered a dominant player in the Transnistrian puzzle with veto power in the OSCE and considerable political and economic leverages over Ukraine and Moldova (notably when it comes to gas supply). Officially, Russia has declared its support for the settlement of the conflict and reintegration of the Republic of Moldova. To this end, Russia has participated in the negotiation process since its commencement.

However, on a more practical level, Moscow has contributed to the existence of the breakaway region, initially by offering support to the Transnistrian troops through the 14th Army, and later on by subsidizing and maintaining the viability of the region's economy. During a relatively long period of time, both the industrial and agricultural sectors of Transnistria have benefited from large Russian subsidies.[33] Moreover, by issuing Russian passports to a significant portion of the enclave's population, Moscow has secured its right to legally interfere in the region's businesses under the guise of defending Russian citizens.[34] Russia has also provided political leaders from Tiraspol with considerable support. Until 2010, Igor Smirnov enjoyed Russian backing, which during the 2011 presidential election was redirected to Anatoly Kaminski, at the time leader of the Obnovlenie party. Furthermore, in addition to providing political and economic support to the separatist regime, Russia is effectively blocking the conflict resolution process by refusing to withdraw its troops from Moldovan territory; in a 2010 German initiative offering President Putin an agreement on EU-Russia security cooperation, one of the conditions is military withdrawal.[35]

Russia has much to gain by supporting the separatist regime and avoiding moving forward with a conflict settlement. First, Russia may satisfy its geopolitical interest by having Transnistria under its political and military control. This way, Moscow holds important leverages in negotiations with both Moldova and Ukraine. Some argue that Russia continues to back the Transnistrian separatists in order to pressure the regime in Chisinau to assume a position of "constitutional neutrality."[36] More important, Russia also holds leverages over Europe, which is interested in diminishing the risk of an outbreak of military confrontations on its immediate border.

To maintain a strong position of influence in the region, Russia has insisted that a reunified Moldova should be in the form of a federation where the Transnistrian leadership is granted a high degree of autonomy and a large influence within the federal state. This way Tiraspol would be able to block any unfavorable decisions within the federation. Furthermore, Russia wants to be a main powerbroker in any settlement between Chisinau and Tiraspol, asserting its role as the main external "guarantor" of the settlement in view of the potentially low viability of the reunified states. In addition, in order to provide alleged reassurance to Tiraspol in case of reunification, Russia has shown willingness to maintain its military forces on Moldovan territory.[37]

Second, Russian oligarchs hold significant economic interests in the region. During the Soviet era, the region was a privileged economic zone within the Moldovan SSR, containing at least 40 percent of Moldova's industrial capacity and the only large power plant in the region.[38] The major Soviet-era industries in Transnistria, like the MMZ steel plant and the Cuciurgan power plant, were "privatized" by Russian oligarchs. In other words, Transnistria's unresolved status allows these oligarchs to reap the profits from Moldovan industries; profits that instead could be reinvested into society.[39]

Organized Crime and Its Main Manifestations

Interrelation Between the Transnistrian Conflict and Organized Crime

Frozen conflicts are known to generate regional instability as a consequence of the close inter-linkage between armed conflicts, organized crime, and political corruption.[40] Moldova, with its Transnistrian conflict, is no exception. Large-scale organized criminal activity in the region is facilitated by weak state structures and poor border management.[41] This has created economic incentives for political elites—especially those from Tiraspol—to avoid actively seeking a negotiated solution to the conflict.[42]

Several factors have contributed to the creation of an environment susceptible to the establishment of organized crime groups in Transnistria—a development beginning in 1992 with the outbreak of military confrontations between the two banks of the Nistru River. Most significantly, the lack of effective legal control over a considerable part of the Moldovan-Ukrainian border has contributed to the growth of organized crime in the region. About a third of Moldova's border with Ukraine is under control of the Transnistrian authorities. Tiraspol has set up its own customs and border control offices both on the border with Ukraine as well as alongside the Nistru River on its alleged border with Moldova.[43] Since Chisinau has not recognized the legitimacy of the unilateral border inspections conducted by the separatist authorities and lacks access to the part of the Ukrainian border under Transnistrian control, it is denied effective control over a significant part of its frontiers. This situation strongly benefits organized crime groups, particularly those involved in smuggling, since these also benefit from the proximity to the Ukrainian seaports Odessa and Ilichiovsk.

Furthermore, the political instability of the Tiraspol regime contributes to a heightened level of criminality in the Transnistrian region. As the future of the region is highly unpredictable and local leaders are preoccupied with personal interests, people are easily lured into criminal activities. For instance, it is common that those involved in smuggling and tax evasion use the fact that the regime is illegal as an adequate moral excuse.[44]

Another issue complicating the fight against organized crime is the lack of the effective application of international agreements, including those covering money laundering, arms or drugs trafficking, and intellectual property rights infringements. Moreover, in Transnistria, international legal instruments regarding extradition, transfer of convicts, and transfer of criminal proceedings and letters of requests do not apply. Nearly all the international treaties Moldova is party to have a reserve clause according to which they apply only in the territory under de facto control of the legal authorities of the country.[45] Other difficulties in combating crimes committed in Transnistria are related to criminals' detention and to the enforcement of sentences issued by local courts. Sometimes criminals can cross to the other side of the river and avoid persecution.[46]

Moreover, people detained and convicted in Transnistria are theoretically entitled to receive compensation from Chisinau authorities for being "illegally" prosecuted, and if refused, to appeal the decision at the European Court of Human Rights.[47]

Specific Features of Organized Crime in Transnistria

Organized crime in Moldova, particularly in the Transnistrian region, can roughly be divided into two main categories. The first category is represented by criminal networks that have evolved from the Soviet "thieves in law" tradition.[48] The second category is organized criminal activity controlled by political and economic elites, partially a remnant of the leadership of the Communist Party in Moldova. Although it cannot be said that these two forms of organized crime are an immediate consequence of the conflict, they have developed over the last two decades and undergone two waves of evolution—conventionally divided between the 1990s and the period afterward.

The situation in Moldova, including Transnistria, in the early 1990s was similar to the one in the other former Soviet republics, characterized by what in Russia has been referred to as *bespredel*—representing both a lack of visible obstacles and the absence of any shared rules or laws.[49] In this period, criminal groups led by "thieves in law" managed to generate large profits and gain significant influence not only in the criminal world but also in the economic and political life of the countries where they operated. From 1993 until 2001 there were six criminal networks led by "thieves in law" in the Republic of Moldova. Each of these criminal leaders appointed local supervisors to the state's 38 districts, and this way they were able to reinforce their positions and ensure effective control over the entire country, including Transnistria. Each group had its own sphere of influence and control. For instance, Vladimir Moscaliciuc's group was involved in motor vehicle thefts and smuggling while Malhaz Djaparidze's group was responsible for drugs and arms trafficking.[50] Criminal operations were facilitated by the unilaterally controlled border as well as the lack of communication between the two parts of the country.

However, as mentioned, more than simply advancing in the criminal world, over time these "thieves in law" started becoming involved in the political life of the region by initiating mutually beneficial relations with politicians and political parties. For instance, in an interview in the Russian newspaper, *Komsomolskaya Pravda*, Grigore Caramalac,[51] a "thief in law" known under the nickname "Bulgarian"—in charge of the wine and oil industry of Moldova—admitted to supporting the Communist Party in the 1997 election campaign by donating US$500,000 and providing offices, transportation, and so on. Caramalac also declared that he used his influence in the south of the country to obtain support for the Communist Party in the 2001 elections.[52]

During this period, clashes among criminal groups over spheres of influence were not uncommon and contract killings became ordinary practice. The victims were not only members of criminal groups, but also businessmen and representatives of the local authorities. On December 20, 1999, two officials from the Transnistrian Ministry of State Security were gunned down along with two suspected criminals. Although this incident received little attention, more prominent cases include the assassinations of Anatol Burduja, head of the Organized Crime Division at the Transnistrian Ministry of State Security, and Victor Constantinov, president of the Transnistrian Association of Industrialists and Businessmen.[53]

With the Communist Party's ascension to power in 2001, there was a shift in the evolution of organized crime in Moldova, where the "thieves in law" structure was eliminated and illegal activities were largely overtaken by the economic elites of Chisinau and Tiraspol. While in power, one of the main priorities of President Vladimir Voronin was the fight against organized crime. Only a few months after his accession to power in September 2001, Voronin established a Coordinating Council for combating corruption and organized crime, which he himself chaired.[54] Furthermore, in June 2002 a law enforcement authority was created in Moldova—the Center for Combating Economic Crimes and Corruption. Reforms progressed with the approval of important national strategies and action plans, including those on fighting corruption in 2004.[55]

Statistics show that Voronin managed to achieve many of his goals, and starting in 2001 the number of crimes—and in particular serious offenses—committed in Moldova steadily decreased.[56] In the last decade, law enforcement measures taken by the authorities led to the arrest and prosecution of several criminal leaders while uprooting a number of criminal networks.[57] However, as mentioned, the actions undertaken by the government, while significantly reducing the level of criminality, were far from eliminating organized crime altogether. Instead, there was a restructuring within organized crime where the initiative of conducting illegal businesses was largely overtaken by economic circles close to the government. As for the old criminal leaders, several ultimately became businessmen while others turned to street crimes.[58]

Smuggling

Since the outbreak of the Transnistrian conflict, smuggling remains the most pervasive crime in the region, mainly as a result of poor border management and high levels of corruption in the breakaway territory. An example that typifies this situation is a protocol signed by the president of Moldova, Mircea Snegur, and the Tiraspol separatist leader, Igor Smirnov, in 1996 on cooperation of customs services. Transnistria agreed to eliminate customs check points within Moldova and to perform joint customs control at the Moldovan-Ukrainian border. In turn, Transnistria is given the right to perform customs clearance using the Republic of Moldova official seals. Once getting hold of the official customs seal, however, Transnistria withdrew from the agreement.[59] Ultimately the signing of the protocol only resulted in the de facto legalization of the immense flows of smuggled goods already passing through the Transnistrian region. In 1998 the total value of imports into the Republic of Moldova (right bank) of goods on which excise duties are imposed (alcohol, oil, tobacco) amounted to around US$108 million, while the value of imports in the Transnistrian region alone reached approximately US$476 million. In other words, taking into account that the secessionist region represents only 12 percent of the territory of Moldova, the figure is more than four times higher in Transnistria than on the right bank.[60] Data collected by EUBAM in 2006–2007 show that the poultry imported into the Transnistrian region was enough for each inhabitant, including newborns, to consume at least 8kg of poultry weekly. Moreover, according to figures on tobacco imports, each person could smoke at least twelve packs of cigarettes weekly.[61]

The above-mentioned data illustrate that a gigantic smuggling scheme was implemented in Transnistria based on the illegal transfer of goods through the region. This mechanism, initiated almost twenty years ago, still generates considerable profits to criminal groups in the region. Moreover, Ukraine seems to be equally affected by this smuggling. In the Black Sea ports of Odessa and Iliciovsk, goods are brought from all over the world and subsequently transported by the Sheriff Company to Transnistria where they are cleared by customs.[62] They are then smuggled back to Ukraine or to the right bank of Moldova. This simple scheme allows criminal groups to avoid tariffs and various controls in Ukraine and Moldova.[63]

These illegal activities have grave and far-reaching consequences beyond the geographic boundaries of the breakaway region of Transnistria. Both Moldova and the Ukraine register considerable losses in import and excise duties. Moreover, smuggled products are usually sold below the open-market price. As a result, legal businesses are forced out of the market and thus the state misses out on revenues in the form of corporate taxes. The possibility of setting lower prices also has an effect on neighboring EU-member countries like Romania; it was recently reported that the smuggling of cigarettes accounts for annual losses estimated at one billion Euros.[64]

Trafficking in Arms, Drugs, and Human Beings

While the conflict in Moldova was relatively short-lived, the absence of a settlement has created a situation that in many ways favors large-scale trafficking in arms, human beings, and drugs. Illegal arms trafficking has until recently been one of the main sources of income for the Transnistrian region, benefiting not only criminal groups but also the Tiraspol authorities.[65] This problem stems from the considerable stock of weapons and ammunition distributed by the 14th Army during the outbreak of the Transnistrian conflict to all those declaring their willingness to participate in the fighting. A large part of the military equipment was never recovered,[66] and according to reports, forty to fifty thousand tons of arms and ammunition that belonged to the 14th Army remained in Transnistria after the breakdown of the USSR. The most important location for these stocks was the Kobasna arsenal, considered one of the largest in Europe during the Cold War.[67] Following the end of the armed conflict, this large stockpile of weapons fell into the hands of criminal groups not only in Transnistria but also in neighboring countries. According to the testimonial of one of the commanders of the Tiraspol garrison, General Mihail Bergman, weapons used in the Transnistrian conflict later appeared in the Ukrainian Odessa port among other places.[68]

Criminal networks were not the only ones to profit from the trade in arms; the Transnistrian separatist leadership provided protection to these illegal activities and were in some cases directly involved in arms smuggling. According to Bergman, a state of chaos was artificially maintained by the Tiraspol leadership with the aim of creating favorable conditions for the illegal trade in arms. One prominent example of how involved the leadership was in smuggling activities was the arrest of Igor Smirnov's son in March 2000, who was detained in Moscow in possession of US$1.2 million obtained from weapons sales.[69]

Furthermore, whereas the conflict in Moldova was relatively short-lived and low in intensity, it indirectly contributed to fueling hot wars in other parts of the world—arms trafficked in the region have been exported to conflict zones. According to Moldovan officials, Transnistrian weapons have been seen in Abkhazia, Chechnya, the Congo, and the Ivory Coast.[70]

While the problem of illegal arms trafficking can be said to stem from the large stocks of weapons left in the region by the Soviet 14th Army, it should be noted that there was also significant production of arms in Transnistria. Between 1995 and 2000, various types of weaponry were produced at Tiraspol-based Bendery Mechanical Factory, the Ribnitsa Metallurgy Factory, and the Elektromash and Elektroagregat factories. The weapons produced included mobile Grad multiple rocket launch systems, mortars, antitank grenade launchers, antipersonnel grenade launchers, machine guns, pistols, and antipersonnel and antitank mines.[71]

Driven by a concern over the extensive smuggling activities and the impact on neighboring EU-states, by the turn of the twenty-first century the EU started to become more actively involved in supporting the combat against organized crime in Moldova. In June 2002, following a brief visit to Moldova and the Transnistrian region, a delegation from the European Parliament issued a report expressing "concern at the existence of a 'black hole' in Europe in which illegal trade in arms, the trafficking in human beings, and the laundering of criminal finance was carried on."[72] The situation has somewhat improved since the establishment of EUBAM in 2005 since major routes for arms trafficking have been put under strict control. As a consequence, criminal groups have been forced to abandon large-scale trafficking operations; there have been no cases of major arms smuggling over the Transnistrian segment of the border between Moldova and Ukraine.[73]

Trafficking in persons and human smuggling[74] through and from Moldova is of central concern and, similar to arms trafficking, can be explained as a negative spillover effect from the Transnistrian conflict. Poor economic performance, poverty, lack of security, and high unemployment are contributing factors to population migration,[75] with figures ranging from 340,000 to 1,000,000 migrants. Approximately 600,000 Moldovans are affected by labor migration, representing one-third of the country's work force.[76] A large part of these migrants are victims of human trafficking. Moreover, human trafficking for sexual exploitation is a problem of special concern in Moldova.[77]

Trafficking in persons and human smuggling is not a problem that can be confined within the national borders of Moldova. Human trafficking is commonly operated by clandestine criminal groups often involved in other illegal activities and is generally part of international criminal networks.[78] Since Romania's admission into the EU, the state's role as an entry point for illegal immigration into the union has grown significantly. Smuggling is facilitated by contacts that international transportation companies based in Romania have managed to establish with forgers and recruiters from countries such as Moldova.[79]

Unlike illegal arms trafficking, this problem equally affects both the right and the left bank of the Nistru River, the difference being in the attitude toward it. In recent years Chisinau has received support and assistance from several international partners in combating human trafficking and a series of institutional and legislative reforms have been implemented. On the other side, the Tiraspol leadership seems to ignore the problem and has made no significant efforts to prevent or combat the practice. Instead, efforts to combat human trafficking are almost exclusively led by NGOs, La Strada being most actively involved. However, the complex political situation in Transnistria and the difficulties associated with dealing with the separatist regime often obstruct NGO efforts. At present, there are no structures in Tiraspol similar to those in Chisinau[80] competent in preventing and fighting human trafficking.

However, even if Chisinau has made efforts to combat human trafficking, the problem persists and major obstacles remain. One of the main hindrances is widespread corruption in the judiciary and police in the region. According to available data, no officials have been convicted or even investigated for being involved in trafficking schemes. Moreover, even on the right side, efforts undertaken in fighting human trafficking decreased in 2011 compared to previous years, and offenses related to forced labor were seldom investigated and reported to law enforcement authorities.[81]

Trade routes crossing through the Republic of Moldova, the proximity of both the EU and two major Black Sea ports, and limited control over a third of the Moldovan-Ukrainian border combine to create extremely favorable conditions for drug trafficking through the separatist region. Criminal groups extensively exploit these opportunities, as confirmed by the increasing number of cases of drug trafficking reported by law enforcement authorities. The seaports of Odessa and Ilichiovsk alone had two tons of cocaine and 759kg of hashish confiscated in 2010. A considerable part of this shipment was destined for EU markets[82] and was supposed to travel through the Republic of Moldova's territory, including its eastern border that is partly controlled by the separatist regime.

In the 2011 Europol Organized Crime Threat Assessment (OCTA) report, Black Sea ports were identified as points of transit and entry for cocaine from Latin America, and Moldova was reported to be an important location for storage and further processing.[83] Although Moldovan authorities have denied these claims, Europol's assessment was reinforced by the interception of a large cocaine load (38 kg) in the Ilichiovsk port in February 2012 that was intended to be received by two Moldovan citizens.[84]

Trade in Nuclear Materials

Besides trafficking in arms, drugs, and human beings, reports point to criminal groups in Transnistria actively involved in affairs related to trading radioactive materials. This claim is supported by a number of cases and detentions with connections to nuclear smuggling in the last ten years. The existence of groups in Transnistria able to modify Alazan rockets (originally used for weather modification) to carry nuclear warheads has been discussed for over a decade. In 2005 the *London Times* reported that an arms dealer in Bender, Transnistria, had offered to sell three Alazan rockets equipped with nuclear warheads to a reporter posing as the representative of an Algerian militant group. The arms dealer ensured that the criminal network he represents is able to ship modified Alazan rockets to Ukraine. Another revelation with regard to nuclear smuggling in Transnistria was made by a *Washington Post* journalist in 2003, who uncovered a document from 2001 stating that Colonel V. Kireyev, a civil defense commander in Transnistria, expressed his concern over the radioactive leakage of the armaments stored in Transnistria.[85] The journalist warned that a large amount of Alazan rockets from Soviet depots in Transnistria had been modified to carry nuclear payloads and were assembled with warheads containing 400 grams of cesium and strontium.[86] Importantly, the head of an OSCE mission to Moldova later questioned the reports of both British and U.S. newspapers, yet no concluding arguments that would verify or falsify these reports were presented.[87]

This trend in radioactive materials smuggling continues to plague Moldova today. In August 2010 Moldovan police discovered a load of 1.8 kg of uranium-238 intended to be sold in Transnistria for nine million Euros.[88] The following June, six people were detained in Chisinau, suspected of smuggling approximately 1 kg of uranium-235. Two of these people were from the Transnistrian region. The price of the goods was valued at over twenty million Euros. According to officials from the Interior Ministry, the uranium came from Russia and the suspects were attempting to sell it to a Muslim citizen of an unnamed African state.[89] The uranium entered Moldova through Transnistria, and it was later discovered that the smugglers were planning to bring in more radioactive substances, including plutonium.[90]

If the reported cases of nuclear smuggling are to be believed, it can be concluded that the operations of criminal groups involved in smuggling radioactive materials are benefiting from the possibilities offered by the breakaway region. They either use the material left in the region from Soviet times, adapting it to market needs such as in the case of Alazan rockets, or use the territory of the region as a secure and convenient channel to trade and deliver illegal substances to other countries.

Other Frauds

One of the main barriers to the settlement of the Transnistrian conflict is the strong economic incentives involved. In spite of the concern expressed by the

Tiraspol leadership with regard to the consequences of the armed conflict, the criminal schemes in the region in the last two decades prove that the leaders were in fact the main beneficiaries of the postconflict situation. With the support and even participation of the separatist leaders, large-scale businesses have been able to take advantage of inadequate control at the Moldovan-Ukrainian border. As a consequence, it is rather difficult to make a clear distinction between businesses and criminal groups involved in trafficking, smuggling, and economic frauds.

The case of natural gas deliveries to the region offers a telling example of the collaboration of businesses and authorities in illegal activities, as well as possible Russian involvement in such criminal enterprises. Moldova, lacking indigenous energy resources, is almost completely dependent on imported energy, mainly in the form of natural gas from Russia. Moldova, including the Transnistrian region, consumes on average 2.5–2.7 bcm of gas annually imported from the Russian company Gazprom—half of it consumed by Transnistria with only 12 percent of the country's territory. Gazprom is running separate accounts for the gas consumed in Transnistria and the rest of Moldova. Whereas the Moldovan government pays all its gas bills to Gazprom, Transnistria has managed to accumulate a debt of more than US$2 billion.[91] Nevertheless, Russia has not undertaken any credible measures to cease this illegal consumption of its gas or recover its debts.[92] But while Russia is not receiving any payment for the gas delivered to Transnistria, the Transnistrian population is in fact paying for the consumed gas to the local authorities, who simply refrain from transferring the collected amounts to Gazprom. According to Evghenii Sevciuc, at that time speaker of the Supreme Soviet in Tiraspol, the Transnistrian administration collected US$27 million for the consumed gas in 2006 and US$18 million in the first quarter of 2007. The money for the Russian gas was never transferred to the supplier, Gazprom, but was embezzled by the Transnistrian Gazprombank,[93] at that time led by Oleg and Marina Smirnov, son and daughter-in-law of Igor Smirnov.

There are also suspicions that Gazprombank was involved in a money laundering scandal where humanitarian aid from Russia was misappropriated by the bank. For years Russia has offered direct humanitarian assistance to the region, mainly as additional payments to the local pension fund. According to official Russian data, from 2007–2010 the total amount of assistance granted to the region was US$55 million.[94] In October 2011 the Investigative Committee of Russia initiated a criminal investigation against Oleg and Marina Smirnov, both Russian citizens. According to Russian law enforcement authorities, a considerable part of the funds intended for humanitarian aid was transferred to Gazprombank, which illegally used it as loans or credits to various entities. Later on, according to the committee spokesperson, the investigated persons received several transfers from a Cypriot company, offering proof that it was a clear case of money laundering.[95]

Another example of how the frozen Transnistrian conflict continues to create opportunities for the local leadership to profit from illegal economic activities is the trade in tobacco products. As a result of a ban imposed several years ago by Igor Smirnov, only cigarettes imported by the Sheriff Corporation are sold in Transnistria.[96] However, it seems that none of the major tobacco producers in Chisinau, Kiev, or Moscow are contracted to sell cigarettes to Sheriff; it would seem that most of the cigarettes sold in Transnistria are counterfeit.[97] This way, the Tiraspol leadership has ensured a constant supply of revenue. In February 2012 the Tiraspol authorities decreased the excise duty on tobacco imports significantly. At the same time, Chisinau increased its excise duties by almost 50 percent, and additional increases are expected. In this scenario the risk of cigarette smuggling from or through the Transnistrian region, mainly to EU countries, increases considerably.[98]

The examples described here show how organized crime in Transnistria has evolved and changed over the years. Criminal groups are no longer focused solely on drug or arms trafficking, or other violent crimes. Organized crime has turned into an extremely diversified semilegal business, with nearly free access to the financial and banking system and widely supported by decision makers in the region.

The Conflict Resolution Process and Its Impact on Criminality in the Region

The Transnistrian conflict is in a sense less complex than the other frozen conflicts in the former Soviet Union. The involvement of external actors, as well as the lack of deep-seated ethnic or religious antagonisms, implies that the conflict should be relatively easy to resolve.[99] Nevertheless, the official positions of the parties to the conflict have been widely disparate, and as such, negotiations have failed to produce any tangible results. Seeing as the parties have not been able to agree even on the most fundamental issues, problems relating to organized crime have been given little or no attention. At the beginning of the 1990s, Tiraspol officials seemed to avoid the issue of organized crime—most likely due to their own involvement in smuggling and arms trafficking. Officials from Chisinau, on the other hand, directed all their focus toward finding a solution to the conflict and believed that once it was settled, its negative consequences, including organized crime, would disappear on their own.[100] Overall, until 2005 the parties had signed approximately 150 documents of which only two dealt directly with combating organized crime. In February 2010 the working group for law enforcement cooperation and the fight against organized crime convened to examine a number of issues related to ensuring public order. Unfortunately, the group has so far convened only once; Tiraspol authorities argue that there is no need for additional meetings.[101] Besides official contacts within the working groups, there is also informal cooperation among law enforcement authorities—however, on a very technical level—with the exchange of operative information when urgently needed for a specific case.[102]

The inability of the parties to find common ground in the negotiations, in addition to the failure of Moldova and Ukraine in their attempts to ensure control over the Transnistrian portion of their common border, led the two countries to seek the assistance of the EU in stabilizing the situation. As a result, EUBAM was launched in December 2005 with a mandate to assist the Moldovan and Ukrainian border and customs authorities in developing border management procedures.[103] As a first step, Ukraine and Moldova adopted a joint statement implementing the customs protocol from 2003. Mechanisms were established facilitating trade between the two sides, as well as enabling information exchange between Ukraine and Moldova, thus facilitating the fight against smuggling and other illegal cross-border activities, while also increasing transparency in trade.[104] A number of other initiatives aimed at facilitating trade and preventing customs fraud, smuggling, and trafficking have subsequently been undertaken with the assistance of EUBAM.[105]

The mandate of EUBAM has continuously been extended and the implications are two-fold. On the one hand, the extension can be interpreted as a sign of the efficiency and success of the instruments and mechanism set up with EUBAM's support. On the other hand, the continued existence of EUBAM implies that there is still a need for it; the problems of smuggling and human trafficking are still present[106] and are likely to persist as long as the conflict remains unsettled. In light of the achievements of EUBAM, one could draw the conclusion that third-party intervention and assistance can often be necessary in frozen conflicts or postconflict states struggling with organized crime. Additionally, this case gives insight into the types of criminal activities that may develop and go unchecked in postconflict societies in which the international community has a less direct presence and interest.

Concluding Remarks

The outbreak of the Transnistrian conflict has no simple or definite explanation. Instead, there are numerous arguments examining the onset of the conflict, and even more explanations for the reasons it persists today. At the end of the 1980s, the grievances of the Russian-speaking minorities in the Transnistrian region resulting from new language laws sparked tensions in the country. However, there were also strong military, political, and later economic interests involved in the outbreak and persistence of the conflict. The 14th Soviet Army, stationed in Transnistria, saw the emergence of a possible conflict in its area of control as a raison d'être while the USSR was disintegrating. After swearing allegiance to the Russian Federation, the Army became a guarantor of Moscow's political interest in maintaining control and influence in the region. Furthermore, the existence of industrial resources in the region provided additional incentives to strive for control over Transnistria.

In this context, it can be questioned whether the Transnistrian conflict was in fact grievance-based, seeing as Russian political, military, and economic support were crucial ingredients in motivating the separatists. At the same time, it is difficult to argue that the conflict was purely greed-driven, particularly because there seems to be no evidence that the separatists were involved in organized criminal activities at the onset of the conflict. Thus, while economic incentives may have played a role, gains from organized criminal activities did not serve as a major goal during the early stages of the separatist movement.

However, as the conflict remained unsettled, one can see a shift in the motivations and interests of the separatists. Whereas the conflict was initially triggered by ethnolinguistic grievances, by the mid-1990s the situation had deescalated and different ethnic communities on both sides of the river seemed to coexist harmoniously. The lack of effective control on behalf of law enforcement authorities resulting from the absence of a settlement offered opportunities for various actors involved in the conflict and for regional crime groups to profit from organized illegal activities. The growth of organized crime created incentives for the political elites of the separatist region to both become involved in, and provide support to criminal activities. The proximity to Europe provided further incentives to engage in illegal activities, opening up the opportunity for the transfer of goods to attractive European markets.

The case of Transnistria illustrates the way in which frozen conflicts can create the perfect environment for the interlinkage of separatist governments and organized crime. Indeed, it has often been difficult to clearly distinguish between the interests of the Tiraspol leadership and the interests of companies or groups with strong criminal profiles, such as the Sheriff Corporation. The proceeds from organized criminal activities formed an incentive for the separatist leaders to avoid seeking a resolution to the conflict, even rejecting a proposal of large autonomy after the cease-fire and instead doubling down on their demand for statehood.

While discussions were held on the settlement of the conflict in Chisinau, Moscow, and other locations, thousands of tons of goods were, and still are, smuggled in and out of Transnistria. A considerable part of the profits from these operations—at least until the 2011 elections—were transferred directly to the Tiraspol leadership.[107]

Yet the question remains whether Transnistrian leaders are now purely motivated by economic benefits in their quest for statehood or if they are still driven by a true desire for self-determination based on ideology. The strong relationship between the Transnistrian separatist leaders and the regime in Moscow might make it difficult to judge the actual intentions of Tiraspol. This close connection could imply that the separatist government is simply being used by Russia to gain influence and promote its interests in the region. On the other hand, it is also possible that the Transnistrian leadership is making use of Russian support to promote its own quest for independence. While it is difficult to identify the true nature of the separatists' motivations, it can be argued that the lack of any serious efforts to combat organized crime on behalf of the authorities indicates that they are indeed driven by economic motives. The prevalence of organized crime in the region is slowing down any development toward independence, seeing as it only increases a dependence on Russia. It is clear that the separatists are increasingly motivated by economic benefits of the organized criminal activities in which they take part.

This situation is not only exacerbating tensions in the region, but it is also impeding Moldova's political and economic stabilization process. Without effective control over the Transnistrian region and the segment of the Moldovan-Ukrainian border located in the separatist region, organized crime networks continue to present a growing threat to the national security of Moldova, as well as other countries in the region.[108] The danger of cross-border organized crime's increasing influence over the Moldovan society, combined with corruption and its extended societal effects, undermines the rule of law and, indirectly, the national security of Moldova as well as the security and stability of the wider region.

Chapter 8

Bosnia-Herzegovina: Where International Wars, Transnational Crime, and Shady Politics Meet

Jana Arsovska

During the past several decades, critical and conflict criminologists have criticized criminology's persistent bias in favor of focusing on crimes of the powerless rather than of the powerful, and on crimes by individuals rather than by governments. Governments seldom define the bad things they do as crimes, thus critical insight into this area is highly needed.[1] In Bosnia-Herzegovina (hereafter Bosnia), one of the former republics of the Socialist Federal Republic of Yugoslavia (SFRY), organized crime and politics appear intrinsically linked in both the traditional "organized crime" and the "white collar crime" sense.[2] Bosnia is therefore an excellent case study to explore the crime-conflict nexus as well as the dynamic interplay between political and economic "rationality" during and following the Yugoslav conflicts.

In the Balkans, the 1990s will be remembered as *Decade Horribilis*; one of lawlessness, armed conflicts, crime, and endemic corruption. Hundreds of thousands of people lost their lives in this period. Although many would argue that war benefits no one, the republics of the SFRY went to war regardless.

This chapter argues that the origins of the conflicts that swept the Balkan region arose from groups seeking the redress of injustice, collective fear, and information failure, as well as flawed political decisions.[3] In the years following the death of communist leader Josip Broz Tito in 1980, Serb nationalists worked hard to reestablish the power Serbia had exercised prior to World War II. These efforts made the other nationalities anxious about the possible emergence of a "Greater Serbia," which gradually led to nationalistic agitation.[4] In April 1987, Slobodan Milošević, Serb Communist Party leader and right-hand man to Serbian president Ivan Stambolić, visited Kosovo, Serbia's poorest province. He was bombarded with accusations by segments of the Serbian population in Kosovo, including the Serbian nationalist movement, that they had been subject to ongoing discrimination and abuse by the ethnic Albanian population. Soon afterward, Milošević gave his historic speech in Kosovo, telling the Serbs, "No one should dare to beat you."[5] Such patriotic speeches and growing "information failure" led to increased tensions between ethnic and religious groups throughout Yugoslavia that prior to the rise of ethnic nationalism were thought to live in brotherhood and unity.

Other scholars have focused on the economic factors that led to the breakup of Yugoslavia.[6] They claim that the Yugoslav government encouraged republics to pursue foreign loans to redress economic concerns, but the loans were unsupervised and made Yugoslavia one of the most heavily indebted states in Europe. The severe economic problems contributed to the violent breakup of Yugoslavia since some people had less to lose. This chapter argues that greed and economic incentives do not appear to have been the initial cause of the Balkan conflicts, including that in Bosnia. They factored in, however, as soon as the conflicts began, and prolonged them by providing an impetus for organized criminal activity and for insurgent groups to become involved in profitable crime. At times of economic repression, the wars enabled the emergence of an alternative system of profit, power, and protection;[7] they provided opportunities for armed groups as well as common people to acquire wealth;[8] and, most important, they allowed criminal segments of society to neutralize their deviant behavior while continuing with their criminal careers.[9]

Organized crime and corruption continued to flourish in Bosnia even after the conflicts ended. This was partly a result of greed, and partly a result of illicit financial incentives serving as a short-term mechanism to "glue" fragile systems together and preventing new waves of violence. In the critical stages of Bosnia's postconflict stabilization, organized crime, criminal-political ties, and elite corruption have led to the establishment of a so-called "negative"— short-term and fragile—peace. The government in Bosnia has been subject to illicit power-sharing and ongoing criminal influences that secure shadow economies, but also the "negative" peace. This chapter argues that this type of "quick fix" could lead to grave institutional and social consequences in the long run.

The War in Bosnia-Herzegovina: Causes and Consequences

The war in Bosnia, which took place between April 1992 and December 1995, has been recognized as an international, territorial, and armed conflict. The war was one of the outcomes of the breakup of the former Yugoslavia. In 1991, the collapse of the federal state culminated in the secession of its more developed republics, Slovenia and Croatia. The conflict in Slovenia came to an end quickly, mainly because Serbian politicians concluded that because there was no Serb minority living in Slovenia, there was no need to invest in the conflict there. Serbia was willing to let Slovenia go without a significant fight in order to focus its limited resources on the creation of a "Greater Serbia," uniting all Serbian-populated territories of the former Yugoslavia. As a result, Croatia experienced armed conflict on its territory during 1991, but the real war started when the multiethnic republic of Bosnia-Herzegovina passed a referendum for independence on February 29, 1992. The referendum was immediately rejected by Bosnian Serb politicians, who had boycotted the referendum and established their own republic.

According to the 1991 census, Bosnia was inhabited by 44 percent Bosniaks (Bosnian Muslims), 31 percent Orthodox Serbs, and 17 percent Catholic Croats; the remainder identified themselves by the nonethnic term "Yugoslav." Historically, these different ethnic and religious groups cohabited in peace. Once manipulative politicians convinced their coethnics that a war for independence and territorial sovereignty was indeed vital for their survival, ethnic security, and future prospects, the "enemy" was dehumanized and the bloodshed began. Following the declaration of independence, Bosnian Serb forces, secretly supported by the Serbian government of Slobodan Milošević and the Yugoslav People's Army (YPA), attacked Bosnia. The war in Bosnia became principally a territorial conflict, initially between the Serb forces, mostly organized in the Army of Republika Srpska (VRS), on the one side, and the Army of the Republic of Bosnia (ARBiH) on the other. Initially, the Croats also aimed at securing parts of Bosnia for Croatia.[10]

As a result, in 1992, Europe experienced the bloodiest war on its territory since World War II. The war was characterized by the destruction of cities, ethnic cleansing, mass rape, and acts of genocide. Events such as the Siege of Sarajevo and the Srebrenica massacre would become iconic of the conflict. The war in Bosnia lasted until 1995 when NATO intervened during Operation Deliberate Force. After this intervention and the signing of the General Framework Agreement for Peace in Bosnia in December 1995, peace negotiations were held in Dayton, Ohio. This peace accord, known as the Dayton Agreement, brought the conflict to an end.[11] During the conflict period, 4.3 million Bosnian citizens were displaced and up to a quarter of a million killed.

The ethnic cleansing of the Bosniak population was only one of the many outcomes of the war. Another consequence was the development of a symbiotic relationship between politics and organized crime. This chapter explains why and how the economic incentives became very important in explaining the war as it progressed, although initially the implanted idea of "ethnic security" and the fear of unjust treatment in the hands of a different ethnic or religious group appear to have been the main factors in the conflict. As political-criminal interrelations developed during the formation of the new Bosnian state, they have left a legacy of institutional ambivalence toward illicit activities. Examples from the Balkan region, including Bosnia, illustrate that temporary accommodations between authorities and organized crime have led to a permanent transformation of state interests into private ones. International police expert Filip De Ceuninck[12] has observed that a significant number of criminal figures in the Balkan region "wear four hats":

> Many of them started as freedom fighters and warlords, and then moved into shady politics. As politicians they stayed in contact with wary businessmen that needed political favors to make their semi-legitimate businesses more profitable. In return the businessmen were financing the political parties. Many politicians—first for state and later on for personal interest—became part of these organized crime networks.[13]

According to Lupsha and Pimentel, the two basic models of the politics-crime nexus are stage-evolutionary and elite-exploitation.[14] The criterion for the dichotomy is the source of illicit power. In the stage-evolutionary model, in pursuit of insurance and protection criminal groups develop upward, from low-level bonding with state institutions to close cooperation with upper ladder bureaucrats. The elite-exploitative model implies a top-down relationship in which criminal organizations are exploited by fraudulent political elites for their own benefits. Both models are relevant for the Balkan context.

Since the war ended, one of the main problems in Bosnia has been the rise in organized criminal activity due to the ability of war profiteers and low-level criminals to become deeply entrenched in politics and business. Nowadays, there are numerous indications that many leading politicians in Bosnia have been involved in a range of criminal activities such as arms, fuel, and cigarette smuggling, drug trafficking, money laundering, embezzlement, and financial manipulations.[15]

It is also safe to argue that during the turbulent 1990s political elites had been strategically exploiting local criminals for their own benefit, including securing votes, raising funds for campaigns, collecting taxes, and supplying paramilitary structures with weapons and human power. Thus the transformation to decentralized economies benefited the old elites who were still functioning within the framework of the new state, and led to the inception of new elites, who positioned themselves outside the established statehood and profited greatly from illegal activities.[16] The outcome, as the authors of a 2010 study put it, is that "The whole state [Bosnia-Herzegovina] is now caught in the vicious circle of politics, mafia and crime."[17] Another consequence has been the expansion of radical Islam and crime-terrorities. These allegations, however, require further systematic analysis.

Nation-Building and the Arms Industry

The UN Embargo

A few important milestones during the Bosnian war are helpful in understanding the rise in organized crime in the country. One of the international community's first reactions to the outbreak of the Yugoslav wars was the arms embargo imposed on all six Yugoslav republics in May 1992.[18] The UN embargo had a detrimental impact on the Army of Republic of Bosnia-Herzegovina since Serbia inherited the lion's share of the former Yugoslav People's Army arsenal.

Before its violent breakdown, Yugoslavia maintained one of the largest armies in Europe. The Yugoslav policy, based on the Total Defense Doctrine, was to engage the entire Yugoslav population in armed resistance, armament production, and civil defense. The YPA was a force of 195,000 soldiers with sophisticated military capabilities and under the central control of Belgrade, capital of Serbia.[19] Additionally, each of the six republics had a Territorial Defense Force (TDF). Some estimates suggest that the two forces had a stockpile of 2.3 million rifles at their disposal.[20] The YPA was largely based on the Soviet model; about 90 percent of the arms were produced domestically. Also, in Tito's time, nothing was discarded. Outdated but functional leftovers from the 1950s and 1960s were conserved and stored in secret warehouses throughout the country.[21] As the wars in the Balkans started, these stockpiles were the primary source of weapons for paramilitary and militia structures, which played an important role throughout the war.

Military production in Yugoslavia was decartelized. About 60 percent of the production was taking place in Serbia, and the rest mainly in Bosnia. According to the Stockholm International Peace Research Institute, some TDF weapons were stored at "decentralized depots through the different republics, including schools and other municipal buildings."[22] Moreover, about 55 percent of the armories of the former Yugoslavia were in Bosnia, owing to its mountainous terrain, but many were under Serbian control. Although Bosnia had a few arms factories on its territory,[23] during the war they were the main targets of the warring parties, and, later on, of NATO air strikes.[24] Most of these factories, it appears, were destroyed.

The Bosnian government lobbied to have the UN embargo lifted. This, however, was opposed by the UK, Russia, and France. The U.S. Congress passed two resolutions calling for the lifting of the embargo, but both were vetoed by President Bill Clinton for fear of creating a rift between the United States and the aforementioned countries. Therefore, in order to push for independence, many politicians, as well as criminals, from the smaller Yugoslav republics engaged in strategic alliances with foreign state and nonstate actors for the importation of weapons and ammunitions. As discussed below, the embargo drove Bosnia into alliances with some of the world's most radical states, as well as terrorist movements, who provided Bosnia with human resources and money.[25]

The Third World Relief Agency (TWRA)

Organized crime quickly became a necessity for the survival of the Bosnian state, rather than a purely profit-driven activity. Weapons smuggling was crucial to the war effort, and the "government" of the Bosniak region was thus directly reliant on organized criminals, or even low-level criminals, to fight the war. As the war progressed in Bosnia, Bosnian Serbs received military supplies from Serbia, while Bosnian Croats received help from Croatia. It appears that the majority of the groups supplying weapons to Bosniaks came from Islamic countries, especially Iran, Turkey, Sudan, and Saudi Arabia.[26] However, the supply of arms to Bosnia was complicated by the country's geographical location. Therefore, the most feasible smuggling routes were those passing over the border with Croatia. Although Croats and Bosniaks were enemies in the regional conflicts, this did not hinder their criminal cooperation.

Commentators claim that between May 1994 and January 1996, Iran supplied the Bosniaks, via Croatia, with about 5,000 tons of arms and ammunition.[27] In fact, one of the largest contingents of weapons that ever entered the Balkan region was in 1994–1995, and it was shipped from Iran to Bosnia through Croatia, as a part of a secret U.S. program helping the Bosnian army. There are allegations that the United States used both "black" (i.e., covert) C-130 transports and back channels, including Islamist groups, to help Bosnia smuggle weapons.[28] Examples such as this show that countries were willing to break their own rules for a seemingly "just cause."

One of the most controversial arms smuggling cases, which illustrates how much the Bosnian government depended on outside aid for weapons, is linked to the name of Sudanese national Elfatih Hassanein. Hassanein founded the Third World Relief Agency (TWRA) in Bosnia in 1987. According to Western officials, the purpose of the organization was the rebirth of Islam in Eastern Europe.[29] In 1995, the TWRA bank records showed that $350 million flowed from the governments of Muslim countries and radical Islamic movements into Bosnia in support of the war. While the agency accepted funds from a variety of sources, Iran, Sudan, and Saudi Arabia were the largest contributors. According to intelligence sources, donations also came from pro-Western countries like Pakistan, Turkey, Brunei, and Malaysia.[30]

Terrorists are also believed to have used the relief agency to get money to the Bosnian government, including Saudi Arabian émigré Osama Bin Laden. The TWRA had ties to Sheik Omar Abdel Rahman—a radical Egyptian convicted of planning terrorist bombings in New York and linked to the group that carried out the World Trade Center bombing in February 1993.[31]

Hassanein built his smuggling business with Islamic activists from Bosnia who had ties to Bosnian president Alija Izetbegović and presently hold senior positions in the Bosnian government. A Western banker cited by the *Washington Post* in 1996 referred to Hassanein as the "bagman" of Izetbegović . "If the Bosnian government said we need flour, he ran after flour. If they said we need weapons, he ran after weapons."

According to intelligence sources, in October 1992 Haris Silajdžić, Bosnia's foreign minister,[32] vouched for Hassanein's credibility as the financial representative of the Bosnian state at the First Austrian Bank. In 1993, Izetbegović wrote a letter assuring the bank that the Sudanese had the support of the Bosnian authorities. In 1992, Hassanein acquired a diplomatic passport and became a Sudanese cultural attaché. This way, cash was transported through Austria and into Croatia and Slovenia without any difficulties. The organization was also moving large amounts of money to Croatia to bribe Croatian officials to allow the weapons to cross their country.[33]

The agency first came to the attention of Western intelligence agencies in late 1992, when transport planes began arriving in Slovenia from the Sudanese capital, Khartoum. The cargo was marked humanitarian aid, but in fact contained 120 tons of assault rifles, mortars, mines, and ammunition from surplus stocks of Soviet weapons.[34] Moreover, Russian-made helicopters ferried some weapons to the Bosniak-controlled towns of Tuzla and Zenica in Bosnia. According to investigators, a Russian-American joint venture called Eco-Trends is believed to have provided the helicopters. In 1993, German police discovered a weapons deal being negotiated in Germany by Bosniaks and Turkish arms dealers. Germany indicted thirty Bosnians and Turks on weapons and racketeering charges in connection with the illegal arms deal worth approximately $15 million. According to August Stern, a prosecutor in the German state of Bavaria, the TWRA was implicated as the financial broker of this deal.[35] Due to a lack of evidence, however, neither Hassanein nor his brother, who was also active in the organization, were charged with any crimes in Austria. The Bosnian government awarded the TWRA a gold medal for its relief work.

The TWRA was not the only Islamic charity operating on the territory of Bosnia. The Bosnian police in 2002 raided the Bosnian offices of Benevolence International Foundation, finding weapons, military manuals, fraudulent passports, and photos of Bin Laden. Another charity was al-Haramain Islamic Foundation, with branches in fifty-five countries and annual expenditure of $57 million. A Bosnian raid on a local branch found tapes calling for attacks on peacekeepers in Bosnia. Most worrying of all, however, is the 2004 arrest of fifteen Bosnian officials who were illegally helping 700 former Islamic fighters with alleged links to terrorist organizations to gain Bosnian citizenship.[36]

All this points to the perplexing linkages between politics, radical Islam, and organized crime in the context of the armed conflict in Bosnia. As literature on greed and grievance in armed conflict suggests, the nexus between organized crime and politics typically arises out of necessity and as a result of an unequal distribution of power, not necessarily because of greed and personal gains. Similarly, radical Islam gained a foothold in Bosnia—as in the case of Chechnya, discussed in Murad al-Shishani's contribution to this volume, because the country was in dire need of military and financial assistance, not necessarily because the Bosniak government supported Wahhabism.[37]

Transnational Ties and the Secret Services

Throughout the past two decades, actors with very diverse profiles have been involved in the arms trade in Bosnia. The list includes politicians, intelligence services, businessmen, criminals, and common people.[38] Going back to the early 1990s, the first weapon smuggling channels in Bosnia appear to have been set up by the head of the Counter-Intelligence Service (KOS), Aleksandar Vasiljevic, a Bosnian Serb.[39] He allegedly made an agreement with Bosnian defense minister Deli Mustafic, a Bosniak, who in 1991 was personally involved in arms smuggling from Vienna to Sarajevo,[40] not to interfere with the shipment of weapons from Serbia through Bosnia to the Serbian-held territories in Croatia. In return, "the secret service deflected some of the weapons to the Bosnian-Muslim army-in-the-making."[41]

Politicians and the secret services have been important players in the arms trade not only on the regional level but also internationally. According to a study by Cees Wiebes, political figures were largely responsible for the smuggling, which was arranged with the help of clandestine agencies from the United States, Turkey, and Iran, and together with a range of radical Islamist groups, including Afghan mujahideen and the pro-Iranian Hizbullah.[42] Arms purchased by Iran and Turkey made their way from the Middle East. Wiebes reveals that the United States was "very closely involved" in the airlift. The volume of weapons flown into Croatia, and later to Bosnia, was enormous, partly because of a Croatian "transit tax." Croatian forces charged 20 to 50 percent of the arms.[43] The Croats themselves also obtained massive quantities of illegal weapons from Germany, Belgium, and Argentina.

There are some documents indicating that when these shipments were noticed, the United States took no action to stop its fund-raising or arms purchases, in large part because of the administration's sympathy for the Muslim government.[44] According to intelligence reports, the German and the British secret services were also aware of the ongoing arms trade. The less publicized assistance from the international community once again illustrates how politics and organized crime intersect on different levels, apparently as a result of "grievance," not necessarily "greed."[45] Such cooperation, as will be illustrated below, has had serious consequences for the fight against organized crime after the war ended.

Moreover, with some foreign assistance, weapons were smuggled from Bulgaria into Yugoslavia, with Bosnia as the final destination. In the fall of 1993, six tractor-trailer trucks carrying 100 mortars, 1,000 mines, and 250 Dragunov sniper rifles for a total price of $670,000 crossed the Bulgarian-Macedonian border. Initially, according to the official documents, the cargo was destined for Albania. On the way, however, the arms cargo disappeared in Macedonia and the trucks returned empty to Bulgaria. Official investigations concluded that the arms were unloaded at Petrovac Airport in Skopje, loaded onto a plane, which had "broken" over Bosnian territories, where it was unloaded.[46]

Arms were also coming into the Balkans, particularly Croatia and Bosnia, from Chile and other parts of South America. In 2008 two Pinochet-era generals were given five-year jail sentences for illegal arms trafficking from Chile to Croatia in 1991. The Chilean shipment of eleven tons of armaments was disguised as humanitarian aid to Sri Lanka. UN officials intercepted the arms in Budapest airport.[47] It is noted that Croatian arms dealers, who also trafficked cocaine from Latin America, were protected by their connections with the Croatian Democratic Union (HDZ), the ruling party under the presidency of Franjo Tuđman.[48] The dealers had connections with the higher echelons of Croatia's Ministries of Defense and Internal Affairs, the customs service, and the secret service. This arrangement was characterized as "a classic example of a well-organized mafia, composed of classic criminals and portions of the state apparatus."[49] Some of these weapons ended up in Bosnia. Serbia too imported weapons illegally, often sharing the same channels with its enemies.[50]

The Serbs, although initially superior, eventually lost momentum as Bosniaks and Croats allied themselves against Republika Srpska in 1994 with the creation of the Federation of Bosnia-Herzegovina. After the war ended, more information started coming out showing how Bosnian politicians and the "international community" were connected to the Bosnian war arms pipeline. In 2007 press reports indicated that the Muslim leader of Bosnia's tripartite presidency, Haris Silajdžić, was under investigation for international arms smuggling. Silajdžić was Bosnian foreign minister during the war. Police are also investigating former Bosnian deputy defense minister Hasan Čengić and Turkish businessman Nedim Suljak. Čengić was closely tied to TWRA.

Furthermore, Bosnian Serb ex-leader Radovan Karadžić stated in front of the International Criminal Tribunal for the Former Yugoslavia (ICTY) that arms smuggled to Muslim areas had prolonged the war. "These weapons were used against us, to kill us. The Serbian side was put in a position to protect their very survival." Karadžić also claimed peacekeepers and aid organizations had provided weapons to his enemy in violation of a UN arms embargo. According to his statement: "Loads and loads of weapons transported by ship and aircraft were funneled into Bosnia from Iran but this could not have been possible without the help of major players."[51]

There is an abundance of evidence indicating the transnational criminal-political-business alliances in Bosnia and the surrounding region initially grew out of necessity to defend the incipient Bosnian state. The highly profitable arms smuggling business was often justified by politicians and common people because it was seen as vital to nation-building. Illicit arms markets deal with a product that is different from other illicit products or services. First, it is essential to understand that the inherent nature of firearms is their ability to take, or protect, human life—to intimidate, threaten, or defend the survival of "imagined communities" including gangs, ethnic groups, and nation-states. Thus, unlike other organized crime commodities (e.g., drugs, cigarettes, or cars) that can be seen as purely economic in nature, arms smuggling is indisputably linked to issues of power and is easier to sustain.[52]

The Arms Trade in Postconflict Bosnia: From Grievance to Greed

The smuggling channels for arms did not disappear after the war ended. After 1996 some arms and weapons started moving from Bosnia to Kosovo in support of the Kosovo Liberation Army (KLA)—a paramilitary group fighting for Kosovo's independence and against the militarily superior Serbia.[53] The KLA, similarly to the Bosnian army, was in a great need of weapons to win the fight for Kosovo's independence and secure the safety of the ethnic Albanian population. In 2001, NATO forces in Bosnia intercepted a large shipment of small arms—including armor-piercing launchers and grenades—intended for ex-KLA guerrillas in Kosovo. The shipment was a part of a smuggling channel, which was organized by the Bosnian Security

Agency (AID, Agencija za istrazivanje dokumentacije), but also included top officials from the Bosnian Ministry of Defense. The AID has since been restructured, and members of the "Kosovo export team" have been undergoing trials in Sarajevo.[54]

The trade in weapons after 2000, in particular, appeared to be quite well-structured and organized. Spanish intelligence suggested that the IRA was buying weapons and ammunition from arms groups based in the Republika Srpska. Such weapons were said to have originated from the former Yugoslav military, the military of Bosnia, and the police.[55] French and Spanish authorities also established links between Croatian arms and explosives, and the Basque separatist ETA. In fact, it was purported that during this time Bosnia and Croatia became major sources of illegal arms for both the IRA and ETA.[56] Interestingly, both allegedly paid for some of these arms with Colombian cocaine. Recent Amnesty International reports claim that weapons from Serbia and Bosnia have been flowing into Liberia and the Democratic Republic of the Congo, fueling the ongoing conflicts in these countries.[57]

Many weapons nevertheless remained in circulation in Bosnia, Croatia, and Serbia, and some were sold on the European black markets, particularly in Amsterdam and Austria.[58] For example, it is reported that almost all murders and suicides committed by firearms in Canton Sarajevo in 2003 were committed with weapons that were not licensed. Also many rapes, robberies, and drug-related crimes were committed with illegally held weapons.[59] In short, criminals, businessmen, and some politicians continued to generate high profits, and "greed" became a more significant factor in explaining the continuation of the arms smuggling business in the region. As sociologist Émile Durkheim once argued, human appetites are unlimited and people always want more, particularly when given the opportunity.

The "freedom fighters" and warlords, many of whom had criminal records even prior to the war, had the knowhow and connections and did not need much to redirect their goals from political to economic ones. Importantly, the role of the criminal segments of society in the regional arms trade strengthened with time, while high-level politicians—some of them former "freedom fighters"—have become slightly less involved in the arms trade due to growing international pressure.

Although the international community turned a blind eye to the illegal arms trade for years, this changed slightly after 2005. The growing export of weapons, particularly to Western Europe and the Western Balkan countries, including Bosnia, attracted significant international attention. As a result, over the last several years, various measures have been undertaken to address the problem of arms trafficking. In 2005–2011 particularly, this led to a number of publicized arrests and confiscations, making illegal arms trading a more visible criminal activity. There were some improvements on the legislative front as well. The communist-era laws on possession of firearms were replaced by much tougher ones. In addition, some of the surplus weapons owned by the national armies of the Western Balkans were destroyed as a part of a U.S.-sponsored program.

Meanwhile, closer cooperation between Serbian, Croatian, and Bosnian law enforcement agencies led to the disruption of several organized groups involved in the smuggling of weapons (mostly handguns and automatic pistols) to Italy, Austria, Great Britain, Ireland, the Netherlands, and farther west. Also, in 2010, the Court of Bosnia-Herzegovina indicted four Bosnian nationals for "illegal production and trafficking in arms and explosives." They were part of an organized crime group which, among other things, produced remotely controlled explosive devices that were smuggled into Serbia with the intention of being transported further to the Netherlands. Both Bosnia and Serbia remain an important part of the so-called Balkan route used to smuggle drugs and arms to Western Europe.

Despite a number of arrests of arm dealers there are still numerous weapons in circulation in the Balkans. According to the 2010 Small Arms Survey, there are about 22 illicit weapons per 100 citizens in Macedonia, 16 in Kosovo, 15 in Montenegro, 13 in Croatia and Bosnia, and 11 in Serbia.[60] Interviewed arms smugglers reported that most weapons now were imported into Bosnia and sold on, or made in official factories and sold through the black market unregistered or unrecorded. It was stated that about 20 percent of weapons made in the factories were sold on illegally.[61] Sources point out that many political figures in Bosnia, but also Kosovo and Croatia, "owe" favors to "criminals" that have helped them obtain weapons and get in power during the times of political instability, so they tolerate their illegal activities, without participating directly in them.[62] In fact many wartime criminals emerged from the war as part of the new elite, having close ties to politicians and the security sector. The complex and preexisting criminal-political ties are one of the reasons why this "business" is difficult to root out completely. Lupsha and Pimentel's stage-evolutionary model of the politics-crime nexus helps in understanding why and how the Balkan region came to experience a more profit-oriented form of weapons smuggling, involving sophisticated organized crime groups that enjoy state protection.

Paramilitary Activities, Extortion, and Racketeering

During conflicts, the line between the legal and the illegal, the admired and the detested, is a thin one. The nexus of gangsters, warlords, and politicians in Bosnia was visible not only in the arms smuggling sector, but in other illicit markets. Many "patriotic" bandits joined the Yugoslav wars and were quickly labeled "heroes" and "freedom fighters," despite the fact that during the same time they were extorting their co-patriots and trading illegal goods with their enemies.

A UN study (S/1994/674/Add.2) from December 1994 identifies 83 separate paramilitary forces operating in the former Yugoslavia during the early 1990s. The most significant units were the Green Berets and the Mujahideen operating in support of the government of Bosnia; the Croatian Defense Forces (Hrvatske obrambene snage, HOS) and Juka's army operating first in support of Bosniaks, and later in support of the Republic of Croatia; and the forces under the command of Arkan (Zeljko Raznatovic) and Vojislav Šešelj—another leader of Serbian paramilitary units—operating in support of the Former Republic of Yugoslavia and the self-declared Serbian Republics in Bosnia and Croatia. According to the study, these forces received attention because of the scope of their military operations; their direct links to their respective governments and militaries; the numerous allegations that these forces committed grave breaches of the Geneva Conventions and other violations of international humanitarian law; and their involvement in a range of other criminal activities. It is interesting to note that these combatants appeared different in their motives and modus operandi. Some were more and some less economically motivated. The motivational differences between the Mujahideen, for example, and the paramilitary groups such as that of "Juka" deserves some analysis.

Mujahideen, or holy warriors, is a term widely used for the Muslim volunteers fighting in the former Yugoslavia. Many of them were veterans of the Afghan war. It is reported that the mujahideen began arriving in Bosnia in June 1992. In 1993, they formed the El Midzahid battalion composed of 3,000 Islamic fighters, which was to serve under the Third Corps of the Bosnian army. Reports indicate that the mujahideen had the support of President Izetbegović and his government. These groups appeared to be less concerned with economic gains. Their main motivation was the spread of radical Islam.

Various sources and anecdotal evidence show that the mujahideen forces came to terrorize the Muslims they had come to protect in an effort to enforce Islamic practices. The Bosnian government tolerated this for a long time because of the need to win the war. Through the years, the Serbs and the Croats

---

YBP Library Services

CONFLICT, CRIME, AND THE STATE IN POSTCOMMUNIST
EURASIA; ED. BY SVANTE CORNELL.
                                Cloth   286 P.
PHILADELPHIA: UNIV OF PENNSYLVANIA PR, 2014

CO-EDITOR: UPPSALA UNIVERSITY. COLLECTION OF NEW
ESSAYS.

  ISBN 0812245652   **Library PO#** GENERAL APPROVAL
                                List   59.95 USD
  5461 UNIV OF TEXAS/SAN ANTONIO   **Disc**   17.0%
  App. Date 4/30/14 CRJ.APR   6108-11 **Net**   49.76 USD

SUBJ: POLITICAL VIOLENCE--ECON. ASPECTS--EURASIA--
CASE STUDIES.

CLASS JC328.6   DEWEY# 364.106095   LEVEL ADV-AC

have argued that the mujahideen presence is evidence that the Bosnian Muslims are intent on turning Bosnia into a fundamentalist Muslim state. The case of Jusuf Prazina (alias Juka) illustrates a different motivation for engaging in armed conflict. Jusuf Prazina was known in Sarajevo as a racketeer and underworld figure before the hostilities broke out in April 1992. Juka was sent to jail five times before the war. However, following the start of the siege of Sarajevo, this patriotic bandit was able to gather 3,000 men willing to defend Sarajevo from the attacks of the VRS.[63] Juka's group, known as the "Wolves," was armed with shotguns and Kalashnikovs.[64] When the conflict started in Bosnia, the government under Izetbegović and its formal army was unorganized. Thus the assistance of private armed groups such as Juka's was welcomed. As a favor, the group's prewar criminality was overlooked.[65]

Juka's forces appear to have played an integral role in defending Sarajevo at the early stages of the conflict. On a number of occasions they participated in actions orchestrated by leaders of other military units closely affiliated with the central government.[66] Juka was proclaimed a hero by the Bosnian press, while the Western media frequently portrayed him as a Robin Hood-style figure.[67] Juka was widely admired among Sarajevo's citizens, even appearing in contemporary patriotic songs.[68] From a criminal with a bad criminal record, Juka quickly became a national hero who, unfortunately, never abandoned his criminal past. [69]

Despite the myth surrounding Juka's heroism, he was known for his brutality not only toward the enemy but also toward his compatriots. He was a local racketeer who for years extorted money from businessmen in Sarajevo for his personal gain. During the war, Juka and his group are also reported to have killed and raped civilians. They allegedly looted houses, stole cars, and handed out Mostar apartments to the Croatian military. According to these confidential reports, he never stopped racketeering and the war just served his purpose. Juka reportedly controlled the Sarajevo black market, which included stolen UN humanitarian supplies.

Due to his success in defending Sarajevo, the Bosnian Government granted Juka the position as Head of the Special Forces during summer 1992. Nevertheless, he reportedly disappointed the Sarajevo authorities and was asked to resign after an allegedly threatening confrontation with Alija Izetbegović. In 1993, Juka officially joined forces with the enemy, the Croatian Defense Council (Hrvatsko Vijeće Obrane or HVO, a military formation in the self-proclaimed Croatian republic in Bosnia, Herzeg-Bosna). After the formal break between Bosniaks and Croats, Juka fought alongside the HVO in Mostar, where he is accused of leading ethnic cleansing operations. Juka lived in a villa on the Dalmatian coast given to him by Croatian authorities and later moved to Liege, Belgium. He was killed there by one of his body-guards in December 1993.[70]

The recruitment of ex-prisoners and criminals in the fight against "state enemies" was very common during the Yugoslav wars. In the fight against Bosnia and Kosovo, Serbia empowered Zeljko Raznatovic, better known as Arkan, and the Serbian "Tigers," some of the most notorious criminals in the Balkan region. Arkan and the "Tigers" were widely known for their brutality and links to the Serbian criminal underworld. They were some of the main smugglers of arms and cigarettes in the country and were involved in extortion, racketeering, and contract killings. Moreover, in Kosovo the KLA cooperated with notorious ethnic Albanian criminals inside and outside of Kosovo. For example, notorious Albanian mafia boss Victor Hoxha was known for collecting money from the Albanian diaspora in Belgium to support the KLA financially. From Belgium, the money was sent to the humanitarian organization Atdheu Thërret (The Motherland calls) set up by the KLA.

In Belgium, Hoxha was known for his involvement in extortion, racketeering, human trafficking, mediation in prostitution, aggravated assaults, and arms smuggling. The "voluntary taxes" he collected from the diaspora were not really voluntary. Confidential intelligence sources point out that if the Albanians did not pay taxes he was leaving bullets in front of their doors as a reminder that they must pay their dues.[71] Similarly to Juka in Bosnia, some of these criminals were seen as heroes by their compatriots. They continued to generate profits by exploiting their own people. Interviews conducted with Albanian offenders have led this author to the conclusion that one of the reasons why these criminals supported their politicians was the hope and expectation that they would be able to expand their criminal empires once these politicians gained power. As a consequence, favoritism continues to flourish in nontransparent postwar Bosnia, making the links between politics and crime stronger and leaving a legacy of institutional ambivalence toward illicit activities. In sum, the case of Juka illustrates that various actors in the war had very different profiles and different motivations, some more and some less economic in nature.

The Drug Trade

In Bosnia, favoritism, patriotism, and strong criminal-political ties are visible in the drug trafficking market. The Balkan route is well known for drug trafficking, particularly since the 1990s. This route involves trafficking goods, particularly heroin, from Turkey to Western Europe. Before reaching Western European distribution centers such as the Netherlands, it often travels via the Balkan countries. Prior to the Balkan conflicts, heroin went mainly through Serbia and Bosnia, but the 1992–1995 wars redirected part of the trade through Macedonia, Kosovo, and Albania. Since the early 2000s, it appears Bosnia once again has gained a prominent role in the drug trafficking chain. INTERPOL currently has a database of more than 280 names of Bosnian citizens involved in the transport and sale of drugs in Western Europe and more than 500 names of ethnic Albanian drug traffickers.[72]

According to intelligence sources, drug traffickers from the Balkan region have moved their criminal empires to Bosnia because of high levels of corruption, lack of transparency, and a weak and fragmented law enforcement and criminal justice system.[73] Not much was known about the Bosnian drug trafficking scene until several arrests in 2009 drew attention to the existence of a large-scale drug trafficking group operating on Bosnian territory.

In February 2009, three men (Açik Can, Hamdija Dačić, and Ljutivia Dačić) were arrested in Bosnia on charges of illegal trade of narcotics in Bosnia, Serbia, Hungary, Austria, Italy, Germany, France, and Spain, money laundering, abuse of position of authority, producing false balance sheets, and tax evasion. Intelligence information from 2009 points out that members of this network have expanded their operations in more than ten countries. The network comprises about 70–80 individuals of different nationalities and is considered one of the most sophisticated drug trafficking groups in the Balkans.[74]

According to EU law enforcement agencies and the Bosnia State Investigation and Protection Agency (SIPA), one of the active leaders involved in this network is an ethnic Albanian man called NK. With his family, including his two sons, and other regional associates, NK has been involved in smuggling of large quantities of heroin. The group has operated mainly from Bosnia, but has kept close ties with smaller groups throughout the Balkan region, including those composed of Serbians, Montenegrins, Turks, and Macedonians. They have also remained in close contact with ethnic Albanians from Germany, Switzerland, Spain, France, Mexico, the United Arab Emirates (UAE), and the United States.

Although born in Kosovo, NK holds dual citizenship in Bosnia and Montenegro. During the early 1990s, police reports show that NK was involved in the cigarette smuggling business, although no charges were brought against him. In 2001, UN Interim Administration Mission in Kosovo (UNMIK) police confiscated contraband cigarettes belonging to NK and his associate EL in the village of Zahać in Kosovo, with a value estimated at thousands of euros. In October 2002, members of the Italian police, while trying to disrupt the main cigarette smuggling routes in Kosovo, searched EL's business premises in Zahać and seized around 280 tons of cigarettes. EL and NK were taken into custody on charges of illegal tobacco production and selling of counterfeit cigarettes, although no trial was subsequently brought. Sources indicate that a large part of this money came into the hands of the KLA, which once more points out the political-criminal ties during times of armed conflict.[75]

After UNMIK placed too much attention on NK in Kosovo, he moved his criminal empire to Bosnia and acquired a Bosnian passport. Since the early 2000s, drug trafficking, particularly heroin, has become NK's primary criminal activity. In fact, this has become a common Balkan trend: although cigarette smuggling remains profitable in the region, many powerful and well-connected individuals who controlled the cigarette smuggling market during the 1990s moved into drug trafficking after 2000. The preexisting connections to influential politicians and customs officials were used to enter into a more lucrative market.[76]

NK's group often works with members of the Dačić family, who operate around Montenegro, Bosnia, and Sandzak, Serbia. The Dačić brothers, Hamdija and Ljutvia Dačić, have a long history of investigations and arrests related to drugs. In February 2009 Hamdija Dačić, who now has a Bosnian passport, was arrested by the Bosnian authorities on charges including drug trafficking and is currently awaiting trial.[77]

Ljutivia Dačić, also known as Haris Zornić, is wanted by German authorities in connection with the illegal trafficking of 46.6 kg of cocaine from Bosnia to Germany and Spain in the early 2000s, and was convicted of illegal weapons possession in Bosnia in 2005. Also arrested in February 2009 was Açik Can, who was born in Germany, but has Turkish citizenship and a permanent residence permit in Bosnia. He has been charged with drug trafficking, money laundering, and tax evasion. Law enforcement agencies indicate that the NK network has cooperated with groups from predominantly Muslim areas. Language and culture have facilitated this cooperation.

From the late 1990s on, members of ethnic Albanian, Montenegrin, and Sandzak criminal groups began selecting Sarajevo as their main place for warehousing and repackaging drugs, mainly heroin and marijuana but also cocaine, for shipments to Western Europe. A widely accepted estimate is that police in any country intercept between 5 and 20 percent of all illegal drugs shipped through that country. This would imply that Bosnia is the transshipment point for approximately 20 to 40 tons of heroin alone.[78] The Center for Investigative Journalism in Bosnia cited Nermin Legumdzija, head of the narcotics division of the Federation of Bosnia police, who explained in February 2009 that drug traffickers stock 100 to 200 kg of heroin and marijuana at all times in and around Sarajevo. The former chief of police in Novi Pazar, Saud Bulić, said in February 2009 that traffickers from his city send 20 to 30 kg of heroin to Sarajevo each week.

Other sources point to similar estimates. Interviews with drug traffickers point out that at least one metric ton of heroin enters Bosnia every month.[79] It is mixed with additives of about 200 kilos and resplit; a ton is exported to Western Europe, while the rest remains in Bosnia for transmission to the Balkan market. These 200 kg sell for approximately three million euros. When asked how this happens, the interviewed offenders stated that those involved have political support not just in Bosnia but in other Balkan countries. In addition, it was noted by the trafficker that much of the money gained was used to fund political parties. The transportation of drugs seems to happen along with legal commodities or alongside weapons or people.

The group of NK also smuggles ecstasy from EU countries to Bosnia, Montenegro, Serbia, and Turkey. Ecstasy smuggling is becoming a more popular business for criminal groups from Bosnia. In fact, police officers note that a lot of synthetic drugs come into Bosnia from the Netherlands where they are mixed with additives and sold on, primarily to end users in western European markets. It is alleged that traffickers get about 500 euros per kilo to transport speed across the border, further noting that one kilo would cost about six to seven thousand euros on the street.[80] Moreover, smuggling acetic anhydride, a main component in the production of cocaine and heroin, is becoming popular. In 2004, Montenegrin police at the Klobuk border crossing between Bosnia and Montenegro confiscated two cisterns that held 360 kg of 99 percent pure methanoic acid and 3,000 kg acetic anhydride. The police arrested two drivers from one of NK's Sarajevan companies. According to police information, the chemicals were ordered by an Austrian company and the customer was a company from Kosovo.[81]

According to Bosnian law enforcement officials,[82] members of NK's group—similar to other criminal organizations operating in the region—are investing in real estate in Bosnia and buying shares of companies in Bosnia,

Montenegro, and EU countries to launder money. NK and his sons own a number of businesses including hotels and a trucking company. NK has had business dealings with influential businessmen including real estate developer FR, who owns Bosnia's most widely circulated daily newspaper and is in negotiations to become Bosnia's new minister of security.[83] The Organized Crime and Corruption Reporting Project (OCCRP) has written extensively on NK connections to two of Bosnia's best-known wartime military leaders, and note that NK's best man is Muhamed Gasi, suspected of being a "capo of the Albanian mafia in Bosnia." The fact that Balkan criminal groups commonly purchase TV stations, shopping malls, hotels, and football clubs and infiltrate deeply into legitimate businesses and politics is a strong indication of the evolution of these criminal networks.[84]

After 2008 NK started attracting attention in Bosnia. The Sarajevo Canton prosecutor's office has consolidated thirteen potential criminal charges against NK and his group. As a result, large amounts of money started moving from Bosnia to Kosovo, most likely with the intention of relocating the criminal empire back to the hometown and gaining the trust of local politicians.[85] The multifaceted criminal-political-business nexus—largely a result of the Balkan conflicts—has turned the region into a safe haven for criminal organizations and has made politicians highly dependent on criminals, particularly white-collar ones.[86]

In June 2012, the White House sanctioned suspected Kosovar Albanian NK for drug trafficking. U.S. president Barack Obama notified Congress, saying he had sanctioned NK under the Kingpin Act, implemented by the U.S. Department of Treasury's Office of Foreign Assets Control (OFAC).[87] Currently, NK is on the run and is suspected to be hiding in Turkey.

Politics, Corruption and White-Collar Crime

Many conflict areas are among those perceived to be the most corrupt in the world. Corruption is seen as an impediment to peacebuilding, since it is linked to organized crime, terrorism, and state failure.[88] When transparency and accountability are absent, the risk of corruption threatens to turn the state apparatus into a tool of enrichment for those in power. Yet, in critical stages of postconflict stabilization, corruption might serve the function of a power-sharing arrangement between conflicting parties, and it might help politicians to buy out potential spoilers of the newly established peace. Illicit financial incentives might serve as a short-term mechanism to glue the fragile system together and prevent future conflicts. Such criminal-political compromises can be observed in Bosnia as well.

The argument made here is that although corruption may have some short-term positive outcomes that are overlooked by scholars and politicians, and while liberalization policies may also foster corruption, in the case of Bosnia and similarly to that of Kosovo, corruption appears to have an overwhelmingly negative impact on the long-term development of the country. It has the potential to lead to the escalation of violence and the creation of a criminalized state. In fact, the pervasiveness of corruption in Bosnia is widely portrayed as a major cause of the country's political and economic setbacks since the 1995 Dayton Accords. The most prominent UN report on peacekeeping operations argues that "support for the struggle against corruption" is the first priority among the "essential complements to effective peacebuilding."[89]

As illustrated above, because of the tight connections between politics and crime, criminals are presently able to operate in Bosnia without difficulties. Although some government attention has been placed on more visible crimes in the Balkan countries due to international pressure, "economic" or "financial" crimes, nevertheless, have been on the rise. The EU in 2003 estimated losses at 150–300 million euros per year, which is roughly equivalent to the annual state budget of Bosnia. A *New York Times* reporter in 1999 reported that nationalist leaders embezzled as much as one billion dollars in public funds and international aid since the signing of Dayton four years earlier.[90] The Guardia de Finanza in Italy compiled a report linking multinational tobacco companies and Balkan governments to cigarette smuggling rings. During the mid- to late 1990s, and even with heightened EU attention, the Western Balkans remained a warehouse facility for smuggled cigarettes throughout Europe. The EU antifraud office estimated the loss of tax revenue to member states was approximately 4.7 billion euros in 1998 alone. One container or truckload of cigarettes was worth approximately one million euros in tax revenue, so it was a very lucrative enterprise for criminal gangs. It has been suggested that the scale and logistical network necessary would not have been possible without the direct involvement of states and multinational companies.[91]

Moreover, since the domestic economic situation in Bosnia remains very bad, economic incentives for crime have become more important in recent years. Investigative agencies point out that the property records of politicians reported to the Central Election Commission (CIK) in Bosnia are in many cases incorrect. The wealth of leading politicians in Bosnia is much higher than that stated in their property records because their property is transferred to other persons, relatives, and bank accounts kept abroad.[92]

According to a 2010 Slovenian study, another problem is that recruitment of new politicians is practically impossible in Bosnia because of nepotism, nontransparent politics, and organized crime. Thus, new politicians may only enter the sphere if approved by the current political elites. As explained previously, connections between crime and politics were created during the period when Bosnia was gaining independence because the leading politicians at that time needed the services of criminal structures. Since then, the connections have become inseparable and can be defined as the "criminalization of politics and politicization of crime."

With "grand" forms of corruption, the problem is not that fraudulent individuals misuse public office, but that corrupt practices affect a whole government, the entire institutional apparatus. In such systems, corrupted practices are institutionalized and deeply embedded in state institutions. When corruption reaches these levels, fraudulent elites have the ability to permanently embed themselves into state institutions, thereby transforming the state into a corruption-addicted social configuration. Prime examples are neopatrimonial states or "parallel states" in which governments, that is, the ruling elite, co-opt key individuals within the state by giving them personal benefits in exchange for their loyalty.[93] The culmination of the institutionalization of corrupt practices leads to state capture, the phenomenon when state institutions embrace criminal organizations and fraudulent purposes.[94]

Although there are many obstacles to anticorruption programs, political will is one of the most fundamental hurdles. Margolies suggests that "the question of state involvement is of particular relevance during or after conflict, when stakeholders may attempt to achieve an agreement at any cost."[95] She argues that if political leaders do not support an anticorruption agenda, it is most likely that anticorruption measures are not going to bring any progress. Political will is unlikely to be present if key political actors themselves are engaged in corrupt activities, as has been the case in Bosnia for a long time. In 2010, the International Institute for Middle-East and Balkan Studies (IFIMES) provided several examples of these criminal-political ties in Bosnia, although none of the actors mentioned in the report have been prosecuted.[96]

Where Is Bosnia Heading?

Bosnia has had a troublesome past. The origins of the war were clearly in line with the "grievance" approach to conflict. The militarized conflict, the wish for autonomy, and the ethnic security dilemmas gradually opened the way for political-criminal alliances in Bosnia. The deficit in weaponry during the Bosnian war and the UN embargo imposed on the former Yugoslavia combined to force Bosnian president Izetbegović to turn to Islamic countries and charities for assistance.[97] It appears that the Bosnian Muslim government in Sarajevo had no choice but to seek assistance from the Islamic world as well as from the international community to secure the Bosniaks' physical survival. Both Bosniaks and Croats had to rely more directly on organized criminals, as these were best placed to mobilize large cadres of fighters quickly.

Hence, organized criminals became central to the war effort early on. Such accommodation between authorities and organized crime have fostered a tolerance of criminal activity among the population, with certain types of crime considered beneficial both for the population's income generation as well as a source of revenue for the state authorities.

These criminal-political alliances continued and even strengthened after the end of the war in 1995. The Dayton Accords created a state that was erroneously expensive to run due to its highly decentralized nature, one where there was no clear power-sharing mechanisms, which contained weak or nonexistent state level institutions and one which was divided along ethnic lines. As time went by, economic incentives became more important than political ones for some actors in Bosnia, since the war brought benefits to segments of Bosnian society, including the political leadership. After the conflict, insurgent and criminal groups have used corruption as a postconflict tactic. Although the motivation for most corruption is conventional financial gain, in a number of cases corruption appears to have been employed to achieve a specific operational end, for example, a short-term truce with a challenger. Since the state had to deal with many spoilers to the peace agreement after the conflict, the creation of ties between politicians, insurgents, and criminal groups seemed inevitable and led to a lack of political will to combat organized crime. This "trinity" consisting of nationalistic parties, a corrupt security sector, and criminal groups has marked postconflict Bosnia.

Moreover, the weakness of Bosnian law enforcement agencies, the deteriorating economic situation, and the political reluctance to face problems related to organized crime all contributed to the development of politicized criminal networks.[98] Bosnia's state authority is organized in a dysfunctional, asymmetrical way: two entities are functioning as if they were individual countries (Republika Srpska and the Bosnia-Herzegovina Federation), and these entities are, moreover, organized on three different levels of authority. This would not be a problem in a modern decentralized state, however, in Bosnia it is a serious problem. The politicization of the police has contributed to deficient law enforcement policies, and criminals have benefited from the fragmented policing structures. In particular, the postwar absence of law enforcement agencies in areas controlled by Bosniaks and Croats greatly facilitated the growth of criminal networks. Thus the growth of organized criminal activity, at first a spillover effect of conflict given the decrease of state control, formed a strong incentive for insurgent groups to become involved in organized crime to reap profits in return for short-term "stability."

Moreover, Bosnia, which has an important role on the Balkan heroin route, has a poor record in controlling drug trafficking. There is no specialized drug enforcement agency either on the state level or within the two Bosnian entities—possibly a result of the lack of political will to deal with these forms of criminality. The effort to contain drug smugglers is left to customs and local police, which have neither the cadres nor the equipment to deal with organized crime groups. Organized crime groups, of course, take advantage of the situation. Once a heroin shipment reaches Serbia, moving it to Croatia either directly or through Bosnia is not a serious challenge.[99]

Since the 2000s, the international community has put some pressure on Bosnia to deal with organized crime and corruption. In Bosnia, most of the help to promote democratic processes has come from abroad. The alleged willingness to focus on countering criminal figures is largely internationally led. At the highest level, the Office of the High Representative (OHR) coordinates the activities of the different international actors and programs. On the military side, NATO's Implementation Force (IFOR), Stabilization Force (SFOR), and the European Union Military Force (EUFOR) have tried to stabilize Bosnia. EUFOR in particular has engaged in the fight against organized crime. During its first mandate EUFOR even set up roadblocks to deter criminals.

Traditional police tasks were taken up by the UN International Police Task Force (UNIPTF) created at Dayton; at its peak it had 2,000 officers. In 2003, the European Union Police Mission in Bosnia and Herzegovina (EUPM) followed with a general mandate to support police reforms and after 2008 their priority has been organized crime. One of its successful international projects in Bosnia was the implementation of the reform of the armed forces in Bosnia.

The engagement of various international actors in Bosnia has been extensive, and the international community has done a lot for the Bosnian government and its people. This pressure no doubt has led to some improvements, however, not every form of criminality was tackled with the same enthusiasm—very much as a result of the ongoing criminalization of the political arena. Criminals have secured places in the parliament in order to obtain political immunity, leading to closer collusion between crime and politics.

While the Bosnian criminal code defines organized crime, measuring the extent and nature of organized crime is difficult. The National Strategy for Fighting Organized Crime and Corruption in Bosnia and Herzegovina 2006–2009 falls short of a systematic threat assessment. Moreover, international actors have repeatedly criticized Bosnian law enforcement as institutionally incapable of prosecuting complicated and high-level cases of crime and corruption.

In parallel, there has been lack of coherence among international programs as well as a lack of appropriate competences and capacities to achieve policy goals. In a number of instances, the international presence has added fuel to the fire and has contributed to the rise of some illegal markets, such as smuggling of cigarettes, human trafficking, and prostitution.[100] Regardless of the obvious failures of the international community in relation to Bosnia, the common feeling is that it should remain present in the country. There are many nationalistic and highly corrupt politicians active in Bosnia that may drive the country downhill, thus the presence of the international community appears necessary.[101] A question often raised at the international level is whether the country can survive as a state. If the international community leaves, will organized crime groups resurface, being able to operate undeterred?

Although there are indications that Bosnia would risk turning into a criminalized state in the absence of international pressure, research regarding victimization published in 2002 shows that citizens in Bosnia, for one or another reason, feel safer than citizens in other European countries. Available data suggest that by 2007 and 2008, neither petty crime nor organized crime was perceived as a big problem in Bosnia, as it may have been in the 1990s. According to a 2009 UNODC study, conventional crime is lower in Bosnia than in many EU states. It is worth noting that since 2009, the international community, including INTERPOL, is of the opinion that some countercrime efforts appear to be improving and the country is more open to cooperation.[102] These are indications that although organized crime remains a serious issue for the future of Bosnia, there is some praiseworthy progress. Yet, one should always be open to the scenario that Bosnia's peace and stability are a result of successful negotiations between politicians, criminals, and insurgents, making the present calm superficial and potentially short-lived.

Chapter 9

The Kosovo Conflict: From Humanitarian Intervention to State Capture

Michael Jonsson

Kosovo has played a central part in the demise of Yugoslavia. It was here that the reemergent Serbian nationalism first reared its head in the late 1980s and it was here that the final act in the violent breakup of Yugoslavia played out. For eight years, the largely pacifist resistance against the nullification of Kosovo's autonomy was led by the Democratic League of Kosovo (LDK) under Ibrahim Rugova. But the lack of any palpable progress gradually shifted support to the more militant Kosovo Liberation Army (KLA), which through violent attacks managed to provoke the Serbian security forces into excessive repression, sparking the Kosovo war in 1998. During this period, the connection between the KLA and ethnic Albanian drug traffickers using the Balkan route was extensively reported in Western media and well known among Western intelligence agencies. Following a short cease-fire and failed negotiations, the war was reignited in March 1999 and concluded by a 78-day aerial campaign led by NATO in 1999. Following this, Kosovo was governed as an international protectorate by UNMIK with an uncertain international status, receiving large amounts of aid and a sizable peacekeeping force, while domestic government agencies were gradually being created and handed increasing power—eventually obtaining "conditional independence" in 2008.

The extensive funding that the KLA received primarily from drug traffick-ers and the Kosovo Albanian diaspora prior to, during, and immediately fol-lowing the end of the conflict has been widely recognized by Western law enforcement and intelligence agencies. Following the end of conflict, the police mission of UNMIK and from 2008 the European Union Rule of Law Mission (EULEX) have made substantial efforts to crack down on organized crime and grand corruption. The results have, however, been limited, in part due to witness intimidation, large-scale riots resulting from the arrest of for-mer KLA members, and a diplomatic prioritization of stability over the rule of law. In spite of vast resources invested in peacekeeping and institution-building, the end result is far from a resounding success, instead illustrating the many challenges to state-building created by the legacies of an extensive crime-insurgency nexus. Thirteen years after the fighting concluded, the risk of state capture by organized crime is significant and the establishment of stable democracy remains elusive.

Actors: LDK and KLA

Whereas competing ethnonationalist narratives over who has the right to govern Kosovo base their claims on historical events spanning centuries, it was developments during the 1980s and 1990s that eventually triggered the Kosovo conflict. In 1974 Kosovo had been awarded status as an autonomous region within Yugoslavia, formally acknowledged in the new constitution adopted that year. This, however, created an imbalance, since Kosovo was effectively awarded the rights of a full republic in the Yugoslav Federation, but on paper remained part of the Serbian Union Republic. Albanians ap-pear to have believed that Yugoslav strongman Josip Broz Tito had promised to upgrade Kosovo to a full republic within the Yugoslav Federation, some-thing that led to large-scale Albanian protests following his death in May 1980.[1] Instead, developments went in the opposite direction, with the rebirth of Serbian nationalism based partly on a narrative of "the sufferings of the Serbian nation," including in Kosovo. In 1987, Slobodan Milošević rose to prominence in Serbian politics partly by exploiting the growing discontent over the situation of Serbs in Kosovo. In 1989, he gave a now infamous speech at the Field of Blackbirds in Kosovo, the site of a historical battle in 1389 between Serbs and Ottoman Turks. The speech came on the heels of a new constitution pushed through by Milošević in early 1989, which drastically reduced the autonomy of the region, leading to extensive protests.[2]

The same year, literary scholar Rugova assumed leadership of the LDK, a newly formed party that resisted the nullification of Kosovo's autonomy. The LDK under Rugova pursued a strategy of pacifist resistance against the Serbian state, setting up a parallel education and welfare system in Kosovo. These institutions were funded largely through the "3 percent fund," which received donations from the Kosovo Albanian diaspora in Western Europe and the United States.[3] Money was collected through fundraisers among the diaspora, with individuals expected to pay up to 10 percent of the profits from companies they owned or 3 percent of their wages, hence giving the fund its name. These donations ranged from voluntary to the verge of extortion, with significant pressure to contribute, not least bearing in mind relatives still residing in Kosovo.[4]

Parallel to the widely supported LDK, the smaller, militant KLA was also created in 1993. Whereas the origins of the KLA are not entirely clear, it appears that the organization gathered a variety of militant groups and individuals that all had one common goal—the liberation of Kosovo through organized armed struggle. Its ranks were filled with a diverse set of characters, ranging from established organized criminals to Marxist-Leninist followers of the late Albanian president Enver Hoxha's ideas of a Greater Albania.[5] However, a majority of its members were young Kosovo Albanians or exiles with no experience of the Yugoslavian political life, which contributed to their more militant strategy and uncompromising approach regarding Serbian authority in Kosovo. By comparison, the vast majority of the LDK leadership had participated in the political life of Yugoslavia, hence giving them a more moderate and political perspective on the possible solution of Kosovo's status. In its early days, the KLA seems to have received a majority of its weapons and training from Albania, which they also used as a rear operating base. As a consequence, the KLA was initially mainly active in southern and western Kosovo.[6] However, for a long time, the Serbian security forces were successful in countering the hit-and-run tactics of the KLA, and as late as 1997 the organization is estimated to have had no more than 150 full-time, armed members.[7]

Whereas the LDK was long the dominant political force and the preferred channel of political resistance in Kosovo, several geopolitical events eventually started shifting popular support toward the more militant approach advocated by the KLA. The Dayton Agreement, which ended the fighting in Bosnia-Herzegovina in 1995, did not reward the patient and pacifist resistance of the Kosovo Albanians with autonomy, leading to widespread disappointment.[8] In 1997, neighboring Albania descended into chaos after extensive pyramid schemes in which large segments of the population had invested money collapsed. During this period, army stockpiles were looted and light weapons were easily and cheaply available, facilitating the arming of the burgeoning insurgency of the KLA based there.[9] Step by step, these events started to tip the scales in favor of the more militant approach sought by the KLA.

Balkan Organized Crime and Kosovo

Parallel to the growing political unrest inside Kosovo, ethnic Albanian organized crime—centered around Albania, but also in Kosovo, northern Macedonia, and southern Serbia—grew and diversified, both geographically and in terms of criminal markets in which they were active.[10] The 1990s and early 2000s saw a steady ascent of Albanian-speaking organized crime, with criminals gradually moving from being the hit men of particularly Italian organized crime groups, into trafficking in drugs and humans, and eventually taking partial control over several illicit markets in Western Europe.[11] There were several domestic, geopolitical, and cultural drivers behind this rapid expansion and diversification. In Albania, the removal of President Hoxha in 1990 and the disbanding of the security service Sigurimi in 1992 left some 10,000 former security officials unemployed, some of whom went into organized crime.[12]

During the 1990s, driven by economic decline, an estimated 600,000 Albanians emigrated to Italy and Greece, where they often became easy recruits for Albanian-speaking organized crime groups. Geopolitically, the UN sanctions against Yugoslavia created ample opportunities to generate income from smuggling through Montenegro. In 1997, massive pyramid schemes in which approximately two-thirds of the population had invested money collapsed, causing major upheavals in the country.[13] Culturally, the Albanian ethos of *kanun*, which emphasizes violent revenge, hospitality, honor, silence, self-reliance, and the subjugation of women, arguably also helped fuel the ascent of Albanian criminals.[14]

Ethnic Albanian criminals frequently engaged in excessive violence, generating notoriety in criminal circles but also attracting extensive law enforcement attention. These networks initially tended to center around extended families or clan structures and emphasized total loyalty, exacting bloody revenge against any defectors or their extended families.[15] During the 1990s, much of the Albanian-speaking organized crime groups engaged mainly in trafficking in women and heroin. In Albania, organized crime early on established links with politicians, and law enforcement officers were reluctant to tackle the problem, since it was believed that major crime figures would simply find ways of short-circuiting the judicial process and officers involved in investigations might be killed.[16] In end-user markets, mainly in Western Europe, law enforcement prosecuted these networks vigorously, but these efforts were hampered due to challenges of translating wiretaps of conversations in Albanian, the code of silence, and the difficulty of planting informants. Italian prosecutor Cataldo Motta, who has worked extensively on combating Albanian organized crime, commented to scholar Jana Arsovska that "We know how to fight against our own mafia, but now we have a new one—and it is a foreign culture we do not understand."[17]

In conclusion, Albanian-speaking organized crime rose to prominence due to several geopolitical and national changes. In parallel, the KLA expanded and recruited some former LDK members as a result of the frustration with the perceived futility of the Kosovo Albanian pacifist resistance against Serbia.[18] Much as the existing literature would predict, the interaction and overlap between these two phenomena proved mutually enabling, making the KLA stronger militarily and later on paving the way for more extensive drug trafficking in the region. In relation to the extensive scholarly debate on motives of rebel groups, it can thus be noted that it was a political grievance—the perceived mistreatment of ethnic Albanians in Serbia—that motivated popular resistance, whereas it was actors with clear greed motives that eventually managed to appropriate this cause.[19]

The Kosovo War, 1998–1999

During 1996 and 1997, attacks by the KLA increased in frequency, on occasion killing members of the Serbian security forces, Serbian civilians, and alleged Albanian "collaborators." Serbian security forces were, however, relatively successful in containing the problem and arresting KLA operatives, making the organization into a minor nuisance rather than a major security threat. It was also during this period that the U.S. special envoy to the Balkans, Robert Gelbracht, labeled the KLA as "without any question a terrorist group," a statement that the Milošević regime may have interpreted as an implicit green light to continue repression.[20] The definitive spark for the war in Kosovo was two consecutive attacks against the family compound of Shaban Jashari, whose son Adem was a local leader of the KLA in Donji Prekaz. A first attack on the family compound in January 1998 was repelled, according to Adem himself, after he received support from "friends from the woods," that is, other KLA fighters. In early March, the Serbian armed forces returned, killing an estimated fifty-eight Kosovo Albanians, including eighteen women and ten children. Amnesty International concluded that the aim of the operation was to "eliminate the suspects and their families."[21]

This event, together with a handful of similar massacres carried out by the Serbian security forces, definitely tipped the scales among the Kosovo Albanian diaspora in favor of supporting violent resistance. The KLA was nevertheless still poorly organized, and its organizational structure in 1998 has been described as "essentially anarchic" and "more resembling an association of clans than a hierarchical military force."[22] Consequently, central command and control of the organization was poor and local commanders initiated attacks without first consulting with the KLA central leadership. Two attacks in June and July of 1998—against a coal mine and a centrally located city in Kosovo respectively—were initiated without consultation with the central KLA command and provoked the first Serbian counteroffensive, which swept away all KLA resistance.[23]

During this period, the KLA was funded through the Homeland Calling Fund. Similar to the "3 percent fund," funding came from the Kosovo Albanian diaspora in Western Europe and the United States, and as violence increased, revenue gradually shifted from the former toward the latter fund. According to some sources, the 3 percent fund was forced to hand over some of its funds to the Homeland Calling Fund.[24] According to German security officials, the KLA received roughly half of its funding directly or indirectly from drug traffickers. In exchange for money, weapons, and material and logistical assistance, drug traffickers were given permission to smuggle drugs through Kosovo and other areas controlled by the KLA.[25]

Whereas often described as pacifist, the LDK set up its own armed wing, known as the Armed Forces of the Republic of Kosovo (FARK). This unit was, however, beset by a number of setbacks. In 1993, almost all its general staff were arrested in Priština, and in fall 1998 several of its members were arrested in Tirana, accused of involvement in a coup attempt against the Albanian government led by Fatos Nano. The leader of FARK, Ahmet Krasniqi, was also killed in Tirana that fall, a murder often attributed to the KLA. FARK nonetheless sent forces into Kosovo to combat Serbian troops during 1998. But relations to the KLA remained tense, with alleged beatings and disarmament of FARK fighters by KLA members. By the fall of 1999, FARK formally dropped its name and joined the general KLA structure.[26]

These seeming contradictions illustrate a central point. Whereas using names suggesting formal, hierarchical organizational structures, the Kosovo resistance built more on the affiliations and animosities between individuals and clans than on discrete bureaucratic organizations. Hence, there was occasional conflict within each group and ad hoc collaborations between them.[27] According to a German intelligence report, for example, a leading KLA member was reported to have informed the Serbs regarding an incoming arms shipment destined for FARK. The same leader is, however, claimed to have put the head of the LDK financial unit in touch with organized crime figures, presumably increasing the incomes of the movement.[28]

The conflict itself developed in fits and starts, with small-scale KLA attacks followed by excessive Serbian counterattacks, intermingled with political and diplomatic efforts aimed at generating international support. In March 1998, Rugova was again elected "president" of Kosovo with 99 percent of the votes cast, and in April 95 percent of the Serbs voted no to any foreign intervention in the Kosovo conflict. By October, under direct threats of NATO airstrikes, Serbian security forces withdrew from Kosovo. In December 1998, in spite of the cease-fire agreement, KLA forces took up positions outside Priština and killed several Serbian teenagers in northern Kosovo, in the so-called Panda Café massacre, followed by the Račak massacre, perpetrated by Serbian forces. In February and March 1999, negotiations were held in Rambouillet in France, during which the Serbian side were offered terms that many analysts believe they could never have accepted, such as NATO troops having free access to Serbian territory. In March 1999, NATO forces initiated an extensive bombing campaign, controversially also attacking nonmilitary targets inside Serbia proper, including Serbian state television. On the ground, the KLA worked as the de facto ally of NATO, directing air strikes and allegedly cooperating with Western special forces inside the territory. By June 1999, after severe damage had been done to its infrastructure, the Milošević regime agreed to a cessation of hostilities.[29] The conflict is estimated to have led to the death of approximately 12,000–14,000 civilians, three-quarters of them ethnic Albanians, whereas only some 400 Serbian military personnel died along with a handful of NATO soldiers.[30]

During the run-up to the war, the U.S. and European approach toward the KLA shifted quickly and dramatically, driven by the perceived inevitability of war combined with NATO reluctance to put "boots on the ground." Hence, whereas Gelbracht labeled the KLA terrorists in February 1998, by May the United States had established high-level contacts with the group, and by July 1999 the special envoy instead reported to the U.S. Congress that the KLA was a "reality on the ground."[31] As a consequence, the U.S. and European countries provided military training to the KLA and did not inhibit its arming and fundraising. In 1998, private military companies from the U.S., UK, and Germany trained KLA fighters in Albania and approximately 400 American Albanians participated in the fighting in the so-called Atlantic Brigade.[32] As opposed to the conflict in Bosnia-Herzegovina, the supply of funds or fighters from transnational Islamist networks seems to have been negligible.

Conflict Actors and Organized Crime: The Role of the KLA

An extensive literature of scholarly research, investigative journalism, and intelligence reports has linked the KLA to ethnic Albanian drug trafficking networks.[33] Funds came from ordinary Albanians in the diaspora as well as drug traffickers. This support was not limited to money, but drug traffickers also sent armed men to fight alongside the KLA, equipped with modern weaponry. Whereas the connection between the KLA and drug trafficking is hard to quantify, there are known court cases from Germany, Italy, and the Czech Republic that all strongly suggest a connection between drug traffickers and the KLA, in the form of monetary support or even buying weaponry, some of it quite heavy.[34] It also seems that drug trafficking correlated with the violence in Kosovo, increasing during the buildup before the conflict and then growing further after the fighting ended.[35] Furthermore there seems to have been a geospatial correlation, with armed resistance from the KLA being the strongest in areas where drug trafficking networks were the most well-entrenched, such as the Drenica Valley and the Dukagjani region.[36] The total amounts collected by the KLA are difficult to estimate. Hence, "guesstimates" vary with an order of magnitude and tend to correlate with the political sympathies of the source. For example, leaked Western intelligence estimates written at the time suggested that as much as 500 million deutsche marks were collected.[37]

By the standards of most insurgencies this would have been a very large sum and it is quite possible that the figure errs on the side of exaggeration.

Last and crucially, Western intelligence agencies clearly seem to have been aware of the connection between the KLA and drug traffickers, not the least since it had been reported as early as 1994.[38] Answering a question from Senator Charles Grassley (R-Iowa), President Clinton admitted during spring 1999 that the DEA and CIA knew that drug traffickers "have contributed at least limited funds and possibly small arms to the KLA." A congressional expert on the drug trade stated anonymously that there was "no doubt that the KLA is a major trafficking organization" and a similarly anonymous State Department official said the United States was doing nothing to stem drug trafficking.[39] European law enforcement agencies were more open in acknowledging these links and active in countering such practices than their U.S. counterparts.[40] Presumably, this was a result of Europe being the main end-user market of heroin trafficked through the region.

Organized Crime in Kosovo Following the End of the Conflict

Following the end of the Kosovo war, it was reported that Kosovo became more open to drug traffickers, as the Serbian police withdrew and the Kosovo Force (KFOR) did not seek to tackle the trade directly.[41] Numerous reports have also indicated that there has been a steep increase in drug, arms, and human trafficking, as well as prostitution, in Kosovo following the end of the war. The demand for the latter may inadvertently have been boosted by the presence of UNMIK personnel. This increase took place in spite of the presence of 25 times more money and 50 times more security personnel per capita being poured into Kosovo than into Afghanistan shortly following the removal of the Taliban.[42] In 2002, the NATO-led KFOR pledged to target organized crime in Kosovo. Simultaneously, diplomats worried that there would be a backlash if prominent Albanian politicians were arrested by international forces on suspicions of involvement in organized crime.[43] Beyond this, there seems to have been competition over both political office and turf, that is, control over illicit sources of income in Kosovo, ranging from drug and human trafficking and extortion, to smuggling of cigarettes and building materials, temporarily increasing local insecurity.[44] A large number of murders were committed following the official end of the war, targeting Serbian civilians and alleged Albanian "collaborators," as well as score-settling between the KLA and LDK, and inside the KLA. The estimated number of murders varies between 470 and approximately 1,000.[45]

Legacies of the KLA-Organized Crime Nexus

Following the end of the conflict, about half the estimated 20,000 members of the KLA returned to their earlier occupations. In mapping the legacies of the KLA, this section focuses on four main pursuits that the other half of the group engaged in: political participation, mainly through the political parties the Kosovo Democratic Party (PDK) and Alliance for the Future of Kosovo (AAK); involvement in the nascent security structures of Kosovo, including the Kosovo Protection Corps (KPC), which later transformed into the Kosovo Security Forces (KSF), the Kosovo Police Service, and the informal "intelligence wing" of the KLA, the National Intelligence Service (SHIK); involvement in armed successor groups in neighboring states such as the National Liberation Army (NLA) in Macedonia and the Liberation Army of Preševo, Medveđa and Bujanovac (UCPMB) in Serbia; and organized crime.[46]

Political Legacies of the KLA

Although the KLA was formally disbanded following the conflict, one way of getting a sense for the legacy of the organization is to track the life stories of prominent former KLA commanders.[47] This section traces the political careers of some of the most prominent KLA commanders, listing credible allegations of their involvement in organized criminality, based on leaked intelligence estimates and criminal investigations, prosecutions, and trials, to evaluate whether the crime-insurgency nexus during the conflict has any bearing on the political situation in Kosovo today.

Hashim Thaçi was spokesperson of the KLA and played a central role during the Rambouillet negotiations, in spite of being only thirty-one. Following the war, he became head of the PDK, and by 2012 he had been prime minister for four years, making him one of the most influential politicians in Kosovo.

During the same period, numerous sources also claim he was one of the central leaders of organized crime in Kosovo. According to a German intelligence report on organized crime in Kosovo, Thaçi was one of the leaders of the so-called "Drenica Group."[48] Likewise, a leaked KFOR intelligence assessment produced around 2004 also named Thaçi as one of a triumvirate of "biggest fish" involved in organized crime in Kosovo.[49] Based on similar intelligence documents and extensive primary sources, a report adopted by the Council of Europe painted an equally critical picture. According to the report, "Thaçi's 'Drenica group' built a formidable power base in the organized criminal enterprises that were flourishing in Kosovo and Albania at the time."[50] Perhaps more damning than the allegations per se—which have circulated for years—was the public nature of the report, its extensive sourcing and the very explicit findings:

> Notably, in confidential reports spanning more than a decade, agencies dedicated to combating drug smuggling in at least five countries have named Hashim Thaçi and other members of his "Drenica Group" as having exerted violent control over the trade in heroin and other narcotics. Similarly, intelligence analysts working for NATO, as well as those in the service of at least four independent foreign governments, made compelling findings through their intelligence-gathering related to the immediate aftermath of the conflict in 1999. Thaçi was commonly identified, and cited in secret intelligence reports, as the most dangerous of the KLA's "criminal bosses."[51]

The most gruesome section of the report recounts how a small subset of prisoners during and after the war were killed and used in human organ trafficking, but does not directly implicate Thaçi in these events. These allegations were originally raised by the former ICTY prosecutor Carla del Ponte, and generated extensive international attention.[52] Politics in Kosovo has been exceptionally exposed to international scrutiny due to the extensive peacekeeping and police presence in the region, and wrongdoings that may have gone unnoticed in other countries are more likely to be brought to public attention here. That being said, it is hard to think of another case where the acting prime minister has simultaneously been identified as a major organized crime figure in an official report published by an international organization.

Ramush Haradinaj was the regional commander of the Dukagjin zone in Kosovo during the war. Following the NATO intervention, he founded and became the leader of the AAK, the second major legacy party of the KLA. Haradinaj became the prime minister in December 2004, but stepped down in March 2005 after being indicted by the ICTY.

As is the case with Thaçi, several intelligence documents and reports claim that Haradinaj is a leading organized crime figure in Kosovo.[53] Spectacular violent incidents and criminal cases further reinforce this impression. In July 2000, Haradinaj and his brother Daut were injured during a shootout with former members of FARK, and Ramush was flown to a U.S. army base in Germany to receive treatment. In 2002, his brother Daut was convicted with four other men for kidnapping, torturing, and killing four former members of FARK. Three years later, three key witnesses and two policemen investigating the case had been murdered.[54] Such events mirrors fears in Albania during the 1990s, where investigators were loath to pursue complex organized crime cases for fear of being subjected to revenge attacks.

Haradinaj had also been investigated by the war crimes tribunal in The Hague, but was acquitted due to insufficient evidence, which may in large part be explained by blatant witness intimidation. In 2010, he was called to a partial retrial by the ICTY for the persecution and abduction of civilians in the Dukagjin area in 1998. Of 100 witnesses, 34 were allowed to conceal their identities, 18 had to be subpoenaed because they refused to appear, and while in court, some witnesses stated openly that they dared not testify. In total, the case against Haradinaj was among the most problematic in the entire ICTY process.[55] Former KLA fighters were reportedly the most frightened among the witnesses and at least three witnesses were murdered prior to the trial. In spite of this, Western diplomats had sought to convince prosecutor del Ponte to refrain from indicting Haradinaj, arguing he played an important role in stabilizing Kosovo.[56] Thus, witness intimidation and victimization, seeming impunity for senior KLA commanders, and Western prioritization of stability over justice were illustrated quite clearly during the course of this case.

Fatmir Limaj was a former commander of the KLA and the deputy president of the PDK. In 2005, Limaj was tried on war crimes charges but acquitted and greeted with street celebrations in Priština. In spite of such suspicions, Limaj became the Minister of Transportation and Telecommunication in Kosovo in 2008–2010, a role that has led to an investigation on suspicion of corruption related to tenders for the construction of roads. As a sign of the sensitivity of the case, Limaj had reportedly been offered a diplomatic post outside Kosovo as part of a "soft landing."[57]

In March 2011, Limaj was again questioned by EULEX, this time related to murders committed during the war.[58] Initially, the former minister claimed immunity under a controversial law that protects members of parliament from prosecution. The constitutional court of Kosovo eventually clarified that the law does not apply to actions taken by MPs outside their responsibilities as parliamentarians and Limaj was put under house arrest in September 2011.[59]

A key witness in the prosecution was Agim Zogaj, initially known as "Witness X," a former KLA member who had kept a careful diary of events during his tenure as a "prison guard," including names of victims and locations of events. Events recorded in his journal were corroborated by physical evidence such as the discovery of bodies at the locations and with the types of injuries Zogaj had described. Zogaj had been residing with his brother in Germany, presumably under the EULEX witness protection program. Only a few weeks after Limaj's arrest, Zogaj was nevertheless found dead in a public park in Germany, from what investigators wrote off as a suicide. However, prior to his death, Zogaj had reported being threatened by the brother of Limaj, who said that Zogaj's family would be killed if he testified. Given events during similar trials and that the family was still residing in Kosovo, these threats presumably seemed highly credible. Zogaj's brother stated that he did not believe his brother had committed suicide or that if he had, he had been pressured into doing so. [60] Following the death of Zogaj, the budget for the EULEX witness protection program was expanded.[61] In late March 2012, the court ruled the late Zogaj's evidence was inadmissible, leading Limaj to be set free pending conclusion of the trial. In November 2012, however, Kosovo's EU-led Supreme Court ordered a retrial, stating that Zogaj's testimony would be admissible.[62] The same month, Limaj was charged by EULEX with organized crime and corruption, largely related to embezzlement of funds during tenders for public contracts.[63]

Xhavit Haliti, former head of logistics for the KLA, by 2011 was a senior parliamentarian for the PDK and a close ally to Prime Minister Thaçi. During the war, Haliti was broadly seen as the main finance and logistics officer of the KLA and as such controlled funds collected through the Homeland Calling Fund. Numerous reports suggest that Haliti siphoned off some of those funds and amassed a personal fortune and turned to organized crime following the end of the war.[64] Haliti is also seen as one of the leaders of the SHIK, the informal intelligence wing of the KLA.[65] This organization has been accused of several murders committed shortly after the end of the formal fighting in Kosovo.[66] Intelligence reports point to him as the "gray eminence" of the party.[67]

These four cases illustrate perhaps the clearest indications of a political legacy of the KLA coupled with credible allegations of involvement in organized crime. A cursory review of other senior KLA commanders reveals a similar, if somewhat less dramatic picture.[68]

Former KLA commanders routinely depict any accusations against them for war crimes or organized criminality as the work of foreign conspiracies and repeat that they fought a just war of liberation.[69] Serbian authorities and individuals have indeed disseminated evidence and allegations that clearly seek to implicate KLA commanders in drug trafficking and war crimes.[70] That said, the number of sources, criminal cases, and secondary evidence substantiating this connection are simply too numerous, varied, and credible to be dismissed. The blatant witness intimidation and victimization during trials against former KLA commanders are particularly disturbing, especially in relation to the future of rule of law in Kosovo. In the Council of Europe report, Marty sums up these events and their implications:

> Everything leads us to believe that all of these men [Haliti, Veseli, Syla, Limaj, and Thaçi, author's clarification] would have been convicted of serious crimes and would by now be serving lengthy prison sentences, but for two shocking dynamics that have consolidated their impunity: first, they appear to have succeeded in eliminating or intimidating into silence, the majority of the potential and actual witnesses against them (both enemies and erstwhile allies), using violence, threats, blackmail, and protection rackets; and second, faltering political will on the part of the international community to effectively prosecute the former leaders of the KLA. This also seems to have allowed Thaçi—and by extension the other members of the "Drenica Group," to exploit their position in order to accrue personal wealth totally out of proportion with their declared activities.[71]

The German intelligence report cited earlier was written in 2005, but reached very similar conclusions. Eerily, it predicted much of what has since come to pass—including the lethal threat against potential witnesses—and concluded that it would be very difficult to establish democracy and rule of law in Kosovo.[72] UNMIK officials interviewed in Priština in 2006 likewise attributed the difficulty of building complex criminal cases to the small size of the country and the clan-based nature of its society, including the fear of violent revenge against witnesses and investigators, or their families.[73]

Much of the reluctance to target former KLA commanders was clearly driven by a fear that such arrests would lead to a popular backlash, jeopardizing stability in Kosovo.[74] The most well-known example of this was the March 2004 riots in Kosovo, when so-called "war associations"—KLA veterans, KLA invalids, and families of the missing—organized widespread demonstrations to protest the arrest of former KLA leaders on domestic and international war crimes charges. Nineteen people were killed during the clashes, more than 900 injured, and 3,600 evacuated.[75] Former KLA commanders have seemingly exploited this fear among the "internationals," in official statements as well as behind-the-scenes maneuvering, using KLA "support groups" to foment unrest in order to exert political pressure. Following the arrest of Limaj in May 2011, war veterans again organized protests involving thousands of demonstrators throughout Kosovo.[76] Commenting on this pattern, Barry Fletcher—then spokesperson of the UNMIK police—in June 2003 noted that one of the greatest challenges to police work in Kosovo was the "Albanian Mafia" using the rhetoric of Kosovo Albanian nationalism: "Whenever we arrest a gang leader, he wraps himself in an Albanian flag and the streets become flooded with demonstrations. This is not a society affected by organized crime, but a society founded on organized crime."[77]

By fall 2012 a number of senior Kosovo politicians were under active investigation, mainly on suspicions of corruption and abuse of political office. While himself being investigated by a team of prosecutors on the basis of the Marty report, Prime Minister Thaçi stated that "I will respect and I will work hard on the motto of zero tolerance of corruption and organized crime anywhere and against whomever." It is, however, telling that the majority of charges being investigated were related to minor offenses while in political office, rather than the more serious allegations of war crimes and organized crime during the conflict.[78] That said, the investigations against Thaçi, Limaj, Bukoshi, and other political powerbrokers in Kosovo represent a sea-change, signaling that Western authorities finally have overcome their trepidation toward enforcing the rule of law in Kosovo, albeit belatedly. That said, more forceful action earlier on had arguably facilitated the investigations greatly and the outcome of the criminal proceedings remain to be seen.

Involvement in the Security Sector in Kosovo

Following the end of fighting, about half the estimated 20,000 KLA fighters went back to their previous occupations, whereas another 5,000 were integrated into the KPC. The KPC initially had an ambiguous mandate, being seen as a civilian rescue service by the internationals and as the future army of Kosovo locally. Since the KPC retained the hierarchy of the KLA, this reinforced the impression of continuity between the organizations.

The "demobilization through transformation" approach taken vis-à-vis the KLA and the KPC, however, proved problematic, partly due to the legacies of the crime-insurgency nexus. Immediately following the conflict, relations between KFOR and former KLA fighters were cordial, almost to a fault. In the early years, KFOR seemed reluctant to tackle crimes perpetrated by KPC members, and UNMIK police officers even claimed that senior KFOR commanders intervened in criminal investigations, demanding the release of arrested KPC officers. Taken together, this created an impression that former KLA commanders were "untouchables," which did nothing to dissuade further criminality on their part.[79] As unrest started brewing in northern Macedonia and eastern Serbia, fomented by the NLA and UCPMB respectively—which showed significant continuity with the KLA and allegedly included members of the KPC—this nevertheless changed and some senior KPC commanders were arrested.[80]

By comparison, the Kosovo Police Service seems to have been more of a mixed story. The KPS did not retain KLA hierarchies and consistently recruited some 15 percent of its cadets from ethnic minorities. There were also screening procedures put in place to avoid recruiting criminal elements into the force. A quota was, however, set for former KLA fighters and there were worries that dual loyalties would develop vis-à-vis UNMIK police and former KLA commanders. In spite of several imperfections, including poor performance during the March 2004 riots, the creation of the KPS is seen as a relative success and it reportedly enjoys the confidence of the Kosovo population, with 56 percent rating its performance as "excellent" or "good" and only 6 percent as "poor."[81]

Interviews with UNMIK officials and investigative journalists in 2006 reinforced this impression, with respondents stating that the KPS did a good job of investigating everyday criminality but were reluctant to investigate organized crime and cases involving senior politicians for fear of repercussions.[82] These findings were echoed four years later in the Council of Europe report, were the KPS was reported to be seen as "decent," whereas judges were "problematic."[83] The ICG likewise reported witnessing cases of suspected political involvement in judicial processes.[84] Beyond this, issues such as political pressure against judges, parliamentary immunity against prosecutions, and the lack of proper equipment may negatively impact the ability of the judicial system to combat crime.

A third, less broadly recognized, legacy of the KLA is the creation of its unofficial "intelligence arm" SHIK, or K-SHIK (Kosovo's National Intelligence Service). The K-SHIK was formed during the Kosovo war with the assistance of the United States and possibly other intelligence services.[85] A former U.S. senior official in Kosovo stated that SHIK turned into an organized crime organization: "At the beginning, there were about 16 chosen by hand— trained, equipped and outfitted and doing good things . . . but what it turned into was a method to maintain control of the crime and the politics in Kosovo."[86] Following the war, SHIK turned its guns against political competitors in Kosovo, mainly representatives of the LDK. Many of the families of the victims believe that the attacks were carried out at the behest of Thaçi.[87] A leaked KFOR targeting folder from 2004 states that Xhavit Haliti, with Kadri Veseli, prepared a "black list" of moderate politicians and that SHIK has strong links with criminal organizations and derives funding from illegal activity and protection rackets.[88] These claims were further corroborated by a 2005 German intelligence report that highlighted its roots in the KLA.[89]

In 2011, Kosovo's political establishment was rocked to its foundation when an individual, Nazim Bllaca, confessed to having been a hit man for SHIK. Bllaca claimed that hundreds of ethnic Serbs and Albanians had been targeted for elimination, admitted to one murder, and testified in a trial against two other suspected SHIK members.[90] As a result of this testimony, by December 2012 five former members of SHIK were being investigated on suspicion of homicide, mainly of former LDK members.[91]

In spite of their troubled legacies and histories of mutual violence, SHIK and its LDK counterpart by 2006 started lobbying for becoming part of the Ministry of the Interior, admitting that they were running full-blown informal intelligence agencies. Obvious challenges included how to weed out criminal elements, avoid transition into organized crime of dismissed officers, and how to get members of the two organizations to cooperate, given the campaign of mutual killings in 1999–2003.[92] By 2009, the conundrum had not been resolved and as a result, the formal Kosovo intelligence agency only had a staff of one.[93]

Armed Groups in Macedonia and the Preševo Valley

Following the end of the war in Kosovo, unrest began brewing in Macedonia's predominantly ethnically Albanian north. The Macedonian NLA was created shortly after the end of the war in Kosovo and overlapped significantly with the KLA. Some founding members were the same individuals and Macedonian Albanians participated in the fighting in Kosovo, just as former KLA fighters flowed across the border in the opposite direction during the skirmishes in Macedonia in early 2001. The campaign in Macedonia drew on the perceived "lessons learned" from the Kosovo conflict and used hit and run attacks to provoke excessive state repression, espoused a modest agenda of equal rights and security for the minority, and hoped to trigger a Western "humanitarian intervention." It was reported that parts of the funds generated by the Homeland Calling Fund were rerouted to the NLA and a fund called National Freedom was set up, mimicking the modus operandi of the

Homeland Calling Fund.[94] The NLA never managed to generate the kind of following the KLA did, the Macedonian government kept its cool, and the international community vehemently opposed its efforts, resulting in the incipient insurgency eventually petering out.

Likewise, the quaintly named UCPMB—based in the southern Serbian Preševo Valley, to the east of Kosovo—relied partly on former fighters from the KLA and followed a similar modus operandi. Former KLA commanders with alleged connections to drug trafficking enlisted in the UCPMB and focused much of their activities on controlling roads that were frequently used for drug trafficking.[95] Like the NLA, the UCPMB also failed to gain significant traction.

Organized Crime in Contemporary Kosovo

In 2007, at the time of increasing international discussions regarding Kosovo's possible independence, the editors of this book warned that Kosovo was at risk of becoming a "criminalized state at the heart of Europe." For many reasons outlined previously in this chapter, the argument was that once independence was achieved, organized crime would project a heavy influence over the political leadership in Kosovo and at worst be in direct collusion with it.[96]

By 2012, however, the organized crime situation in Kosovo presented a mixed picture, with low levels of violent crime but extensive indications of market-based organized criminality and low levels of interdictions of trafficked goods and criminal prosecutions. Homicide rates were down from 11.8 per 100,000 inhabitants in 2000 to around 3 per 100,000 in 2009, slightly higher than the regional average, but a mere fraction of postconflict countries in areas such as Central America.[97] On the other hand, according to several international organizations, market-based crimes involving both illicit and excise duty goods are a significant problem. In the 2011 European Organized Crime Threat Assessment, for example, Albanian-speaking organized crime in general and Kosovo in particular are singled out as central in trafficking, especially of drugs.[98]

Likewise, these organized crime groups have reportedly expanded their trade into new types of narcotics and there seems to be a direct continuity with the former KLA: "Albanian speaking organized crime is truly poly-drug and poly-criminal. Within the EU, Albanian speaking groups are active in the fields of cocaine, heroin, synthetic drugs and cannabis trafficking. . . . Some of their proceeds are reportedly destined for support organizations for the former Kosovo Liberation Army."[99]

Trafficking in human beings is also reported to be a major problem.[100] These findings are echoed in several similar reports, including from the UNODC and Interpol.[101] In a report on the rule of law in Kosovo, the ICG notes that "small-scale crime is not a big problem: the challenge is instead large-scale organized crime, trafficking and corruption." The report notes that the drug trade is highly organized, reliant on high-level corruption and close to destination markets. It points out that the KPS has a limited ability to fight such crimes and that many sources believed that the government prefers a weak judiciary, since it facilitates corruption.[102] The post-conflict situation enabled the operational capacity of these groups, allowing them to avoid extradition and obtain false identities. Following the conflict, individuals needed only two witnesses to confirm their identity, enabling criminals to obtain documents in several names or even new identities altogether.[103] More recently, Albanian criminals have become increasingly involved in organized crime in the United States, focusing on multicommodity crime.[104]

These problems are likely to increase as the international presence is gradually drawn down and to become further compounded by the very weak economy. Unemployment today stands at around 70 percent for the population under 30, much of the licit urban economy is centered on catering to well-paid "internationals," and development assistance represents 21 percent of the national budget.[105] Whereas Kosovars have been vocally critical of the international presence, it is not clear how the local economy will be able to subsist without it. Hence there is a very real risk of an eventual economic downturn that may generate willing recruits for organized crime networks.

Established in 2008, with its 2,500 staff the EULEX represents both an acknowledgement of the troubling situation regarding organized crime in Kosovo and a robust attempt to tackle the problem. Fielding almost one police officer, prosecutor, and judge per thousand inhabitants in Kosovo, this aim should have been achievable. Four years into its existence, EULEX has investigated corruption, organized crime, and war crimes, achieving convictions of some former foot-soldiers for the KLA, but it still has not been able to convict any senior commander from the KLA. Some former employees of EULEX are deeply pessimistic of its prospects of success.[106] The cases reviewed in this study illustrate the problems of the timing and sequencing of the deployment of EULEX. It took over following the departure of UNMIK, which suffered both from external pressures to abstain from prosecuting senior KLA commanders and limited technical capacity. For instance, the files handed over from the outgoing UNMIK mission to EULEX have been described as "300,000 pages in disarray."[107] The perceived impunity of KLA commanders in the early 2000s, witness intimidation, and murders and attacks against investigators has arguably hampered the ability to carry out complex investigations of war crimes and organized criminality, as has the deterioration of useful physical evidence, which inevitably occurred during the nine years from the end of the conflict until EULEX creation. Hence, whereas EULEX is the right answer to the right problem, its delayed creation is likely to limit its potential positive impact.

Countering organized crime in Kosovo should have been achievable—the territory and population are small, the international presence extensive, the stakes of the countries involved large, and the mandate and duration of the peacekeeping mission extensive. That international state-building in Kosovo still presents very mixed results is a humbling reminder of both the complexity of such endeavors and the limited capability of international organizations to achieve them.

Conclusions

In relation to the theoretical framework outlined at the outset of this book, the Kosovo case confirms some of its hypotheses and diverges from others. As outlined earlier, the conflict began due to grievances related to the revocation of regional autonomy and as a classical ethnic conflict over who should rule the region. But the main actor on the Kosovo Albanian side maintained close links with drug trafficking networks from its very creation. Hence, the conflict did not necessarily increase the level of organized criminality but rather hindered it, since the small region was flooded with Serbian security forces during the conflict. Due to the short duration of the conflict, insurgent involvement in organized criminality did not increase, nor did motives necessarily change notably. There were certainly instances of war profiteering among KLA commanders—including siphoning off funds donated to the struggle—but these patterns of behavior did not necessarily differ significantly from their behavior prior to the war.[108] This highlights a crucial general implication. Most studies on the connection between organized crime and civil war have tended to focus on long-duration conflicts in large countries, often in regions with preexisting production of narcotics and other valuable commodities. In such conflicts, illicit activities and the insurgency tend to develop in tandem in peripheral regions, with increasing insurgent involvement in organized crime driven by growing financing requirements. Over time, combatant motives shift from providing collective political goods toward obtaining personal economic gain, as a military victory remains elusive while they are continuously exposed to increasing amounts of illicit incomes.[109] In Kosovo, the crime-insurgency nexus was established before the outbreak of large-scale conflict and the fighting itself was too short-lived for motives to change substantially. This connection, however, certainly had some military implications, making the KLA much stronger than it would otherwise have been. The group expanded from perhaps 500 fighters in early 1998 to at least 6,000 combatants by mid-1999 and up to 20,000, counting individuals who provided logistical support or participated in a single armed confrontation.[110] Yet the KLA never turned into any formidable fighting force like other drug-funded groups, but clearly would have lost the war but for the intervention of NATO.[111]

Instead, it was mainly after the end of conflict that the crime-insurgency nexus came to play a crucial role. Initially, drug trafficking increased, local turf wars were fought over the control of the illicit economy, and legacy organizations such as the NLA threatened to destabilize northern Macedonia. All of these effects were, however, contained by the peacekeeping forces, even though disarmament, demobilization, and reintegration (DDR), security sector reform (SSR), and rule of law functions were certainly executed far from perfectly.

The most insidious legacy, however, is the connection between organized crime and leading political parties, with former KLA commanders amassing personal fortunes, gaining extensive political influence, and acting with seeming impunity. This situation has been maintained through witness intimidation, political influence over the judiciary, parliamentary impunity from prosecution, and an underfunded Customs Service. Whereas EULEX is now making a last-ditch effort to tackle this situation, for a long time the international community clearly prioritized stability over rule of law. As a result, Kosovo has transitioned from a humanitarian intervention to what seems to be full-blown state capture, a follow-on effect of a crime-insurgency nexus that so far remains underemphasized both in the academic literature and seemingly in the premission planning of peacekeeping operations.

Winning Ugly, Losing the Peace

In their influential book *Winning Ugly: NATO's War to Save Kosovo*, Daalder and O'Hanlon in 2000 reviewed the decision to intervene in Kosovo and the military conduct of the war in detail. They use the term "winning ugly" partly due to the decision to bomb nonmilitary targets inside Serbia proper, but largely gloss over the arguably ugliest aspect of the intervention—the decision to collaborate with an armed group using terrorist tactics and funded in part by drug trafficking. Written directly following the end of the conflict, Daalder and O'Hanlon only briefly mention the suspicions of funding through drug-trafficking and the risk that the KLA would carry out retaliatory killings, but are largely dismissive of the importance of such problems, arguing that they pale in comparison with the risk of ethnic cleansing in 1998–1999. [112] The short- and long-term consequences of this decision have been analyzed in this chapter, suggesting that the postconflict reconstruction of Kosovo has been severely hampered by legacies of the KLA, creating spillover effects for the entire region. Hence, whereas the military intervention did fulfill its purpose, the state-building efforts arguably have not.

There is thus a clear policy implication from the Kosovo conflict—in choosing what allies to work with on the ground during limited interventions, Western militaries should be keenly aware that these actors are likely to become influential political actors following the end of fighting. In working with organized criminals or political extremists, Western militaries thus risk paving the way for their ascent to power in postconflict societies. What is militarily convenient and tactically effective during the conflict can thus prove politically embarrassing and strategically counterproductive after the fighting has ended.

In some conflicts, simply defeating the incumbent regime is all the intervening forces are willing to commit to. The geopolitical location of Kosovo and the long-term international commitment suggest that the aims and hopes were set higher here. In spite of the hardwon lessons of Kosovo, the fallacy of collaborating with "my enemy's enemy" have continued to dog Western interventions during the past decade, from Afghanistan to Iraq and most recently in Libya, with similarly effective battlefield outcomes but troubling long-term consequences.

Although it would be appealing to end on a positive note, the evidence presented above makes this difficult. Insofar that the aim of the NATO intervention was to stop the risk of genocide, it was largely successful. Insofar that it also aimed to create democracy and rule of law in Kosovo, the United States and its NATO allies seem to have lost the peace almost as resoundingly as they won the war.

Chapter 10

Conclusions and Implications for Conflict Resolution and Peacekeeping

Svante Cornell and Michael Jonsson

The chapters in this study illustrate the depth of the interaction between organized crime and armed conflict in postcommunist Eurasia. They also show that this interaction can take a number of forms, with varied implications; conclusions that inform the academic debate on armed conflict, but also have significant implications for humanitarian interventions, peacekeeping interventions, and negotiated solutions of "frozen" conflicts.

These chapters have in general corroborated the propositions that were outlined at the outset. Indeed, they overwhelmingly suggest that conflict is not caused by organized crime, but feeds organized crime; and that insurgent groups overall find it impossible to pass on the opportunity to engage in this lucrative activity. The chapters are more equivocal on the possible changes of motivations in insurgent groups. Indeed, the picture here is mixed, while an important finding is that groups appear capable of moving back and forth between a more ideological and a more economic motivation over time. Moreover, the chapters are practically unanimous in pointing to the substantial and adverse impact of the crime-conflict nexus on the postconflict period, particularly on efforts to rebuild functional state institutions. These findings, and the nuances brought forward by the contributions to this volume, are summarized in the following section. Overall, the findings cast substantial doubt over the central assumptions in the established literature on the political economy of war. The focus on preexisting natural resources or "economic endowments" over endogenous war economies, the emphasis on structure over agency, "greed" as a cause of civil war onset, the assumption of armed groups as unitary actors, and motives as unchanging over time are all severely questioned by the findings of this book.[1] In fact, natural resources were notably insignificant as a source of financing in most of these cases, the actions of armed groups were far from predetermined by the structure in which they acted, and several groups showed signs of both motive changes and internal fractions. In most of these conflicts, control of the state, rather than external resources, was notably central to the postconflict period. Hence, whereas the political economy was central to these conflicts, its forms and consequences were far more complex and nuanced than suggested by the existing literature. Likewise, in an era of decreasing numbers of active civil wars, a concomitant shift in research focus away from conflict causes and dynamics and toward war-to-peace transitions and postconflict state-building clearly seems warranted. These conclusions have important policy implications. Indeed, at their most basic, they emphasize the entrenchment of organized crime in societies affected by armed conflict, an entrenchment that is exacerbated in situations where conflicts become protracted or unresolved—and where situations emerge where forces on all sides benefit economically from the lack of resolution. This could be called the opportunity cost of unresolved conflict.

More specifically, the contributions to this volume suggest that the political economy of armed conflict remains poorly understood. Indeed, the book is replete with examples of how international policymakers neglect—and sometimes purposefully avoid—addressing the rise of organized crime in conflict areas with substantial international presence, with clear adverse consequences. Afghanistan and Kosovo are the most glaring examples. When, several years later, organized crime is gradually factored into policy-making, it is often too late: efforts to prosecute politicians with criminal connections failed to prevent such forces from continuing to wield power in Kosovo; efforts to ramp up anticorruption in Afghanistan and to focus on interdiction have yielded few results; and the EUBAM mission in Transnistria has failed to make a significant impact on the character of the separatist regime of that territory. Thus, one of the major lessons from the conflicts surveyed is the importance of increasing the awareness of the role of economic factors in armed conflict. If policymakers ask the right questions at the outset, they have a greater chance to devise policies that, at a minimum, do not inadvertently contribute to the growth of organized crime, and at best, integrate efforts to mitigate its expansion in their broader policies.

These conclusions are of relevance in particular for peacekeeping missions. Understanding of the mission environment is not merely a theoretical question for peacekeepers, as it could affect the very security of a mission itself. Understanding the economic forces at play in a conflict zone is crucial for a peacekeeping operation, especially in a time when most peacekeeping operations include police forces. In particular, it is crucial in determining the success or failure of SSR efforts, lest they inadvertently help criminalized groups assert control of major state institutions, or the state itself. The perhaps most thorny question is what implications this should have for the mandate of peacekeeping operations—where opinions differ on whether combating organized crime should be made into a core function or even ignored altogether. Depending on resources and the individual context, the answer may differ; but the point is that the question is far from peripheral, as the answer could go far in determining the chances of success of an operation, and the challenges it is likely to face.

Implications for the Understanding of Armed Conflict

This study set out with a series of propositions on the relationship between armed conflict and organized crime. Most of these were proven correct in the Eurasian context; others are more difficult to trace, while the empirical material suggests issues that were not necessarily foreseen by the theoretically derived literature on the subject.

Conflict Is Not Caused by Organized Crime

The study's first proposition was that the origins of conflict are based on grievance and not greed. Indeed, all conflicts in this study have their origin in political incompatibilities, not the quest for greed on the part of an insurgent force.

This argument is more watertight in some cases than others. In the Abkhazian and South Ossetian conflicts, it is clear that economic interest related to organized crime had little, if anything, to do with the ethnic tensions that plunged Georgia into armed conflict in the late 1980s and early 1990s. Likewise, the conflict in Kosovo appears to have been caused by growing ethnic animosities between Albanians and Serbs, even though Kosovo Albanian crime groups were well established by the outbreak of the conflict in 1998 and helped finance the fighting. In Tajikistan, the civil war emerged in 1992, long before large-scale trafficking of opiates from Afghanistan had begun to develop. As for the IMU, the forces that founded this movement under different names around the time of the breakup of the Soviet Union had a clearly ideological, religiously motivated agenda. In all of these cases, the conflicts were caused by ideological grievances, not the quest for economic profit. Likewise, the war in Bosnia-Herzegovina was clearly an ethnopolitical conflict, even though substantial war profiteering occurred during the war. Chechnya stood out among the ethnic republics in Russia by the absence of strong economic motives behind the quest for sovereignty. Indeed, the conflict was deeply rooted in the history of the 1944 deportations and a strong belief that the Chechen people could find a future only in the absence of Russian domination.

On a methodological note, these case studies illustrate a fundamental weakness in the purely structural and quantitative approach to research on the onset of conflict. Most of these conflicts were caused by ethnopolitical security dilemmas, coupled with state weakness that arose following the breakup of the former Soviet Union and Yugoslavia, and were mostly financed by revenue streams other than natural resources, such as sanctions busting, drug trafficking (as opposed to drug production), diaspora, and co-religionist or external state sponsorship. Such factors are not captured by studies that compare "atypical grievances" (usually measured as ethnic diversity, level of democracy, Gini coefficients for income inequality) or "atypical opportunities" (usually measured as dependence on commodity exports or types of natural resources, unemployment levels, and state expenditures, to name a few). In a nutshell, both the possible causes of political incompatibilities and sources of rebel financing are thus too numerous and difficult to quantify adequately in panel data cross-country models (regardless if they seek to explain motives of armed groups or simply the "feasibility" of conflict), restricting both the validity and explanatory power of such studies.[2]

The two conflicts that have less of a crystal clear picture are those in Afghanistan and Transnistria. In Afghanistan, the main question is if the entire period from 1979 to the present is defined as a single conflict over the government of Afghanistan, or whether it is divided into a myriad of smaller conflicts, something that could extend into dozens of different conflicts, given the bewildering complexity of short-term allegiances between warring parties there. In sum, if the conflict is defined as a single one, it is clear that the emergence of the Mujahideen groups following the Soviet invasion had very little to do with any economic incentives. Indeed, their emergence was solely political and ideological in nature. However, if one separates the jihad against the Soviet occupation and the subsequent civil war into two separate conflicts, the picture is less clear-cut. Thus, when the Soviet forces retreated, the various Mujahideen factions were already deeply involved in the drug economy. Was the fact that they began fighting each other instead of coalescing to form a new government in Afghanistan related only to their ideological, political, or personal differences and animosities? Or was it rather a function of their rivalry for the control of the incomes of the drug economy? This question, which was not one customarily asked during the Afghan civil war, cannot be readily answered without much deeper field studies in Afghanistan, although anecdotal evidence suggests that rivalry over drug cultivation areas and trafficking routes did play a role in at least some conflicts between Mujahideen commanders. Indeed, if events following the NATO intervention in 2001 are any guide to motives during the preceding civil war, such considerations probably played a central role.[3] Nevertheless, it remains the case that these conflicts were not caused primarily by the drug trade; the drug trade may have affected the calculus of these groups, which makes any such eventuality rather a question of a change in motivational structures, discussed later.

The second case where the proposition can be questioned is Transnistria. Indeed, the Transnistrian conflict was less ethnic in character than those in the Balkans and Caucasus. Transnistria remains a multiethnic territory, and ethnic Moldovans are the largest population group there, comprising about 40 percent of the population, followed by Ukrainians and Russians. As such, several scholars have identified this conflict as more political than ethnic in nature. The quest for control over the industrial resources of the Transnistrian region—which could be characterized as greed rather than grievances—may have formed an impetus for secession. That said, there is no evidence that any organized criminal intent was involved in this early period. Moreover, it is clear that ethnolinguistic tensions from 1990 to 1992, together with the emboldening support for the separatists from Russia and especially the 14th Army, formed the most significant motivations for the separation of Transnistria from Moldova. Hence, while some economic elite calculations may have been involved in the calculus, there is little to suggest organized criminal proceeds were one of them, anymore than the quest for power and influence can be termed a factor in all insurgent forces, and geopolitical considerations on behalf of the Russian side clearly played a central role.

Conflict Leads to a Growth in Organized Crime—Postconflict Period More Mixed

The study's second proposition was that the conditions of armed conflict provide an impetus for organized criminal activity. This proposition has been vindicated, given the very visible growth of organized crime in all conflict zones since the outbreak of conflict. However, it is necessary to note that simply observing a growth in organized crime in the conflict zones will not suffice, given that the entire postcommunist area has experienced a substantial growth of organized criminal activity. Hence, to show a link between armed conflict and organized crime, it is necessary to show that organized crime has affected conflict zones considerably more than it has affected comparable regions not affected by conflict, thereby isolating the impact of the independent variable. And in this context, the answer to the question is less unequivocal. The conflict zones in fact break down into two categories: those that have very substantially seen an increase in organized crime, and those where such an increase cannot be proved. Importantly, the former outnumber the latter.

The conflict zones where conflict has had a measurably substantial effect on organized crime are Afghanistan, Tajikistan, South Ossetia, Bosnia-Herzegovina, Chechnya, Kosovo, and Transnistria. In Afghanistan, the numbers practically speak for themselves: the drug industry, small to almost nonexistent at the outset of the conflict, now represents a value equal to half the country's legal economy. The opium industry has reached proportions unthinkable in any country earlier, and appears to keep growing under circumstances of insurgency.[4] Indeed, since the mid-1980s, conflict and the drug economy have gone hand in hand, with nothing so far succeeding in breaking this vicious circle.

Tajikistan presents a somewhat similar picture, but with a twist. Here, the descent of the country into civil war, coupled with the proximity to Afghanistan and substantial interaction between Afghan and Tajik armed factions, led to a rampant rise in drug trafficking in the country. These factions included the IMU as well. Unlike Afghanistan, Tajikistan's conflict has found a somewhat lasting settlement; nevertheless, the drug industry has continued to rage. There is thus a new focal point of Eurasian organized crime, encompassing Afghanistan, Tajikistan, and the northwestern border areas of Pakistan.[5]

South Ossetia and Transnistria present a parallel, yet different picture. While organized crime has boomed in these territories, they function as enclaves of organized crime on the outskirts of Europe, in a sense utilizing their relatively stable uncontrolled status over a number of years to fulfill a criminal economic niche that other, recognized states cannot easily fulfill—at least not in such proximity to Europe. Indeed, the territories neighboring the two conflict zones—Romania, Moldova, Ukraine, and Georgia—are gradually reforming and Europeanizing; as this process develops, the two conflict zones seem to ever more consolidate a role as organized crime enclaves that, unlike Afghanistan and Tajikistan, espouse a multicriminal profile. It is not just drugs that find a haven in these territories, but human trafficking, arms smuggling, consumer goods smuggling, and counterfeiting of U.S. dollars, to name only a few prominent aspects.[6] In Kosovo and Bosnia-Herzegovina, extensive peacekeeping operations—including sizable policing units—have brought violent crime to low levels, but numerous reports and supporting evidence indicate that both territories play a role in market-based criminality that is entirely disproportionate to the size of their populations and territory. However, all unresolved conflict zones have not been affected to the same systematic extent by organized crime capture of unrecognized states. In Abkhazia and Nagorno-Karabakh (not studied in detail here because it is primarily an interstate conflict), the levels of organized crime in the respective territories are high, but not dramatically different from the average of the postcommunist area. In Moldova, violent organized crime flourished during the 1990s, but during the 2000s these networks were diminished and criminality in the entire country shifted toward more economic and white collar crimes, which remained at very high levels. The North Caucasus has also seen the growth of organized crime, but its link to conflict has varied over time. Chechnya became a hub for crime very much as a result of its attempted secession in the 1990s, but levels of organized crime soon boomed in the remainder of the North Caucasus as well. The insurgency, in turn, has existed in a symbiotic relationship with the general lawlessness of the region.

Insurgents Do Tend to Involve in Organized Crime

The study's third proposition was that the growth of organized criminal activity forms a strong incentive for insurgent groups to involve increasingly directly in organized crime to reap profits. The study finds that this is indeed the case in most conflict zones. It is the case for the major actors in the conflict zones of Greater Central Asia, including Afghanistan, Tajikistan, and the IMU. In these conflicts, there appears to be a systematic involvement of insurgent groups in the Afghan narcotics trade. Indeed, given the fact that the conflicts in Afghanistan and Tajikistan occurred in a context of state collapse, involvement in the drug trade appears to have become practically a sine qua non for insurgents to continue to have a meaningful political and military existence. As the cases of Chechnya, the IMU, and the Taliban illustrate, however, the degree of insurgent involvement can vary over time, and is very much related to the availability of alternative funding. When donations from the Gulf region have been forthcoming, for example, insurgent involvement in organized crime has tended to decline, and vice versa.

In the unresolved territorial conflicts of the eastern fringes of Europe, the situation is more mixed, as the conflict zones fall into two categories. In South Ossetia, Kosovo, Bosnia-Herzegovina, Transnistria, and Georgia prior to the 2003 Rose Revolution, the evidence suggesting the comprehensive involvement of political elites in organized crime is overwhelming.[7] That said, the short duration of the armed phase of these conflicts, however, meant that insurgents rapidly transitioned into political actors—legitimate ones in the cases of Bosnia-Herzegovina, Kosovo, and Georgia, and illegitimate ones in the cases of South Ossetia and Transnistria. But on the other hand, there is less evidence that the political leadership of either Abkhazia (or Nagorno-Karabakh) have been permeated by organized criminal interests to a level comparable to that in either Kosovo, South Ossetia, Bosnia-Herzegovina, or Transnistria. Indeed, this finding is related to the differences between the territories' political systems. As far as the four post-Soviet conflicts are concerned, there is a striking correlation between the level of Russian intervention in the governance of the unrecognized entities and their level of organized crime. Both South Ossetia and Transnistria have extremely high levels of Russian interference in their internal affairs, to the extent that the leadership of the two entities can be said to be much more dependent on Moscow than on their own populations. By contrast, the leaderships of Abkhazia and Nagorno-Karabakh have a much more developed connection to the narrow ethnic populations they claim to represent; in the case of Karabakh, the leadership is intricately linked to that of Armenia. While speaking of democracy in ethnically cleansed territories would be a misnomer, it is clear that the Abkhaz and Nagorno-Karabakh leaderships do have a substantial level of legitimacy within the ethnic Abkhaz and Karabakh Armenian populations, as both have contested elections and real political competition.[8] This does not appear to be the case in either South Ossetia or Transnistria, where populations have little influence over the political elite. Hence, it appears that the level of external, in this case Russian, involvement in a conflict zone is directly linked to the criminalization of that conflict zone. A similar pattern can be seen in Chechnya, where the involvement of both Russian forces and the pro-Moscow administration of Ramzan Kadyrov in organized crime are well known.

In South Ossetia and Transnistria, as well as in Tajikistan, Russian involvement in "peacekeeping" missions often seems to have aided and abetted organized criminal involvement.[9] It does not seem that Western interventions have necessarily been successful in decreasing levels of organized crime, but at the very least, Western peacekeepers themselves do not seem to have been actively involved in this type of crime, with some notable exceptions.

In sum, it is clear that insurgent parties' levels of involvement in organized crime in conflict zones in postcommunist Eurasia are high. However, the caveat that needs to be inserted is that the degree of involvement depends on the perceived need for international recognition. Territories run by what is essentially "proxy regimes" for a foreign power, such as South Ossetia and Transnistria, have seen the highest and most systematic levels of criminal involvement. But in territories where a politically motivated elite with strong connections to its own society maintains power and seeks international (particularly Western) acceptance and recognition, involvement in organized crime has tended to be lower. Abkhazia (and Nagorno-Karabakh) hold parallels to the Zapatista rebellion in Mexico in the 1990s, which purposefully sought to avoid involvement in the narcotics trade, although it had extremely good opportunities to do so, in order to safeguard its domestic and international standing.

Kosovo and Bosnia-Herzegovina do not fit either mold entirely, as post-conflict elites in these territories were highly dependent on the West, while their involvement in organized crime appears to have been substantial. In Kosovo in particular, the leadership curiously did not appear concerned that its criminalization would impede its efforts to achieve international recognition. In the end, however, that assessment proved entirely correct, suggesting that the dependency was a two-way affair. In both Kosovo and Afghanistan, criminalized elites appear to have more or less kept Western forces hostage, succeeding in minimizing damage from allegations of criminal involvement, while continuing to receive large amounts of aid. This can be partially explained by Western countries clearly prioritizing stability over rule of law directly following the end of the conflicts and perhaps also a reluctance to reveal embarrassing details about their former de facto allies, even though this now appears to be changing, at least in Kosovo.[10]

Insurgent forces that have sought political recognition exclusively in non-Western states, in particular Islamist groups in Greater Central Asia, appear to see little reason not to involve in the drug trade. The same could be said for Transnistria and South Ossetia, decidedly anti-Western political entities whose ties with Moscow appear not to be compromised by organized criminal links to the political leadership.

As argued in Chapter 1 of this volume, insurgency financing is not merely an automatic function of what "economic endowments" were available at the outset of the conflict. Instead, insurgents pursue several types of funding, many of which are not captured by macroeconomic statistics (such as diaspora funding, extortion, kidnappings, local "taxation," and so forth). What types of funding they obtain may also impact their motives, as illustrated by the case of the IMU, Tajikistan, and to some extent Afghanistan in this volume. This contradicts much of the purely quantitative approaches to analyzing the economics of civil wars, since such studies either do not adequately measure the sources used to fund rebels, or cannot account for shifting types of financing and motives during the duration of the conflict.

Motivational Change: A Mixed Picture

The study's fourth proposition was that insurgent groups are likely, once involved in organized crime, to see their motivational structures affected to some extent, with elements of the group acquiring an economic motivation that compounds or supplants the ideological one. This idea is perhaps the most difficult one to prove, given that evidence of the actual motivational structures of an organization is extremely difficult to substantiate. Indeed, are the leaders of South Ossetia and Transnistria, or the neo-Taliban insurgency in Afghanistan, involved in organized crime mainly to finance their operations, or to amass profit? The picture appears to diverge substantially among the conflict zones.

In Afghanistan's post-Taliban environment, the question is complicated by the permeation of the entire political spectrum by the drug trade. Asking whether the neo-Taliban insurgency is motivated primarily by ideology or profit could be countered by asking the same question about Afghanistan's state officials. In all, there is no clear conclusion on the motivations of the Afghan insurgents.[11] Their involvement in the drug trade is undeniable; on the other hand, the amorphous nature of the insurgency and the unclear hierarchical and command structures make the question impossible to answer on an organizational basis. It is most likely that the insurgency is composed of a range of various motivations, from the purely ideological to the purely criminal. Much the same can be said about Tajikistan, with the difference that the conflicting parties were all gradually integrated into the government. This integration, in turn, carried with it the legalization of their position and influence; field commanders appear not to have been much affected by their previous ideological allegiances, and continued to reap profits from organized crime following their inclusion into the state. The gradual collapse of the ideological nature of the Tajik opposition leaders and the waning of the Islamist forces in the politics of the country cannot only be ascribed to the population's war fatigue or government repression. Indeed, it must to a significant extent be explained by the co-optation of its leaders into the governing structures, with apparent approval of their continued involvement in organized crime, suggesting the weakness of their ideological motivation.[12] It can be noted here that in situations of state collapse, involvement of armed groups in organized crime does not necessarily undermine the legitimacy of those groups. This is especially so if civilians have developed "coping economies" reliant on illicit economies and some share of the proceeds of crime trickle down to civilians through patron-client networks, while the negative effects of drug consumption occur mainly abroad. Indeed, this seems to be the conclusion by Tajikistan's population, whose tolerance toward the leadership's criminal links and growing authoritarianism appears to be determined by the priority not to revert to war, but also by the economic necessities.

As for the IMU, the history of this organization prior to Operation Enduring Freedom reads as a textbook example of one whose motivational structures gradually altered, changing the nature of the entire movement from an ideological to a criminal direction. However, following the death of its military leader, Juma Namangani, in 2001 and its subsequent loss of control of drug trafficking routes, the remnants of the IMU under its ideological leader, Tohir Yoldash, increasingly blended into the region-wide, transnational Salafist movement, which received financial backing from Gulf-based donors. Following the death of Yoldash in 2009, the rump IMU has again established itself in northern Afghanistan and southern Tajikistan and has reportedly become increasingly involved in the drug trafficking industry. This case illustrates a central problem with the "continuity hypothesis" implicitly underpinning quantitative research on conflict duration, that is, the idea that the motives of armed groups remain unchanging during the entirety of a conflict, as well as the idea of armed groups as unitary, homogenous actors.[13] Instead, analysis of civil wars must allow for the possibility that motives may change due to shifts in the leadership of armed groups or their operational context and pay greater attention to intramovement cohesiveness and fractions.[14] This reinforces the basic assumption in Makarenko's crime-terror nexus that motives of armed groups can change due to involvement in organized crime.[15] However, more analysis needs to be devoted to what makes armed groups become less motivated by economic motives and the importance of individual leaders in shaping the motives of the group.

In the territorial conflicts in western Eurasia, the picture is more mixed. Here, as the previous section has suggested, the conflicts fall into several categories. Abkhazia appears to be the least affected by criminal involvement on the part of the leadership. In the cases of South Ossetia and Transnistria, the extremely close connections between Moscow and the leaderships of Tiraspol and Tskhinvali complicates a thorough analysis of their motivations. Indeed, as they are not independent actors, their very allegiance to the ideological causes they claim to espouse—independence from Moldova and Georgia, respectively—must be put in doubt. Given that they answer primarily to Moscow and not their own populations, their general motivation is difficult to determine. Are they using Moscow's support for the purpose of strengthening their enclave's independence? Or are they using their territory's position to strengthen Russia's position in the "near abroad"? Their involvement in organized crime in fact appears to be an indication that could help understand their motivations. Had they been solely motivated by a political agenda, they would likely have sought to prevent the extensive criminalization of their territories, which has negative effects for their international legitimacy, further cementing their dependence on Russia. Indeed, the high levels of organized crime are an indication of the leaderships' ulterior motive. Interestingly, the dependence on Russia by client regimes such as that in South Ossetia, or the Kadyrov regime in Chechnya, goes both ways. It is well-established that the elites in Grozny and Tskhinvali have made a practice of diverting the large financial flows of subsidies from Moscow to their own narrow interests. For Ossetian and Chechen client regimes, the lure of appropriating the millions of dollars simply delivered from Moscow trumped even the ease with which they could finance themselves through organized crime.

In the final analysis, the criminalization of these unresolved conflicts has gone hand in hand with Russia's growing involvement in and control over the conflict zones. It is therefore clear that in more than one way, the motivation of the separatist leadership has changed considerably since the emergence of conflict in the late 1980s.

The Postconflict Period: The Decay of the State

The last proposition argued that an extensive crime-insurgency nexus increased the risk of state weakness or state failure, as well as a "criminalization" of the state itself, especially if the insurgents became political leaders following the end of active conflict. In Afghanistan, Tajikistan, and Kosovo, government forces at top levels suffer from systematic involvement in organized crime; in Bosnia-Herzegovina, the problem is only slightly less prevalent. In Georgia, the same was true until the remarkable anticorruption efforts of the Saakash-vili administration. In South Ossetia and Transnistria, and to a lesser degree in Abkhazia, leaders of the unrecognized entities depended largely on organized crime. In Chechnya, the insurgents turned Russian proxies did the same. Thus, in all the conflicts studied, with the exception of the IMU, former insurgents did in fact become leading politicians, which is otherwise a fairly uncommon outcome of civil wars.[16] While they differ substantially among themselves, these conflicts point to the problem of the crime-conflict linkage in a postconflict situation. Indeed, they indicate that the problem of criminalized conflict parties is unlikely to go away simply because a conflict has moved toward a political solution.[17]

Only two countries could clearly be labeled "failed" states or regions—Afghanistan and the North Caucasus, with Tajikistan a possible candidate.[18] With its raging civil war, Afghanistan clearly does not hold a monopoly on violence and the state lacks legitimacy among a significant share of its population. In the North Caucasus, there is still a simmering low-intensity insurgency, levels of violence are high, and the local Moscow-supported government lacks legitimacy among large segments of the population, primarily in Chechnya but also in Dagestan. In Tajikistan, the government is at pains delivering basic services to its population, and its legitimacy is extremely low.

In most other regions studied, the state is weak but not failing, largely thanks to external support from Moscow, Brussels, or Washington. Homicide rates are surprisingly low in most of these regions, indicating that the state does indeed hold a monopoly on violence. Legitimacy varies across the different countries, being the lowest in South Ossetia and Transnistria (together with Afghanistan and the North Caucasus). Public goods deliveries have been problematic, partly as a result of extensive corruption in relation to major infrastructure projects, and residents often have to pay for services such as health care, which are formally supposed to be provided free or for a nominal fee. That said, the situation regarding the delivery of public goods is not necessarily worse in these postconflict territories than in, for example,

Kyrgyzstan, reflecting instead the problematic transition from authoritarian command economies to semidemocracies with supposedly capitalist systems.[19] The viability of these postconflict societies seems to be conditional on continued external support, and if the West were to withdraw support from Bosnia-Herzegovina, Kosovo, or Afghanistan, or if Russia would cease to uphold the regimes in Transnistria, South Ossetia, or Abkhazia, it is difficult to see how these economies could become self-supporting and it seems quite possible that levels of violence would increase significantly.

Instead, the most significant legacy of the crime-insurgency nexus has been the extensive "criminalization" that has occurred in most of these states. This is arguably the result of a combination of structural conditions that facilitated the emergence of organized crime entities—discussed in Chapter 1; the crime-insurgency nexus during the conflicts; and the fact that all these conflicts (save for the IMU and Chechnya following the second war) resulted in peace agreements or prolonged cease-fires where insurgents came into senior positions of power. For example, in Moldova, the dominant role of the Sheriff Corporation and its ties to the Smirnov family has been widely publicized. In Kosovo, chilling accusations against senior politicians from international actors have practically become routine.[20] In Afghanistan, parts of the governing coalition have repeatedly been accused of having established a strong interest in poppy cultivation.[21] In Georgia, the Interior and Security Ministries prior to the 2003 Rose Revolution were deeply implicated in organized crime, including the running of heroin laboratories in the Pankisi Gorge bordering the North Caucasus.

Interestingly, whereas much of the contemporary literature on the political economy of civil war has focused on preexisting commodities as a source of insurgency financing, these cases illustrate the continuing challenges created by the crime-insurgency nexus during postconflict situations or in situations of "frozen conflicts."

A basic challenge is that individuals that were insurgency leaders during the conflicts have used their accumulated economic, political, and military capital to gain political influence and continued control of illicit and legal economies following the end of the conflicts.[22] Likewise, less than subtle policies have been used to uphold this system—immunity of members of parliament from prosecution, witness intimidation, and law enforcement weakness or corruption have become commonplace in most of the postconflict societies.

The mechanisms through which this occurred have been analyzed in detail in the case studies but deserve brief mention here. In the Russian-backed conflicts (Transnistria, South Ossetia, and Abkhazia), insurgency leaders with implicit or overt Russian support became political leaders of de facto miniature states. In Tajikistan and Afghanistan, warlords were invited into fragile government coalitions by virtue of their firepower and ability to ensure a modicum of stability and enforce any agreements struck with the central government. In Kosovo, this deal was less explicit, but former KLA leaders used the specter of renewed ethnic hostilities to counter efforts by the international community to rein in their organized crime activities and seemingly used the proceeds of crime to create political platforms.[23]

In countries that saw major Western interventions, the transition from "war economies" to what is perhaps most aptly termed "peacekeeping economies" has entailed a great deal of focus on controlling revenue streams that are specific to postconflict reconstruction. This seems to have played a significant role as sources of financing. This includes internationally funded infrastructure projects in Kosovo and aid projects and the private security companies protecting them in Afghanistan. Likewise, the unresolved territorial conflicts in Western Eurasia have developed their own type of political economy, benefitting the leadership while choking normal entrepreneurial behavior.[24] As illustrated in the chapter on Moldova in this volume, this has more recently come to include smuggling of licit goods through Transnistria to avoid taxation and numerous other white collar crimes that rely on external aid or require control of the state itself.

These patterns offer fundamental theoretical implications. First, the literature on war economies, including discussions on changes of motivation and intramovement factionalism, must be expanded to the postconflict setting as well, rather than focusing on conflict onset or duration alone, which has mainly been the case to date.[25] Second, the excessive focus on natural commodities or set economic endowments should be broadened, since insurgencies typically generate new forms of endogenous revenue streams, including sources of funding that are particular to the conflict—arms trafficking, diaspora support, external state sponsorship—or postconflict situation—infrastructure projects funded by international financial institutions, diversion or armed extortion of development aid, and so on. Hence, it is impossible to understand the conflict dynamic and the postconflict reconstruction by looking merely at preexisting, unchanging natural resources in isolation. Third and finally, the international community should devise clearer strategies for dealing with economic agendas as part of the peacekeeping missions, including how to address illicit economies, employment for ex-combatants, the role of potential spoilers motivated by maintaining wartime revenue streams, and the generation of sustainable growth. This should be of particular importance to peacekeeping missions, since not much can be done to alter preexisting natural resources or economic endowments, whereas issues pertaining to postconflict reconstruction aid are directly under the purview of peacekeeping and peace-building missions. This facet further reinforces the existing acknowledgement of the importance of improving civilian-military collaboration in contemporary peacekeeping missions.

Implications for Conflict Resolution

The conclusions of this study have significant policy implications for the international community's response to armed conflict, involving both conflict resolution efforts and peacekeeping operations.

The Opportunity Cost of Unresolved Conflict

A first implication of the territorial conflicts in the western part of the post-communist area is that the lack of speedy resolution of these conflicts has contributed significantly to the entrenchment of organized crime in the conflict zones, leading the territories to find a niche in the global illicit economy and providing for increased stakes on the part of forces on both sides of the conflict in the status quo—thereby making conflict resolution more difficult. The policy implication is that allowing a conflict to remain unresolved and protracted, as has been the case in the post-Soviet ethnopolitical conflicts, implies an opportunity cost; it creates additional problems that impede the resolution of the conflict at a later stage and the building of normal statehood in the rump parent states, as the cases of Georgia and Moldova illustrate.[26]

Understanding the Political Economy of Armed Conflict

In spite of the very substantial role organized crime has played in most of the conflicts discussed in this study, the international community's efforts to bring an end to these conflicts has in general failed to incorporate this predicament. Indeed, an understanding of the political economy of armed conflict appears to have been underemphasized in the international community's efforts at conflict resolution and where considered, insufficiently elaborated and analyzed.

Afghanistan stands out as only a partial exception. In Afghanistan, Western support for the jihad against the Soviet occupation in the 1980s turned a blind eye to the growing involvement of the mujahideen in opium trafficking. Again, in the aftermath of the collapse of the Taliban regime, the international coalition explicitly favored counterinsurgency at the expense of counternarcotics. While perhaps initially necessary to succeed in fighting the neo-Taliban insurgency, this approach ignored the linkages between the narcotics industry and the insurgency.[27] At present, the haphazard way in which the international community has approached counternarcotics in Afghanistan has undermined both the efforts of rebuilding Afghanistan and achieving success in the counterinsurgency, as well as ensuring a legitimate and functioning government.[28] Thus, counternarcotics initially was downplayed, followed by a counterproductive emphasis on eradication. It was then largely ignored again, until the Obama administration ramped up interdiction efforts. In the meantime, both the Afghan government elite and the Taliban insurgency grew dependent on the drug industry, negating any hope for success in counternarcotics.

Transnistria also is a partial exception: the EUBAM mission, explicitly designed to combat the illicit economy of Transnistria, indicates a belated understanding of the organized criminal element of the conflict. As with interdiction in Afghanistan, this nevertheless came more than a decade after the end of hostilities. In Kosovo, the UNMIK police unit represents an effort to more directly tackle the issue of criminality in a region that the international community more directly controlled, but the track record of this institution was disappointing, owing both to political prioritization of stability over rule of law—as in Afghanistan—and arguably a somewhat limited technical capability on behalf of the institution itself. The establishment of EULEX in 2008 represents a serious effort to tackle the issue of war crimes and impunity directly, but the long time that elapsed following the end of conflict, coupled with a very visible history of witness intimidation and perceived impunity of former KLA commanders, makes this effort highly challenging.[29] By contrast, in the conflicts in the South Caucasus, the political economy of the conflicts has hardly been integrated in the international community's efforts—which themselves have been relatively half-hearted.

Finally, little can be said regarding Tajikistan and the IMU, as international community involvement was rather low-key in both cases. Suffice it to note that the United States and UN spent important resources building up Tajikistan's DCA, which was for a time—when it served the short-term purposes of the country's leadership—run by a suspected drug lord.

This experience suggests that the international community has not sufficiently factored in the role of criminalized parties to conflict into their conflict resolution strategies. This, in turn, has the potential to significantly impede postconflict reconstruction and development, not to speak of the normalization of the postconflict territory's economy and political system. In the future, both in these and other conflicts, it will be imperative for the international community to include analysis of this aspect into any efforts to seek a resolution to conflicts, as well as in postconflict reconstruction and development strategies. Nitzschke and Studdard argue that this implies that third-party monitoring of natural resources, generating quick employment as part of DDR programs, acknowledging that shadow economies sometimes play an important role as coping economies for civilians, and equitable sharing of incomes from natural resources need to be part of peace-building efforts.[30] To this, one could ask that prior to deployment, the political economy of civil wars needs to be better understood, and during deployment, considered strategies need to be implemented to deter and repress organized criminality on behalf of former rebel leaders, particularly when they come into political office.

This may appear difficult, but several concrete steps can be employed in this regard. First of all, diplomats, NGOs, and others involved in the conflict resolution processes will need to develop greater understanding of the economic agendas of conflict parties, involving both insurgents and, in many cases, elements of governments. As such, better resources will need to be geared toward understanding the motivations of parties to conflict. This should involve going beyond the political declarations of the respective parties, and seeking independently to determine the level and character of their economic motivations, if any. Specifically, predeployment mission planning should analyze the financing sources of insurgents, identifying key units and actors responsible for fundraising and logistical support. Furthermore, high-risk areas both in terms of regions (from where illicit revenue streams may emanate, either through lootable commodities or established smuggling routes) and high-risk areas of the economy that are vulnerable to criminal involvement (which can include large infrastructure projects, smuggling of licit but high-value goods such as petrol or cigarettes, agencies managing aid flows, and so on) should be identified. This task is challenging, but from the experience of the present authors in having analyzed the financing of several different armed groups, much information can in fact be gathered through open sources alone.[31] Whereas one cannot expect to have a perfect intelligence assessment prior to deployment, establishing a baseline that can be improved following deployment ensures that relevant questions are being asked from the outset of the mission, rather than forced upon the peacekeeping mission by events on the ground.[32] As these parties are by no means coherent and uniform, it will be necessary to study intraparty cohesion in order to determine possible factions with lesser or greater criminal involvement and the risk for formation of financially motivated spoiler groups.[33]

Specifically, individuals or actors that have amassed large fortunes during the conflict may seek to use this as a means to establish a political powerbase, either formally through party financing or informally through bribery or paying of standing militias, or simply financing ongoing criminal operations. Beyond logistics or financial officers, regional midlevel commanders deserve particular attention, since they often have direct knowledge of and control over trafficking operations, but are usually not offered special incentives to lay down their arms in the postconflict settlement. Only having undertaken this task, through intelligence gathering and other methods, will it be possible to ascertain whether the declared aims of the conflicting parties correspond to the true motives of their leaders. This will in turn enable the formulation of corresponding policies to resolve the conflict in question. For example, the issue of potential "spoilers" may include not only actors that are disappointed with the political settlement of the conflict, but also actors that may want to continue using violence to maintain a profitable war economy.[34] Whether this will imply the employment of positive or negative economic incentives is an issue to be handled in specific cases. Suffice it to note here that several paths of action are available to the international community once it has ascertained the economic interests of a group of individuals in a conflict. These range from eliminating these individuals through military action or arrest; over the freezing of their assets; to the exact opposite, namely "buying" these groups with economic incentives or providing them with a safe exit from the conflict zone with part of their assets. This latter option may be deemed unethical, but may be the lesser evil compared to a festering unresolved conflict situation.[35] In any case, the understanding of the political economy of armed conflict is imperative for any steps to be taken in conflicts where parties are affected by organized criminal involvement.

Implications for Peacekeeping

The results of this study have implications for peacekeeping operations. These break down primarily into two categories: understanding of mission environment, and the mandate of peacekeeping operations.

Understanding of Mission Environment

A first and obvious conclusion, very much in line with the discussion of implications for conflict resolution, lies in the mission understanding of peacekeeping operations. Just as any diplomats seeking to work positively in a conflict zone affected by organized crime, the imperative for peacekeepers to understand the criminal aspects of a given situation is even more acute. This is the case not least to ensure the very security of these peacekeeping forces.

Peacekeepers are not normally trained in understanding the political economy of the territories where they are deployed. But if deployed in a territory where the armed forces involved in the conflict are involved in organized crime, peacekeepers are at risk of finding themselves in the middle of criminal operations that they are not trained to address. For instance, when engaging in SSR it becomes essential to ensure that peacekeeping operations (PKOs) do not inadvertently help turn organized criminals into the future police force, intelligence agency, and military forces of the territory being stabilized. Likewise, when carrying out DDR programs, a firm understanding must be in place that "recidivism" need not include only remobilization into political violence, but may just as well involve transitions into criminal violence and organized criminality.[36]

Aside from preventing PKOs from pursuing their purpose, this could cause dangers for the peacekeeping forces themselves. Specifically, revenue streams generated by insurgent groups may be channeled into regional successor organizations as occurred in Serbia and Macedonia following the Kosovo conflict; intra-insurgency turf wars over control of illicit markets may erupt; miniature conflicts may start aimed at maintaining vital trafficking routes; or criminally motivated splinter groups may form. Hence, understanding the crime-insurgency nexus ahead of deployment can help PKOs understand the mission environment and prepare for possible contingencies motivated more by personal economic motives than by the nominal political conflict or "master cleavage," which may in and of itself have been formally resolved.

A second aspect of this problematique is the potential involvement of individual peacekeepers in organized crime. If officers and leaders are unaware of the criminal context, they may not be able to prevent the occasional peacekeeper succumbing to the temptation of colluding with criminal forces. In places such as Afghanistan, the temptation to facilitate a shipment of heroin may be an example, which could be better avoided if the criminal aspects are included in the mission planning. Suspected cases of this are common— the involvement of UN peacekeepers in mineral extraction in the Congo and

Ukrainian peacekeepers' involvement in cigarette and fuel smuggling in Ko-sovo, to name a few. [37] A specific variation of this problem occurs when the presence of peacekeeping forces actively spurs the market for prostitution, which has occurred in the Balkans. Indeed, it has been found that the traf-ficking of women for the purpose of prostitution increased with the arrival of peacekeepers in Bosnia-Herzegovina and Kosovo.[38] The responses of the higher commands to the problem of prostitution ranged from quietly endors-ing it as harmless entertainment for the troops, to outright prohibition. In most cases, the linkages between prostitution and systematic organized crime were not fully understood, contributing to the problem. Indeed, the pres-ence of peacekeepers could end up boosting the revenues of organized crime groups in conflict zones, as well as serious human rights violations against victims of human trafficking.

Mandate of Peacekeeping Operations

A much more difficult question is whether the mandate of peacekeeping forces needs to be amended to take into account the criminal aspect of a conflict situation. More to the point, the question is whether peacekeepers' mandates should include countercriminal operations. Indeed, at first sight, this may seem logical. If organized crime is indeed a source of financing for armed groups, and if the salience of organized crime in a conflict zone un-dermines the prospects of building sustainable political and economic de-velopment, then it may seem appropriate that peacekeepers should have the suppression of organized crime as a part of their mandate.

Yet this raises serious questions. First of all, peacekeeping forces are nor-mally military in nature, and military personnel are not usually trained for law enforcement operations, which is what the countering of organized crime implies. Even if most peacekeeping missions today include a law enforcement component, these face numerous challenges. First, there may not be an ap-plicable legal regime, intelligence records may be entirely missing or not col-lected in an actionable manner, and an entire criminal justice system needs to be set up. Likewise, complex criminal cases may take years to build up, whereas police officers sent on peacekeeping missions typically rotate on an annual or twice-annual basis. And as the case-studies on Kosovo and Afghan-istan in this volume illustrate, when military and law enforcement priorities are perceived to be in conflict, the former tends to take precedence.

Second, in the case that peacekeepers have the countering of organized crime in their mandate, this could have substantial implications for their security. If conflicting parties are indeed criminalized, they would likely see little problem in the presence of peacekeepers as long as they can continue pursuing their criminal operations. But if these criminal profits would be threatened by peacekeepers, the attitude of conflicting parties toward them might change; they may hence be targeted in an entirely different manner. Likewise, if transitional justice agreements involve strict asset confiscation laws, criminal elements may be unwilling to lay down their arms, putting the entire peace agreement in jeopardy. Particularly given the casualty aversion of Western powers, this could pose a serious problem to the continuation of such missions. This would in turn imply that much larger numbers of peacekeepers would be required in a conflict zone should the mandate include organized crime. However, as this book has illustrated, if the aim of a peacekeeping mission is not simply to stop the immediate bloodshed but also to build a modicum of sustainable states, economically and judicially, such problems cannot simply be wished away, but require a considered, balanced approach. In Kosovo, Western neglect of the criminalization of the elite led to the establishment of a quasi-criminalized state in Europe. Perhaps worse, in Afghanistan, the failure to address the opium economy's deep impact on Afghanistan's government contributed directly to endangering the entire objective of the mission, namely the establishment of a state that could prevent Afghanistan from once again becoming a haven for terrorism.

Hence, a difficult balance needs to be struck between keeping the peace and upholding the law, which will vary from case to case. First, to realistically be able to diminish the impact of organized criminality, PKOs need to be sufficiently extensive and appropriately equipped and trained. Furthermore, the likely length of deployment needs to be foreseen to last at least into the medium term. A compromise version may exist, where peacekeepers do not confront organized crime directly, in order not to undermine the coping economies of local civilians and risk losing their support, but move aggressively to ensure that central government officials are not involved in organized crime. A sequenced approach may also be possible, which focuses on ensuring military security initially and gradually expands law enforcement operations. None of this is easy and obvious negative contingencies may arise. But as Kosovo and Afghanistan illustrate, prioritizing security over the rule of law until the latter becomes too problematic to ignore can undermine the prospects of success for even the best-resourced PKOs. Therefore, a conscious strategy should be developed, rather than reflexively turning a blind eye to

the problem of organized crime while praying that it does not reach systemi-
cally destabilizing levels or undercuts the legitimacy of the regime that the
operation supports.

Conclusions

This study has shown that organized crime is much more of a salient factor in
armed conflict in the postcommunist conflict zones of Eurasia than normally
assumed. Furthermore, the involvement of insurgent forces in organized
crime and questions surrounding their potential motivational changes suggests that this is not a trivial matter. Likewise, there is a decisive area-specific
aspect to these conflicts. The character of these conflicts impacted the war
economies that developed—the sudden eruption of conflict following the
breakdown of multiethnic "empires" created a situation where fighting forces
needed to be mobilized quickly, creating an opening for organized criminal
networks. This was further facilitated by the "thieves in law" tradition that had
developed in the former Soviet Union and cultural ethos such as the *kanun*
tradition in the Balkans. Likewise, the relative absence of lootable resources
shifted focus of the war economies to trafficking of legal and illegal goods
and in some instances diaspora or transnational external funding, primarily
to Muslim parties such as the Bosniaks, Chechens, and Afghans. The relative
strength of the state and the extensive postconflict reconstruction aid that
flowed into several of these regions (primarily Bosnia-Herzegovina, Kosovo,
and Afghanistan) made control of the state as such a central aim during the
postconflict phase. Last, the geographical proximity of Western Europe, both
as an end-user market of smuggled goods and an intervening political and
military actor, clearly impacted the conflict dynamics and postconflict settlements. Taken together, this suggests that rather than searching for a single
"political economy" framework, future research should focus on midrange
theories or at least state the scope conditions of their findings.

Several of the case-studies identify multiple occasions of intramovement
factionalism and defections, with internal or local rivalries often awarded as
much time and resources as the formal "master cleavage" of the conflict. This
suggests that the main trend in studies of conflict economies may be over-
emphasizing structure—such as what commodities are available in a conflict
zone—and missing the agency of the armed actors, and what their main motives are, as illustrated by their actions on the ground.

Indeed, serious and systematic organized crime forms a key factor in the political economy of armed conflict. Indeed, as Naím has argued, various aspects of globalization have facilitated transnational crime—increased ease, lowered transaction costs, and increased volumes of cross-border trade, migration, communication, financial flows, and exchanges of ideas that facilitate licit and illicit commerce alike.[39] This arguably helps to explain the increased international focus on transnational organized crime, especially in postconflict societies, as illustrated by the most recent World Development Report.[40] It appears clear that the importance of this factor implies that it deserves a much more central role in the international community's understanding of armed conflicts, as well as needing to be factored into the international response to conflict situations. If not, future PKOs are doomed to repeat the mistakes of omission carried out by their predecessors, with predictable consequences of transitions from political conflict to criminal capture of the state.

Notes

Chapter 1. The Nexus of Crime and Conflict

1. Jeanne K. Giraldo and Harald A. Trinkunas, "The Political Economy of Terrorist Financing," in *Terrorist Financing and State Responses: A Comparative Perspective*, ed. Jeanne K. Giraldo and Harald A. Trinkunas (Palo Alto, Calif.: Stanford University Press, 2007), 7–20.

2. One the most notorious commodity-financed civil wars is the conflict in the Democratic Republic of Congo, sometimes referred to as "Africa's first World War"; see Léone Ndikumana and Kisangi F. Emizet, "The Economics of Civil War: The Case of the Democratic Republic of Congo," in *Understanding Civil War: Evidence and Anlysis*, vol. 1, *Africa*, ed. Paul Collier and Nicholas Sambanis (Washington, D.C.: World Bank, 2005), 64.

3. As Snyder and Bhavnani point out, even though alluvial diamonds are correlated with a higher risk of civil wars, most significant producers of such gemstones have not experienced civil wars since the end of World War II, which they explain with access to supplementary non-lootable sources of revenue and prudent investment in the military and social welfare. Rick Snyder and Ravi Bhavnani, "Diamonds, Blood and Taxes: A Revenue-Centered Framework for Explaining Political Order," *Journal of Conflict Resolution* 49, 4 (2005): 563–97.

4. See Jeremy Weinstein, *Inside Rebellion: The Politics of Insurgent Violence* (New York: Cambridge University Press, 2007) on Peru; Francisco Gutiérrez Sanin, "Telling the Difference: Guerrillas and Paramilitaries in the Colombian War," *Politics and Society* 36, 3 (2008) on Colombia; Jonathan Goodhand, "Corrupting or Consolidating the Peace? The Drugs Economy and Postconflict Peacebuilding in Afghanistan," *International Peacekeeping* 15, 3 (2008): 405–25.

5. In Colombia, the best publicized case of a drug-financed long-duration civil war, the paramilitary AUC and more recent successor groups originally fought to recapture control over vital drug cultivation areas. Over time, however, various militias under the

AUC umbrella engaged in a wide variety of illicit economic activity, from extorting multinational corporations to capturing government tenders for public projects. See Mauricio Romero Vidal, ed., *La Economía de los paramilitares* (Bogotá: Editorial Debate, 2011).

6. Michael L. Ross, "Oil, Drugs and Diamonds: The Varying Roles of Natural Resources in Civil Wars," in *The Political Economy of Armed Conflict*, ed. Karen Ballentine and Jake Sherman (Boulder, Colo.: Lynne Rienner, 2003), 47–70; Michael L. Ross, "What Do We Know About Natural Resources and Civil War," *Journal of Peace Research* 41, 3 (2004): 337–56; Michael L. Ross, "How Do Natural Resources Influence Civil War? Evidence from Thirteen Cases," *International Organization* 58 (Winter 2004): 35–67; James D. Fearon, "Why Do Some Civil Wars Last So Much Longer Than Others?" *Journal of Peace Research* 41, 3 (2004): 275–301.

7. Whereas research in this field has expanded rapidly, there is still far from unanimity regarding the exact impact of various types of "lootable" commodities. Ross argues that "contraband financing" (including gemstones, timber, and drugs) is correlated with longer-duration civil wars, but questions the direction of causality, arguing that contraband financing may increase due to civil war rather than the other way around. Michael L. Ross, "A Closer Look at Oil, Diamonds, and Civil War," *Annual Review of Political Science* 9 (2006): 265–300. Lujala distinguishes between these different types of "contraband" and finds that drug financing is associated with lower combat intensity, whereas gemstone mining inside the conflict area more than doubles the number of combat deaths. Paivi Lujala, "Deadly Combat over Natural Resources: Gems, Petroleum, Drugs and the Severity of Armed Conflict," *Journal of Conflict Resolution* 53, 1 (2009): 50–71.

8. Ross, "How Do Natural Resources Influence Civil War?" 43; D. Scott Bennett and Alan C. Stam, "The Duration of Interstate Wars, 1816–1985," *American Political Science Review* 90, 2 (1996): 239–57.

9. One crucial distinction here is that between *means* and *motives*. Some scholars take the fact that an armed group is financed through, for example, drug trafficking as prima facie evidence of its motives, whereas others argue that such financing can simply be a means to an end, and that complementary indicators, such as modus operandi, target selection, and internal incentives offered to combatants need to be factored into such an analysis. For an illustration of these diverging approaches, see Michael P. Roth and Murat Sever, "The Kurdish Workers Party (PKK) as a Criminal Syndicate: Funding Terrorism Through Organized Crime, a Case Study," *Studies in Conflict and Terrorism* 30, 10 (2007): 901–20; Michael Jonsson and Svante Cornell, "Examining PKK Financing," *Jane's Intelligence Review* (April 2008).

10. Weinstein, *Inside Rebellion*.

11. Ted R. Gurr, *Peoples Versus States: Ethnopolitical Conflict and Accommodation at the End of the 20th Century* (Washington, D.C.: U.S. Institute of Peace Press, 2000); Michael E. Brown, "Causes and Implications of Ethnic Conflict," in *Ethnic Conflict and International Security*, ed. Michael E. Brown (Princeton, N.J.: Princeton University Press, 1993); Stephen Van Evera, "Hypotheses on Nationalism and War," *International*

Security 18, 4 (1994): 5–39; David A. Lake and Donald Rothschild, "Containing Fear: The Origins and Management of Ethnic Conflict," *International Security* 21, 2 (1996): 41–75.

12. David Keen, "The Economic Functions of Violence in Civil Wars," *Adelphi Papers* 38, 320 (1998); Paul Collier and Anke Hoeffler, *Greed and Grievance in Civil War* (Washington, D.C.: World Bank, October 2001); Mats Berdal and David M. Malone, "Introduction," in *Greed and Grievance: Economic Agendas in Civil Wars,* ed. Mats Berdal and David M. Malone (Boulder, Colo.: Lynne Rienner, 2000), 1–18; Ballentine and Sherman, *The Political Economy of Armed Conflict.*

13. H. I. Grossman, "Kleptocracy and Revolutions," *Oxford Economic Papers* 51 (1999): 267–83; Collier and Hoeffler, *Greed and Grievance in Civil War.*

14. Collier and Hoeffler, *Greed and Grievance in Civil War,* 2.

15. David Keen, "Incentives and Disincentives for Violence," in Berdal and Malone, *Greed and Grievance,* 19–42.

16. Collier and Hoeffler, *Greed and Grievance in Civil Wars,* 1.

17. Ibid., 16.

18. Aspinall, for example, argues that it is not only the presence of natural resources that triggers conflict, but how the proceeds of these resources are spent (e.g., if they are not benefiting the local population, such resources may reinforce a "discourse of deprivation") and whether there are local ethnic political entrepreneurs who can mobilize resistance against such patterns or resource extraction. Focusing on the rise of the Free Aceh Movement (GAM) in Aceh, Indonesia, Aspinall points out that similar natural resources were also available in Riau and East Kalimantan, but no conflict erupted there. Edward Aspinall, "The Construction of Grievance: Natural Resources and Identity in a Separatist Conflict," *Journal of Conflict Resolution* 51, 6 (2007): 950–72.

19. Karen Ballentine and Heiko Nitzschke, "Beyond Greed and Grievance: Policy Lessons from Studies in the Political Economy of Armed Conflict," *International Peace Academy Policy Report* (October 2003): 1.

20. Ross, "What Do We Know," 337–38.

21. Ibid., 338.

22. Christopher Cramer, "Homo Economicus Goes to War: Methodological Individualism, Rational Choice and the Political Economy of War," *World Development* 30, 11 (2002): 1845–64.

23. Paul Collier and Anke Hoeffler, "Beyond Greed and Grievance: Feasibility and Civil War," *Oxford Economic Papers* 61, 1 (2009): 1–27.

24. Cf. Romero Vidal, ed., *La Economía de los paramilitares*; Michael Jonsson and Svante Cornell, "Countering Terrorist Financing: Lessons from Europe," *Georgetown Journal of International Affairs* 8 (Winter/Spring 2007); Feargal Cochrane, Bahal Baser, and Ashok Swain, "Home Thoughts from Abroad: Diasporas and Peacebuilding in Northern Ireland and Sri Lanka," *Studies in Conflict and Terrorism* 32, 8 (2009): 681–704.

25. Philippe Le Billon, "The Political Ecology of War: Natural Resources and Armed Conflicts," *Political Geography* 20, 5 (2001): 561–84.

26. Ross, "Oil, Drugs and Diamonds," 47–70.

27. Moisés Naím, *Illicit: How Smugglers, Traffickers and Copycats Are Hijacking the Global Economy* (New York: Anchor, 2005).

28. Macartan Humpreys, "Natural Resource, Conflict, and Conflict Resolution," Santa Fe Institute/Javeriana University Workshop, Obstacles to Robust Negotiated Settlements, Bogotá, May 29–31, 2003.

29. Fearon, "Why Do Some Civil Wars Last So Much Longer Than Others?" 283–84.

30. Ross, "What Do We Know," 344–45.

31. Svante E. Cornell, "Narcotics and Armed Conflict: Interaction and Implications," *Studies in Conflict and Terrorism* 30, 3 (2007): 207–27.

32. I. William Zartman, "The Timing of Peace Initiatives: Hurting Stalemates and Ripe Moments," *Global Review of Ethnopolitics* 1, 1 (2001): 8–18.

33. Rachel Ehrenfeld, *Narcoterrorism* (New York: Basic Books, 1990); Chris Dishman, "Terrorism, Crime and Transformation," *Studies in Conflict and Terrorism* 24, 1 (2001): 43–58; Glenn E. Schweitzer, *A Faceless Enemy: The Origins of Modern Terrorism* (Cambridge: Perseus, 2002), 287–89; Tamara Makarenko, "Crime, Terror, and the Central Asian Drug Trade," *Harvard Asia Quarterly* 6 (Spring 2002); also Ekaterina Stepanova, *Rol' narkobiznesa v politekonomii konfliktov i terrorizma* (The Role of Drugs in the Political Economy of Conflict and Terrorism) (Moscow: Ves Mir, 2005), with English summary, 302–10; Pablo Dreyfus, "Sendero Luminoso: ¿Un caso de Narcoterrorismo?" *Boletín Saap, Sociedad Argentina de Análisis Político* 8 (1999); Luis Alberto Villamarin, *Narcoterrorismo: La guerra del nuevo siglo* (Madrid: Nowtilus, 2005).

34. The analytical construction of the crime-terror nexus was originally conceptualized specifically for terrorism. However, it captures the dynamic of all politically motivated nonstate violent actors, including separatist and insurgent groups whether or not they use terrorist tactics. The study thus does not differentiate among groups based on whether they use terrorist tactics.

35. Tamara Makarenko, "A Model of Terrorist-Criminal Relationships," *Jane's Intelligence Review* (August 1, 2003).

36. Sherzod Abdukadirov, "Terrorism: The Dark Side of Social Entrepreneurship," *Studies in Conflict & Terrorism* 33, 7 (2010): 603–17.

37. Phil Williams, "Transnational Criminal Organizations and International Security," *Survival* 36, 1 (1994): 96.

38. Bruce Hoffman, *Inside Terrorism* (New York: Columbia University Press, 1998), 43.

39. Williams, "Transnational Criminal Organizations and International Security," 96.

40. Phil Williams, "Terrorist Financing and Organized Crime: Nexus, Appropriation or Transformation?" in *Countering the Financing of Terrorism*, ed. Thomas J. Biersteker and Sue Eckert (London: Routledge, 2008), 131–32.

41. Kimberley Thachuk, "Transnational Threats: Falling Through the Cracks?" *Low Intensity Conflict & Law Enforcement* 10, 1 (2001): 51.

42. World Bank, *World Development Report 2011* (Washington, D.C.: World Bank, 2011).

43. Alain Labrousse, *Géopolitique des drogues* (Paris: Presses Universitaires de France, 2004), 72; Jeanne K. Giraldo and Harald A. Trinkunas, "The Political Economy of Terrorist Financing," in Giraldo and Trinkunas, *Terrorist Financing and State Responses*, 7-20.

44. Tamara Makarenko, "Terrorism and Transnational Organized Crime: Tracing the Crime-Terror Nexus in Southeast Asia," in *Terrorism and Transnational Violence in Southeast Asia: Challenges to States and Regional Stability*, ed. Paul Smith (Armonk, N.Y.: M.E. Sharpe, 2004).

45. Thomas M. Sanderson, "Transnational Terror and Organized Crime: Blurring the Lines," *SAIS Review* 24 (Winter/Spring 2004); Thomas J. Biersteker and Sue Eckert, "Conclusion: Taking Stock of Efforts to Counter the Financing of Terrorism and Recommendations for a Way Forward," in Biersteker and Eckert, *Countering the Financing of Terrorism*, 289-304.

46. Barbara Harriss-White, "Globalization, Insecurities and Responses: An Introductory Essay," in *Globalization and Insecurity: Political, Economic and Physical Challenges*, ed. Barbara Harriss-White (New York: Palgrave, 2002); H. Richard Fridman and Peter Andreas, eds., *The Illicit Global Economy and State Power* (Lanham, Md.: Rowman and Littlefield, 1999).

47. Phil Williams, "Transnational Criminal Networks," in *Networks and Netwars: The Future of Terror, Crime and Militancy*, ed. John Arquilla and David Ronfeldt (Santa Monica, Calif.: RAND, 2000), 61-97. Melvin Levitzky, "Transnational Criminal Networks and International Security," *Syracuse Journal of International Law and Commerce* 30 (Summer 2003): 227-40; Svante E. Cornell, "Crime Without Borders," *Axess Magazine* 6 (2004): 18-21.

48. Moisés Naím, *Illicit: How Smugglers, Traffickers, and Copycats Are Hijacking the Global Economy* (New York: Anchor, 2005).

49. Tamara Makarenko, "A Model of Terrorist-Criminal Relationships"; Makarenko, "The Crime-Terror Continuum: Tracing the Interplay Between Transnational Crime and Terrorism," *Global Crime* 6 (Spring 2004).

50. Adapted from Tamara Makarenko's concept of the crime-terror nexus; see Makarenko, "A Model of Terrorist-Criminal Relationships."

51. Dishman, "Terrorism, Crime and Transformation."

52. Chester G. Oehme, III, "Terrorists, Insurgents and Criminals—Growing Nexus?" *Studies in Conflict & Terrorism* 31, 1 (2008): 80-93.

53. Makarenko, "Crime, Terror, and the Central Asian Drug Trade."

54. Makarenko, "The Crime-Terror Continuum"; Schweitzer, *A Faceless Enemy*, 287-89.

55. Independent Monitoring Commission for Northern Ireland, *Seven Report of the Independent Monitoring Commission*, London, October 2005, 18-20.

56. Jonsson and Cornell, "Examining PKK financing"; Gutiérrez Sanin, "Telling the Difference."

57. Gutiérrez Sanin, "Telling the Difference." In a separate article, Gutiérrez Sanin also argues that it was the formal, hierarchical organization of FARC that meant it was

less affected by motivational changes than Taliban networks in Afghanistan. Francisco Gutiérrez Sanin and Antonio Giustozzi, "Networks and Armies: Structuring Rebellion in Colombia and Afghanistan," *Studies in Conflict and Terrorism* 33, 9 (2010): 836–53.

58. Jonsson and Cornell, "Countering Terrorist Financing."

59. Jacob N. Shapiro, "Terrorist Organizations' Vulnerabilities and Inefficiencies: A Rational Choice Perspective," in Giraldo and Trinkunas, *Terrorist Financing and State Responses*, 56–71.

60. Cf. Weinstein, *Inside Rebellion*.

61. John T. Picarelli and Louise I. Shelley, "Organized Crime and Terrorism," in Giraldo and Trinkunas, *Terrorist Financing and State Responses*, 46–47.

62. Picarelli and Shelley, "Organized Crime and Terrorism," 54. While the term "terrorism financing" may suggest small-scale, secretive, and urban cells using terrorist tactics, their survey includes several armed groups that are better characterized as full-blown insurgencies, such as the Tamil Tigers. As such, this argument is fully applicable to the aim of this book.

63. Karen Ballentine, "Beyond Greed and Grievance: Reconsidering the Economic Dynamics of Armed Conflict," in Ballentine and Sherman, *The Political Economy of Armed Conflict*, 262n1.

64. Pierre-Arnaud Chouvy, *Les Territoires de l'opium: Conflits et trafics du Triangle d'Or et du Croissant d'Or* (Geneva: Olizane, 2002), 43–67.

65. Mary B. Anderson, *Do No Harm: How Aid Can Support Peace—or War* (Boulder, Colo.: Lynne Rienner, 1999).

66. Michael P. Roth and Murat Sever, "The Kurdish Workers Party (PKK) as a Criminal Syndicate: Funding Terrorism Through Organized Crime: A Case Study," *Studies in Conflict and Terrorism* 30, 10 (2007): 901–20; Arabinda Acharya, Syed Adnan Ali Shah Bukhari, and Sadia Sulaiman, "Making Money in the Mayhem: Funding Taliban Insurrection in the Tribal Areas of Pakistan," *Studies in Conflict and Terrorism* 32, 2 (2009): 95–108; Gutiérrez Sanin, "Telling the Difference."

67. Alain Labrousse, "Colombie: Le Role de la drogue dans l'extension territoriale des FARC-EP (1978–2002)," *Géopolitique des drogues Illicites*, Hérodote 112 (Paris: Découverte, 2004).

68. Vladimir N. Brovkin, "Corruption in 20th Century Russia," *Crime, Law and Social Change* 40 (2003): 195–230.

69. Boris Mikhailichenko, "Mezh dvuh Yaponchikov," *Moskovskiye Novosti* 28 (2004).

70. For an overview, see Gennadii F. Khokhriakov, "Organizovannia Prestupnost' v Rossii: 60–e-pervaia polvina 90–kh godov," *Obschestvennye nauki i sovremennost'* 6 (2000): 62–74; "Organized Crime in Russia from the 1960s Through the First Half of the 1990s," *Sociological Research* 41, 5 (2002): 5–29; Virginie Colloudon, *La Mafia en Union Soviétique* (Paris: Lattès, 1990).

71. James O. Finckenauer and Yuri A. Voronin, *The Threat of Russian Organized Crime* (Washington, D.C.: National Institute of Justice, 2001), 5.

72. Mark Galeotti, "The Mafiya and the New Russia," *Australian Journal of Politics and History* 44, 3 (1998): 415–29; J. Michael Wallner and Victor J. Yasmann, "Russia's Great Criminal Revolution," *Journal of Contemporary Criminal Justice* 11, 4 (1995).

Chapter 2. Afghanistan's Endless Conflict and the Development of the Opium Industry

This chapter relies on previous work by the author, and benefited from contributions of researchers affiliated with these projects. Klas Marklund contributed to drafting an earlier version of this chapter. Tamara Makarenko and Maral Madiyeva also contributed to earlier studies, in particular a report for UNODC that the author co-wrote with Niklas Swanström, which this chapter draws on.

1. UN Office on Drug Control and Crime Prevention, *Illicit Drug Situation in the Regions Neighbouring Afghanistan and the Response of ODCCP*, 2002, 3.

2. UNODC, "The Opium/Heroin Market," in UNODC, *World Drug Report 2011* (Vienna: UNODC, 2011), http://www.unodc.org/documents/data-and-analysis/WDR2011/The_opium-heroin_market.pdf.

3. Larry P. Goodson, *Afghanistan's Endless War* (Seattle: University of Washington Press, 2001), 58–67.

4. Gilles Dorronsoro, *Revolution Unending: Afghanistan: 1979 to the Present* (London: Hurst, 2005), 146; Ishtiaq Ahmad, *Gulbuddin Hekmatyar: An Afghan Trail from Jihad to Terrorism* (Islamabad: STEP, 2004); Svante E. Cornell, "Taliban Afghanistan: A True Islamic State?" in *The Limits of Culture: Foreign Policy, Islam, and the Caspian*, ed. Brenda Shaffer (Cambridge, Mass.: MIT Press, 2007).

5. The discussion regarding the involvement of various economic contributors to the Afghan conflict and their agenda is outside the focus of this chapter. For more information see Christopher M. Blanchard, *Afghanistan, Narcotics, and U.S. Policy* (Washington, D.C.: Congressional Research Service, Report for Congress, 2005); George Crile, *Charlie Wilson's War: The Extraordinary Story of How the Wildest Man in Congress and a Rogue CIA Agent Changed the History of Our Times* (New York: Atlantic, 2003); John K. Cooley, *Unholy Wars: Afghanistan, America and International Terrorism* (London: Pluto, 2002).

6. Goodson, *Afghanistan's Endless War*, 64–68.

7. Ahmad, *Gulbuddin Hekmatyar*, 10–16.

8. Michael Griffin, *Reaping the Whirlwind: The Taliban Movement in Afghanistan* (London: Pluto, 2001).

9. Svante E. Cornell, "Pakistan's Foreign Policy: Islamic or Pragmatic?" in Shaffer, *The Limits of Culture*.

10. Brian Glyn Williams, "Writing the Dostumname: Field Research with an Uzbek Warlord in Afghan Turkistan," *Central Eurasian Studies Review* 6, 1/2 (Fall 2007).

11. See Cornell, "Taliban Afghanistan" in Shaffer, *The Limits of Culture*.

12. Antonio Giustozzi, *Koran, Kalashnikov, and Laptop: The Neo-Taliban Insurgency in Afghanistan* (New York: Columbia University Press, 2008), 80–86; Shahid Afshar,

Chris Samples, and Thomas Wood, "The Taliban: An Organizational Analysis," *Military Review* (May–June 2008), http://www.humansecuritygateway.com/documents/ MILRE VIEW_Taliban_Organizational_Analysis.pdf.

13. Bill Roggio, "Pakistan's ISI, Quetta Shura Behind Rabbani's Assassination, Afghan Officials Say," *Long War Journal* (October 2, 2011), http://www.longwarjournal.org/ threat-matrix/archives/2011/10/pakistans_isi_quetta_shura_beh.php.

14. Gary Reid and Genevieve Costigan, eds., *Revisiting the Hidden Epidemic: A Situation Assessment of Drug Use in Asia in the Context of HIV/AIDS* (Melbourne: Burnet Institute, 2002), 20.

15. UNODC, *The Opium Economy in Afghanistan: An International Problem* (New York: UN, 2003), 88. See also the useful overview in Gretchen Peters, *How Opium Profits the Taliban*, Peaceworks 62 (Washington, D.C.: U.S. Institute of Peace, 2009), 7–16.

16. UNODC, *Illicit Drug Situation in the Regions Neighboring Afghanistan and the Response of ODCCP* (Vienna: UNODCCP, 2002), 5.

17. David MacDonald, *Drugs in Afghanistan* (London: Pluto, 2007), 88–89.

18. UNODC, *The Opium Economy in Afghanistan*, 90.

19. Aleksandr Knyazev, *K Istorii i Sovremenomy Sostoyaniyu Proizvodstva Narkotikov v Afganistane i ikh rasprotranenie v Sentralnoi Azii* (Bishkek, 2003), 14.

20. Kosimsho Iskandarov, "Narcobusiness in Tajikistan and Its Relation to the Afghan Conflict," *Central Asia and Caucasus* 5 (1999).

21. Barnett R. Rubin, "The Political Economy of War and Peace in Afghanistan," *World Development* 28, 10 (2000): 1789–1803.

22. Goodson, *Afghanistan's Endless War*, 97–103.

23. Alfred W. McCoy, *The Politics of Heroin: CIA Complicity in the Global Drug Trade*, 2nd rev. ed. (Chicago: Lawrence Hill, 2003), 504–6.

24. Rubin, "The Political Economy of War and Peace in Afghanistan."

25. UNODC, *The Opium Economy in Afghanistan*, 90; McCoy, *The Politics of Heroin*, 484–85.

26. For an excellent overview of the dynamics of opiate production in the Golden Crescent and Golden Triangle, see Pierre-Arnaud Chouvy, *Les Territoires de l'opium: Conflits et trafics du Triangle d'Or et du Croissant d'Or* (Geneva: Olizane, 2002).

27. Alexander L. Zelichenko, *Afganskaya Narkoekspansiya,1990-x gg. i Problema Natsionalnoi Bezopasnosti Kirgizstana* (The Afghan Narco-Expansion of the 1990s and the Problem of Kyrgyzstan's National Security) (Bishkek: Kyrgyz Slavonic University Publications, 2003), 28.

28. Johan Engvall, "The State Under Siege: The Drug Trade and Organised Crime in Tajikistan," *Europe-Asia Studies* 58, 6 (2006).

29. Alfred W. McCoy, "Opium History, 1940 to 1979," A Quick History of Opium, http://www.a1b2c3.com/drugs/opi002.htm; Cooley, *Unholy Wars*.

30. James Rupert and Steve Coll, "U.S. Declines to Probe Afghan Drug Trade," *Washington Post*, May 13, 1990, A1. See Peters, *How Opium Profits the Taliban*, for the Western tendency to downplay the problem.

31. Ikramul Haq, "Pak-Afghan Drug Trade in Historical Perspective," *Asian Survey* 36, 10 (October 1996): 945–63; Ahmad, *Gulbuddin Hekmatyar*, 41–42.

32. See, e.g., Zelichenko, *Afganskaya Narkoekspansiya, 1990–x*, 27.

33. Knyazev, *K Istorii i Sovremenomy*, 14.

34. Griffin, *Reaping the Whirlwind*, 153.

35. Peters, *How Opium Profits the Taliban*, 10–11.

36. Ahmed Rashid, *Taliban: Islam, Oil, and the New Great Game in Central Asia* (London: Tauris, 2000), 119; Griffin, *Reaping the Whirlwind*, 154.

37. Rashid, *Taliban*, 166.

38. McCoy, *The Politics of Heroin*, 508–9.

39. Rashid, *Taliban*, 164

40. UNDCP, *Global Illicit Drug Trends 2001* (New York: UN, 2001), 39.

41. Observatoire Géopolitique des Drogues, *The World Geopolitics of Drugs*, 1995/96 Annual Report, http://www.ogd.org/rapport/gb/RP09_1_AFGH.html.

42. BBC News, October 26, 1997.

43. Transnational Institute, "Merging Wars," 11.

44. U.S. Department of State, Bureau for International Narcotics and Law Enforcement Affairs, *International Narcotics Control Strategy Report, 1998* (Washington, D.C.: Department of State, February 1999); http://usembassy.state.gov/afghanistan/wwwhnr 98.html.

45. Griffin, *Reaping the Whirlwind*, 220.

46. "Afghanistan's Taliban Bans Heroin," *Associated Press*, February 29, 1999.

47. UNDCP, *Global Illicit Drug Trends 2001*, 35.

48. Rashid, *Taliban*, 164.

49. David Mansfield and Adam Pain, *Evidence from the Field: Understanding Changing Levels of Opium Poppy Cultivation in Afghanistan*, Briefing Paper Series, Afghanistan Research and Evaluation Unit, November 2007.

50. Ahto Lobjakas, "NATO Sees 'Tribal' Nature to Taliban Insurgency," *RFE/RL*, July 20, 2007.

51. "Afghan Drug Trade Closely Linked to Taliban Insurgency," *USINFO*, June 26, 2007.

52. Aisha Ahmad, "Afghanistan's Narco-Economy," 2005.

53. Peters, *How Opium Profits the Taliban*, 20.

54. *United States v. Bashir Noorzai*, U.S. District Court, Southern District of New York, S1 05 Cr. 19, April 25, 2005.

55. Sally Neighbor, "Taliban's Heroin, Inc.," *Australian*, May 21, 2010; Peters, *How Opium Profits the Taliban*, 20.

56. Gretchen Peters, *Seeds of Terror: How Drugs, Thugs and Crime Are Reshaping the Afghan War* (New York: St. Martin's, 2010), 101.

57. Del Quentin Wilber, "Afghan Farmer Help Convict Taliban Member in U.S. Court," *Washington Post*, December 23, 2008.

58. Rajeev Syal, "Wikileaks Cables: 'Taliban Treats Heroin Stocks like Savings Accounts,'" *Guardian*, December 20, 2010.

59. James A. Piazza, "The Opium Trade and Patterns of Terrorism in the Provinces of Afghanistan: An Empirical Analysis," *Terrorism and Political Violence* 24 (2012): 213–34.

60. Giustozzi, *Koran, Kalashnikov, and Laptop*, 88.

61. Peters, *Seeds of Terror*, 102.

62. Ibid., 25, 102–3; Peters, *How Opium Profits the Taliban*, 6.

63. Peters, *Seeds of Terror*, 24.

64. David Mansfield, "Responding to Risk and Uncertainty: Understanding the Nature of Change in the Rural Livelihoods of Opium Poppy Growing Households in the 2007/08 Growing Season," Report for the Afghan Drugs Inter Departmental Unit of the UK Government, July 2008, 40–44.

65. Maria Abi-Habib, "Afghan Air Force Probed in Drug Running," *Wall Street Journal*, March 7, 2012; Spencer Ackerman, "Afghan Air Force: Flying Drug Mules That Fuel Civil War," *Wired.com*, March 8, 2012.

66. Tom Lasseter, "Afghan Drug Trade Thrives with Help, and Neglect, of Officials," *McClatchy Newspapers*, May 10, 2009.

67. Graeme Smith, "Afghan Officials in Drug Trade Cut Deals Across Enemy Lines," *Globe and Mail*, March 21, 2009.

68. James Risen, "Reports Link Karzai's Brother to Drug Trade," *New York Times*, October 4, 2008; Lasseter, "Afghan Drug Trade Thrives"; Tom Lasseter, "Karzai's Brother Threatened McClatchy Writer Reporting Afghan Drug Story," *McClatchy Newspapers*, July 2, 2009; "U.S. Warns Karzai's Brother Could Become Target," *Reuters*, March 30, 2010; Steve Coll, "Kandahar," *New Yorker*, April 2, 2010; Matthieu Aikins, "Who Killed Ahmed Wali Karzai," *Foreign Policy*, July 12, 2011.

69. "Afghan President Hamid Karzai Chooses Warlord as Running Mate," *Associated Press*, May 4, 2009.

70. Rashid, *Taliban*; Ikram Sehgal, "The New 'Great Game," *Defence Journal* (August 2003), http://www.defencejournal.com/2003-08/abm-a.htm; Jerome Starkey, "Former Warlord to Fight Karzai in Afghanistan Polls," *Independent*, March 9, 2009.

71. Ahmed Rashid, "Chief Ousted as British Troops Head for Afghan Drug Region," *Telegraph*, December 23, 2005.

72. Jean MacKenzie and Abaceen Nasimi, "Tensions Between U.S., Kabul, Likely to Worsen," *New Haven Register*, January 28, 2009.

73. Thomas Schweich, "Is Afghanistan a Narco-State?" *New York Times Magazine*, July 27, 2008.

74. Ali Jalali, "Afghanistan Beyond Bonn," address to W.P. Carey Forum, Central Asia-Caucasus Institute, Washington D.C., December 7 2005, http://www.silkroadstudies.org/new/inside/forum/WPC_2005_1207.htm.

75. Vanda Felbab-Brown, "Afghanistan: When Counter-Narcotics Undermines Counter-Terrorism," *Washington Quarterly* 28, 4 (2005): 55–72.

76. James Risen and Carlotta Gall, "An Afghan's Path from U.S. Ally to Drug Suspect," *New York Times*, February 2, 2007; James Risen, "Propping Up a Drug Lord, Then

Arresting Him," *New York Times*, December 11, 2010; Jeff Stein, "CIA Hired Karzai Brother Before 9/11, Woodward Says," *Washingtonpost.com*, September 30, 2009.

77. Jalali, "Afghanistan Beyond Bonn."

Chapter 3. Tajikistan: From Drug-Insurgency to Drug-State Nexus

1. Luigi De Martino, "Tajikistan at a Crossroad: Contradictory Forces at the Heart of the Tajik Political System," in *Tajikistan at a Crossroad: The Politics of Decentralisation*, ed. Luigi De Martino (Geneva: CIMERA, 2004), 152–53; Jesse Driscoll, "Inside the Leviathan: Coup-Proofing After State Failure," unpublished paper, Stanford University, October 18, 2008.

2. Kathleen Collins, "The Logic of Clan Politics: Evidences from the Central Asian Trajectories," *World Politics* 56, 1 (2004): 224–61.

3. Aziz Niyazov, "Tadzhikistan: konflikt regionov" (Tajikistan: Conflict of Regions), *Vostok* 2 (1997): 94–107.

4. Letizia Paoli, Irina Rabkov, Victoria A. Greenfield, and Peter Reuter, "Tajikistan: The Rise of a Narco-State," *Journal of Drug Issues* 37, 4 (Fall 2007): 954.

5. Driscoll, "Inside the Leviathan," 6.

6. Jesse Driscoll, "Commitment Problems or Bidding Wars? Rebel Fragmentation as Peace-Building," paper for the 14th World Convention of the Association for the Study of Nationalities, New York, April 19, 2009.

7. The decline in output in Tajikistan was much sharper and more sustained than elsewhere in the region. By 1996, it was less than 40 percent of its 1989 value.

8. Olivier Roy, *The New Central Asia: The Creation of Nations* (London: Tauris, 2000), 139–42.

9. U.S. Department of State, Bureau for International Narcotics and Law Enforcement Affairs, *International Narcotics Control Strategy Report, 2001* (Washington, D.C., 2002), 128–29.

10. Kirill Nourzhanov, "Saviours of the Nation or Robber Barons? Warlord Politics in Tajikistan," *Central Asian Survey* 24, 2 (2005): 119.

11. Erica Marat, "State-Crime Nexus in Central Asia: State Weakness, Organized Crime, and Corruption in Kyrgyzstan and Tajikistan," Silk Road Paper, Central Asia-Caucasus Institute-Silk Road Studies Program, Uppsala, October 2006, 111–12.

12. In January 2002 Qurbon Cholov and another PFT warlord, Saidsho Shamolov, were dismissed from leadership positions in the border control committee. It was reported that both were involved in activities from drug and arms smuggling to kidnapping and assassinations. For more, see ICG, "Tajikistan's Politics: Confrontation or Consolidation?" *ICG Asia Briefing* (May 19, 2004).

13. Paoli et al., "The Rise of a Narco-State," 969.

14. Shirin Akiner, *Tajikistan: Disintegration or Reconciliation?* (London: Royal Institute of International Affairs, 2001), 73–74.

15. Nourzhanov, "Warlord Politics in Tajikistan," 120.

16. Khudoberdiyev was killed by his partner in an internal conflict in 2001. Boimatov was killed in an armed skirmish with government forces in 1997.

17. Nourzhanov, "Warlord Politics in Tajikistan," 119.

18. Cf. Mancur Olson, *Power and Prosperity: Outgrowing Communist and Capitalist Dictatorships* (New York: Basic Books, 2000), 1–24.

19. See, e.g., Akiner, *Tajikistan: Disintegration or Reconciliation.*

20. Ahmed Rashid, *Jihad: The Rise of Militant Islam in Central Asia* (New Haven, Conn.: Yale University Press, 2002).

21. Ibid.

22. See also Tamara Makarenko, "Crime, Terror and the Central Asian Drug Trade," *Harvard Asia Quarterly* 6, 3 (2002).

23. Svante E. Cornell, "The Narcotics Threat in Greater Central Asia: From Crime-Terror Nexus to State Infiltration?" *China and Eurasia Forum Quarterly* 4, 1 (2006): 43.

24. "Tajikistan: Leading Politician Faces Extradition," *IWPR Central Asia Reporting,* December 14, 2004, http://iwpr.net/?p=rca&s=f&o=162091&apc_state=henirca200412; "Tajik Opposition Leader Arrested," *IWPR Central Asia Peace Reporting,* April 29, 2005, http://iwpr.net/?p=rca&o=238840&apc_state=henirca2005. The Tajik Supreme Court later sentenced him to twenty-three years in prison.

25. He was later moved to the Leninabad region in northern Tajikistan.

26. Author's interviews with Kyrgyz law enforcement officials, Bishkek, February 2006.

27. "Tajikistan: President to Head East as Battle for Badakshan Control Continues," *Eurasianet,* September 14, 2012, www.eurasianet.org/node/65914.

28. Driscoll, "Inside the Leviathan," 37.

29. See UNODC, *World Drug Report 2011* (Vienna: UNODC, 2011), 71.

30. Some sources even estimate that about 100 tons of heroin are smuggled through Tajikistan each year. See Filippo De Danieli, "Counter-Narcotics Policies in Tajikistan and Their Impact on State Building," *Central Asian Survey 30,* 1 (2011): 129–45; Paoli et al., "The Rise of a Narco-State," 951–80; ICG, "Tajikistan: The Changing Insurgent Threats," *ICG Asia Report* 205 (May 24, 2011); UNDP on heroin trade in Tajikistan, http://europeandcis.undp.org/files/uploads/CA%20HDR/ oxford%20analytica%20–%20 Tajikistan.pdf.

31. UNODC, *World Drug Report 2011,* 72.

32. S. Frederick Starr, "Clans, Authoritarian Leaders and Parliaments in Central Asia," Silk Road Paper, Uppsala: Central Asia-Caucasus Institute-Silk Road Studies Program, June 2006, 12.

33. Paoli et al., "The Rise of a Narco-State," 966.

34. Ibid., 967.

35. De Danieli, "Counter-Narcotics Policies in Tajikistan," 141.

36. "OSCE Holds Training Seminars on Fights Against Human Trafficking in Northern Tajikistan," OSCE press release, July 3, 2003, http://www.osce.org/tajikistan/55459.

37. Johan Engvall, "The State Under Siege: The Drug Trade and Organised Crime in Tajikistan," *Europe-Asia Studies* 58, 6 (2006): 845.

38. For this distinction between centralized and decentralized authoritarian rule, see Johan Engvall, "Kyrgyzstan: Anatomy of a State," *Problems of Post-Communism* 54, 4 (2007): 42.

39. Driscoll, "Inside the Leviathan," 30.

40. Ibid. Driscoll notes that among the most prominent locations are Darband, controlled by Mullo Abdullo; Tavildara, the home of Ziyoev; and the Leninsky district, no more than 20 kilometers from downtown Dushanbe and ruled by Rakhmon "Hitler" Sanginov.

41. Kenzhaev was assassinated in the build-up to the 1999 presidential elections.

42. Driscoll, "Inside the Leviathan."

43. Anvar Karimov, "Bez shtanov, a ego karmany prodolzhaet vyvorachivat" (Without pants, but continues to turn out his pockets), *Charogi Ruz* 3 (2004): 11; Marat, "The State-Crime Nexus in Central Asia."

44. Engvall, "The State Under Siege," 846.

45. With a 3,000–man force directly subordinate to Mirzoyev, the presidential guard was the country's strongest and best equipped security force.

46. Before 1992, it was known that Mirzoyev had previously been arrested for racketeering and during that time he practically controlled the central parts of Dushanbe. Nikolai Vavilov, "V rezul'tate boev v Dushanbe i ego okrestnostyakh uzhe imeyutsya zhertvy" (There are already victims as a result of fighting in Dushanbe and its surroundings), *Nezavisimaya gazeta*, August 12, 1997.

47. Akiner, *Tajikistan: Disintegration or Reconciliation*, 71.

48. Maral Madi, "Who Is the New Director of the Tajik Drug Control Agency?" *Central Asia-Caucasus Analyst*, March 24, 2004, www.cacianalyst.org/view_article.php?articleid=2230; "Tajikistan Capital's Mayor Involved in Drug Business," *Pravda*, July 30, 2001.

49. Cornell, "The Narcotics Threat in Greater Central Asia," 54.

50. Marat, "The State-Crime Nexus in Central Asia," 113.

51. Driscoll, "Inside the Leviathan."

52. See *Asia-Plus*, "General Suhrob Qosimov Sends in His Resignation," March 13, 2007, www.asiaplus.tj/en/news/36/164662.

53. See Henry Hale, "Democracy or Autocracy on the March? The Colored Revolutions as Normal Dynamics of Patronal Presidentialism," *Communist and Post-Communist Studies* 39, 3 (2006): 305–29.

54. Driscoll, "Inside the Leviathan," 38–39.

55. Alexander Sodiqov, "High-Profile Death Raises Questions in Tajikistan," *Central Asia-Caucasus Analyst*, August 19, 2009, www.cacianalyst.org/?q=node/5164; ICG, "Tajikistan: The Changing Insurgent Threats."

56. ICG, "Tajikistan: The Changing Insurgent Threats," 2.

57. Ibid.

58. "Tajikistan: Will Ceasefire End Deadly Conflict in Gorno-Badakshan?" *Eurasianet*, July 25, 2012.

59. Cornelius Graubner, "Central Asia: A Look at Sources of Violence and Instability," *Eurasianet*, August 7, 2012.

60. For the dynamics, see, e.g., Keith Darden, "Blackmail as a Tool of State Domination: Ukraine Under Kuchma," *East European Constitutional Review* 10, 2–3 (2000): 67–71.

61. Kairat Osmonaliev, "Interrelationship Between Drug Trafficking and Corruption in Central Asia," Public Speaking Series, Social Research Center, American University-Central Asia, Bishkek, March 15, 2006, http://src.auca.kg/images/stories/files/report-Osmonaliev-english.pdf.

62. ICG, "Drugs and Conflict," *ICG Asia Report* 25 (November 26, 2001): 15–16.

63. Roger N. McDermott, "Border Security in Tajikistan: Countering the Narcotics Trade?" Conflict Studies Research Center, October 2002, http://da.mod.uk/CSRC/Home/CentralAsia/K36.

64. Ibid., 7.

65. Jean-Christophe Peuch, "Central Asia: Charges Link Russian Military to Drug Trade," *RFE/RL*, June 8, 2001.

66. Ibid.

67. See *BBC*, "Russian Held in Tajik Heroin Boost," April 26, 2004.

68. Author's interview with Western intelligence official, 2006.

69. UNDP, *Central Asia Human Development Report* (Bratislava: UNDP, 2005), 121; UNODC, *World Drug Report 2011*, 63.

70. Kairat Osmonaliev, "Developing Counter-Narcotics Policy in Central Asia," Silk Road Paper, Central Asia-Caucasus Institute-Silk Road Studies Program, Uppsala, January 2005, 22.

71. De Danieli, "Counter-Narcotics Policies in Tajikistan," 129–45.

72. Ibid., 133.

73. Author's interview with Western intelligence official, 2006.

74. Paoli et al., "The Rise of a Narco-State," 957.

75. *Reuters*, "Remote Tajik Outpost on Front Line of Drugs War," June 11, 2008.

76. See World Bank on HIV/AIDS in Tajikistan, http://lnweb18.worldbank.org/ECA/ECSHD.nsf/0/814FDCE14FDAF46585256C83006D9373?Opendocument.

77. UNDP on heroin trade in Tajikistan, http://europeandcis.undp.org/files/uploads/CA%20HDR/oxford%20analytica%20–%20Tajikistan.pdf.

78. UNODC, *Afghanistan's Opium Survey 2006* (New York: UN, 2006).

79. Marat, "The State-Crime Nexus in Central Asia," 108.

80. Recall Eric Hobsbawm's classical discussion in *Bandits* (London: Weidenfeld and Nicolson, 1969).

81. For more details on the politics-crime-business merger, derived from a detailed case study of Kyrgyzstan, see Johan Engvall, *The State as Investment Market: An*

Analytical Framework for Interpreting Politics and Bureaucracy in Kyrgyzstan (Uppsala: Department of Government, 2011).

Chapter 4. The Islamic Movement of Uzbekistan

1. Vitaly Naumkin, "Militant Islam in Central Asia: The Case of the Islamic Movement of Uzbekistan," Berkeley Program in Soviet and Post-Soviet Studies Working Paper Series, Spring 2003, 20-21.

2. Michael Fredholm, "Uzbekistan and the Threat from Islamic Extremism," Conflict Studies Research Centre Report K39, Royal Military Academy, Camberley, March 2003, 4.

3. Ahmed Rashid, *Jihad: The Rise of Militant Islam in Central Asia* (New Haven, Conn.: Yale University Press, 2002), 147.

4. Naumkin, *Militant Islam in Central Asia*, 39; Rashid, *Jihad*, 159-60.

5. Alfred Appei and Peter Skorsch, *Report of the EC Rapid Reaction Mechanism Assessment Mission: Central Asia, Border Management* (Brussels: EC, June 2002), 24-27.

6. Tamara Makarenko, "Crime, Terror and the Central Asian Drug Trade," *Harvard Asia Quarterly* 6, 3 (2002): 1-24; Naumkin, *Militant Islam*, 40; Fredholm, "Uzbekistan and the Threat from Islamic Extremism," 6.

7. Naumkin, *Militant Islam*, 40.

8. David Leheny, "Tokyo Confronts Terror," *Policy Review* 110 (December 2001/ January 2002).

9. Ahmed Rashid, "They're Only Sleeping: Why Militant Islamicists in Central Asia Aren't Going to Go Away," *New Yorker*, 14 January 2002.

10. See an account of the episode that is likely highly "embellished" in Greg Child, "Fear of Falling," *Outside Magazine*, November 2000. Intelligence sources from the region suggest the climbers did not heroically flee their captors but were rescued. Also Fredholm, "Uzbekistan and the Threat from Islamic Extremism," 7.

11. Rashid, *Jihad*, 176-78.

12. See, e.g., Alisher Khamidov, *Countering the Call: The U.S., Hizb-ut-Tahrir, and Religious Extremism in Central Asia*, Analysis Paper 4 (Washington, D.C.: Brookings Institution, July 2003).

13. See Naumkin, 42.

14. *Moya Stolitsa*, Bishkek, 30 August 2002; also discussion in Naumkin, *Militant Islam*, 42.

15. Naumkin, 43.

16. See Bakhrom Tursunova and Marina Pikulina, "Severe Lessons of Batken," Conflict Studies Research Centre Report K 28, Royal Military Academy, Camberley, November 1999), 8.

17. Tamara Makarenko, "Traffickers Turn from Balkan Conduit to 'Northern' Route," *Jane's Intelligence Review* 13, 8 (August 2001).

18. See Uppsala Silk Road Studies Drugs database, http://www.silkroadstudies.org/database.htm.

19. For more information, http://www.un.org.kg. The project was discontinued

October 1999. "Conference on Drug Traffic Ends," *RFE/RL Kyrgyz Report*, October 8, 1999.

20. UNDCP, *Global Illicit Drugs Trends 2001* (New York: UN, 2001), 39.

21. See Maral Madi, "Drug Trade in Kyrgyzstan, Structure, Implications, and Countermeasures," *Central Asian Survey* 23, 3-4 (December 2004).

22. Ibid., 10

23. Kozhanov and Avdeeva, "Ekho Batkena," *Vecherny Bishkek*, September 7, 1999; Otorbayeva, "Batkenskiy Dnevnik," *Vecherny Bishkek*, September 3, 1999.

24. See Mahmadamin Mahmadaminov, "The Development of the Islamic Movement of Uzbekistan (Turkestan)," Central Asia-Caucasus Institute, Johns Hopkins University, 2003.

25. See Madi, "Drug Trade in Kyrgyzstan" 5; also Kairat Osmanaliev, *Organizovanya Prestupnost' v Kirgizskoi Respublike* (Organized Crime in the Kyrgyz Republic) (Bishkek: Mol, 2002).

26. See, e.g., Fredholm, "Uzbekistan and the Threat from Islamic Extermism," 9-10.

27. Makarenko, "Traffickers Turn from Balkan Conduit to 'Northern' Route"; Madi, "Drug Trade in Kyrgyzstan," 7.

28. *Associated Press*, May 25, 2001.

29. "Narcotic Flood Threatens to Wash Away Central Asian Stability," *Times of Central Asia*, December 30, 2000.

30. Personal communications from international drug control officials, Washington, May 2001; Tamara Makarenko, "Crime and Terrorism in Central Asia," *Jane's Intelligence Review* (July 2000).

31. Ralf Mutschke, "The Threat Posed by the Convergence of Organized Crime, Drugs Trafficking and Terrorism," statement; Donnie R. Marshall, Drug Enforcement Administration administrator, testimony; both U.S. House Judiciary Subcommittee on Crime, December 13, 2000, http://usinfo.state.gov/topical/pol/terror/00121301.htm.

32. Bolot Januzakov, quoted in Glenn E. Curtis, *Involvement of Russian Organized Crime Syndicates, Criminal Elements in the Russian Military, and Regional Terrorist Groupings in Narcotics Trafficking in Central Asia, the Caucasus, and Chechnya* (Washington, D.C.: Library of Congress, Federal Research Division, October 2002), 14.

33. Makarenko, "Crime, Terror, and the Central Asian Drug Trade."

34. Ibid.

35. Personal communication; also *Bloomberg News*, March 12, 2002.

36. Ikbol Mirsaitov and Alisher Saipov, "Ex-Gunmen of the Islamic Movement of Uzbekistan Claim That Their Organization Is No More," *Fergana News*, April 16, 2006, http://enews.fergananews.com/article.php?id=1386.

37. See, e.g., Jacob Zenn, "The Indigenization of the Islamic Movement of Uzbekistan," *Terrorism Monitor* 10, 2 (January 26, 2012); Khan Zeb Burki, "Rise of Taliban in Waziristan," *The Dialogue* 5, 3 (July–September 2010): 188–211.

38. Ronald Sandee, "The Islamic Jihad Union," NEFA Foundation, October 14, 2008, 1–2.

39. Kamal Hyder, "Uzbeks Outstay Pashtun Welcome," *Al Jazeera*, March 28, 2007.

40. Carlotta Gall, "A Taliban Leader in Pakistan Says He Would Aid Bin Laden," *New York Times*, April 21, 2007.

41. Burki, "Rise of Taliban," 199; Hassan Abbas, "South Waziristan's Maulvi Nazir: The New Face of the Taliban," *Terrorism Monitor* 5, 9 (May 14, 2007).

42. Syed Saleem Shahzad, "Baitullah: Dead or Alive, His Battle Rages," *Asia Times*, August 8, 2009.

43. Mona Kanwal Sheikh, "Disaggregating the Pakistani Taliban," Danish Institute for International Studies Brief, September 2009, 5.

44. Zenn, "The Indigenization," 2.

45. Abubakar Siddique, "IMU's Evolution Branches Back to Central Asia," *RFE/RL*, April 19, 2012.

46. Zenn, "The Indigenization."

47. "German, Afghan Offensive in North Targets IMU," *RFE/RL*, July 23, 2009.

48. Siddique, "IMU's Evolution."

49. Bill Roggio, "ISAF Kills IMU/Taliban District Commander in Afghan North," *Long War Journal*, December 3, 2012, http://www.longwarjournal.org/archives/2012/12/isaf_kills_imutaliba.php.

50. Jacob Zenn, "IMU Reestablishes Bases in Northern Afghanistan," *Central Asia-Caucasus Analyst*, February 8, 2012, http://www.cacianalyst.org/?q=node/5710.

51. "Treasure Names Terrorist Financiers in South Asia," Investigative Project on Terrorism, September 29, 2011, www.investigativeproject.org/3208/.

52. Amir Mir, "TTP Using Uzbeks to Conduct Terrorist Attacks," *News International Pakistan*, December 18, 2012.

53. "Shifting Afghan Drug Trade Threatens Central Asia," *Reuters*, January 18, 2011.

54. Thomas M. Sanderson, Daniel Kimmage, and David A. Gordon, *From the Ferghana Valley to South Waziristan: The Evolving Threat of Central Asian Jihadists* (Washington, D.C.: CSIS, March 2010), 15.

Chapter 5. From Chechen Mafia to the Islamic Emirate of the Caucasus: The Changing Faces of the Insurgency-Organized Crime Nexus

1. See Paul B. Hanze, "The Demography of the Caucasus according to 1989, Soviet Census Data," *Central Asian Survey* 10, 1–2 (1991): 155.

2. Barasbi Baytugan, "al-Quqaz al-Shamali (The North Caucasus)," *Journal of Soviet Affairs* (Arabic Version) (Institute for Study of the USSR-Munich) 27–28 (1970): 51.

3. For historical accounts on the North Caucasians resistance see John F. Baddeley, *The Russian Conquest of the Caucasus* (New York: Russell & Russell, 1969); Moshe Gammer, *Muslim Resistance to the Tsar: Shamil and the Conquest of Chechnia and Daghestan* (London: Routledge, 2003).

4. Aleksei Malashenko, "Islam in Northern Caucasus," *Prism* 11, 2 (1996), http://Soros.org//Monitor; Alexandre Bennigsen, "Mullahs, Mujahidin and Soviet Muslims," *Problems of Communism* 33 (November–December 1984): 28–44; Alexandre Benningsen, "Muslim

Guerrilla Warfare in the Caucasus (1918–1928)," *Central Asian Survey* 2, 1 (1983): 45–56; Chantal Lemercior-Quelquejay, "Sufi Brotherhoods in the USSR: A Historical Survey," *Central Asian Survey* 2, 4 (1983): 1–35.

5. Larisa Ruban, "Growing Instability in the North Caucasus: A Major Threat to Russian Regional Security," *Caspian Cross Roads Magazine* 3, 2 (1997), www.ourworld. comuserve.com.

6. Sergei Arutiunov, "Ethnicity and Conflict in the Caucasus," in *Ethnic Conflict and Russian Intervention in the Caucasus* ed. Fred Wehlin, Policy Paper 16, University of California-Irvine, 1995, 15–19.

7. Rajan Menon and Graham E. Fuller, "Russia's Ruinous Chechen War," *Foreign Affairs* 79, 2, (2000): 34.

8. Ibid.

9. Interview with Dzhokhar Dudayev, *Asharq al-Awsat* (Arabic Daily) (London), June 28, 1992, 8.

10. On Dudayev's policies see Carlotta Gall and Thomas De Waal, *Chechnya: A Small Victorious War)* London: Pan, 1997), 120–30.

11. Ibid., 124, 128–30.

12. Svante E. Cornell, "The Narcotics Threat in Greater Central Asia: From Crime-Terror Nexus to State Infiltration?" *China and Eurasia Forum Quarterly* 4, 1 (2006): 37–67.

13. Julie Wilhelmsen, *When Separatists Became Islamists: The Case of Chechnya* (Kjeller: Norwegian Defense Research Establishment, 2004).

14. Lorenzo Vidino, "The Arab Foreign Fighters in Chechnya and the Sacralization of the Chechen Conflict," *Al-Nakhlah, the Fletcher School Online Journal for Issues Related to Southwest and Islamic Civilisation* (Spring 2006): 2.

15. Paul Tumelty, "The Rise and Fall of Foreign Fighters in Chechnya," *Terrorism Monitor* 4, 2 (January 26, 2006).

16. Wilhelmsen, *When Separatists Became Islamists*, also Svante E. Cornell, "The War Against Terrorism and the Conflict in Chechnya: A Case for Distinction," *Fletcher Forum of World Affairs* 27, 2 (Fall 2003): 171.

17. Miriam Lanskoy, "Daghestan and Chechnya: the Wahhabi Challenge to the State," *SAIS Review* 22, 2 (Summer/Fall 2002): 167–92.

18. Nom de guerre of Samir Saleh Abdullah Al-Suwailem.

19. Menon and Fuller, "Russia's Ruinous Chechen War," 35–36.

20. Maitham al-Junabi, "The Geostrategic Dimensions of Caucasian Problem," *Rimal* 6 (Moscow, 2006).

21. See Peter Baker, "Putin Moves to Centralize Authority; Plan would Restrict Elections in Russia," *Washington Post*, September 14, 2004; "Putin Wins Power to Appoint Regional Governors," *Voice of America*, December 3, 2004.

22. "Kadyrov Vows to Prosecute Federal Commanders for Abuses," *Chechnya Weekly*, 7 December 2006.

23. Kevin Daniel Leahy, "Kadyrov's Bluff," *Central Asia-Caucasus Analyst* 8, 10 (May 17, 2006): 7.

24. See, e.g., Oleg Antonenko, "Chechnya: Gde konchayetsya konstitutsiya i nachinayetsya shariat?" (Chechnya: Where Does the Constitution End and Shari'a Begin?), *BBC Russian Service*, December, 26 2008.

25. See Svante E. Cornell, *The "Afghanization" of the North Caucasus: Causes and Implications of a Changing Conflict* (Carlisle, Pa.: U.S. Army War College Strategic Studies Institute, 2012).

26. Ibid.; Paul Goble, "Kabardino-Balkaria Highlights Putin's 'Failure' in the Caucasus," *Window on Eurasia*, January 23, 2008.

27. *Economist*, January 27, 2011.

28. Mairbek Vatchagaev, "Russian Security Services Responsible for Majority of Kidnappings in the North Caucasus," *Eurasia Daily Monitor* 9, 48 (March 8, 2012).

29. Anatol Lieven, "Nightmare in the Caucasus," *Washington Quarterly* 23, 1, (2000): 146–47; Thomas Goltz, "Chechnya and the Bear's Long Shadow," *The Nation*, February 10, 1997.

30. Interview with Aslan Maskhadov conducted by the *al-Muslmoon Newspaper* (Jeddah, Saudi Arabia in Arabic), April 11, 1998, 1.

31. Interview with Shamil Basayev conducted by, *al-Bayan Newspaper* (Dubai, in Arabic), February 3, 2000, 37.

32. For information about Arab fighters in Chechnya see Murad Batal Al-Shishani, "The Rise and Fall of Arab Fighters in Chechnya," in *Volatile Borderland: Russia and the North Caucasus*, ed. Glen E. Howard (Washington, D.C.: Jamestown Foundation, 2012), 286–316.

33. Julia Novitskaia and Stewart Prest, *Criminogenic Early Warning and Indicator Survey: Russia 1991–1997*, Country Indicators for Foreign Policy (Ottawa: Carleton University, 2004), 31.

34. See "Country Information: Russia Federation—North Caucasus," Food and Agriculture Organization, http://www.fao.org/emergencies/country-information/list/europe/russianfederation/en/.

35. See Jamestown Foundation, "Rights Activists Say Corruption in Chechnya is an 'Unwritten Rule," *Eurasia Daily Monitor* 7, 20 (January 29, 2010. }

36. Olof Staaf, "Moscow Unable to Afford New Development Program for the North Caucasus," *Central Asia-Caucasus Analyst* 13, 11 (August 17, 2011); "Moscow Hosts Rally Under the Motto 'Stop Feeding Caucasus!'" *Caucasian Knot* (October 22, 2011), http://rf.eng.kavkaz-uzel.ru/articles/18748/

37. Charles W. Blandy, "North Caucasus: On the Brink of Far-Reaching Destabilisation," Conflict Studies Research Centre Report, Caucasus Series, Royal Military Academy, Camberley, August 2005, 6.

38. Tom Hunter, "Russia's Mafias: the New Revolution," *Jane's Intelligence Review* (June 1997).

39. Nicholas Marsh, "The Russian Mafia—How Much Power Beneath the Hype?" *Regional Studies* (UK Defence Forum), February 1998.

40. "'Mafia', 'mafiya': In many languages, the Italian word 'mafia' is used more frequently than 'organised crime.' The term first appeared in Sicily in the 1860s, where it had a quite specific meaning. Later it entered other languages and was used more broadly to refer to criminal societies and associations which behaved in similar ways and engaged in similar criminal activities—providing 'protection,' operating 'vice industries,' trafficking in illegal drugs, etc. 'Mafia' was adopted into Russian, too"; ibid., 15.

41. Roustam Kaliyev, "Russia's Organized Crime: A Typology Part I: How the Mafias Were Formed," *Eurasianet* Commentary, January 30, 2002, http://www.eurasianet.org/departments/insight/articles/eav013102.shtml

42. Ibid.

43. Ibid.

44. All this background information is available in Thomas Petrov and Alexey Gordon, "End of Chechen Mafia 'Wise Guy'," *Russian Mafia*, April 26, 2011, http://www.rumafia.com/material.php?id=267.

45. Ibid.

46. Mark Galeotti, "'Brotherhoods' and 'Associates': Chechen Networks of Crime and Resistance," *Low Intensity Conflict & Law Enforcement* 11, 2 (2002): 344.

47. Ibid., 344.

48. Ibid., 350.

49. See Lawrence Uzzell, "Reports Question Death of Chechen Prisoner," Jamestown Foundation, *North Caucasus Analysis*, December 31, 2004.

50. Galeotti, "'Brotherhoods' and 'Associates'," 344.

51. See Cornell, *The 'Afghanization' of the North Caucasus*; Sanobar Shermatova, "The Secret War Between Russian Intelligence Agencies," *Moscow News*, August 8, 2000; Khassan Baiev, Nicholas Daniloff, and Ruth Daniloff, *The Oath: A Surgeon Under Fire* (New York: Walker, 2004).

52. Galeotti, "'Brotherhoods' and 'Associates'."

53. Amjad Jaimoukha, *The Chechens: A Handbook* (London: Routledge, 2005); Moshe Gammer, *The Lone Wolf and the Bear: Three Centuries of Chechen Defiance of Russian Rule* (London: Hurst, 2006), 194–97.

54. Alexander Janda, Norbert Leitner, and Mathias Vogl, eds., *Chechens in the European Union* (Vienna: Austrian Federal Ministry of the Interior, 2008).

55. Galeotti, "'Brotherhoods' and 'Associates'," 345.

56. John Russell, "Mujahedeen, Mafia, Madmen: Russian Perceptions of Chechens During the Wars in Chechnya, 1994–96 and 1999–2001," *Journal of Communist Studies and Transition Politics* 18, 1 (2002): 73–96.

57. Graham H. Turbiville, Jr., "The Chechen Ethno-Religious Conflict, Terrorism and Crime," *Military Review* 74, 3 (1994).

58. Andrew Meier, "The Real Reason Yeltsin Invaded: The Chechen Mafia," *New Republic*, April 24, 1995, 16.

59. Russell D. Howard and Colleen M. Traughber, "The 'New Silk Road' of Terrorism and Organized Crime: The Key to Countering the Terror-Crime Nexus," in *Armed Groups: Studies in National Security, Counterterrorism and Counterinsurgency,* ed. Jeffrey H. Norwitz (Newport, R.I.: U.S. Department of Defense, Naval War College, 2008), 377.

60. Cornell, "The Narcotics Threat in Greater Central Asia," 50.

61. Galeotti, "'Brotherhoods' and 'Associates.'"

62. Kaliyev, "Russia's Organized Crime."

63. See Murad Batal al-Shishani, "Russian Policies in the North Caucasus Fuels a New Generation of Insurgents," *Central Asia-Caucasus Analyst* 13, 3 (February 16, 2011).

64. Ibid.

65. Cornell, "The Narcotics Threat in Greater Central Asia," 61.

66. See al-Shishani, "Russian Policies in the North Caucasus."

67. See Valery Dzutsev, "Numbers of Casualties in the North Caucasus in 2011 Rise," *Jamestown Foundation Blog,* January 9, 2012.

68. Petrov and Gordon, "End of Chechen Mafia 'Wise Guy.'"

69. Ibid.

70. Cornell, "The Narcotics Threat in Greater Central Asia," 50.

71. Ibid., 57.

72. Kathy Lally, "Russia Backs Resorts to Stem Terrorism," *Washington Post,* November 4, 2012.

Chapter 6. Georgia's Conflicts: Abkhazia and South Ossetia

1. As in Kosovo, revoked autonomy and perceived hostility against national minorities thus became one of the causes of the conflict.

2. The USSR had been abolished during the civil war in Tbilisi.

3. Pavel Baev, "Civil Wars in Georgia: Corruption Breeds Violence," in *Potentials of Disorder,* ed. Jan Koehler and Christoph Zürcher (Manchester: Manchester University Press, 2003), 129.

4. David Darchiashvili, "Georgia: A Hostage to Arms," in *The Caucasus: Armed and Divided,* ed. Anna Mateeva and Duncan Hiskock (London: Saferworld, 2003), 2–3.

5. Svante Cornell, Niklas Swanström, Anara Tabyshalieva, and Georgi Tcheishvili, "A Strategic Conflict Analysis of the South Caucasus with a Focus on Georgia," Silk Road Paper, Central Asia-Caucasus Institute and Silk Road Studies Program, Uppsala, June 2005, 29.

6. For a detailed account of organized crime penetration of the Georgian state, see Louise Shelley, "Georgian Organized Crime," in *Organized Crime and Corruption in Georgia,* ed. Louise Shelley, Eric R. Scott, and Anthony Latta (New York: Routledge, 2007).

7. Georgi Glonti, "Organized Crime in Georgia," *Trends in Organized Crime* 9, 2 (2005): 69–70.

8. Gavin Slade, "Georgia and Thieves-in-Law," *Global Crime* 8, 3 (2007): 273–74.

9. Glonti, "Organized Crime in Georgia," 75.

10. Gavin Slade, "The Threat of the Thief: Who Has Normative Influence in Georgian Society?" *Global Crime* 8, 2 (2007): 173–74.

11. Alexandre Kukhianidze, "Corruption and Organized Crime in Georgia Before and After the 'Rose Revolution,'" *Central Asian Survey* 28, 2 (2009): 218–20.

12. Charles H. Fairbanks, Jr., "Weak States and Private Armies" in *Beyond State Crisis: Postcolonial Africa and Post-Soviet Eurasia in Comparative Perspective*, ed. Mark R. Beissinger and Crawford Young (Washington, D.C.: Woodrow Wilson Center Press, 2002), 129–37.

13. Baev, "Civil Wars in Georgia," 140.

14. Ibid., 131–40.

15. Christoph Zürcher, "Georgia's Time of Troubles, 1989–1993," in *Statehood and Security: Georgia After the Rose Revolution*, ed. Bruno Coppieters and Robert Legvold (Cambridge: American Academy of Arts and Sciences, 2005), 93–94; Thornike Gordadze, "Russian-Georgian Relations in the 1990s," in *The Guns of August 2008: Russia's War in Georgia*, ed. Svante E. Cornell and S. Frederick Starr (Armonk, N.Y.: M.E. Sharpe, 2009).

16. Baev, "Civil Wars in Georgia," 131–40.

17. Kukhianidze, "Corruption and Organized Crime in Georgia," 220.

18. Zürcher, "Georgia's Time of Troubles," 97.

19. Alexandre Kukhianidze, Alexandre Kupatadze, and Roman Gotsiridze, *Smuggling Through Abkhazia and South Ossetia Regions of Georgia* (Tbilisi: Transnational Crime and Corruption Center Georgia Office, 2004), 23.

20. Glenn E. Curtis, *Involvement of Russian Organized Crime Syndicates, Criminal Elements in the Russian Military, and Regional Terrorist Groups in Narcotics Trafficking in Central Asia, the Caucasus, and Central Asia* (Washington, D.C.: Library of Congress, 2003); Jaba Devdariani and Blanka Hancilova, "Georgia's Pankisi Gorge: Russian, US and European Connections," *Center for European Policy Studies Policy Brief* 23 (June 2002).

21. Cornell et al., "A Strategic Conflict Analysis," 17, 29.

22. Svante E. Cornell, "The Growing Threat of Transnational Crime," in *The South Caucasus: a Challenge for the EU*, ed. Dov Lynch (Paris: EU Institute of Security Studies, 2003), 27.

23. Darchiashvili, "Georgia: A Hostage to Arms," 2–3.

24. Kukhianidze, "Corruption and Organized Crime in Georgia," 221.

25. Interview, Alexander Kukhianidze, Director of Transnational Crime and Corruption Center (TraCCC), Georgia Office, Tbilisi, May 10, 2007.

26. Darchiashvili, "Georgia: A Hostage to Arms," 4.

27. Interview, Alexander Kukhianidze.

28. Interview, Anonymous Expert, Tbilisi, May 18, 2007.

29. Cornell et al., "A Strategic Conflict Analysis," 29.

30. Interview, Alexander Kukhianidze.

31. Cornell et al., "A Strategic Conflict Analysis," 29.

32. Cory Welt, "Political Change and Border Security Reform in Eurasia: The Case of Georgia," *Nonproliferation Review* 12, 3 (2005): 513–14.

33. Cornell, "The Growing Threat of Transnational Crime," 35.

34. Just as the temporal breakdown of civil order in Albania during 1997–98 led

to looting of local arms caches, which flowed into Kosovo and helped ignite the conflict there, Georgian, Abkhazian and South Ossetian paramilitaries armed themselves through looting former USSR weapons and purchases of arms from the Russian army.

35. Cornell, "The Growing Threat of Transnational Crime," 35–36.

36. Louise Shelley and Robert Orttung, "Criminal Acts: How Organized Crime Is a Nuclear Smuggler's Best Friend," *Bulletin of the Atomic Scientists* (September/October 2006): 22–23.

37. Alexander Kupatadze, "Organized Crime and the Trafficking of Radiological Materials," *Nonproliferation Review* 17, 2 (2010): 222, 229–31.

38. Stacy Closson, "Networks of Profit in Georgia's Autonomous Regions: Challenges to Statebuilding," *Journal of Intervention and Statebuilding* 4, 2 (2010): 180–91.

39. Kukhianidze et al., *Smuggling Through Abkhazia and South Ossetia Regions of Georgia*, 30.

40. Closson, "Networks of Profit in Georgia's Autonomous Regions," 186; Theresa Freese, "A Report from the Field: Georgia's War Against Contraband and Its Struggle for Territorial Integrity," *SAIS Review* 25, 1 (2005).

41. International Crisis Group, *Avoiding War in South Ossetia* (Brussels: ICG, 2004), 10.

42. Welt, "Political Change and Border Security Reform in Eurasia," 522.

43. John Mackedon, "The Surprise of Abkhaz Elections," *Central Asia-Caucasus Analyst* (October 20, 2004).

44. ICG, *Abkhazia: Deepening Dependence* (Brussels: ICG, 2010), 6–7.

45. Ibid., 5.

46. ICG, *Abkhazia Today* (Brussels: ICG, 2006), 15.

47. UN Security Council, *Report of the Secretary-General on the Situation in Abkhazia, Georgia*, January 13, 2006, S/2006/19, and June 26, 2006, S/2006/435.

48. Maia Mindorashvili, "Gangster Wars in Abkhazia," *Central Asia-Caucasus Analyst* (June 20, 2001).

49. Kukhianidze et al., *Smuggling Through Abkhazia and Tskhinvali Region of Georgia*, 23, 29.

50. Interview, Alexander Kupatadze, Ph.D. candidate, School of International Relations, St. Andrews University, Tbilisi, September 11, 2006.

51. Interview, Anonymous Expert, Tbilisi, September 11, 2006.

52. Kukhianidze et al., *Smuggling Through Abkhazia and Tskhinvali Region of Georgia*, 22.

53. Ibid., 22.

54. Ibid., 27, 34.

55. Ibid., 13–14.

56. Interview, Alexander Kukhianidze, May 10, 2007.

57. Kukhianidze et al., *Smuggling Through Abkhazia and Tskhinvali Region of Georgia*, 14–15.

58. Kosta Dzugayev, "South Ossetia's President Clamps Down," Institute for War and Peace Reporting, July 4, 2003.

59. Ibid.

60. Zaal Anjaparidze, "South Ossetian Elections Follow Moscow's Script," *Eurasia Daily Monitor*, May 28, 2006; Vladimir Socor, "Moscow's Fingerprints All over South Ossetia's Referendum," *Eurasia Daily Monitor*, November 15, 2006.

61. ICG, "Avoiding War in South Ossetia," 11.

62. Roman Gotsiridze, "Economic and Social Consequences of Internal Conflicts in Georgia," Parliament Budget Office of Georgia, 2003, 22.

63. ICG, *South Ossetia: The Burden of Recognition* (Brussels, ICG, 2010), 4.

64. Alexander Skakov, "South Ossetia: Aftermath and Outlook," Russian Expert Group Report 2011/1, Carnegie Moscow Center, 2011.

65. Interview, Anonymous Expert, Tbilisi, September 11, 2006.

66. "Georgian Foreign Minister Protests Arms Deliveries to South Ossetia," *Civil Georgia*, January 18, 2006.

67. ICG, "Avoiding War in South Ossetia," 10.

68. Kukhianidze et al., *Smuggling Through Abkhazia and Tskhinvali Region of Georgia*, 19.

69. Shida Kartli borders South Ossetia and is the region through which smuggled goods were transported on their way to Tbilisi.

70. ICG, "Avoiding War in South Ossetia," 10.

71. Kukhianidze et al., *Smuggling Through Abkhazia and Tskhinvali Region of Georgia*, 25.

72. Ibid, 19.

73. Interview, Anonymous Expert, Tbilisi, May 18, 2007.

74. David Darchiashvili and Givi Tevzadze, *Building Democracy in Georgia; Ethnic Conflicts and Breakaway Regions in Georgia* (Stockholm: International Institute for Democracy and Electoral Assistance, 2003), 12–13.

75. Interview, Alexander Kupatadze, Tbilisi, September 11, 2006.

76. Closson, "Networks of Profit in Georgia's Autonomous Regions," 193.

77. ICG, "Avoiding War in South Ossetia," 11–14.

78. "Government Intensifies Anti-Smuggling Measures in Shida Kartli," *Civil Georgia*, March 13, 2005.

79. Interview, Alexander Kukhianidze, Tbilisi, May 10, 2007.

80. Closson, "Networks of Profit in Georgia's Autonomous Regions," 194.

81. World Bank, *Fighting Corruption in Public Services: Chronicling Georgia's Reforms* (Washington, D.C.: World Bank, 2012), 15.

82. Kukhianidze, "Corruption and Organized Crime in Georgia," 226.

83. Transparency International Corruption Perception Index, http://www.transparency.org/policy_research/surveys_indices/cpi.

84. For an extensive account of Georgia's police reform, see Alexander Kupatadze, Giorgi Siradze, and Giorgi Mitagvaria, "Policing and Police Reform in Georgia," in Shelley et al., *Organized Crime and Corruption in Georgia*.

85. World Bank, *Fighting Corruption in Public Services*, 16–17.

86. Matthew Devlin, "Seizing the Reform Moment: Rebuilding Georgia's Police, 2004–2006," *Innovations for Successful Societies*, Princeton University, 2010.

87. World Bank, *Fighting Corruption in Public Services*, 38–43.

88. Welt, "Political Change and Border Security Reform in Eurasia," 515–18.

89. Ibid., 516.

90. Welt, "Political Change and Border Security Reform in Eurasia," 521–22.

91. U.S. Embassy cable, "Georgia: Border Control Changes Worry," 09TBILISI207, February 5, 2009.

92. World Bank, *Fighting Corruption in Public Services*, 91–99.

93. Vicken Cheterian, "Georgia's Rose Revolution: Change or Repetition? Tension Between State-Building and Modernization Projects," *Nationalities Papers: The Journal of Nationalism and Ethnicity* 36, 4 (2008); Lincoln A. Mitchell, "Compromising Democracy: State Building in Saakashvili's Georgia," *Central Asian Survey* 28, 2 (2009).

94. Louise Shelley, "Introduction," in Shelley et al., *Organized Crime and Corruption in Georgia*, 7–9.

95. Interview, Anonymous Expert, Tbilisi, May 18, 2007.

96. "Top Police Officials Sacked in Shida Kartli," *Civil Georgia*, March 13, 2005.

97. "Chief of Military Police Becomes Deputy Defense Minister," *Civil Georgia*, August 30, 2006.

98. Welt, "Political Change and Border Security Reform in Eurasia," 511.

99. Kakha Jibladaze, "Smuggling and Corruption Continue to Plague Georgia," *Central Asia-Caucasus Analyst* (March 23, 2005).

100. Interview, Alexander Kupatadze, September 11, 2006.

101. Ibid.

102. Kukhianidze, "Corruption and Organized Crime in Georgia," 228.

103. See Niklas Nilsson, "Georgia's Rose Revolution: The Break with the Past," in Cornell and Starr, *The Guns of August 2008*.

104. Brian Whitmore, "Medvedev Gets Caught Telling the Truth," *RFE/RL*, November 22, 2011.

105. Bruno Coppieters, "Locating Georgian Security," in Coppieters and Legvold, *Statehood and Security*, 356–57.

Chapter 7. Moldova: The Transnistrian Conflict

1. Law regarding languages spoken on the territory of Moldovan SSR 3465-XI, September 9, 1989, http://lex.justice.md/index.php?action=view&view=doc&lang=1&id=312813.

2. Oazu Nantoi, "Conflictul Transnistrean—anul 2010" (Transnistrian Conflict—year 2010), Institutul de Politice Publici, 2010, http://www.ipp.md/public/files/Publicatii/2010/1Nantoi_pdf.pdf.

3. Vladimir Soloviov, "Otechestvo s organichennoy otvetstvennostyu" [Limited liability country], *Komersant* 30, 934 (August 2011), http://www.kommersant.ru/doc/1685540.

4. The urban to rural population breakdown in Transnistria is 68 to 32 percent. Most often quoted proportions for ethnic breakdown are Moldovans 30 percent, Ukrainians 28 percent, and Russians 26 percent. Minority groups also include Bulgarians, Jews, and Poles. Most Moldovans live in villages (often ethnically homogeneous); the Russian-speaking population mainly live in the cities.

5. Christopher Borgen, "Thawing a Frozen Conflict: Legal Aspects of the Separatist Crisis in Moldova: A Report from the Association of the Bar of the City of New York," *Record of the Association of the Bar of the City of New York* 61 (2006): 13–14.

6. Alexander Bogomolov, Igor Semyvolos, and Victor Pushkar, "Transnistria Assessment Mission Report—Transnistrian Crisis: Human Dimension," December 2008–February 2009, 10–11, www.peaceportal.documents/130276236/a08b7fb3-a8a1-451e-b8f4-526d3c1deca4.

7. Borgen, "Thawing a Frozen Conflict," 14.

8. Pal Kolsto, ed., *National Integration and Violent Conflict in Post-Soviet Societies: the Cases of Estonia and Moldova* (Lanham, Md.: Rowman & Littlefield, 2002), 235.

9. Mikhail Bergman, "Vozhd' v chuzhoy staye" (Leader in Alien Parcel), *Chelovek i ego prava* 17–34, Tiraspol, 2005, http://sborka.syno-ds.de/lindex/Lindex4/Text/9220.htm; Charles King, "The Moldovans: Romania, Russia and the Politics of Culture," *Foreign Affairs* (November–December 2000): 192.

10. Ibid., 192.

11. *Ilaşcu and Others v. Moldova and Russia*, European Court of Human Rights, App. 48787/99, Strasbourg (July 8, 2004), http://cmiskp.echr.coe.int/tkp197/view.asp?item=1&portal=hbkm&action=html&highlight=Ilascu&sessionid=94148198&skin=hudoc-en.

12. Charles King, "The Benefits of Ethnic War Understanding Eurasia's Unrecognized States," *World Politics* 53 (July 2001): 533.

13. The Agreement on Principles of Peace Settlement of the Armed Conflict in the Transnistrian Region of the Republic of Moldova on July 21, 1992, http://www.operationspaix.net/ DATA/DOCUMENT/1651~v~Accord_de_cessez_le_feu_entre_la_Transnistrie_et_la_Moldavie_du_21_juillet_1992_-_document_en_russe_ anglais_roumain.pdf.

14. Most definitions of civil wars use 1,000 battle-related deaths during a calendar year as a criterion for whether a conflict is classified as a war.

15. Elena Gorelova and Galina Şelari, "Costurile conflictului transnistrean şi beneficiile soluţionării lui" (Costs of Transnistrian Conflict and Benefits of Its Resolution), Center for Strategic Studies and Reforms, Chişinau, 2009, 8.

16. Tomasz Karniewicz, Marie Petrovicka, and Natasha Wunsch, "The EU and Conflict Resolution in Transnistria," *New Dimensions of Security in Europe* (Dresden: Technische Universität Dresden, 2010), http://tu-dresden.de/die_tu_dresden/zentrale_einrichtungen/zis/newseceu/outcomes/papers_folder/PolSec_20EU%20and%20Transnistria.pdf.

17. Félix Buttin, "A Human Security Perspective on Transnistria Reassessing the Situation Within the 'Black Hole of Europe,'" *Human Security Journal* 3 (February 2007).

18. Nicu Popescu, "Noile oportunitati de solutionare al problemei transnistrene prin mecanismele Europei moderne" (New Opportunities of Solving the Transnistrian Problem Following the Mechanisms of a Modern Europe), Insistutul de Politici Publice, 2003, 4, http://www.policy.hu/npopescu/publications/ue_trans.pdf.

19. Kolsto, ed., *National Integration and Violent Conflict*, 236.

20. Victor Osipov, "Transnistrian Conflict Settlement: Towards Genuine Reintegration of the Country," lecture, Center for Strategic and International Studies, Washington, D.C., May 3, 2010, http://csis.org/files/attachments/100503_osipov_speech.pdf.

21. Bogomolov, Semyvolos, and Pushkar, "Transnistria Assessment Mission Report," 13.

22. Bernard Aussedat, "How Can Confidence and Security Be Restored in Moldova?" in *OSCE Yearbook* (Baden-Baden: Nomos Verlagsgesellschaft, 2009), 191–99, http://www.core-hamburg.de/documents/yearbook/english/09/Aussedat-en.pdf.

23. Interview with representative of Ministry of Foreign Affairs and European Integration of the Republic of Moldova, January 2012, Chisinau.

24. Matthew Rojansky, "Prospects for Unfreezing Moldova's Frozen Conflict in Transnistria," Congressional Briefing, Carnegie Endowment for International Peace, U.S. Commission on Security and Cooperation in Europe, June 14, 2011, http://carnegie endowment.org/files/Rojansky_Transnistria_Briefing.pdf.

25. Mikhail Bergman, "Yevgeniy Shevchuk boretsya s mafiosnym naslediem Smirnova-Antiufey"va" (Evghenii Sevciuc Fears Smirnov-Antiufeev's Criminal Legacy), Lenta PMR, January 2012, http://tiras.ru/evrazija/33610–mihail-bergman-evgeniy-shevchuk-boretsya-s-mafioznym-nasllediem-smirnova-antyufeeva.html.

26. Vladimir Sokolov, "Pridnestryove popalu pod sledstvenniy komitet" [Transnistria got the attention of the Investigative Committee], *Komersant* 156 (4697), August 2011, http://www.kommersant.ru/doc/1757073.

27. Tudor Iaşcenco, "Transnistria—afacerea profitabilă a clanului Smirnov" (Transnistria—a Profitable Business for Simrov's Clan] *Centrul de Investigaţii Jurnalistice*, http://www.investigatii.md/index.php?art=514.

28. Sevciuc's pre-electoral statement displayed on his party's Web site http://www.vozrojdenie-pmr.ru/index.php?id=69.

29. Ghenadii Kuzmiciov was appointed head of the Transnistrian customs committee at the time he was under criminal investigation, charged with two different criminal offenses. Later, Svetlana Climencova was appointed first deputy head of the committee, despite the fact that her husband was recently convicted of bribery in Belarus. Head of Combating Economic Frauds and Corruption, Anna Ianciuc, was serving a term in prison for robbery.

30. "Spionii se ascund printre ONG-uri" (Spies Are Hiding Among NGOs, *moldova.org*, July 19, 2006 http://politicom.moldova.org/news/spionii-se-ascund-printre-onguri-14515-rom.html.

31. Michael Bobick, "Profits of Disorder: Images of the Transnistrian Moldovan Republic," *Global Crime* 12, 4 (November, 2011): 258.

32. Alina Radu, "Afacerea transnistreană în băncile din Austria" (Transnistrian Venture in Austrian Banks), *Ziarul de Gardă* 62 (November, 2005), http://www.zdg.md/62/investigatii/.

33. Borgen, "Thawing a Frozen Conflict," 64–68.

34. Iașcenco, "Transnistria—afacerea profitabilă a clanului Smirnov."

35. Svante E. Cornell, "No Reset in the Post-Soviet Space," *Journal of International Security Affairs* 20 (2011).

36. Ibid.

37. John Löwenhardt, *The OSCE, Moldovan and Russian Diplomacy in 2003* (The Hague: Clingendael Institute, April 2004), Dutch original published in *Internationale Spectator*, The Hague, April 2004; Russian draft memorandum on the basic principles of the state structure of a united state in Moldova (Kozak Memorandum), http://eurojournal.org/comments.php?id=P107_0_1_0_C.

38. Borgen, "Thawing a Frozen Conflict," 14.

39. Vladimir Socor, "Frozen Conflicts: A Challenge to Euro-Atlantic Interests," in *A New Euroatlantic Strategy for The Black Sea Region*, ed. Ronald D. Asmus, Konstantin Dimitrov, and Joerg Forbrig (Washington, D.C.: German Marshal Fund of the United States, 2004), 127.

40. King, "The Benefits of Ethnic War," 524–52.

41. Witold Rodkiewicz, ed., *Conflictul Transnistrean după 20 de ani* (Transnistrian Conflict After 20 Years) (Chisinau: IDIS Viitorul, 2011), 8–10, http://www.viitorul.org/public/3585/ro/STUDIU_TRANSNISTRIA.pdf.

42. King, "The Benefits of Ethnic War," 524–52.

43. EUBAM, *Progress Report 2005–2010—Main Achievements in Border Management by the Partner Services in Five Years of EUBAM Activity* (Odessa: EUBAM, 2011), 15, http://eubam.org/files/AOSU%20Progress%20Report%20final.pdf.

44. Interview with a resident of Transnistria, December 2011, Dnestrovsk.

45. For instance, this sort of reservation is made by the Republic of Moldova to most Council of Europe conventions on criminal matters, http://conventions.coe.int/Treaty/Commun/ListeTraites.asp?CM=8&CL=ENG.

46. Interview with former officer of the Ministry of Interior, Republic of Moldova, December 2011, Chisinau.

47. *Ilașcu and others v. Moldova and Russia*.

48. "Thief in law" is a term used in the Soviet Union and later in CIS republics for a criminal with large or superior authority in the criminal underworld. Thieves in law have their own very strict code of conduct ("Poniatya") which in fact represents their law. There is a well-defined hierarchy in criminal networks led by a thief in law, strictly followed by its members. According to the code of conduct the members of this network must have no ties to the government, meaning they cannot serve in the army or cooperate with officials while in prison. They must also have served several jail sentences before they merit this "distinction."

49. Bobick, "Profits of Disorder," 246.

50. Gheorghe Papuc, "Conceptul combaterii crimei organizate în Republica Moldova" (The Concept of Combating Organized Crime in the Republic of Moldova), *Scientific Yearbook 5* (Chisinau: Police Academy, 2004): 21.

51. "Wanted Persons," INTERPOL, last modified 2012, http://www.interpol.int/Wanted-Persons/(wanted_id)/1999-2969.

52. Elena Alexandrova, "Biznesmen Grigoriy Karamalak: v Moldove razdavlen ves' chestnyy biznes" (Businessman Grigorii Karamalak: The Honest Business Is Crushed in Moldova) *Komsomoliskaya Pravda*, February 23, 2005, http://kp.ru/daily/23467/37138/.

53. Oazu Nantoi, "Conflictul din zona de est a Republicii Moldova : Aspecte economice" (Conflict in the Eastern Zone of the Republic of Moldova: Economic Aspects), *transnistria.md*, http://transnistria.md/ro/articles/0/541/.

54. Decree of the President of the Republic of Moldova238-III on Constituting Coordination Council in the Issues of Corruption Combat (September 21, 2001).

55. Parliament decision 421-XV on National Anti-Corruption Strategy and Action Plan, December 16, 2004, http://www.edu.md/file/docs/File/2A496d01.pdf.

56. Criminality in the Republic of Moldova, National Bureau of Statistics, Chisinau, 2010, http://www.statistica.md/public/files/publicatii_electronice/Infractionalitatea/Criminalitatea_editia_2010.pdf p.42.

57. Papuc, "Conceptul combaterii crimei organizate în Republica Moldova," 21.

58. Interview with former officer of the Ministry of Interior, December 2011, Chisianu.

59. Igor Boţan, *Procesul de negociere ca modalitate de amînare a soluţionării problemei* (Negotiation Process as a Way of Postponing Problem Solving), Centrul de Investigatii Strategice si Reforme Chişinau, 2009, 22.

60. Nantoi, "Conflictul din zona de est a Republicii Moldova. Aspecte economice."

61. Vladimir Soloviov, "Otechestvo s organichennoy otveststvennostyu".

62. Stiven Lee Myers, "Ukraine Battles Smugglers as Europe Keeps Close Eye," *New York Times*, May 28, 2006.

63. Interview with Alexandr, resident of Transnistria.

64. Rodkiewicz, "Conflictul Transnistrean după 20 de ani," 10.

65. Achilles Skordas, "Transnistria: Another Domino on Russia's Periphery?" *Yale Journal of International Affairs* 1, 1 (Summer/Fall 2005): 33-34.

66. "Aspectul militar în soluţionarea conflictului din zona de Est a Republicii Moldova" (The Military Aspects of the Conflict Settlement in the Eastern Part of the Republic of Moldova), Institute for Public Policies, April 3, 2001, 13-15, http://ipp.md/lib.php?l=ro&idc=162&year=2001.

67. Committee on the Honouring of Obligations and Commitments by Member States of the Council of Europe, "Functioning of Democratic Institutions in Moldova," document 9418, Parliamentary Assembly of the Council of Europe, Strasbourg, April 23, 2002, http:// www.assembly.coe.int/Mainf.asp?link=/Documents/WorkingDocs/Doc02/EDOC9418.htm.

68. Bergman, "Vozhd' v chuzhoy staye".

69. Oazu Nantoi, "Conflictul din zona de est a Republicii Moldova. Aspecte eco-nomice" (Conflict in the Eastern Zone of the Republic of Moldova: Economic Aspects, transnistria.md, http://transnistria.md/ro/articles/0/541/.

70. Buttin, "A Human Security Perspective," 17.

71. "Aspectul militar în soluționarea conflictului din zona de Est a Republicii Mol-dova," 10.

72. Jan Marinus Wiersma, "Report from the Chairman," PE 318.227, European Par-liament ad hoc delegation to Moldova, European Parliament, 2002.

73. Interview with representative of the Bureau of Reintegration of the Republic of Moldova, January 2012, Chisinau.

74. It is important to distinguish between human smuggling, referring to facilita-tion of illegal entry of migrants into a country, and trafficking in persons, which entails exploitation and forced labor of the migrants. Europol, "EU Organised Crime Threat Assessment 2009," 20–21 The Hague, https://www.europol.europa.eu/sites/default/files/publications/octa2009_0.pdf.

75. . Council of Europe (Octopus Programme), "Organised Crime Situation Report 2005," Strasbourg, December 2005, 53.

76. Mihail Şalvir, "Tendințe şi Politici Migraționiste în Regiunea Mării Negre: ca-zurile R. Moldova, României şi Ucrainei" (Migration Trends and Policies in the Black Sea Region: Case Studies of Moldova, Romania and Ukraine), Institute for Develop-ment and Social Initiatives (Chisinau: IDIS Viitorul, 2008), http://www.viitorul.org/public/1675/ro/Migratia_rom_final.pdf.

77. U.S. Department of State, "Trafficking in Persons Report 2011," http://www.state.gov/j/tip/rls/tiprpt/2011/164232.htm.

78. Mihaela Vidaicu si Igor Dolea, "Combaterea traficului de fiinte umane" (Com-bating Trafficking in Human Beings) Institutul National de Justitie, Chisinau, 2009, http://www.unodc.org/documents/human-trafficking/Combating_Trafficking_-_Mol-dova.pdf.

79. Europol, "EU Organised Crime Threat Assessment 2009," 31.

80. Buttin, "A Human Security Perspective," 19.

81. U.S. State Department, Moldova, Background Note, Fact Sheet, 2012, The U.S. Embassy in Moldova, Alexei Mateevici Str., #103, Chisinau.

82. Annual report, EU Border Assistance Mission to Moldova and Ukraine (EUBAM 2010): 6 http://www.eubam.org/files/MR_2011_ENG_FINAL_EUBAM.pdf.

83. Europol,"EU Organised Crime Threat Assessment 2011," 10.

84. Moldoveni reținuți în Ucraina: Transportau 38 kg de cocaină în ananaşi [Mol-dovans arrested in Ukraine while transporting 38 kg of cocaine hidden in pineapples] Jurnal TV, February 2012, http://jurnal.md/ro/news/moldoveni-re-inu-i-in-ucraina-transportau-38-kg-de-cocaina-in-anana-i-215761/.

85. Brian Johnson Thomas and Mark Franchetti, "Radioactive Rockets 'For Sale' in Breakaway Soviet Republic," Times, May 8, 2005.

86. Joby Warrick, "Dirty Bomb Warheads Disappear," *Washington Post*, December 7, 2003.

87. Johnson Thomas and Franchetti, "Radioactive Rockets 'For Sale."

88. "Smuggled Uranium-238 Seized in Moldova," *BBC News Europe*, August 24, 2010, http://www.bbc.co.uk/news/world-europe-11074645.

89. "Six Moldovan 'Uranium Smugglers' Arrested," *BBC News Europe*, June 29, 2011.

90. Interview with the representative of the Bureau of Reintegration of the Republic of Moldova, January 2012, Chisinau.

91. Ioannis F. Vichos and Anna Adaktilidou, "Moldova's Energy Strategy and the 'Frozen Conflict' of Transnistria," *AKEM European Energy Policy Observatory*, February 21, 2011.

92. Valeriu Prohnițchi, "Rusia, Moldova și suportul economic pentru Transnistria" (Russia, Moldova and the Economic Support for Transnistria), *Expert-Grup*, August 22, 2011, http://expert-grup.org/?go=news&n=214&nt=4.

93. Tudor Iașcenco, "Transnistria—afacerea profitabilă a clanului Smirnov" (Transnistria—a Profitable Business for Simrov's clan), *Centrul de Investigații Jurnalistice*, http://www.investigatii.md/index.php?art=514.

94. Press release, Russian Parliament, http://www.duma.gov.ru/news/274/67369/?s phrase_id=192690.

95. "Syna Igora Smirnova khotyat doprosit' prinuditel'no" (The Son of Igor Smirnov Will Be Interrogated), *BBC Russia*, November 28, 2011.

96. Interview with a resident of Transnistria, December 2011, Tiraspol.

97. Soloviov, "Otechestvo s organichennoy otveststvennostyu".

98. "Contrabanda cu țigări din Transnistria ar putea crește. Autoritățile au redus de aproape trei ori accizul la țigaretele de import în zonă" (The level of cigarette smuggling in Transnistria could increase. Authorities diminished three times the excise duty on imports of tobacco products to the region), *PUBLIKA.MD*, February 22, 2012, http://www.publika.md/contrabanda-cu-tigari-din-transnistria-ar-putea-creste_716911.html.

99. Victor Osipov Deputy Prime-Minister of the Republic of Moldova, "Transnistrian Conflict Settlement: Towards a Genuine Reintegration of Moldova," Lecture, Center for Strategic and International Studies, Washington, D.C., May 3, 2010.

100. George Bălan, "Place of the Confidence Building Process in the Policy of Solving the Conflict in the Eastern Region of Moldova," case study, IPP, Chisinau, 2010, 3.

101. Interview with representative of Bureau of Reintegration, Republic of Moldova, January 2012, Chisinau.

102. Interview with a representative of the Bureau of Reintegration of the Republic of Moldova, January 2012, Chisinau.

103. EUBAM, *Progress Report 2005–2010*, 5, http://eubam.org/files/AOSU%20Progress%20Report%20final.pdf.

104. Ibid., 16.

105. The operation carried on in 2011(AKKERMAN), has led to numerous

detections of smuggling activities (85 cases of tobacco smuggling resulting in seizures worth more than 14.5 million pieces), irregular migration (29 cases), and customs fraud (272 cases). It also resulted in seizures worth EU 3.2 million. In addition, 16 criminal cases of international scope were initiated. See EUBAM, Report on 8th Joint Border Control Operations AKKERMAN, 2011, Odessa, http://www.eubam.org/files/Akkerman_ENGL.pdf.

106. EUBAM, *Progress Report 2005–2010*, 22–23.

107. Alina Radu, "Afacerea transnistreană în băncile din Austria" (Transnistrian Venture in Austrian Banks) *Ziarul de Gardă* 62 (November 2005), http://www.zdg.md/62/investigatii/.

108. 1.3.8 Section, Threat posed by organized crime and corruption, National Security Concept of the Republic of Moldova, Law 112 from May 22, 2008.

Chapter 8. Bosnia-Herzegovina: Where International Wars, Transnational Crime, and Shady Politics Meet

1. For more on conflict, critical and social movement theories, and interaction between politics, terrorism, and organized crime, see William Chambliss, *On the Take: From Petty Crooks to Presidents* (Bloomington: Indiana University Press, 1978); Wolfgang Benedek, Christopher Daase, Vojin Dimitrijevic, and Petrus van Duyne, eds., *Transnational Terrorism, Organized Crime and Peace-Building: Human Security in the Western Balkans* (New York: Palgrave, 2010); Rob Watts, ed., *International Criminology* (London: Routledge, 2009).

2. Sheelagh Brady, "Organised Crime in Bosnia and Herzegovina: A Silent War Fought by an ambush of Toothless Tigers or a War Not Yet Fought?" EU Police Mission in Bosnia Herzegovina, October 2012.

3. As noted in Chapter 1 of this volume, traditional conflict theory has focused on a "grievance" approach to explain the causes of conflict. Ted R. Gurr, *Peoples Versus States: Ethnopolitical Conflict and Accommodation at the End of the 20th Century* (Washington, D.C.: U.S. Institute of Peace Press, 2000).

4. Patricia Kollander, "The Civil War in Former Yugoslavia and the International Intervention," in *Reflections on the Balkan Wars*, ed. Jeffrey S. Morton et al. (London: Palgrave, 2004), 3–23.

5. BBC Documentary, *The Death of Yugoslavia: Part 1, Entering Nationalism*, 1995. This documentary was used as evidence during the ICTY trials. It provides a well-documented chronological overview of the origins, causes, and consequences of the Yugoslav conflicts.

6. Morton et al., *Reflections on the Balkan Wars*.

7. David Keen, "Incentives and Disincentives for Violence," in *Greed and Grievance: Economic Agendas in Civil Wars*, ed., Mats Berdal and David D. Malone (Boulder, Colo.: Lynne Rienner, 2000), 19–42.

8. Paul Collier and Anke Hoeffler, "Greed and Grievance in Civil War," World Bank, Washington, D.C. October 2001, 16.

9. Alexander Alvarez, "Adjusting to Genocide: The Techniques of Neutralization and the Holocaust," *Social Science History* 21 (Summer 1997): 22.

10. *UN ICTY Prosecutor v. Mladen Naletilic, aka "Tuta" and Vinko Martinovic, aka "Štela,"* IT-98-34T, March 31, 2003.

11. The Dayton Agreement should not be viewed outside the context of diplomatic efforts in the region during its formation. The Agreement ended the war, but has not contributed to the modernization and progression of Bosnia.

12. Personal interview, Brussels, September 2007.

13. Personal interview, EU police mission Proxima, Belgian police expert Filip De Ceuninck, September 2008.

14. Peter A. Lupsha and Stanley A. Pimentel, "The Nexus Between Crime and Politics: Mexico," *Trends in Organized Crime* 3, 1 (1997): 65–67.

15. Cornelius Friesendorf et al., "Bosnia and the Art of Policy Implementation: Obstacles to International Counter-Crime Strategies," in Benedik et al., *Transnational Terrorism, Organized Crime and Peace Building*, 265–86; Brady, "Organised Crime in Bosnia and Herzegovina."

16. Brady, "Organised Crime in Bosnia and Herzegovina."

17. "The Vicious Circle of Politics, Mafia and Crime," International Institute for Middle-East and Balkan Studies (IFIMES), September 7, 2010, http://www.ifimes.org/default.cfm?Jezik=En&Kat=10&ID=548.

18. Bosnia and Herzegovina, Croatia, Macedonia, Montenegro, Serbia (including Kosovo and Vojvodina), and Slovenia. On September 25, 1991, the UN Security Council passed Resolution 713 imposing an arms embargo on all former Yugoslavia.

19. Mark Bromley, *UN Arms Embargoes: Their Impact on Arms Flows and Target Behaviour. Case Study: Former Yugoslavia, 1991–96* (Stockholm: Stockholm International Peace Research Institute, 2007), 200.

20. Ibid. See also E. Kauer, "Weapons Collection and Destruction Programmes in Bosnia and Herzegovina," in *Small Arms—Big Problem, a Global Threat to Peace, Security and Development*, ed. P. Hazdra (Vienna: Schriftenreihe der Landesverteidigungsakademie, 2007), 81–103.

21. These caches were de facto controlled by Slobodan Milosevic, president of Serbia.

22. Bromley, *UN Arms Embargoes*, 4.

23. The target for the Bosnian defense industry was an enormous output of both small arms and light weapons (SALW) and heavy weapons of all types. Also, more than 50,000 people were employed by Bosnia arms factories. Kauer, "Weapons Collection and Destruction Programmes," 82.

24. Ibid., 83.

25. Mincheva G. Lyubov and R. Ted Gurr, "Unholy Alliances: Evidence of the Linkages Between Trans-State Terrorism and Crime Networks: The Case of Bosnia," in Benedik et al., *Transnational Terrorism, Organized Crime and Peace-Building*, 194.

26. Ibid. See also Cees Wiebes, *Intelligence and the War in Bosnia: 1992–1995* (Berlin: Studies in Intelligence History, 2006).

27. Dejan Anastasijevic, "Organized Crime in the Western Balkans," paper presented at the First Annual Conference on Human Security, Terrorism and Organized Crime in the Western Balkan Region, Human Security, Terrorism and Organised Crime in the Western Balkans (HUMSEC), 2006. 15p.

28. Richard J. Aldrich, "America Used Islamists to Arm the Bosnian Muslims: The Srebrenica Report Reveals the Pentagon's Role in a Dirty War," *Guardian*, April 21, 2002.

29. It is not clear if Sudan formally backed the agency, but Western intelligence officials say Hassanein is believed to have been responsible for the Sudanese Islamic Front policy in Bosnia, Afghanistan, and Pakistan.

30. The details of the case were provided by Austrian investigators working on this case.

31. Intelligence agencies say they have tapes of telephone calls by Rahman to agency office, in which he discussed its commitment to sell the sheik's videotapes in mosques around Europe.

32. In the 2006 elections, Silajdžić was elected Bosniak member of the presidency of Bosnia and Herzegovina for four years in the rotating presidency.

33. A senior Western diplomat in the region said the Clinton administration knew about the TWRA and its activities. Wiebes, *Intelligence and the War in Bosnia*. See Brady, "Organised Crime in Bosnia and Herzegovina."

34. John Pomfret, "Bosnia's Muslims Dodged Embargo," *Washington Post*, September 22, 1996, A01.

35. Ibid.

36. Various cases on linkages between trans-state terrorism and criminal networks are discussed in Lyubov and Gurr, "Unholly Alliances."

37. Readers should bear in mind that during communism differences in religion, tribe, ethnicity, and tradition were strongly repressed to promote equality and unity. This is why I argue that religion did not take an integral part in the lives of the Bosnian people, and it was misused during the postcommunist era. Young people in Bosnia and Kosovo were wearing crosses without understanding their true meaning.

38. Brady, "Organised Crime in Bosnia and Herzegovina."

39. Center for Study of Democracy, "Partners in Crime: The Risk of Symbiosis Between the Security Sector and Organized Crime in Southeast Europe," CSD Report 13, Sofia, 2004, 47.

40. Wiebes, *Intelligence and the War in Bosnia*, 180.

41. CSD, "Partners in Crime," 47. Read more about the Serbian Secret Security Services in "Intelligence and the War in Bosnia." Professor Cees Wiebes of Amsterdam University has had unrestricted access to Dutch intelligence files.

42. Wiebes, *Intelligence and the War in Bosnia*, 180–82.

43. See also Brady, "Organised Crime in Bosnia and Herzegovina."

44. Aldrich, "America Used Islamists to Arm the Bosnian Muslims"; Pomfret, "Bosnia's Muslims Dodged Embargo."

45. While some countries were supportive of Bosnia, the secret services of Ukraine, Greece, and Israel were arming the Bosnian Serbs. Mossad was especially active and concluded a deal with the Bosnian Serbs at Pale involving a large supply of artillery shells and mortar bombs. In return they secured safe passage for the Jewish population out of the town of Sarajevo. Pomfret, "Bosnia's Muslims Dodged Embargo."

46. CSD, "Partners in Crime," 47; Jana Arsovska and Panos Kostakos, "Illicit Arms Trafficking and the Limits of Rational Choice Theory: The Case of the Balkans," *Trends in Organized Crime* 11, 4 (2008): 352–87.

47. "Ex-Weapons Director Convicted of Chile Arms Trafficking to Croatia," *Santiago Times*, January 31, 2008; "Menem Acquitted of Arms Smuggling," *Argentina Independent*, September 2011, www.argentinaindependent.com/tag/croatia/.

48. Glenn E. Curtis and Tara Karacan, *The Nexus Among Terrorists, Narcotics Traffickers, Weapons Proliferators, and Organized Crime Networks in Western Europe*, U.S. Federal Research Division Reports (Washington, D.C.: Federal Research Division of the Library of Congress, 2002), 11.

49. Ibid.

50. Anastasijevic, "Organized Crime in the Western Balkans."

51. "Karadzic Says Arms Smuggling Prolonged the War in Bosnia," *Ekathimerini*, February 16, 2010.

52. Arsovska and Kostakos, "Illicit Arms Trafficking."

53. Brady, "Organised Crime in Bosnia and Herzegovina."

54. Anastasijevic, "Organized Crime in the Western Balkans."

55. Brady, "Organised Crime in Bosnia and Herzegovina."

56. Ibid.

57. Amnesty International, "Democratic Republic of Congo: Illegal Arms Exports Fuelling Killings, Mass Rape and Torture," 5 July 2005, http://www.amnesty.org/fr/library/asset/AFR62/008/2005/fr/944ed2e3-d4d1-11dd-8a23-d58a49c0d652/afr620082005en.html.

58. Arsovska and Kostakos, "Illicit Arms Trafficking."

59. Ibid.

60. *Small Arms Survey 2010*, Cambridge University Press, 2010; Benedek et al., *Transnational Terrorism, Organized Crime and Peace-Building*.

61. Brady, "Organised Crime in Bosnia and Herzegovina."

62. Personal interview, regional security consultant, Macedonia, 2008.

63. Vildana Selimbegović, "Bacio je samo jednog snajperistu," *Dani* 259 (May 31, 2002).

64. Ibid. See also UN Security Council, *Final Report of the United Nations Commission of Experts established pursuant to security council resolution 780 (1992)* (S/1994/674/Add.2 (Vol. I)), "Special Forces in Bosnia, Croatia," annex III A, December 28, 1994.

65. "Juka of Sarajevo," *Vreme News Digest Agency*, January 10, 1994.

66. Vildana Selimbegović, "Kako je pjevao četnicima," *Dani* 260 (June 7, 2002).

67. "Juka of Sarajevo."

68. Selimbegović, "Kako je pjevao četnicima."

69. Selimbegović, "Bacio je samo jednog snajperistu."

70. UN Security Council, *Final Report of the United Nations Commission of Experts*.

71. Personal investigation of files and discussions with police officers in Belgium (Federal Police), 2006–2007.

72. Confidential INTERPOL Report 2009. Also reported by Organized Crime and Corruption Reporting Project (CIN), http://69.16.245.159/~reportin/occrp/index.php/ccwatch/cc-watch-indepth/503-naser-kelmendi-from-kosovo-inmate-to-sarajevo-businessman.

73. See Anastasijevic, "Organized Crime in the Western Balkans"; Friesendorf et al., "Bosnia and the Art of Policy Implementation."

74. For more about the NK case see Jana Arsovska, "Networking Sites—Criminal Group Expands Across the Balkans," *Jane's Intelligence Review* 21, 12 (2009), 43–47; Center for Investigative Reporting, "Naser Kelmendi: From Kosovo Inmate to Sarajevo Businessman," Sarajevo, November 16, 2009.

75. Based on confidential police file on the illegal activities of NK, France 2009.

76. See, for example, the case of Stanislava Cocorovska, responsible for trafficking half a ton of cocaine—the largest cocaine seizure in the Balkan region—from Venezuela to Greece, via Bar in Montenegro, Kosovo, and Macedonia.

77. Dačić was also arrested in November 1999 by Italian authorities with 12.75 kg heroin and was sentenced to eight years, but escaped from an Italian prison. Sarajevo police arrested him in September 2002, but he was released because Italy could not extradite him.

78. Center for Investigative Reporting, "Naser Kelmendi."

79. Brady, "Organised Crime in Bosnia and Herzegovina."

80. Ibid.

81. Confidential police report on the activities of NK and his associates, France 2009. The report contains the findings of several Western European law enforcement agencies, including Germany, Austria, Bosnia, France, and others.

82. Personal interview, May 2009.

83. Valerie Hopkins, "US Blacklists Balkan Businessman Naser Kelmendi," *Hetq Online Investigative Journalism*, June 4, 2012, http://hetq.am/eng/news/15172/us-blacklists-balkan-businessman-naser-kelmendi.html.

84. Brady, "Organised Crime in Bosnia and Herzegovina."

85. Based on hypotheses by law enforcement officials from Western countries during an expert workshop on ethnic Albanian organized crime in Ohrid, Macedonia, April 2009.

86. Sanders Huisman (IPIT, Kernteam Noord Oost Nederland), Public Administration, Corruption and Organised Crime in Albania, CIROC workshop, June 9, 2004.

87. Hopkins, "U.S. Blacklists Balkan Businessman Naser Kelmendi."

88. Philippe Billon, "Corrupting Peace? Peacebuilding and Post-Conflict Corruption," *International Peacekeeping* 15, 3 (2008): 344–61.

89. Ibid.

90. Brady, "Organised Crime in Bosnia and Herzegovina."

91. Ibid.

92. "The Vicious Circle of Politics, Mafia and Crime."

93. J. McFarlane, "Corruption and the Financial Sector: The Strategic Impact," *Dickinson Journal of International Law* 19, 1 (2000): 47–48.

94. Louise Shelley, "Restoring Trust for Peace and Security," presentation at 14th International Anti-Corruption Conference, Bangkok, 2010, 2.

95. Amy Margolies, "Peacebuilding and Anti-Corruption: Room for Collaboration?" *New Routes* 14, 3 (2009): 34–37.

96. Ibid. The report claims that since the beginning of democratic changes, power has been mainly in the hands of national/nationalist parties. Even parties that were not nationalistic at the time of their establishment gradually became so, such as Milorad Dodik's Alliance of Independent Social Democrats (SNSD) and the Party for BiH (SBiH) led by Haris Silajdžić. Regardless of Silajdžić's alleged involvement in many affairs, he has never been processed before the judicial bodies of Bosnia for connections with "sophisticated crime," including white-collar and organized crime. According to the IFIMES report, there have been allegations that Dodik has also been misusing his political power. The most illustrative example is his award of a contract to a Slovenian company from Maribor without having carried out an (international) invitation to tender. This puts under question the transparency of a contract award for the construction of the Banja Luka-Doboj highway. According to the International Institute for Balkan Studies, the record in the number of criminal charges and court proceedings against politicians in Bosnia is held by the president of the Croatian Democratic Union, Dragan Čović. The report argues that the involvement of Čović and close collaborators in criminal activities has resulted in criminalization of the Croatian nation in Bosnia, which again can lead to further escalation of conflicts in the area.

97. Benedek, *Transnational Terrorism, Peace Building and Organized Crime*, 194–95.

98. M. Abazović, *Neorganizirano Društvo Preduvjet Organiziranosti Kriminala*, Kriminalističke Teme (Sarajevo: Fakultet kriminalističkih nauka, 2003), 3–4; Bojan Dobovshek, "Organised Crime as a State Capture Problem in Countries in Transition," in *Research Conference on Organized Crime at the Bundeskriminalamt in Germany*, ed. Tottel Ursula and Buchler Heinz (Köln: Luchterhand, 2010), 72–94.

99. Anastasijevic, "Organized Crime in the Western Balkans."

100. Peter Andreas, "The Clandestine Political Economy of War and Peace in Bosnia," *International Studies Quarterly* 48, 1 (2004): 46.

101. "The Vicious Circle of Politics, Mafia and Crime."

102. Friesendorf et al., "Bosnia and the Art of Policy Implementation," 283.

Chapter 9. The Kosovo Conflict: From Humanitarian Intervention to State Capture

1. Tim Judah, *Kosovo: War and Revenge*, 2nd ed. (New Haven, Conn.: Yale University, Press, 2002), 43.

2. Ivo H. Daalder and Michael E O'Hanlon, *Winning Ugly: NATO's War to Save Kosovo* (Washington, D.C.: Brookings Institution Press, 2000), 6–11.

3. Stacy Sullivan, *Be Not Afraid, for You Have Sons in America* (New York: St. Martin's, 2004), 97.

4. Judah, *Kosovo: War and Revenge*, 68–70. For example, during field research in Priština in 2006, several respondents spontaneously mentioned that there were s ongoing discussions regarding what businessmen and leading organized crime figures did or did not contribute to the 3 percent fund (author's interviews). As mentioned by Arsovska in the chapter on Bosnia-Herzegovina in this volume, money was also often extorted rather than donated, with fairly explicit threats issued by leading organized crime figures in, for example, Belgium.

5. Andreas Heinemann Grüder and Wulf-Christian Paes, *Wag the Dog: The Mobilization and Demobilization of the Kosovo Liberation Army*, Brief 20 (Bonn: Bonn International Centre for Conversion, 2001), 10–12.

6. Sullivan, *Be Not Afraid*, 95.

7. Judah, *Kosovo: War and Revenge*, 118.

8. Heinemann Grüder and Paes, *Wag the Dog*, 12.

9. Chris Smith and Domitilla Sagramoso, "Small Arms Trafficking May Export Albania's Anarchy," *Jane's Intelligence Review* 11, 1 (1999), 24–28; Christopher Jarvis, "The Rise and Fall of the Pyramid Schemes in Albania," IMF Working Paper 99/98, Washington, D.C., 1999.

10. It should be noted here that extensive involvement in organized crime was far from unique to Kosovo or ethnic Albanians, but widespread in large parts of the former Yugoslavia. The extensive involvement of Serbian paramilitary and state actors has been extensively catalogued by Arsovska in the chapter on Bosnia-Herzegovina in this volume, in Misha Glenny, *McMafia: A Journey Through the Global Criminal Underworld* (New York: Random House, 2008) and Mary Kaldor's seminal work, *New and Old Wars: Organized Violence in a Global Era* (Stanford, Calif.: Stanford University Press, 1999). The focus here on the political and criminal violence exercised by ethnic Albanian groups thus in no way negates similar and often worse crimes committed by their Serbian adversaries. Instead, it is simply a choice made in order to analyze how these actions impacted the KLA and its legacy organizations in Kosovo.

11. Jana Arsovska and Mark Craig, "'Honourable' Behaviour and the Conceptualization of Violence in Ethnic-Based Organized Crime Groups: An Examination of the Albanian Kanun and the Code of the Chinese Triads," *Global Crime* 7, 2 (2006): 214–46.

12. Jana Arsovska, "Albanian Crime Laid Bare: The Developments of Albanian Organized Crime Groups in the Balkans," *Jane's Intelligence Review* 19, 2 (2007): 36–40.

13. Jarvis, "Rise and Fall."

14. Arsovska and Craig, "'Honourable' Behaviour."

15. Jana Arsovska "Code of Conduct: Understanding Albanian Organized Crime" *Jane's Intelligence Review* 19, 8 (2007): 46–49.

16. Jana Arsovska and Dimal Basha, "Bare Trap: Albanian Police Step Up Co-Operation" *Jane's Intelligence Review* 23, 6 (2011): 40–43.

17. Arsovska, "Code of Conduct."

18. Heinemann-Grüder and Paes, *Wag the Dog*, 12.

19. Cf. Weinstein, who argues that greed-motivated groups frequently tend to "crowd out" competing grievance-motivated armed groups. Weinstein claims groups that possess "economic endowments" can recruit "opportunistic joiners" faster. However, the KLA overtook the LDK using a combination of violence against its competitors and demonstrating the relative success of its methods, after LDK's pacifist resistance had yielded very few palpable results, rather than simply out-competing the LDK by offering wages to its recruits. Jeremy Weinstein, *Inside Rebellion: The Politics of Insurgent Violence* (New York: Cambridge University Press, 2007).

20. Heinemann-Grüder and Paes, *Wag the Dog*, 12.

21. For an extensive account of these events, see Human Rights Watch, "Humanitarian Law Violations in Kosovo," *Human Rights Watch* 10, 9 (October 1998), which also cites an earlier Amnesty report.

22. Judah, *Kosovo: War and Revenge*, 147. See ICG, "What Happened to the KLA?" *Balkans Report* 88, March 3, 2000.

23. Judah, *Kosovo: War and Revenge*, 169–70.

24. Loretta Napoleoni, *Terrorism Incorporated: Tracing the Dollars Behind the Terrorist Networks* (New York: Seven Stories Press, 2005), 171–72; Zoran Kusovac, "Another Balkans Bloodbath?" *Jane's Intelligence Review* 10, 3 (1998), 9–12.

25. Marc Galeotti, "Albanian Gangs Gain Foothold in European Crime Underworld," *Jane's Intelligence Review* 13, 11 (2001), 25–27.

26. Heinemann-Grüder and Paes, *Wag the Dog*, 10–11.

27. In this case, Xhavit Haliti and Bujar Bukoshi, the main financial officers for the KLA and LDK respectively, seem to have cooperated, while Haliti at the same time betrayed an arms shipment intended for FARK, and Bukoshi seemingly rejected the leadership of Rugova inside LDK. Intelligence reports indicate that the men later cooperated in setting up a business venture in Priština following the war.

28. KFOR, "Target Folder Xhavit Haliti," Secret Rel USA KFOR, and NATO, March 10, 2004, 3; Bundesnachrichtendienst Analyze vom 20.02.2005, German Intelligence Report 2005, 9–10.

29. Heinemann-Grüder and Paes, *Wag the Dog*, 12–16.

30. Daalder and O'Hanlon, *Winning Ugly*, 193, reports approximately 10,000 casualties.

31. Ibid., 15.

32. Heinemann-Grüder and Paes, *Wag the Dog*, 12–16.

33. Bundesnachrichtendienst Analyze; Heinemann-Grüder and Paes, *Wag the Dog*, 13; "What Is Happening to Albanian Cadres?," *Jane's Terrorism and Security Monitor*

(April 15, 2005); Thomas M. Sanderson, "Transnational Terror and Organized Crime: Blurring the Lines," *SAIS Review* 24, 1 (2004): 52; Roger Boyes and Eske Wright, "Drugs Money Linked to Kosovo Rebels," *Times of London*, March 24, 1999; Peter Klebnikov, "Heroin Heroes," *Mother Jones*, January/February 2000.

34. Klebnikov, "Heroin Heroes."

35. Ibid.; Ken Layne, "The Crime Syndicate Behind the KLA," *Mother Jones*, April 8, 1999.

36. Heinemann-Grüder and Paes, *Wag the Dog.*

37. Ibid., 13.

38. Layne, "Crime Syndicate." In the article, Layne cites articles from 1994 detailing how ethnic Albanian networks were shipping drugs to Italy and arms to Bosnia-Herzegovina, with some of the proceeds being used to buy weapons for "the brewing war in Kosovo."

39. Klebnikov, "Heroin Heroes."

40. Cf., for example, Boyes and Wright, "Drugs Money Linked to Kosovo Rebels," who cite law enforcement officials from several European countries.

41. Klebknikov, "Heroin Heroes." In the article, a State Department official is quoted as saying, "We do care about [KLA drug trafficking]. It is just that we've got our hands full trying to bring peace there."

42. Rebecca Thornton, "Endgame in Kosovo," *Prospect Magazine*, May 26, 2007.

43. Paul Ames, "NATO Pledges to Crack Down on Organized Crime in Kosovo," *Associated Press*, March 12, 2002.

44. The Center for Geopolitical Drug Studies, "Dangerous Liaisons," *Geopolitical Drug Newsletter* 1 (October 2011).

45. Dick Marty, *Inhuman Treatment of People and Illicit Trafficking in Human Organs in Kosovo* (Strasbourg: Council of Europe, Committee on Legal Affairs and Human Rights, 2010), 9. See also U.S. Embassy cable, "Hitman's Confession Shakes Kosovo Political Establishment," December 1, 2009.

46. This division follows a 2000 ICG report, which argued the KLA continued through political parties, military, police and security service, and organized crime. Today, sufficient evidence exists of the overlap in manpower, leadership, and fundraising channels to include the NLA and UCPMB in this list of KLA successor organizations. ICG, "What Happened to the KLA?" 2.

47. Cf. Human Rights Watch, *Under Orders: War Crimes in Kosovo* (New York: HRW, 2001). This report lists senior KLA commanders, some included in the following section.

48. Bundesnachrichtendienst Analyze, 4.

49. Paul Lewis, "Report Identifies Hashim Thaçi as 'Big Fish' in Organized Crime," *Guardian*, January 24, 2011.

50. Marty, *Inhuman Treatment of People and Illicit Trafficking*, para. 63.

51. Ibid. paras. 66–67. Five drug enforcement agencies and at least four intelligence agencies (German, Italian, British, and Greek) are used as sources for these claims,

including first-hand interviews with the authors of the Bundesnachrichtendienst report cited elsewhere in this chapter.

52. Andrew Rettman and Ekrem Krasniqi, "Thaçi Camp Hits Back at Organ Trafficking Allegations," *EU Observer,* December 21, 2010.

53. Bundesnachrichtendienst Analyze, 22. According to the report, "In the Decani region the clan-based structure of the Haradinajs engages in the entire spectrum of criminal, political and military activities that influences all of Kosovo. The group has circa 100 members and are active in drug- and weapons smuggling and the illegal trade duty-obliged merchandise."

54. Jeta Xharra, Muhammeth Hajrullahu, and Arben Salihu, "Kosovo's Wild West," *Balkan Investigative Research Network,* April 18, 2005.

55. Matthew Brunnwasser, "Death of War Crimes Witness Casts Cloud over Kosovo," *New York Times,* October 6, 2011.

56. Marlise Simons, "Former Leader in Kosovo Acquitted of War Crimes," *New York Times,* April 4, 2008.

57. ICG, "The Rule of Law in Independent Kosovo," *Europe Report* 204, May 2010, 4.

58. Nebi Qena, "Senior Kosovo Leader to Be Tried for War Crimes," *Guardian,* September 2, 2011.

59. Petrit Collaku and Artan Mustafa, "EULEX Urges Limaj to Face War Crimes Trial," *Balkan Insight,* June 15, 2011; Fatmir Aliu, "Kosovo Court Ruling Heightens Arrest Risk for Limaj," *Balkan Insight,* September 21, 2011.

60. Genc Nimoni, "How Witness X's Diary Unlocked Kosovo's Klecka Case," *Balkan Insight,* October 20, 2011; Brunnwasser, "Death of War Crimes Witness."

61. Lawrence Marzouk, "UK Criticizes Kosovo Witness Protection System," *Balkan Insight,* December 1, 2011.

62. Agence France-Presse, "Kosovo Court Orders Retrial of Ex-Rebel for War Crimes," November 20, 2012.

63. DPA International English Service, "EU Prosecutors Charge Top Kosovo Politician for Corruption," November 16, 2012.

64. Bundesnachrichtendienst 2005, 11. According to the report: "[Haliti] is connected to money laundering, drug- weapons- human and fuel smuggling, trade in women and the prostitution business and belongs to the inner circle of the Mafia. As a key figure in OC he constantly moves (moved) large sums of money." See also KFOR 2004 "Target Folder Xhavit Haliti" , 3.

65. Paul Lewis, "Report Identifies Hashim Thaçi as 'Big Fish' in Organized Crime," *Guardian,* January 24, 2011.

66. KFOR 2004 "Target Folder Xhavit Haliti", 3.

67. Bundesnachrichtendienst Analyze, 8–9.

68. Agim Ceku was head of staff for the KLA and became first head of the KPC following its establishment. Serbia has issued an Interpol Red Notice against him on charges of war crimes and he has been detained in Slovenia, Hungary, and Bulgaria, but

never indicted by the ICTY. Ekrem Rexha, commander of the Pastrik zone, was killed in May under unclear circumstances. Rrustem Mustafa, commander for the Llap zone, became an MP for PDK. In 2009, he was convicted of torture of detainees in 1998–1999 by EULEX. Sami Lushtaku was the commander of the Drenica zone and an MP. In 2011 he was charged with issuing death threats against a leading Kosovo journalist. Kadri Veseli was the head of SHIK. Together with Thaçi, he is implicated in the organ harvesting allegations presented in the Council of Europe report (2010).

69. In reaction to the Council of Europe report, Thaçi, for example, stated it was "slanderous Serbian propaganda" and threatened to sue its author Dick Marty for defamation. Mark Lowen, "Report Reignites Kosovo Organ Trafficking Claim," *BBC*, January 25, 2011; Rettman and Krasniqi, "Thaçi Camp Hits Back at Organ Trafficking Allegations."

70. The Serbian Information Agency (BIA), for example, published a report on organized crime in Kosovo in 2003, listing 147 individuals and their alleged involvement in war crimes and organized criminality, presumably based in part on Serbian intelligence files. Written in English and extensively citing Western media, the report was clearly intended primarily for external consumption. BIA, "Albanian Terrorism and Organized Crime in Kosovo and Metohija," Belgrade September 2003.

71. Marty, "Inhuman Treatment of People," 15, para. 69.

72. Bundesnachrichtendienst Analyze, 5–6, 26. According to the report: "Regarding the key players (multifunctional persons, among others Haliti, Thaçi, Haradinaj and LLuka), only the thinnest lines divide politics, business and internationally operating OC-structures in Kosovo. The criminal networks standing behind [these persons] require political instability. These structures have no interest in the construction of a functioning governmental order, through which their flourishing business may be limited. The OC is rather creating for itself a suitable political environment, which also is shown by the establishment of individual OC-actors in politics. Against this background, it will probably be difficult for the international community to establish rule of law and democratic structures in Kosovo" (author's translation).

73. Author's interview with UNMIK official, Priština, June 2006.

74. Klebnikov, "Heroin Heroes."

75. Andreas Heinemann Grüder and Igor Grebenschikov, "Security Governance by Internationals: The Case of Kosovo," *International Peacekeeping* 13, 1 (2006): 53–54.

76. "Thousands Protest Against Arrest of KLA Veterans," *Balkan Insight*, March 29, 2011.

77. Jana Arsovska, "Albanian Crime Laid Bare: The Developments of Albanian Organized Crime Groups in the Balkans," *Jane's Intelligence Review* 19, 2 (2007): 36–40.

78. BBC Monitoring Service, "Daily Profiles Kosovo Officials Under Investigation for Corruption, Other Crimes," October 5, 2012.

79. Ibid., 47

80. Heinemann-Grüder and Grebenschikov, "Security Governance by Internationals," 46–47, both paras.

81. Ibid., 50–51.

82. Author's interviews in Priština, June 2006.

83. Marty, "Inhuman Treatment of People," 8, para. 10. The report particularly highlighted the problem of witness protection, which was also borne out by events related to the Limaj case.

84. ICG, "The Rule of Law," 4.

85. Matt McAllister, "Kosovo's Mafia: Assassinations and Intimidations," *Global Post*, May 4, 2011. The article ascribes this claim to Kadri Veseli, former SHIK head, as well as "half a dozen sources," including another SHIK operative, a former KLA fundraiser, a Western diplomat, and Kosovar political analysts.

86. Ibid. The official also claimed SHIK was sponsored by the CIA.

87. Ibid.; U.S. Embassy cable, "Hitman's Confession."

88. KFOR, "Target Folder Xhavit Haliti," 4.

89. Bundesnachrichtendienst Analyze, 18. According to the report: "The SHIK developed in its present form in the second half of 1999 in Pristian on Thaçi's initiative. Thaçi and Haradinaj, among others used it to recruit suitable candidates for the Kosovo Police Service and TMK [the Albanian acronym for KPC, author's remark]. In reality, the service is primarily involved in spying activities, intimidation and physically eliminating democratic forces."

90. McAllister, "Kosovo's Mafia: Assassinations and Intimidations"; U.S. Embassy cable, "Hitman's Confession."

91. BBC Monitoring Service, "Daily Profiles Kosovo Officials Under Investigation."

92. Jeta Xharra, "Kosovo's Intelligence Services Come in from the Cold," *Balkan Investigative Research Network*, December 23, 2005.

93. Lucia Montanaro, "The Kosovo State-Building Conundrum: Addressing Fragility in a Contested State," FRIDE Working Paper 9, October 2009, 6.

94. Nicholas Wood, "Albanian Exiles Threaten to Escalate War," *Guardian*, May 21, 2001.

95. See also Wood, "Albanian."

96. Svante Cornell and Michael Jonsson, "Creating a State of Denial," *International Herald Tribune*, March 22, 2007.

97. ICG, "The Rule of Law," 3. The comparable figure for most Central American countries is 40–50 homicides per 100,000 inhabitants annually.

98. EUROPOL, "OCTA 2011: EU Organised Crime Threat Assessment," EUROPOL, 2011, 14. According to the report: "The continued prominence of Western Balkans in heroin trafficking, despite the existence of more direct routes through South East Europe and, indeed, the fact that traffic must leave the EU in order to enter these countries, points to the existence of substantial criminal logistics in the region. . . . Multinational criminal groups assembled on the basis of ethnicity are concentrated in the Kosovo region, the former Yugoslav Republic of Macedonia and Albania in particular."

99. Ibid., 15.

100. Ibid., 20.

101. UNODC, for example, estimates that the opiate market in Southeastern Europe

(including drugs trafficked through the region) was worth $2.5 billion and with Albanian drug traffickers benefiting substantially from heroin trafficked to Italy and Germany as well. *World Drug Report 2011* (Vienna: UNODC, 2011), 83–84.

102. ICG, "The Rule of Law," 1–3.

103. Jana Arsovska, "Sixth Form: Ethnic Albanian Criminals Thrive in New York," *Jane's Intelligence Review* 23, 1 (2011): 44–47.

104. Arsovska, "Sixth Form."

105. Montanaro, "The Kosovo State-Building Conundrum," 13.

106. Andrea Capussela, "Eulex in Kosovo: A Shining Example of Incompetence," *Guardian*, April 9, 2011.

107. Marty, "Inhuman Treatment of People," 8, n3.

108. Ibid., 12, paras. 31–32, 36: "The evidence we have uncovered is perhaps most significant in that it often contradicts the much-touted image of the Kosovo Liberation Army, or KLA, as a guerilla army that fought valiantly to defend the right of its people to inhabit the territory of Kosovo. . . . The reality is that the most significant operational activities undertaken by members of the KLA—prior to, during and in the immediate aftermath of the conflict—took place on the territory of Albania, where the Serb security forces were never deployed."

109. Tamara Makarenko, "The Crime-Terror Continuum: Tracing the Interplay Between Transnational Organized Crime and Terrorism," *Global Crime* 6, 1 (2004): 139–45.

110. Heinemann-Grüder and Paes, *Wag the Dog.*

111. Daalder and O'Hanlon, for example, note the KLA had "only a few thousand rag-tag fighters into 1999," *Winning Ugly*, 16.

112. Ibid., 152, 215.

Chapter 10. Conclusions and Implications for Conflict Resolution and Peacekeeping

1. This literature includes, among others, Paul Collier and Anke Hoeffler, *Greed and Grievance in Civil War* (Washington, D.C.: World Bank, October 2001); James D. Fearon, "Why Do Some Civil Wars Last So Much Longer Than Others?" *Journal of Peace Research* 41, 3 (2004): 275–301; Jeremy Weinstein, *Inside Rebellion: The Politics of Insurgent Violence* (New York: Cambridge University Press, 2007); Paul Collier and Anke Hoeffler, "Beyond Greed and Grievance: Feasibility and Civil War," *Oxford Economic Papers* 61 (2009): 1–27.

2. Cf. Collier and Hoeffler, *Greed and Grievance in Civil War*, and Collier and Hoeffler, "Beyond Greed and Grievance" for two of the most influential versions of these arguments. Similar approaches are still being used, for example, Krishna Chaitanya Vadlamannati, "Why Indian Men Rebel? Explaining Armed Rebellion in the Northeastern States of India, 1970–2007," *Journal of Peace Research* 48, 5 (2011): 605–19. Fearon also made an oft-cited observation that civil wars financed by "contraband" tended to last four times as long as other conflicts. Most of the conflicts in this volume were, however, to some extent financed by "contraband," but only one (in Afghanistan) lasted longer than the median 6.0 or mean

8.8 years, suggesting that this result may indicate simply that in long-duration civil wars, the armed parties, including their financing sources, simply become better known. Fearon, "Why Do Some Civil Wars Last So Much Longer Than Others?"

3. Jonathan Goodhand, "Corrupting or Consolidating the Peace? The Drugs Economy and Postconflict Peacebuilding in Afghanistan," *International Peacekeeping* 15, 3 (2008): 405-25.

4. Opium production decreased somewhat in Afghanistan in 2007-2010, but still accounted for more than 60 percent of world production. The Taliban strongholds of Helmand and Kandahar provinces alone accounted for three-quarters of production in the country, and almost half the entire world production. UNODC, *World Drug Report 2011* (Vienna: UNODC, 2011), 59, table 13.

5. Available data also indicate that law enforcement capacity among Central Asian countries is very weak. Notably, whereas Iran alone accounted for 89 percent of world seizures of opium and Afghanistan and Pakistan 5 and 4 percent respectively, the five Central Asian countries together accounted for less than 0.7 percent in 2009. Likewise, for heroin and morphine, Iran seized more than twelve times the amounts of these five countries, Afghanistan more than twice as much, and Pakistan more than the five taken together. UNODC, *World Drug Report 2011*, 62-63, map 10, fig. 30.

6. See the chapters in this volume on Georgia by Niklas Nilsson and Moldova by Alexandru Molcean and Natalie Verständig for a full review of organized criminality in these regions.

7. See Dick Marty, "Inhuman Treatment of People and Illicit Trafficking in Human Organs in Kosovo," Council of Europe, Committee on Legal Affairs and Human Rights (Strasbourg: Council of Europe, 2010) on Kosovo; and Peter Andreas, "The Clandestine Political Economy of War and Peace in Bosnia," *International Studies Quarterly* 48, 1 (2004): 31 on Bosnia.

8. Freedom House, "Freedom in the World: Disputed Territories," Freedom House, 2012, http://www.freedomhouse.org/report/freedom-world/freedom-world-2012.

9. See Johan Engvall, "The State Under Siege: The Drug Trade and Organised Crime in Tajikistan," *Europe-Asia Studies* 58, 6 (2006): 851. Also see the discussion in Engvall's chapter on Tajikistan in this volume.

10. Andreas Heinemann-Grüder and Igor Grebenschikov, "Security Governance by Internationals: The Case of Kosovo," *International Peacekeeping* 13, 1 (2006): 46-47. With the establishment of EULEX and its 2,500 staff in 2008, the EU seems to be making a last ditch effort to address this challenge, but results so far are disappointing, the seeming prospects for success dim, and former employees of the mission question the capacity of the mission itself. Andrea Capussela, "Eulex in Kosovo: A Shining Example of Incompetence," *Guardian*, April 9, 2011.

11. Former counterinsurgency advisor David Kilcullen, however, points out that the opium economy has been formally embraced as part of the five-point Taliban "ideology." David Kilcullen, *The Accidental Guerrilla: Fighting Many Small Wars in the Midst of a Big One* (Oxford: Oxford University Press, 2006), 58.

12. Also see Jesse Driscoll, "Commitment Problems or Bidding Wars? Rebel Fragmentation as Peace Building," *Journal of Conflict Resolution* 56, 1 (2012): 118–49.

13. See Paul Collier, Anke Hoeffler, and Måns Söderbom, "On the Duration of Civil War," *Journal of Peace Research* 41, 3 (2004), which builds on the assumption of unchanging motives over time; Anthony Vinci, "Greed-Grievance Reconsidered: The Role of Power and Survival in the Motivation of Armed Groups," *Civil Wars* 8, 1 (2006): 25–45, on the assumption of armed groups as unitary actors.

14. For some initial approaches in this vein, see Theodore McLauchlin and Wendy Pearlman, "Out-Group Conflict, In-Group Unity? Explaining the Effects of Repression on Intra-Movement Cooperation," *Journal of Conflict Resolution* 56, 1 (2012): 41–66, and Driscoll, "Commitment Problems or Bidding Wars?."

15. Tamara Makarenko, "Crime, Terror, and the Central Asian Drug Trade," *Harvard Asia Quarterly* (Spring 2002).

16. In an analysis of terrorist groups (which include both smaller terrorist networks and full-blown insurgencies, such as the LTTE in Sri Lanka, FARC in Colombia, Shining Path in Peru, and PKK in Turkey), Crunin, for example, finds only two successful cases among some thirty groups—ANC in South Africa and Irgun in Israel, Audrey Kurth Crunin, "How al Qaeda Ends: The Demise and Decline of Terrorist Groups," *International Security* 31, 1 (2006): 19, table 1.

17. For a preliminary discussion of these issues, see Heiko Nitzschke and Kaysie Studdard, "The Legacies of War Economies: Challenges and Options for Peacemaking and Peacebuilding," *International Peacekeeping* 12, 2 (2006): 222–39. Whereas Nitzschke and Studdard point to some of the issues raised in this chapter, we expand the discussion by focusing on other sources of financing than natural resources, outline practical options for and challenges to tackling organized crime, discuss the issue of former rebel leaders as political actors, and emphasize the ambiguous role of postconflict reconstruction aid.

18. For the purposes of this section, "failed states" are defined following standard definitions, i.e., states that fail in one or several of the following regards: (1) maintain a monopoly on violence; (2) have a basic modicum of legitimacy among their populations; (3) deliver basic public goods such as education and health care, or basic infrastructure such as electricity, running water, and roads. Whereas there is a vigorous debate on how to define "state failure," these criteria are broadly agreed on, even though how to measure them operationally is subject to extensive debate. See Stewart Patrick, "'Failed' States and Global Security: Empirical Questions and Policy Dilemmas," *International Studies Review* 9, 4 (2007): 649–50.

19. Johan Engvall, "The State as an Investment Market: An Analytical Framework for Interpreting Politics and Bureaucracy in Kirgizistan," Ph.D. dissertation, Department of Government, Uppsala University, 2011.

20. Marty, "Inhuman Treatment of People and Illicit Trafficking."

21. Gretchen Peters, *Seeds of Terror: How Drugs, Thugs and Crime Are Reshaping the*

Afghan War (New York: St. Martin's, 2010); Thomas Schweich, "Is Afghanistan a Narco-State?," *New York Times Magazine,* July 27, 2008.

22. See, e.g., Andreas, "The Clandestine Political Economy of War and Peace in Bosnia," 31.

23. Heinemann-Grüder and Grebenschikov "Security Governance by Internationals."

24. Charles King, "The Benefits of Ethnic War: Understanding Eurasia's Unrecognized States," *World Politics* 53 (July 2001): 524–52.

25. For an exception to the predominant focus on the conflict itself, see Nitzschke and Studdard, "The Legacies of War Economies."

26. For a similar argument directed specifically at the "frozen" conflicts in the region, see King, "The Benefits of Ethnic War."

27. Goodhand, "Corrupting or Consolidating the Peace?"

28. Schweich, "Is Afghanistan a Narco-State?"

29. See the chapter on Kosovo by Michael Jonsson in this volume for a fuller elaboration of this argument. Cf. also, for example, Marty, "Inhuman Treatment of People and Illicit Trafficking" on the issue of organized criminality during the conflict, and Capussela, "Eulex in Kosovo," for a skeptical view of the prospects for EULEX success.

30. Nitzschke and Studdard, "The Legacies of War Economies."

31. Michael Jonsson and Svante Cornell, "Countering Terrorist Financing: Lessons from Europe," *Georgetown Journal of International Affairs* 8 (Winter 2007); Michael Jonsson and Svante Cornell, "Examining PKK Financing," *Jane's Intelligence Review* (April 2008); Michael Jonsson, Christian N. Larson, and Nir Artzi, "Tax Evasion: Dealing with the Shabab's Financing," *Jane's Intelligence Review* (February 2011).

32. Cf. Heinemann-Grüder and Grebenschikov, "Security Governance by Internationals," for an example of how largely foreseeable legacies of the war economy impeded DDR and particularly SSR initiatives in Kosovo.

33. See Jacob N. Shapiro, "Terrorist Organizations Vulnerabilities and Inefficiencies: A Rational Choice Perspective," in *Terrorist Financing and State Responses: A Comparative Perspective,* ed. Jeanne K. Giraldo and Harold A. Trinkunas (Palo Alto, Calif.: Stanford University Press, 2007), 56–71, which argues that financial units and logistics officers are particularly likely to become motivated by personal economic gain. See also Jonsson and Cornell, "Countering Terrorist Financing," for an example of the emergence of such "spoilers" following the Good Friday agreement in Northern Ireland.

34. Stephen J. Stedman, "Spoiler Problems in Peace Processes," *International Security* 22, 2 (1999): 5–53.

35. See Jake Sherman, "Burma: Lessons from the Cease-Fires," in *The Political Economy of Armed Conflict: Beyond Greed and Grievance,* ed. Karen Ballentine and Jake Sherman (Boulder, Colo.: Lynne Rienner, 2003), 225–55.

36. This is discussed in Nat J. Colletta and Robert Muggah, "Context Matters: Interim Stabilisation and Second Generation Approaches to Security Promotion," *Conflict, Security and Development* 9, 4 (2009): 425–53.

37. See, e.g., "UN Covered Up Claims Corrupt Peacekeepers Sold Arms to Rebels in DR Congo," *Daily Mail*, April 28, 2008, and "Ukrainian KFOR Peacekeeper Charged with Bribery," *Balkan Insight*, January 17, 2011.

38. On Kosovo, see, e.g., Lucia Montanaro, "The Kosovo State-Building Conundrum: Addressing Fragility in a Contested State," FRIDE Working Paper 9, October 2009.

39. Moisés Naím, *Illicit: How Smugglers, Traffickers and Copycats Are Hijacking the Global Economy* (New York: Anchor, 2005).

40. World Bank, *World Development Report 2011* (Washington, D.C.: World Bank, 2011).

Contributors

Jana Arsovska, a native of Macedonia, teaches in the Sociology Department at the John Jay College of Criminal Justice, where she teaches courses on International Criminal Justice and Balkan Crime and Justice. She also teaches a sociology course at Otisville Correctional Facility in New York. She holds a Ph.D. in Criminology from the Catholic University of Leuven, where she studied the role of cultural codes in the evolution of ethnic Albanian organized crime groups. Currently she is working on several international projects: "The role of West African women in transnational human trafficking networks"; "The expansion of Radical Islam in Kosovo and Macedonia"; and "Migration and transnational crime: Albanian organized crime in NYC." She has acted as a consultant on Albanian/Balkan organized crime for organizations such as the World Bank, UN, DCAF, and West Sands Advisory LLP. Prior to her current post, she worked for the European Forum for Restorative Justice and underwent training at INTERPOL. She is a member of the Executive Committee of the Standing Group on Organised Crime. She has published numerous articles on Balkan criminality in scholarly peer-reviewed journals and intelligence magazines such as *Jane's Intelligence Review*. She is co-editor of the book *Restoring Justice After Large-Scale Conflict: Kosovo, Congo and the Israeli-Palestinian Case* and is currently finalizing her new book, Decoding Albanian Organized Crime.

Svante Cornell is Research Director of the Central Asia-Caucasus Institute & Silk Road Studies Program Joint Center, a Joint Research and Policy Center affiliated with Johns Hopkins University-SAIS, Washington, D.C., and the Stockholm-based Institute for Security and Development Policy, of which he is a co-founder. He was educated at the Middle East Technical University, Ankara, and received his Ph.D. in Peace and Conflict Studies from Uppsala University. He was awarded an honorary doctoral degree by the Azerbaijani Academy of Sciences in 1999. He is an Associate Research Professor at Johns Hopkins-SAIS, where he teaches courses on the Caucasus and the Turkic world. He previously served as Course Chair for the Caucasus at the Foreign Service Institute, and as Associate Professor of East European Studies and Government at Uppsala University. His main areas of expertise are security issues, broadly defined, and state-building in the Caucasus, Turkey, and Central Asia. He is the author of *Small Nations and Great Powers*, the first comprehensive study of the post-Soviet Caucasus, *Azerbaijan Since Independence*, and more than fifty academic and policy articles, including in journals such as *World Politics*, *Journal of Democracy*, *Current History*, *Foreign Policy*, *Orbis*, *Journal of Peace Research*, *Studies in Conflict and Terrorism*, *Middle East Policy*, and *Middle Eastern Studies*. His op-eds have appeared in major American and European newspapers.

Johan Engvall is a postdoctoral researcher at the Uppsala Center for Russian and Eurasian Studies (UCRS) and a Research Fellow with the Central Asia-Caucasus Institute & Silk Road Studies Program. He holds a Ph.D. in political science from the Department of Government, Uppsala University. His main areas of expertise are the domestic political systems of post-Soviet countries, particularly Central Asia. He has authored numerous articles on Central Asian affairs in journals such as *Europe-Asia Studies*, *Problems of Post-Communism*, and *Nordic Journal of East European Studies*. His dissertation, "The State as an Investment Market: An Analytical Framework for Interpreting Politics and Bureaucracy in Kyrgyzstan," was published by Uppsala University in 2011.

Michael Jonsson is a Research Fellow with the Institute for Security and Development Policy and a lecturer at the Department of Government at Uppsala University. He holds a B.A., M.A., and Ph.D. in Political Science from Uppsala University, a B.A. in Economics from Stockholm University, and an M.S. in Foreign Service from Georgetown University, where he was also a Fulbright Scholar. He has written extensively on the interlinkages of economic crimes, insurgencies and organized crime, among others, for *Georgetown Journal of International Affairs*, *Journal of Money Laundering Control*, and *Survival*. He is the founder and owner of the AML/CFT Group in Washington, D.C., where he has worked as a consultant for the International Monetary Fund and the Swedish Defense Headquarters. He has also provided consulting and training to the World Bank, the Swedish Police, the Folke Bernadotte Academy and the Swedish Economic Crimes Bureau, and other organizations. His opinion pieces have been published by the *International Herald Tribune* and leading Swedish news dailies such as *Dagens Nyheter* and *Svenska Dagbladet*.

Alexandru Molcean is a project coordinator at the Institute for Security and Development Policy. He is predominantly involved in the Transnational Organized Crime Initiative coordinating a research project regarding the threats that transnational criminal networks pose to democratic processes. Prior to his involvement with ISDP, he worked as head of the International Legal Cooperation Division in the Ministry of Justice of the Republic of Moldova. He also has experience as a legal adviser to other government institutions such as the Ministry of Finance and Customs Service. He has been a member of the Council of Europe Committee of Experts on the Operation of European Conventions in the Penal Field and co-authored, among others, a handbook on mutual legal assistance to enhance the cooperation of relevant Moldovan authorities with their foreign partners. He holds a B.A. in International Public Law from Moldovan State University and an M.A. in Public Administration from the Academy of Public Administration of the Republic of Moldova.

Niklas Nilsson is a Research Fellow with the Central Asia-Caucasus Institute & Silk Road Studies Program, and a Ph.D. candidate and Lecturer in Political Science at Uppsala University and Södertörn University. He is Associate Editor of the *Central Asia-Caucasus Analyst*, the Joint Center's biweekly electronic journal. His research interests include foreign policy analysis and international relations with a focus on the South Caucasus and the Black Sea/Caspian region. He has published extensively on Caucasian affairs, including in edited volumes and peer-reviewed academic journals such as *Ethnopolitics* and *Demokratizatsiya*.

Murad Batal al-Shishani is an expert on Islamic groups that operate in the Middle East or North Caucasus. He has garnered significant experience as a researcher, field journalist, analyst and writer. He holds an M.A. in Political Science, and is author of a book on the Islamic groups in Chechnya and on the insurgency in Iraq. His forthcoming book in Arabic covers the geopolitics of

Al Qaeda. He has written numerous articles and taken part in a multitude of studies in the last ten years, in both Arabic and English, for several prestigious publications. Among the publications he has contributed to are *Terrorism Monitor, Central Asia-Caucasus Analyst, Prague Watchdog, Al-Siyassa Al-Dawliya, Shu'un al-Aawsat, CTC Sentinel, Afaq al-Mustaqbal,* and *Journal of Democracy.* He has contributed to prestigious online publications such as BBC News Online, Open Democracy, and many others. He regularly writes articles for newspapers, contributing an in-depth bi-weekly article to the London-based *al-Hayat,* and a weekly column to the Jordanian daily *al-Ghad.* He frequently appears on the BBC World Service program, where he takes part in the analysis of news stories related to his specialization.

Natalie Verständig is a Junior Research Fellow with the Central Asia-Caucasus Institute & Silk Road Studies Program Joint Center. She holds a B.A. from the Interdisciplinary Center (IDC), Herzliya, Israel, in Government, Diplomacy and Strategy, with specialization in International Relations and Middle Eastern studies. She has published several commentaries for the ISDP on security developments in the Middle East.

Index

Acknowledgments

This book encapsulates the research conducted at the Central Asia-Caucasus Institute & Silk Road Studies Program on organized crime, conflict, and the state in Eurasia over the past decade. In analyzing specific security threats across postcommunist space, our researchers over time came to identify drug trafficking, state capture, political corruption, weakness of the judiciary, frozen conflicts, large-scale financial crimes, faltering international support, and ungoverned spaces as the primary challenges to peace, stability, and prosperity in the region. Many of these problems have their roots in the "triple transitions" and civil wars that followed the break-up of the Soviet Union and Yugoslavia, and their enduring nature cannot be fully understood without first explaining how these challenges originally arose as a consequence of crime-conflict collaboration during a time of war. This volume, then, represents an attempt at summarizing what we have learned regarding the contemporary security problems confronting these regions, but also at explaining the roots of these challenges and why they have remained largely unresolved, in spite of today being widely recognized.

The research for this book chiefly takes its base in a research project funded in 2005–2007 by the Swedish Emergency Management Agency (SEMA), since renamed the Swedish Civil Contingencies Agency. At SEMA, the editors would like to thank Maria Monahov and Ebba Hallsenius, as well as director of research Bengt Sundelius, for the generous support provided for this project. This book, while belated indeed, is a more than anything a product of that research project.

The book also builds on the larger research program on narcotics and organized crime in Eurasia conducted at the Silk Road Studies Program, dating back to 2002, when it received funding by SEMA and the Office of the Swedish Drug Policy Coordinator. In the years that passed, the program also received funding from various institutions, including the Swedish Agency for International Development, the U.S. government, and the UN Office on Drugs and Crime. Moreover, the book would not have seen the light of day without continuous institutional support for the Joint Center's work by the Swedish Ministry for Foreign Affairs and the Smith Richardson Foundation.

As the book has drawn on the work conducted over almost a decade by a varied group of researchers, we owe an intellectual debt to all those that were involved in that research program. Niklas Swanström, presently Director at the Institute for Security and Development in Stockholm of which the Silk Road Studies Program is a part, co-chaired the program and contributed research particularly on Central Asian affairs. From 2008 onward, Walter Kegö led the work on organized crime at ISDP, contributing important insights. Louise Shelley, an early leader in the research on organized crime, has inspired us and shared her valuable advice at many occasions. Tamara Makarenko, one of the first scholars to bring attention to the crime-terror nexus and the author of numerous studies on the topic, was a senior research fellow with the program, and contributed greatly to several earlier research products that inform this book. Anna Jonsson Cornell, also a senior research fellow, produced important work especially on human trafficking. Similarly, Erica Marat served for several years as a research fellow with the program, writing several key studies on the interrelationship of crime and the state in Eurasia. Moreover, several junior fellows contributed important research as well as research assistance. Emin Poljarevic conducted field research in Kosovo and Moldova—together with Klas Kärrstrand in the latter case—and produced valuable reports that inform this book. Klas Marklund contributed text to an earlier draft of the chapter on Afghanistan. Maral Madi and Emma Björnehed contributed research assistance in the early years of the program. Finally, the editors would like to thank the fantastic crew at the University of Pennsylvania Press, especially Bill Finan and Alison Anderson but also its anonymous reviewers, for their patience with us.

The editors and authors are also grateful to the numerous individuals across Eurasia who met with us, and who shared their insights and knowledge about these sensitive issues. These persons know who they are, but shall remain unnamed. Last, the editors would also like to thank our respective families for their patience with our constant travels and their enduring support.